INDIA–AFGHANISTAN

This book is a searing history of Indo-Afghan relations. It looks at how Afghanistan, once the heartland of India, has now been reduced to a troubled cousin in the contemporary era. Drawing on archival records, as well as ancient Greek, Sanskrit, Chinese, and Persian literature, the book traces the history of Afghanistan from ancient times up to the recent Taliban takeover of the country in 2020. It presents an analytical history of race, culture, and belonging in a world shaken and transformed by colonization. The author provides a new interpretation of the region and discusses South Asia's courteous racial etiquette.

An indispensable read, the book will be useful for students and researchers of history, Middle East and Central Asian studies, international relations, politics, development studies, and Asian studies.

Saroj Kumar Rath has written extensively on the history of Afghanistan's responses to the world. His prize-winning history *Fragile Frontiers: The Secret History of Mumbai Terror Attacks* (2014) has been used as course material at leading universities in Europe, Asia, and America. A specialist in South Asia's security history, he teaches at the University of Delhi.

"Saroj Kumar Rath's *India–Afghanistan* is a recommended read for anyone, scholars, thinkers, diplomats, and students alike, seeking to know the original character of Afghanistan and her umbilical interaction with India. Retrieved from the womb of the historical past and shaped like careful foliation, it tells India's place in Afghan history. *India–Afghanistan* is told with authority, depth and wit, and the ease of reading a good novel, and that makes it a great history."

Mahmoud Masaeli, *Persian Scholar and Retired Professor of International Law and Relations, Carleton University and University of Ottawa, Canada*

INDIA–AFGHANISTAN

From Common Inheritance
to Contested Histories

Saroj Kumar Rath

LONDON AND NEW YORK

Designed cover image: Getty Images

First published 2026
by Routledge
4 Park Square, Milton Park, Abingdon, Oxon OX14 4RN

and by Routledge
605 Third Avenue, New York, NY 10158

Routledge is an imprint of the Taylor & Francis Group, an informa business

© 2026 Saroj Kumar Rath

The right of Saroj Kumar Rath to be identified as author of this work has been asserted in accordance with sections 77 and 78 of the Copyright, Designs and Patents Act 1988.

All rights reserved. No part of this book may be reprinted or reproduced or utilised in any form or by any electronic, mechanical, or other means, now known or hereafter invented, including photocopying and recording, or in any information storage or retrieval system, without permission in writing from the publishers.

Trademark notice: Product or corporate names may be trademarks or registered trademarks, and are used only for identification and explanation without intent to infringe.

British Library Cataloguing-in-Publication Data
A catalogue record for this book is available from the British Library

ISBN: 978-1-041-03003-4 (hbk)
ISBN: 978-1-041-04287-7 (pbk)
ISBN: 978-1-003-62767-8 (ebk)

DOI: 10.4324/9781003627678

Typeset in Sabon
by Deanta Global Publishing Services, Chennai, India

To

Professor Kapil Kapoor

The sheer Sire, who inspired this book in his novel, unspoken way.

CONTENTS

Foreword by Professor P. Radhakrishnan   *viii*
Preface   *xi*
Acknowledgements   *xxxii*
Abbreviations   *xxxiv*

1	Explaining Ancient Connection	1
2	The Contested Histories: Journeying Through the Ages	31
3	Special Symmetry in the Modern Era	53
4	Testing Time for Perpetual Friendship	89
5	The Dimensions of Choices in Bilateral Relations	129
6	Navigating the Chessboard in the 21st Century	155
7	From Grandeur and Glory to an Oscillating Bond	175

Bibliography   *183*
Index   *194*

FOREWORD

Saroj Kumar Rath's *India–Afghanistan: From Common Inheritance to Contested Histories* is not just a much-debated issue and freshly marshalled evidence; more importantly, it is a fascinating tale of India's ancient past and the evolution of the modern era. Saroj's earlier book *Fragile Frontiers: The Secret History of Mumbai Terror Attacks* (2014) has been my recommended read for politicians and college students alike, seeking to know about the security history of South Asia: how it began and how it evolved up to the Mumbai Terror Attacks, especially against the backdrop of the United States' war on terror in the Afghan arena, the passionate and colourful characters who played vital roles, and the contesting views of the global dilemma for India. *India–Afghanistan* returns to the same story, albeit with far more intensity, high-quality historical craft, and the usual flamboyance of storytelling style. The satisfying part about this research work is that it covers one of the centrally important topics in the Indian national story and the most popular yet so far neglected history of India and Afghanistan. I can vouch for this, having read and to some extent been involved in their making.

As an aside, Saroj's *Fragile Frontiers: The Secret History of Mumbai Terror Attacks* is unique, and I have not come across any book of such rigour and scope.

Saroj is one of the most deeply immersed of all Indian historians in this history and has collaborated with or mentored what seems to be almost all others who study it seriously. He applied on-field information from a vast array of sources like contemporary scribes, writers, authors, historians, travellers, and original court materials to explain and bring out the chronicle, which sends the readers to the core of the subject and gives us a lively sense of their character, as well as the taunt and tenor of their journey not only within the geographic limits of India--Afghanistan but also over the contextual issues of India's relations with other countries like Russia, the United States, China, and Pakistan, in recent decades. It is no surprise that this unfolding story is rich, especially as a treasure trove of archival sources, illuminating historical episodes, and unconventional anecdotes.

It is a story about ancient identity, colonial perception, and change and continuity. For Indians who might think that India's Afghanistan connection is merely political and geographical, Saroj reminds us

> A simple glimpse into the annals of classical Greek and Indian literature offers numerous mute milestones, which endorse the fact that India and Afghanistan, before the demarcation of modern boundaries and the artificial erection of the Durand line, shared nearly everything for millennia.

Saroj provided new interpretations on the prevalent narratives like the medieval invaders who used Afghanistan as a springboard to attack India for many centuries were Turks and not Afghans, as claimed by historians. He further emphasized that the invincibility of Afghans as asserted by numerous authors, which became a dominant narrative over time, is a myth, and the interpretations of scholars that Afghanistan was the graveyard of empires is mere hearsay without academic scrutiny. Such myth-busting provides much of the fascination of the book. But there is also something captivating in how Saroj portrays Afghanistan as a land integral to India's spiritual journey for millennia.

While on occasion, Saroj has presented newly declassified archival records as they allow readers to have their views on subjects ranging from Pashtunistan to Chinese predatory policy in the pan-handle region of Badakhshan, his own position on Indo-Afghan ties is on the side of change. He was guided by ethical precepts and moral methods while explaining serious issues in rude terms. At times, however, the serious content within cannot help but bring on a certain hilarity, as in the chapter where the literature review is conducted and also when he explains the series of diplomatic failures faced by the Indian Embassy in Kabul and the Ministry of External Affairs in New Delhi. The first chapter, which cites numerous contemporary Greek works, unusual histories, and peculiar interpretations, is the most important of all chapters as it explains the pristine character of Afghanistan hitherto untouched by any historian in a brute didactic fashion sufficient for a lift of eyebrows of historians.

The value of this book for policymakers and the public is not just the narrative about ancient common inheritance and counter-narratives; it is in the lesson of how the issue was left out of popular debate and how many of our historians and civil bureaucrats refused to see beyond colonial literature and the way they often worked in trying to bring the public along with them. Readers of *India–Afghanistan: From Common Inheritance to Contested Histories* will unravel unexplored histories but will also find enjoyment and be enriched by the benefit of knowing the evolution of India–Afghan relations. I dedicate this book to all scholars, in particular, our highly competitive knowledge-seeking Millennials of the Wonderland.

Professor P. Radhakrishnan
Indian Social Thinker and Former Professor
Madras Institute of Development Studies

PREFACE

Rig Veda, the earliest known religious text, passionately debates matters involving Gandhara, which reiterates India's ancient engaging contact with Afghanistan. In the subsequent era, one can find countless original literary sources, all of which effortlessly explain Indo-Afghan similes. It is an undoubted fact that Afghanistan shares cultural patterns and history with India, and the religious affinities between the ancestors of the current Indians and Afghans are one of the historically well-established realities.

Starting from the writings of Greek philosopher-historian Herodotus to Sanskrit scholar Panini and then the pious Chinese visitor Hiuen Tsang, every scholar liberally elucidated the age-old association between the peoples of the two countries. In the annals of Afghan history, India is its civilizational base, a fact corroborated by contemporary scholars and their authorized ancient texts. In the Bamiyan hill range, many noble images and statues were made by Hindu Rajas, especially by the five brothers or *Pandavas* of *Mahabharata* fame. Archaeological reiteration of India's civilizational acquaintance with Afghanistan is abundant. Shortughai, deep inside Northern Afghanistan, bears testimony to the Indus civilization's extended bazaar.

Afghanistan was in the midst of the Indus Valley civilization. Ancient cities like Shortughai and Bamiyan are two centres where Indo-Afghan connections are evident. The Khyber Pass and Bolan Pass used to be the exclusive historical routes for traders, travellers, learners, as well as advancing armies to reach India. The Chinese used to take a slightly different route to reach India. Hiuen Tsang started from Shanxi, China, and took the route through Afghanistan to reach India. Therefore, Afghanistan used to be the first door to enter the heartland of India.

So many cultural commonalities existed between the two countries that the very names – India and Afghanistan – were attributed to the same source, which was Persian and Greek philological-colloquial expression. Both countries derived their names from the Persian and Greek languages.

The Greeks, mostly the learned ones, were the first group of scholars to be overawed and overwhelmed by the astonishing civilizational wisdom of India. There was intense curiosity among the Greek scholars to know more about India and understand the immense wonderland that it represented. They breathlessly admired the sheer concentration of philosophers, learned men, knowledge, and learning of science, mathematics, and philosophy in India. The Grecians were awed by India's wealth, town planning, flora and fauna, fabulous creatures, and the surprising sophistication of its common citizens. For nearly a millennium starting in 500 BC, there was also a cut-throat competition among Greek scholars to undertake field visits and conduct studies and inquiries before writing about and decoding the high culture of India.

The Chinese, mostly monks, were the second group of celebrated scholars who set foot on the soil of India with the explicit intent to augment intellectual wisdom and to sharpen the quest for philosophical inquiry. They were amazed by the socio-cultural setup and stayed for decades to study religion and philosophy in India. While doing so, they left behind a wealth of historical records and volumes of original religious-philosophical interpretation and information about the daily life of Indians. Since all the Grecian and Chinese scholars either crossed through Afghanistan to reach India or visited Gandhara during their stay in India, their writings inform us about the history of Afghanistan and testify to historical linkages between the two countries.

The two countries used to share the same landmass, the same kings, similar population, and homogeneity of religion. A simple glimpse into the annals of classical Greek literature and ancient Indian manuscripts offers numerous mute milestones, which endorse the fact that India and Afghanistan used to share nearly everything for millennia before the demarcation of modern boundaries and the artificial erection of the Durand Line.

The Durand Line disturbed the ancient connections between India and Afghanistan. Named after British Col. Mortimer Durand, who negotiated a frontier agreement between India and Afghanistan in 1893, the Durand Line was rejected by Afghanistan in 1947 because the agreement, as per the Afghan Government, lapsed when the British transferred control to Pakistan in 1947. The Durand Line does not extend the full distance of the boundary between Afghanistan and Pakistan. The western terminus of the line is the junction of the Iran–Afghanistan–Pakistan borders. The eastern terminus is the junction of the Afghanistan–Pakistan–India borders. From the eastern terminus of the line eastward to the junction of the Afghanistan–China–India borders, the boundary is undefined by any agreement. Most of the Durand Line has been demarcated on the ground. The entire stretch between the western terminus of the line and a point northwest of Parachinar, as well as a small sector in the vicinity of the Khyber Pass, is demarcated; the remainder is undermarked. As the 1893 British India–Afghanistan Agreement explains, the eastern terminus of the Durand Line is the junction of the Afghanistan–Pakistan–India borders. According to the Government of India's record, India shares a 106-kilometre border with Afghanistan.

When Islam hurtled at the doorstep of India, especially during the early 8th century CE, Afghanistan was the western exterior of India. Afghans stood like a mighty wall against the sword of Islam. The advent of Islam and the advancement of the marauding sword of the Islamic army ravaged both Afghanistan and India equally.

Numerous attempts to subdue Afghanistan and overrun India ended in the loss of men, materials, and resources before imminent failures. In the year 644 CE under Caliph Osman, Abdullah bin-Amar led an intelligence mission by land through Persia and Afghanistan to Sind and Hind. After his return, he reported to Damascus, the Caliph's headquarters, that in Hind, 'A small army will soon be annihilated there, and a large army will soon die of hunger'.

But gradually, Islam consolidated its foothold in Afghanistan, and the new religion's entry changed the region for the better as well as for the worse. When Islam penetrated the region, under the Persian Samanid dynasty, which lasted from 874 CE to 999 CE, Afghanistan was part of a new Persian renaissance in arts and letters. This association proved beneficial for India–Afghanistan relations as the Persian language later reached India and brought the two countries closer again on a linguistic basis. For the next 300 years, the Eastern Afghan tribes led by Turkic commanders periodically invaded India, conquered Delhi, and created vast Indo-Afghan empires. These were peculiar periods of domination and counter-domination of each other's territories.

Afghanistan became the springboard for the Turks to start a campaign against India. The five dynasties of the Sultanate era and the Mughals ruled India for the next 750 years. Hindi was one of the 11 prevalent languages in Kabul, while Persian was the court language in India. The combination of Hindi and Persian gave birth to Urdu.

These homilies and bonds were cut adrift once Nadir Shah won Afghanistan and brought his rule up to the bank of the Indus in 1739. He attacked India and undertook killing and looting on an unimaginable scale. A few years later, in 1747, Nadir Shah was assassinated and the Afghans under Ahmed Shah united to rule their own country. Ahmed Shah led many campaigns against India. Indo-Afghan relations remained entangled in a series of Indo-Afghan Wars and Anglo-Afghan Wars for the next two centuries.

By 1947, India gained independence while Afghanistan had already been freed much earlier after the third Anglo-Afghan War in 1919. Afghanistan was eager to renew its age-old relations with India, and the presence of Indians in Afghanistan was all-pervasive until the civil war that started in 1979. Although no official census has been carried out by the Royal Afghan Government, according to a 1972 report from the Indian Embassy in Kabul, the approximate number of Afghan Hindus and Sikhs of Indian origin is said to be 20,000.[1] They were mostly residing in Kabul, Kandahar, Jalalabad, and Ghazni. While the majority of them had been settled there for generations, some migrated from the North West Frontier Province in 1947, at the time of the partition of India, and had since acquired Afghan nationality. In 1971, the number of Indian families (not the native Indian-Afghans) in Afghanistan was nearly 370. The total population of Indians and their families was estimated to be 1600.

Some reports suggest that during the late 1980s, there were about 500,000 Indians scattered across Afghanistan.[2] By the year 1990, the number reduced to a mere 45,000.[3] The emigrants mostly belonged to the category of retail shopkeepers and general merchants dealing in clothes and other consumer items. Most of those individuals had become naturalized Afghan citizens. Many Hindus once formed Afghanistan's intellectual backbone. Now, most of them are shopkeepers. The number reduced further to 30,000 by the end of 1992.[4]

The country's Islam was moderate, based on the Sunni Hanafi sect. However, after the Mujahideen civil war and the rise of the Taliban in 1994, a harsh form of Islam was introduced, forcing most people of Indian origin to flee the country by 1998. Then, the number dwindled to 1200 families, including about 6500 Sikhs and Hindus.[5]

After the Taliban took control of Afghanistan, there was large-scale migration and a drastic reduction in the number of people of Indian origin in Afghanistan. According to the estimate of the Indian Embassy in Kabul, those who remained in Afghanistan numbered about 1000, mostly residing in Jalalabad and Kabul, while the rest were scattered in other parts of Afghanistan.[6]

In April 2001, the Taliban regime issued an order imposing new restrictions on the Hindus and Sikhs in Afghanistan. As per this edict, the male Hindus were debarred from wearing either salwar kameez or white turbans. They were directed to wear a black cap and put a red tilak on their foreheads when they went out of their homes as marks of identification. Hindu women too, when going out of their homes, were asked to drape themselves fully in a yellow cloth and wear an iron necklace. All Hindus were also required to display a yellow flag on their houses. Muslims and Hindus were debarred from residing in the same house. Many Afghan Hindus and Sikhs had moved out of Afghanistan before 11 September 2001.

The lone Sikh senator in Afghanistan's parliament, Mr Avtar Singh, who was killed in the 2018 Jalalabad attacks, explained before his death about the absence of government aid to the minorities of the country. According to an estimate by the Department of State, Government of the US, in 2011, there were three active gurdwaras in Kabul and ten in other parts of the country; there were 64 gurdwaras throughout the country before the Mujahideen era when many were seized. There are five remaining Hindu mandirs in three cities: two in Kabul, one of which shares a wall with a mosque, one in Jalalabad, one in Helmand, and one in Kandahar. Eighteen others were previously destroyed or rendered unusable due to looting during the civil war.

The continuous and steep rise of violence against the Hindus and Sikhs; the onset of neo-fundamentalist intolerance towards Indians; and the absence of support from any source evaporated the number to approximately 2000 Sikhs and approximately 100 Hindus in 2011.[7] In 2017, as per the Indian Mission, which maintains a database on Indians staying in Afghanistan, though many Indians don't register with the mission, there are estimated to be about 2500 Indians in the country, though only about 850 are registered with the Mission. Most of the Indian diaspora are engaged as professionals in banks, IT firms, construction companies, hospitals, NGOs, telecom companies, security companies, universities, Government of India-sponsored projects, the Government of Afghanistan, and UN Missions.[8]

In 2020, just over 600 Hindus and Sikhs lived across Afghanistan; two major attacks, one in Jalalabad in 2018 and one in Kabul in 2020, have killed about 50, leaving practically every family scarred.[9] The strong, centuries-old Sikh and Hindu presence in Afghanistan was decimated during recent years as pandits, professionals, and community leaders fled the country and the Taliban cracked down on non-Muslims.

Considering the geostrategic significance and despite the dismal ground situation, in the contemporary era, India–Afghanistan relations have long been a much-hyped subject among the academic and strategic circles in India. People-to-people relations between the two countries, which used to be two-way flamboyance until the onset of Taliban rule in 1996, have in the subsequent years primarily been driven by *Bollywood* films and Afghan refugees in India. The Bollywood influence in Afghanistan is tremendous.

Afghans learn Hindi because of *Bollywood*. Pakistan's former Inter Services Intelligence (ISI) Chief Lt. Gen. Asad Durrani noticed that during a 2015 visit to Herat, while he was speaking to his friend Gen. Aziz Khan, a 10-year-old girl overheard them speaking in Urdu, so she turned around and said *Namaste* (palms joined together and greeting with a *Namaste*). Lt. Gen. Durrani said, *kyun bhai kaha se sikha* (from where have you learned this joining of hands and *Namaste*). *TV dekhte hain na* (we watch television), she said.[10]

All academic institutions, think tanks and media groups in India have been running virtual Afghanistan–Pakistan desks and employing a varied number of subject experts to a surprising proportion when compared with other subjects. Masquerading as subject experts in India, people from all walks of life, starting from film stars to fashion designers and social workers to self-appointed social media activists, have been writing, talking, commenting and deliberating on India's relations with Afghanistan. However, the ancient Indo-Afghan landscape is hitherto unexplored by any historian or contemporary chronicler. So far, no systematized effort has ever been made by any scholar to explain how the two ancient nations were behaving during olden times or in the modern era. The subject of India–Afghanistan relations is an automatic yet undesirable hostage to post-1978 events.

During the summer of 2019, when I sent an article on Indo-Afghan relations covering the era starting from 1947 to 1979 to the prestigious *India Quarterly* journal, the rejection from a subject expert reviewer was accompanied by the advice to read J.N. Dixit's *Afghan Diary: Zahir Shah to Taliban* and Avinash Paliwal's *My Enemy's Enemy: India in Afghanistan from the Soviet Invasion to the US Withdrawal*. When I sent a piercing note reiterating the fact that neither the subject expert nor the editor of *India Quarterly* had read both the suggested books, since Dixit's book is a personal memoir about the period 1981–1985 and Paliwal's book is about post-1979 Indo-Afghan relations, which were mostly based on hearsay and secondary materials, the editor went on the back foot and agreed to reconsider the piece. Although the editor sent the piece to another 'subject expert', by then the editor's pride was bruised, and she rejected the paper on trivial grounds. Even experts in India are still trying to have a full understanding of the trajectory of Indo-Afghan relations.

The prevalent perception among Indian scholars that there is a plethora of research on Indo-Afghan relations is widespread. Therefore, every time a 'subject expert' blithely tried to opine about the availability of numerous research studies and books on Indo-Afghan relations, I used to ask him/her to specify the title of the book or research, the name of the author, the place of publication, and the name of the library housing such books or journals. Their answer naturally ended with more confusion and an absence of substance. This is especially true because nobody has ever worked on this topic, and there is no such work available in India or any part of the world. Probably, the contemporary generations of scholars in India have yet to embark on a rigorous research undertaking on the subject to match the teeming intellectual energy of India's ancient past.

Some of the good books on Afghanistan were written by Arab writers. Sir H. Elliot, in his note titled *India as known to the Arabs During the First Four Centuries of the Hijri Era*, wrote that *Mujmal-ut Tawarikh* of Abul Hasan bin Muhammad Ameen Gulistana; *Futuhu-i-Buldan* of Biladuri; *Chach-nama* translated from the Arabic by Muhammad Ali bin Hamid bin Abu Bakr Kufi;[11] and *Jami-ut Tawarikh* of Rashiduddin, all these Arabic sources deal with the course of Arab conquests in Sind. The *Chach-nama* deals more fully with the same subject, and the Arabic original of this work must have been written soon after the events it records, though the Persian version, which is the only one known to us, is of a later date. Citing all these sources, Sir H. Elliot concluded,

> The Arab occupation of Sind was but temporary, it was the precursor, not the commencement, of Musalman rule in India. On the retreat of the Arabs the government of the country reverted to native princes, and notwithstanding the successes of Mahmud of Ghazni, the land remained practically independent until its absorption into the Empire during the reign of Akbar in 1592 AD.[12]

Arab philosophers and geometricians have divided the land of Hind into nine unequal parts, giving each part a separate name, as appears from the Arabic source called *Batanjal*.[13] Their geographic expression of Hindustan started from the beginning of China through Tibet, and the country of the Turks, to Kabul, Badakshan, Turkharistan, Bamiyan, Ghur, Khurasan, Gilan, Azerbaijan, Armenia, Rum, to the country of the Franks and Galicia in the west.[14]

The Moroccan author Abu Abdullah Muhammad, known to us as 'Al-Idrisi' was employed by King Roger II of Sicily in the year 1145 CE. Roger II hired Al-Idrisi to create an updated world map. Al-Idrisi sent travellers and geographers around the world to gather knowledge for this updated map. He completed his book titled *Nuzhat-ul-Mushtak fi Ikhtirakh-ul Afak* or *The Delight of Those Who Seek to Wander through the Regions of the World* in the year 1154. He wrote, 'The people of Kandahar are often at war with those of Kabul, which is an Indian city, large and well built, bordering upon Tukharistan'.[15]

In the modern era, Gurudev Rabindranath Tagore's *Kabuliwala* is set against the backdrop of modern Kolkata in the eastern part of India. Bollywood, which is in Mumbai, the Western part of India, engaged megastar Amitabh Bachchan in the film *Khuda Gawah* to play the role of a *Pathan* from Kabul, who comes to India to settle a score with his fiancée's enemy.

There are many books published by colonial authors who completed their work while in the service of the East India Company or the service of the British Crown. At times, the Company or the Crown commissioned research or writing through their military officers or civil bureaucrats. A Lieutenant General in the Royal Artillery in the British Army, Sir George MacMunn, like his other colonial counterparts, embarked upon the journey of academic narrative building when he wrote the book *Afghanistan From Darius to Amanullah* in 1929. As a British Army officer, Lt. Gen. MacMunn was well-versed in military exploits. He had little exposure to Indian and Afghan history; therefore, in his work, he never provided citations, references or sources in his entire book and enlisted only nine books in his bibliography, which he admittedly consulted while writing his *Afghanistan From Darius to Amanullah*. Out of the nine books, except for Ferishta's work and the Persian source *Sair-ul-Mutaqareen*, the rest of the seven books were written by colonial authors.[16] In other words, Lt. Gen. MacMunn never consulted Indian or Afghan sources while writing his book.

MacMunn's scholarship, like that of his other colleagues, was limited to the task of proving the Aryan invasion theory in India. Nonchalantly, he wrote, 'Coming of the Aryan waves through the Afghan passes to India'.[17] 'The Aryan race started moving from the Central Asian Stepps, impelled perhaps by Tatar pressure, and split into the three streams of accepted theory'.[18] For nearly two centuries, the British and some Indian historians tried to portray the narrative that the Aryans were outsiders who invaded India which was famously known as the 'Aryan invasion theory'. The Aryan invasion theory was mostly based on unscrutinized historical materials and unsubstantiated claims without any scientific rationale. The colonial agenda was to rob Indians of their ancient identity and replace the local religion with Christianity, as they have done in other parts of the world.[19] Therefore, the colonial authors, followed by Indian historians, tried hard to prove that 'Aryans came to India from Central Asian Stepps and they invented Hinduism in India only'.[20] Colonial writers and their Indian counterparts refused to scrutinize the fact why Sanskrit was not present in Central Asian Stepps from where the Aryans headed towards India. All these authors advanced the theory that the Aryans devised their language 'Sanskrit' in India only, not in Central Asian Stepps, and they developed a culture alien to their homeland, which they left behind. MacMunn's biases can be further confirmed in his other book *The Martial Races of India*, where he stated:

> The white races that forced their way through the mountains of Solomon from Central Asian Stepps, evolved a faith which we call Hinduism but which they do not. They impinged on a far older faith.[21]

Scientific studies conducted by modern scholars deciphered 'ancient genomes from the Indus Valley Civilization', which 'had little if any Steppe pastoralist-derived ancestry.[22] The study contradicts the hypothesis that the shared ancestry between early Iranians and South Asians reflects a large-scale spread of western Iranian farmers east'.[23] Sampled ancient genomes from the Iranian plateau and Indus Valley proved the fact that the two sets of civilizations were unconnected with each other.

Lt. Gen. MacMunn, in his book, delink Afghanistan from India by proving the theory that Afghans were of Semitic origin. He stated that 'there is every possibility that the Afghans, that is to say, the Abdalis, are of Hebrew origin'[24] and 'their physiognomy would point much more to Judah than to Israel'.

Lt. Gen. MacMunn's inveterate hatred towards India can be easily judged from his writings. He wrote, 'Our energies in India have let the education that is so essential pass to the clever un-manly classes, who cannot alone use it effectively', and

> the ineffective outlook of the Gandhi mind would but throw the country back, would get rid of the West and its millions of miles of life-giving water, its thousands of miles of rail that prevent famine, and would bring it where it was, like China with her bandits and war-lords.[25]

Western writers, along with their Indian counterparts, generally confine their research on Afghanistan to the recent few centuries, especially after the full grip of Islam in Afghanistan, and they present Afghanistan as a landlocked country of Islamist tribes. Dutch historian Jos J.L. Gommans, in his *The Rise of The Indo-Afghan Empire, c. 1710–1780* confined his research to 70 years only and presented Afghanistan as a successful Islamic empire, which not only gained parity with India but also defeated Indian kings comfortably. Gommans's thesis was based on his understanding that the Durrani-Afghans had created a new empire and formulated a 'new imperial tradition on the basis of long-standing Perso-Islamic ideas of legitimate rule'.[26] He wrote, 'Afghan tribes, originally located in their mountain strongholds of Roh but increasingly spreading out towards India, were particularly well suited to outmanoeuvre the Mughals'.[27] Although he quoted Abul Fazl, who explicitly enmeshed modern-day Afghanistan and India, Gommans followed in the footsteps of colonial authors and did not properly scrutinize the historical identity of the Afghans.

T.A. Heathcote, the military historian and expert on the British military, was another colonial historian who wrote extensively about the British Army's strategic thinking and exploits. His book *The Afghan Wars, 1839–1919* is, as with many other British authors, an attempt to glorify Britain's involvement in Afghanistan. The book is all about Britain's Great Game struggle,[28] the three Afghan Wars that were waged by the British empire from Indian soil and the consequent final disconnect with Afghanistan. The first Anglo-Afghan War, which was intended to make Afghanistan a client state, turned out to be an utter military disaster. The famous painter Elizabeth Butler aptly painted *End of War*, where she depicted an exhausted, tired, and defeated William Brydon, the assistant surgeon, the only British soldier who managed to return alive on the back of an unwilling horse to the safety of Jalalabad Fort at the end of the war on 13 January 1842. Heathcote portrayed the second Anglo-Afghan War as a successful punishing adventure as the Treaty of Gandamak signed on 26 May 1879 turned Afghanistan into a client state of the British empire. Heathcote absorbed the demoralizing British defeat at Maiwand on 27 July 1880 and the subsequent withdrawal of British forces from Afghanistan as a British military strategy.[29] British strategic thinkers felt that a subsidiary buffer state, i.e. Afghanistan, was established between the British Indian Empire and Russian predatory eyes. This buffer state theory was giving much consolation to the British, and the arrangement was in vogue for the next 40 years until the third Anglo-Afghan War that was fought in 1919. After the second Anglo-Afghan War, the British gained control over the foreign affairs of Afghanistan and, therefore, they managed to draw and ratify the artificial Durand Line in 1893. However, soon the third Anglo-Afghan War was fought and the Afghans regained not only their freedom but also removed the last vestiges of British influence. By 1921, Afghanistan signed the Treaty of Friendship with the Soviet Union, turning the British gain in the Great Game struggle into a fiasco.

Rob Johnson's *The Afghan Way of War Culture and Pragmatism: A Critical History* also belongs to the same category. Johnson was a former British Army officer who joined Oxford University as a 'Lecturer' in the History of War Department. Johnson drew upon the archives of the much-mined India Office as well as private collections. Most of the consulted papers were secondary sources. The work of Rob Johnson is mostly based on the Great Game struggle and not on India–Afghanistan relations. For the Soviet experience in Afghanistan, he found extensive resources from the Cold War International History Project. All are secondary. He used anthropological texts, notably A.S. Ahmed's articles and books – all secondary. His bibliography is the most extensive, not necessarily primary sources, as most of them are secondary sources. In any case, the book was inspired by B.H. Liddell Hart's *The British Way in Warfare* published in 1934 and also represents a continuing imitation of Russell Weigley's *The American Way in War* and a similar study by British military historian David French in his two books *The British Way of War Reconsidered* and *The British Way in Counterinsurgency*.

William Dalrymple's *Return of a King: The Battle for Afghanistan 1839–1842* also belongs to the same genre of work where British actors dominate the British–Afghan relations debate. Dalrymple powerfully portrayed the genesis of the Great Game struggle.[30] He explained extremely well how the Afghan empire changed hands from one ruler to another. But despite accessing numerous Persian sources, his thesis is a mere summary of the British side of the story regarding the first Anglo-Afghan War.

All these works explained British interaction with Afghanistan in threadbare detail and portrayed Afghan history through the prism of Islam or Abrahamic religion. Although there are sprinklings of explanations about India's ancient character, such explanations are mostly presented in denial mode. There is a complete lack of research on the subject of India and Afghanistan's mutual relations.

A few decades after the partition of India, Pakistan tried to make Afghanistan a client state or a strategic backyard. Pakistan pursued a 'strategic depth' policy in Afghanistan, which propelled much research on the subject.[31] The Soviet departure from Afghanistan and Taliban takeover of the country in 1996 dampened the spirit of scholars on Afghanistan. Except for ace Pakistani journalist Ahmed Rashid, no other scholar worked on Afghanistan in those days.

Ahmed Rashid published the most popular book on Afghanistan titled *Taliban: Militant Islam, Oil and Fundamentalism in Central Asia* in 2000, just ahead of the 9/11 attacks. He had been working as a reporter in Afghanistan when the Taliban ruled the country and when no other journalist or academic was showing any interest in the subject. Therefore, when 9/11 happened and when the whole world wanted to understand the Taliban, Ahmed Rashid's book naturally became the best source material. Timing apart, the book is an honest academic endeavour. I have had many interactions with Ahmed Rashid to get an overview of Afghan politics.[32] Peter Hopkirk was the only other scholar who published an important book *The Great Game: The Struggle for Empire in Central Asia* in the year 1994. Hopkirk's book is extremely important because, as fate favoured the author under an unlikely situation, President Najibullah, who had taken asylum in the United Nations compound in Kabul for more than four years starting 16 April 1996 after the overthrow of his government, embarked upon the task of translating Hopkirk's book into Pashtu. As reported by the *New York Times* merely a week after Najibullah's death, 'Mr. Najibullah told United Nations officials that he wanted Afghans to read the Hopkirk text because of what they would learn from it about the 19th-century struggle between imperial Britain and imperial Russia for influence in Afghanistan'.[33] Najibullah clearly stated that the book is about Britain and Russia's struggle for influence in Afghanistan and not on Indo-Afghan relations. On the morning of 27 September 1996, the day the Taliban conquered Kabul, an assassination squad snatched him from the UN compound. Najibullah, who was also known as 'The Ox', was castrated and shot. Finally, his executioners – members of a Pakistani-backed militia – hung his mutilated body from a pillar on one of Kabul's busiest roundabouts. Hopkirk grieved when he told *The Times* reporter, 'I am not sure what became of Najibullah's translation. I know that it found its way to India where his wife and children had been given asylum. Sadly, after that, the trail goes cold'.[34] Hopkirk published six other books, including the important work *Foreign Devils on the Silk Road: The Search for the Lost Cities and Treasures of Chinese Central Asia* published in 1980. A former Pakistani spy, Mohammad Yousuf, and his co-author Mark Adkin published the revealing *Afghanistan: The Bear Trap, The Defeat of a Superpower* in 2001. Yousuf was a senior Pakistani military officer on deputation to train Mujahideen forces in Afghanistan, who were fighting against Soviet occupation in Afghanistan. This valuable book is a glimpse into the Pakistani role in supporting the US scheme of checkmating Soviet Russia in Afghanistan.

Once it was ascertained by the US intelligence that the 9/11 attacks were orchestrated from Afghan soil, the world's academia again turned its attention to Afghanistan. The US war on terror and the North Atlantic Treaty Organization's participation in Afghanistan propelled extraordinary research on the subject, and scores of good books published by eminent scholars on Afghanistan adorned the Afghan section of libraries across the world. Ahmad Rashid published two extremely well-written books, *Descent into Chaos: The United States and the Failure of Nation Building in Pakistan, Afghanistan, and Central Asia* and *Pakistan on the Brink – The Future of Pakistan, Afghanistan and the West*. Famous Afghan specialist Amin Saikal published *Modern Afghanistan: A History of Struggle and Survival*. Award-winning journalist Steve Coll wrote *Ghost War: The Secret History of the CIA, Afghanistan and Bin Laden*, which became an overnight bestseller. Kathy Gannon's *'I is for Infidel'* received unusual limelight.

As the book-writing spree continued, I was engaged by various institutes to review books written by Afghan experts. For the *Journal of International and Global Studies* published by Lindenwood University, I reviewed two important works. The first one was *Afghanistan to 2015 and Beyond* edited by Toby Dodge and Nicholas Redman, and the second was Astri Suhrke's *When More is Less: The International Project in Afghanistan*. For the *World Affairs* journal, I reviewed Radha Kumar and Kailash Prasad's *Afghanistan 2012: Looking to the Future*.

Carlotta Gall's *The Wrong Enemy: America in Afghanistan 2001–2014*; David Sanger's *The Inheritance: The World Obama Confronts and the Challenges to American Power*; Syed Saleem Shahzad's *Inside Al Qaeda and the Taliban: Beyond bin Laden and 9/11*; Bob Woodward's *Obama's War*; and Adrian Levy's *The Exile* are some of the best investigative books on the subject. I had the good fortune of long conversations with Syed Saleem Shahzad (who was kidnapped and killed in Pakistan), Adrian Levy, and email correspondence with Ahmed Rashid.

B.D. Hopkins's *The Making of Modern Afghanistan* was shaped by the colonial knowledge of Afghanistan and the Great Game struggle, which dealt with British interaction with Afghanistan. Other than providing a few pages on the geographical background of Afghanistan, Ali Ahmed Jalali's *A Military History of Afghanistan: From the Great Game to the Global War on Terror* covers the period starting from 1747. Like many other books, the scope of these two works is never Indo-Afghan relations. Kaushik Roy's *War and Society in Afghanistan*; M. Hassan Kakar's *Afghanistan: The Soviet Invasion and the Afghan Response, 1979–1982*; and Victoria Schofield's *Afghan Frontier: Feuding and Fighting in Central Asia/At the Crossroads of Conflict* – all based on secondary sources – have touched various aspects of the Afghan landscape but are far detached from the subject of Indo-Afghan relations.

The scope of all these books has remained within the modern era. Although brilliantly written, all these books deal with popular subjects like the Great Game struggle; the post-1979 military adventures of the Soviet Union in Afghanistan; and the United States' war on terror after the 9/11 attacks. All these books are fantastically written and very important works in their own right, which contributed to the scholarship on the subject but were far detached from the scope of 'Indo-Afghan relations'.

The issue of the 'Great Game' is purposefully left out in this book as the subject has nothing to do with India and Afghanistan relations. The Great Game struggle started with the sighting of the Russian agent Captain Vitkevitch near eastern Persia in 1837 by the British political agent Lieutenant Henri Rawlinson. British military-political strategists had long suspected Russian intentions to threaten their Indian possession – the jewel in the crown – through Afghanistan.

This British–Russian shadow fight in Afghanistan was dubbed as Great Game. British East India Company's Captain Arthur Conolly and Lieutenant Henry Rawlinson jointly coined the phrase 'Great Game' in 1840. In July 1840, Captain Conolly first used the phrase when he wrote a letter to Lieutenant Rawlinson in which he stated 'You've a great game, a noble game, before you'.[35] The sighting of a Russian agent sent chilling waves through the British camp. On 1 November 1837, immediately after the detection of a Russian agent on the soil of Afghanistan, Rawlinson headed straight back to Teheran and brought the news of the existence of the Russian delegation to Afghanistan to Sir John MacNeill – the British Ambassador in Teheran.

MacNeill, in turn, sent two messengers to Lord Palmerston in London and to the new Governor General of India, Lord Auckland, in Calcutta.

The British ambassador in Tehran reported, 'The Russians have formally opened their diplomatic intercourse with Kabul. Captain Victevitch, alias Omar Beg, a soonee Mahommedan subject of Russia, had been accredited, I am informed, as charge d'affaires to Ameer Dost Mohammed Khan'.[36] Rawlinson's sighting of Vitkevitch seemed to validate all the over-heated fears of his boss, MacNeill, Lord Ellenborough, and other British policymakers who had long feared that the Russians wanted to take over Afghanistan and use it as a base for attacking British India.[37] The Russian officer Captain Victevitch was not headed to India. His mission was to undermine British interests in Afghanistan and forge an alliance between the Tsar and Dost Mohammad. The British, in return, wanted to stop Russian overtures in Afghanistan.

This vicious spy-fight and proxy war continued for the next 63 years. It had nothing to do with India or Indian interests. It was a pure British–Russian competition to gain control of Afghanistan. Rudyard Kipling's novel *Kim*, which was published first in a magazine and then as a book during 1900–1901 glamorized the Great Game.[38] Kipling used the phrase Great Game a total of 16 times in his novel. But as already explained, the subject is foreign to the scope of this study and it has no connection whatsoever with this manuscript. As explained in great detail, the theme Great Game struggle is outside the domain of Indo-Afghan relations. It was a story of the Russo-British fight. Therefore, this manuscript does not delve into the subject of the Great Game struggle. Contrary to the Great Game debate, which was unsuitably fitted by many scholars into India's Afghan relations, the subject of Pashtunistan is very much part of Indo-Afghan relations. Therefore, the manuscript deals adequately with the Pashtunistan issue.

Based mostly on original ancient literature and relying heavily on authorized hitherto unknown archival documents, this work is exclusively about India–Afghanistan relations. South Asia's history, although ancient in age and authentic in character, is highly contested in academia and grossly misunderstood by the Western world. Due to a misconstrued portrayal of India, modern scholars have discounted India's role in the complex Afghan imbroglio that has persisted in the country for the past four decades. Despite the volume of research available in the West about India's ancient civilizational prowess, Western scholars have always preferred to view India's intellectual tradition through the eyes of folklore, tall tales, and hearsay. Since Western history, Greece apart, is more recent when compared with other civilizations, which is a mere 2000 or 2500 years old, they may even have municipality certificates and other written documentary evidence of their history.[39] The West has been a scriptural civilization. But India's sources are different.

Legends, race memory, which people store in their minds, memorization of canonical texts, graves and samadhis, ruins and monuments, folk songs, and oral history are the backbone of Indian history.

From time to time, knowledgeable explanations have been provided by Indian scholars against modern Western scholars' brazen and unsubstantiated accusations. This attitude towards Indian civilization is connected with a retrospective vindication of British rule. This is also linked with the fairly common back-handed compliment paid to Jawaharlal Nehru as 'India's last Governor-General'. The idea is that the momentum of the British ethos survived during the leadership of the most British of Indian politicians. All this would have very little immediate significance if it were not for the fact that there is today a lobby in the United States which has linked ideas. British eccentricities of opinion can be dismissed as of minor importance.[40]

India, the cradle of ancient civilization and the powerhouse of scholarly debate, is left out of meaningful Afghan-related academic discussion at the present time due to the neglect and inability of contemporary historians. A serious flaw in the historical interpretation of Afghanistan by contemporary global historians is the deliberate and ignoble absence of India's connection. The history of Afghanistan, from an ancient sophisticated Hindu civilization to a flourishing culture of Buddhism to a frenzied form of Islam, is short-circuited into a troubled land steeped in chaos and disarray.

India's bilateral relations with Afghanistan, particularly after the country's independence, are prejudicially viewed from the prism of a Great Game struggle involving the United States, Soviet Russia, China, and Britain. Owing to the birth of Pakistan between India and Afghanistan and because of the changing dynamics of geostrategic significance, analysts and foreign policy observers erroneously yet consistently hyphenate India's Afghan policy with Pakistan. Curiously, there is nearly no scholarly discussion about India's early relations with Afghanistan. Both countries' excellent mutual relations, common adherence to doctrinal principles like non-aligned ideology, anti-colonialism and promotion of world peace have been conveniently ignored. As former President S. Radhakrishnan opined in Kabul in 1963, 'the relations which are so cordial and happy between our two countries – there is not one problem which is dividing us or giving us concern'.

Considering the absence of Indo-Afghan research from ancient times to the modern era, the scope of this manuscript ranges from ancient antiquity to the contemporary era. This book is an attempt to understand the ancient historical linkages between India and Afghanistan and provide a first-ever chronological explanation of the historical journey of the two countries. Empirically, the study deals with the evolution of India's Afghan policy. It identifies historical catalysts that contributed to the deterioration of ancient bonds and linkages. Intricate issues such as the erection of the Durand Line

– the boundary line between Afghanistan and British India, which became a dispute encyclopaedia - from the outset; the creation of Pakistan and its impact on Indo-Afghan relations; and the ethnic-religious factors responsible for the topsy-turvy India–Afghanistan relations in the recent past are also deliberated.

For the ancient and medievalist explanations, I have incorporated almost all relevant sources authored/compiled by Greek, Chinese, Sanskrit, and Persian scholars. The manuscript methodically explains how Afghan people were obsessed with Magadh, which is not a peripheral state. The manuscript discusses extensively how a portion of the *Rig Veda* was composed in Afghanistan and how the *Mahabharata* was deeply affiliated with the Afghan landscape. It shows how Gautama Buddha's appeal still reverberates across Afghan soil. These subjects are pan-Indian in their appeal and influence the Indian thought system. In other words, all over India, people are well acquainted with Afghan topography as their folklore and philosophy are intrinsically associated with Afghanistan.

Despite destruction attempts, Buddha's colossal statues still adorn the cliffs of Bamiyan Valley. The city of 'Balkh' in the heart of Afghanistan used to be called 'Little Rajgriha' owing to the heavy concentration of Buddhist viharas and also the former's resemblance to Rajgriha, the Magadhan town in the heart of India.

For the modern era, I have accessed archival sources available in India, America, and Britain. Using these archival sources, the book explores how India and Afghanistan conducted themselves during the early years after the establishment of formal diplomatic relations. The study inquires into the question of how Afghanistan's multilateral relations with great powers and neighbouring countries had no impact whatsoever on bilateral relations with India.

After independence, although the formal signing of the friendship treaty with Afghanistan happened in January 1950, Wing Commander Rup Chand was appointed as Ambassador of India to Afghanistan in June 1948. The Indian Embassy in Kabul reported that India's relations, especially trade relations, were hostage to India–Pakistan relations, on the one hand, and Afghanistan–Pakistan relations, on the other.

Perhaps the Afghans feel that only the creation of an independent state of Pakhtoonistan from Chitral to Baluchistan with a contiguous border with India at one end and an outlet to the sea at the other can remove the thorn from the sides of the Indo-Afghan trade and provide a condition for its development to the maximum heights. Even during the early days of independence, Indian diplomats showed a desire 'to play [a] legitimate and well-deserved role in the reconstruction and development of the economic life of both Pakhtoonistan (shattered by over a 100 years of war which the British waged there) and Afghanistan'.

India's position on the Durand Line was that the line was not calculated to demarcate the boundary between India and Afghanistan but to delimit the sphere of influence of the Amir's authority in the tribal area. This fact has been patently admitted even by a pro-Pakistani person like Sir Olaf Caroe in his book *The Pathans*. Therefore, as per India's policy, 'it is wrong for Pakistan to assert that [the] Durand Line constituted an international frontier between pre-partition India and Afghanistan'.

The year 1978 was a watershed in the Indo-Afghan relationship. Afghanistan was about to enter a new phase, an era of predatory foreign intervention and internal chaos. For the next 11 years, up to 1989, Afghanistan witnessed an unprecedented power struggle, the involvement of foreign fighters, and civil strife. India was unprepared for the massive change that was about to take place in Afghanistan. Although diplomatic cables sent from the Indian Embassy and Consulates in Afghanistan explained the change with captivating details, unlike the pre-1978 era, a convincing bilateral relationship was absent, and there was also a frequent change in New Delhi's position *vis-à-vis* the Afghan government.

By 16 February 1989, the Soviet Union announced the return of its last soldier from Afghan soil. India supported the Soviet-backed government while establishing contacts with the leaders of the Resistance Movement against the Soviet Union. India sided with President Najibullah despite Afghan public opinion against him and even though the Mujahideen started a Jihad against the Soviet-backed Najibullah. The international community and even some Soviet observers expected that after Moscow's withdrawal, President Najibullah's days were numbered. Contrary to everyone's estimation, President Najibullah's forces proved sturdier than expected. They possessed vast arsenals of Soviet-supplied weapons. Najibullah was finally killed in September 1996 by the Taliban. These were challenging years for the Indian staff. They were in the midst of war. Death used to lurk on the doorstep.

With the takeover of Kabul by the Taliban militia on 27 September 1996, a new dimension had been added to the unstable condition in Afghanistan. Pakistan thought that it had successfully removed India from the soil of Afghanistan, which was true on paper. India continued to recognize the government of Professor Burhanuddin Rabbani, and although regular contact was not possible, relations continued to flourish at various levels.

This book negates the popular perception that India lost contact with Afghanistan during the decade of the 1990s. It provides in great detail how India's contact with Afghanistan continues despite the loss of formal diplomatic contact with the pariah Taliban administration in September 1996.

It elucidates how, despite the loss of contact with Afghanistan twice during the 1990s, India remained an important arbiter and a tested friend. India continued to maintain contact with the Ahmed Shah Massoud-led Northern Alliance. The Taliban overran Kabul in September 1996 and established an ultra-Islamic government that was recognized only by Saudi Arabia, Pakistan, and the United Arab Emirates.

When the 9/11 attacks happened and the world grappled with the fact that the attack originated from the trenches of Afghanistan, the US response eclipsed every other aspect *vis-à-vis* Afghanistan. The Durand Line had reduced Afghanistan to a landlocked country. Considering the inhospitable terrain in Central Asia and Iran's pariah status among the comity of nations, Afghanistan is heavily dependent on Pakistan to transit materials from India and from elsewhere. The US and NATO countries, during the war on terror in Afghanistan, entirely relied on Pakistan to transfer materials through the Karachi Port. On 21 November 2001, amidst America's 'Operation Enduring Freedom' in Afghanistan that started on 7 October 2001, India's Special Envoy on Afghanistan Mr. S.K. Lambah led a diplomatic mission to Kabul. From the same date, the Liaison Office of the Ministry of External Affairs became operational in Kabul. Since then, Indo-Afghan relations have grown with time.

India developed air connectivity with Kabul and Kandahar, which reduced this dependency to a considerable level. The air route not only augmented Indo-Afghan connections but also facilitated the entire world to reach Afghanistan by transiting through India.

To remove the Pakistani monopoly in dictating global transit to Afghanistan, India invested heavily in the development of Shahid Beheshti Port in Chabahar in cooperation with the Government of the Islamic Republic of Iran. During the visit of Prime Minister Narendra Modi to Tehran in May 2016, the contract on Chabahar was signed which, *inter alia*, comprises an investment of $85 million for equipping the port. The contract also comprises the provision of credit of approximately $150 million for the development of the first phase of Shahid Beheshti Port at Chabahar. The Trilateral Transit Agreement (Chabahar Agreement) was signed by the three Transport Ministers of India, Iran, and Afghanistan in the presence of Prime Minister Narendra Modi, President Dr Hassan Rouhani, and President Ashraf Ghani in May 2016. The Indian company, India Ports Global Limited, took over port operations in December 2018 and has been successfully handling cargo since then. The US has shown an understanding of the importance of the Chabahar Port operations for continued humanitarian supplies to Afghanistan and to provide Afghanistan with economic alternatives. Afghanistan has also started using the port facility. It sent its first export consignment to India through Chabahar Port in February

2019. Besides the Indian exports of food products, the port has also handled several shipments and trans-shipments from Russia, Brazil, Thailand, Germany, Ukraine, and the UAE.

India benefited from the outcome of the US policy response and managed to reorient Indo-Afghan relations. India's investment in the reconstruction of Afghanistan and enrichment of bilateral relations, including the signing of the Strategic Partnership Agreement, were important landmarks in Indo-Afghan relations.

In April 2021, nearly two decades after the war and ravage, President Joe Biden announced the withdrawal of all combat troops from Afghanistan by 11 September 2021. It was the declaration of an end to America's longest war. During the two decades of fighting, nearly 2400 American troops had died in Afghanistan. The conflict had cost about $2 trillion. The US was still to find a suitable strategy on how to deal with terrorist groups like al-Qaeda when 3500 US troops and 7000 NATO soldiers left Afghanistan to honour the troop withdrawal deadline.

The American presence in Afghanistan proved to be a great boon for India. Considering India's traditional long-term relations with anti-Taliban groups in Afghanistan and because of the Taliban's proximity to Pakistan, India never developed relations with the Taliban. Now, US troops have left Afghanistan and the Taliban regained power with the active backing of Pakistan in August 2021. India's investment and fantastic relations with Afghanistan were disturbed after the Taliban takeover of Kabul in August 2021. All these developments ceased, and India's foreign relations with Afghanistan are in tatters.

Flight operations to Afghanistan also ceased, and India, like many other countries, closed its Embassy in Kabul and Consulates in Kandahar, Herat, and Mazar-e-Sharif. The topsy-turvy turf of Afghanistan again proved challenging for India. Bilateral relations ended abruptly. Nevertheless, India's post-2021 Taliban engagement reflects a pragmatic shift driven by security and strategic imperatives. While eschewing formal recognition, India has pursued dialogue, prioritizing counterterrorism and humanitarian aid. Initial contacts in Doha transitioned to tangible assistance, including food, medicine, and COVID-19 vaccines. The establishment of a technical team in Kabul facilitated aid distribution and on-ground monitoring. Crucially, high-level meetings, such as the one in Dubai on 8 January 2025, where India's Foreign Secretary Vikram Misri met acting Foreign Minister of Afghanistan Maulvi Amir Khan Muttaqi, underscore deepening engagement, focusing on bilateral relations, regional stability, and the strategic importance of the Chabahar Port. India's approach balances security concerns, particularly the prevention of anti-India terror emanating from Afghan soil, with the necessity of maintaining a degree of influence. This engagement, though delicate, aims to safeguard India's regional interests and age-old contacts amidst a volatile geopolitical landscape.

Notes

1. Annual Report for 1971 from Kabul, MEA, GOI, File No. HI/1011 (14)/72-I, 1972, National Archives of India.
2. Reuters, Times of India, 22 November 2006.
3. Report of the High-Level Committee on Indian Diaspora, 'Afghanistan, Central Asia and Iran', Chapter 2, 2001, p. 7.
4. *SL and Others (Returning Sikhs and Hindus) Afghanistan v. Secretary of State for the Home Department*, CG, 2005, UKIAT 00137, United Kingdom: Asylum and Immigration Tribunal/Immigration Appellate Authority, 7 October 2005, available at: http://www.unhcr.org/refworld/docid/43fc2d7911.html
5. *SL and Others (Returning Sikhs and Hindus) Afghanistan v. Secretary of State for the Home Department*, CG, 2005, UKIAT 00137, United Kingdom: Asylum and Immigration Tribunal/Immigration Appellate Authority, 7 October 2005, available at: http://www.unhcr.org/refworld/docid/43fc2d7911.html
6. Report of the High-Level Committee on Indian Diaspora, 'Afghanistan, Central Asia and Iran', Chapter 2, 2001, p. 7.
7. International Religious Freedom Report for 2011, Afghanistan, Section I. Religious Demography, Bureau of Democracy, Human Rights and Labor, Department of State, Government of USA, 2011, https://2009-2017.state.gov/j/drl/rls/irf/2011religiousfreedom/index.htm?dlid=192917#wrapper
8. MEA, India-Afghanistan Relations, October 2017.
9. Mujib Mishal and Fahim Abed, India Offers Escape to Afghan Hindus and Sikhs Facing Attacks, *New York Times*, 19 July 2020.
10. A.S. Daulat, Asad Durrani, and Aditya Sinha, *Spy Chronicles: RAW, ISI and the Illusion of Peace* (Noida: HarperCollins Publishers, 2018), p. 237.
11. A full translation of the whole work into French was published in Paris in 1836 and 1840 by M. Jaubert, and from this the following extracts have been translated into English; John Dowson ed., *History of India as Told By Its Own Historians: The Muhammadan Period*, Vol. I (Lucknow: Kitab Mahal, 1869), p. 131.
12. John Dowson edt., Op cit., p. 44.
13. The book *Batanjal* or the complete title *Kitab batanjal al-hindi fi'l-khitif min al-amtfial* is Al-Biruni's Arabic version of Patañjali's *Yogasutra*; Al-Biruni's Arabic version of Patañjali's *Yogasutra*; Shlomo Pines and Tuvia Gelblum, *Bulletin of the School of Oriental and African Studies, University of London*, Vol. 29, No. 2 (1966), pp. 302–325.
14. John Dowson edt., Op cit., p. 44.
15. John Dowson ed., Op. cit. p. 92.
16. MacMunn stated that 'the Cambridge History of India is the last word in summarizing and coordinating all that has gone before, and that for the ordinary student neither the basic Ferishta nor the Sair-ul-Mutaqerin need be opened again'. He consulted 1. 'History of the Sikhs', Cunninghame (Murray); 2. 'The War in Afghanistan', John William Kaye (Bentley); 3. 'Forty-one Years in India', Lord Roberts (Macmillan); 4. 'Neville Chamberlain', Forrest (Blackwood); 5. 'The Life of Abdurrahman', an edited autobiography (Murray); and 6. 'The Amir Abdurrahman', Stephen Wheeler (Bliss, Sands & Foster).
17. George MacMunn, *Afghanistan From Darius to Amanullah* (London: G. Bell & Sons, 1929, p. XI.

18 George MacMunn, Op. cit., pp. 8–9.
19 David R. Syiemlieh ed., *On the Edge of Empire: Four British Plans for North East India, 1941–1947* (New Delhi: Sage Publications, 2014); R. Coupland, *The Future of India* (London: Oxford University Press, 1943), p. 164; Andrien, Kenneth, and Adorno, Rolena (eds.). *Transatlantic Encounters: Europeans and Andeans in the Sixteenth Century* (Berkeley: University of California Press, 1991); Jawaharlal Nehru, *Discovery of India* (New Delhi: Penguin, 2004), pp. 68–146.
20 George MacMunn, *The Martial Races of India* (London: Sampson Low Marston and Company Limited, 1933), p. 6.
21 George MacMunn, *The Martial Races of India*, p. 6.
22 Vasant Shinde et al., Ancient Harappan Genome Lacks Ancestry from Steppe Pastoralists or Iranian Farmers, *Cell*, 5 September 2019, pp. 17–19, DOI: https://doi.org/10.1016/j.cell.2019.08.048
23 Vasant Shinde, Ancient Harappan Genome Lacks Ancestry, p. 19.
24 Vasant Shinde, Ancient Harappan Genome Lacks Ancestry. p. 19.
25 George MacMunn, The Martial Races of India, Sampson Low Marston and Company Limited, 1933, p. 359.
26 Jos J.L. Gommans in his *The Rise of The Indo-Afghan Empire, c. 1710–1780*, p. 4.
27 Jos J.L. Gommans in his *The Rise of The Indo-Afghan Empire, c. 1710–1780*, p. 4.
28 T.A. Heathcote, *The Afghan Wars, 1839–1919* (London: Osprey Publishing, 1980), p. 19.
29 Heathcote, *The Afghan Wars, 1839–1919*, p. 32.
30 William Dalrymple, *Return of a King: The Battle for Afghanistan 1839–1842* (New Delhi: Bloomsbury, 2013), pp. 74–134.
31 Mirza Aslam Beg, General Zia-ul-Haq's high-profile army chief, was credited with the authorship of 'strategic depth' in the early 1980s; Saroj Kumar Rath, *Fragile Frontiers: The Secret History of Mumbai Terror Attacks* (London: Routledge, 2014), p. 16.
32 Author's meeting with Ahmed Rashid on 25 January 2011 in Jaipur; and subsequently, an email exchange on various dates.
33 John F. Burns, Afghanistan Reels Back into View, *New York Times*, 6 October 1996.
34 Tarquin Hall, The Great Game That Is Still Being Played, *The Times*, 29 April 2006.
35 John William Kaye, *Lives of Indian Officers*, Vol. II (London: W.H. Allen and Co., 1867), p. 101.
36 National Archives of India, Foreign, Secret Consultations, 17 October 1838, Nos 53–54.
37 William Dalrymple, *Return of a King: The Battle for Afghanistan 1839–1842* (New Delhi: Bloomsbury, 2013), pp. 79–82.
38 Rudyard Kipling, *Kim* (New York: Doubleday Page & Co., 1912), p. 181.
39 Kapil Kapoor and Michael Danino, Why Sanskrit is Not a Dead Language, nor the Language of Gods, Part I, Indian Institute of Technology, Gandhinagar, 11 January 2023, available at https://www.youtube.com/watch?v=BvYkT5J4Nqk&list=PLRfu94TCePTt0JaPrZfTiQTNu9dlT-xiB&index=1
40 A.K. Damodaran, Additional Secretary, 'Hinduism, Truth & Corruption', D.O. No. 479/AS/82, 3 April 1982, Cabinet Secretariat, Bikaner House Annex, Shahjahan Road, New Delhi, File No. FIII/103(16)/82, Note on 'Hinduism, Truth and Corruption Prepared by Cabinet Secretariat', MEA, GOI, National Archives of India (NAI), 1982.

ACKNOWLEDGEMENTS

Since 1991, I have been studying the contour of Afghanistan, the trajectories of ethnic groups, militant organizations, and people of Afghanistan. Since 2009, eminent scholar and International Criminal Tribunal for the Former Yugoslavia Judge, Prof. Chikako Taya, joined me in my research pursuit on Afghanistan. Ever since Prof. Taya joined our collective research, she has brought tremendous energy, scholarly innovations, and critical thinking to the subject. Twice, she facilitated my visits to Afghanistan. Besides my search for literature on the topic in India, I have visited libraries and archives across Europe and America to unravel source materials linked with Afghanistan.

However, prolonged study of the subject convinced me that scholars worldwide have already researched nearly all aspects of Afghan history – except one area – i.e. Indo-Afghan relations. It was surprising to find that one of the most popular topics, Indo-Afghan relations, was spared by scholars for academic research. Despite my own involvement in research on the topic for decades, I was nearly unaware of many facets of Indo-Afghan relations – especially about the information available in Greek, Chinese, Persian, and Sanskrit sources. This was primarily because modern scholars entirely rely on English literature and, to some extent, French work for source materials, which characterized Afghan history from a colonial prism and blurred the ancient characteristics of Afghanistan.

I embarked on this complex research only with the sole inspiration of Prof. Kapil Kapoor. The legendary Sanskrit scholar, originally an English literature Professor at the Jawaharlal Nehru University, inspired me in his quintessential style – 'We are representatives of a donor culture, not of a *katora* (beggar) culture'. In his roaring voice, he speaks the plain truth about the ancient character of India, which included Afghanistan. During one of the discussions at his abode at New Delhi's Indraprastha Extension, he told me that his ancestors belonged to Afghanistan. This book's writing and review process extended to over seven years, and Prof. Kapoor remained the unflinching guiding light during the entire span of labour. The ethical values and scholarly strength which he infused in me helped me see the light after the tunnel and finalize this book.

Shri Salman Rashid, Pakistani travel writer, historian and fellow of the Royal Geographical Society, stirs curiosity, enthusiasm, and conviction in me to write this book. The doyen of Indian history, Shri Rashid, instills great pride in ancient India's wisdom. He introduced me to the vista of Greek and Chinese fascination for ancient India's grandiose lifestyle, philosophy, and science and guided me in understanding Afghanistan's place in Indian history. Readers may understand the depth of his scholarship when they read the book as I have quoted him extensively.

Routledge's review process was so rigorous and educative for both the reviewers as well as for the author that thrice during the review and copyediting, the project was almost in the morgue. Resuscitation of the work was possible only at the behest of scholarly editor Dr Shashank Sinha *Sahib*. Like Prof. Kapoor, Dr Sinha is an unconventional scholar, who believes in ethics and risks.

Adwiteya Riti Rath, the mewing daughter, who came to this world in 2018, was three months old when I went for a three-week field trip to Europe and America. My field visit was not approved by *Riti*, and as a protest, she stopped taking food (breastfeeding only) and reduced her weight to tell her tale when I returned home. Owing to my vanishing acts and sudden reappearance during research when I had to bite the dust of archives, libraries, battlefields and cities in various countries, *Adyan Rigsadi Rath*, our son, used to think as if I was working as a spy for an intelligence agency. Mony, my wife, single-handedly set the stage for an enabling environment to meet the challenges of research, writing, and publication. When a bigger crisis used to substitute a smaller one and tried to asphyxiate the project, Mony used to be the fresh oxygen to breathe.

As a happy coincidence, during my writing, the Indian Council for Culture Research offered me a small grant to undertake research and write on the subject in *Hindi*, which augmented and helped my archival inquiry and field research. A few people helped me from behind the curtain. They wish not to make their names public. I owe a lot to them, and I can only remain indebted to them for their embrace.

ABBREVIATIONS

ADB	Asian Development Bank
ANSF	Afghan National Security Forces
APTTA	Afghanistan-Pakistan Transit Trade Agreement
ATTA	Afghanistan Transit Trade Agreement
CENTO	Central Treaty Organization
CIA	Central Intelligence Agency
CRC	Central Revolutionary Council
DNA	Deoxyribose Nucleic Acid
HI	Hekmatyar-Hizb-i-Islami-Hekmatyar (Party of Islam)
HII	Harakat-i-Inquilab-i-Islami (Islamic Revolutionary Forces)
HI-Rabbani	Hezb-i-Islami-Rabbani (Party of Islam)
ISI	Inter Services Intelligence
ITEC	Indian Technical and Economic Cooperation
IUM	Ikhwan-ul-Musalmeen
JI	Jamiat-i-Islami (Islamic Society)
JNM	Jabha-i-Nijat-Milli (Afghan National Liberation Front)
KDP	Khalq Democratic Party
KGB	Committee for State Security
MMI	Mahaz-i-Milli Islam (National Islamic Front of Afghanistan)
NA	Northern Alliance
NAM	Non Alignment Movement
NATO	North Atlantic Treaty Organization
NDS	National Directorate of Security
NEFA	North East Frontier Agency
NFLA	National Front for the Liberation of Afghanistan

NWFP	North West Frontiers Province
OSGAP	Office of Secretary-General in Afghanistan and Pakistan
PDPA	People's Democratic Party of Afghanistan
RPO	Regional Passport Office
RAW	Research and Analysis Wing
SEATO	South East Asia Treaty Organization
TAP	Turkmenistan-Afghanistan-Pakistan
TAPI	Pipeline Consortium Ltd
TAPI	Turkmenistan-Afghanistan-Pakistan-India
UNCOA	United Nations Coordinator's Office in Afghanistan
UNGA	United N General Assembly
USSR	Union of Soviet Socialist Republic

1
EXPLAINING ANCIENT CONNECTION

A simple glimpse into the annals of classical Greek and Indian literature offers numerous mute milestones, which endorse the fact that India and Afghanistan, before the demarcation of modern boundaries and the artificial erection of the Durand Line, shared nearly everything for millennia.

Racially, Indians and Afghans are akin, for the old Aryan stock dominates the two countries.[1] Greek historian Herodotus (484–424 BC) referred to the people living in and around the rivers Helmond, Haroot-rud, Farrah, Khash, and Kabul as Aryans by race.[2]

Civilizationally, as French archaeologists have unearthed contact between the Afghan city of Shortugai, situated on the eastern edge of the Amu Darya basin, and mature Harappan cities of India, the inextricable link dates back to 3500 BC.[3] The discovery of Mehrgarh, a few miles below the Bolan Pass, by French and Pakistani archaeologists supplemented the bond story, which they claimed was flourishing in 6400 BC.[4] Bolan Pass is one of the gateways to India, widely used by Arabs and Western travellers, traders, and invaders. Recent scientific research pushed the common India–Afghanistan Harappan civilizational tie to 7500 BC, while the year 3000 BC was stated as the beginning of the end of the Harappan era.[5]

Evidence of unbroken chronological religious affinity between the two countries is reiterated by the discovery of Harappan-era terracotta models of carts at the Afghan city of Shortugai, along with its contemporary Indian cousins at Mohenjo-Daro, Harappa, Lothal, Surkotada, and Kalibangan.[6] *Rig Veda*, the earliest known religious text, talks about the good wool of the sheep of Gandhara.[7] Gandhari lambs were famous for their wool. In the typical Vedic conversation, 'Romasa boasted to her husband Bhavayavya

DOI: 10.4324/9781003627678-1

of Sindhu: Mount up. Embrace me closely. I am voluptuous in venery. My vulva is buxom and is covered with hair like that of the lamb of Gandhara'.[8] *Atharva Veda*, another sacred religious text of India written along with *Rig Veda*, mentions the Gandharis with the Mujavats, apparently as a despised people[9] *Zend-Avesta*, the holy book of Zoroastrians, endorses the prevalence of Hindu civilization in the Helmond River basin and Kabul, which 'in fact in the two centuries before and after Christ were known as "White India", and remained more Indian than Iranian'.[10]

Sage Panini (550–490 BC), in his Sanskrit magnum opus *Ashtadhyayi*, the first-ever grammatical treatise of the world, provided rich geographical information[11] and topographical data from his time. It is interesting to note that Panini was residing at the border of present-day Afghanistan and, therefore, his explanation throws authentic light on the land and its people. Panini was a resident of Salatura.[12] The village has been identified with Lahur, a small town 4 miles north-west of Ohind, at the angle of the river Kabul meeting the Indus.[13] Being a resident of the region, Panini had a grasp of the geography, people, religion, and rulers present there.

His grammatical treatise *Ashtadhyayi* is not a rote textbook on Sanskrit grammar but a literary encyclopaedia comprising the minutest details about the last DNA sequence of not only contemporary humans but also of plants and animals. As a philologist, Panini never lost sight of providing information about the meaning and reason behind the naming of cities, towns, villages, places, rivers, forests, mountains, and oceans. Since grammar regulates the names, Panini discussed the names and their formation liberally in his treatise. Along with grammar, the subject of history is also richly benefited because while discussing the names, Panini talks about the social life and historical background under which a particular name is fixed for a place, person or thing.

Living in the age of Mahajanapadas, Panini offered a rare glimpse into the history of the region when he said, the 'western-most point of India is Prakanva (Fergana[14])'.[15] Herodotus named this place Parikanioi. Panini informs us that 'Rishi Praskanva used to live in this city and from this name is derived Prakanva'.[16] Panini wrote, 'South of Ferghana lay Kamboja[17] which is identified with Badakshan-Pamir region'.[18] An early Vedic tribe, Kambojas are mentioned in a list of ancient Vedic teachers given in the Vamsa Brahmana of the *Sama Veda*, where it is said that Kamboja is the son of Upamanyu.[19] *Rig Veda* mentions Sage Upamanyu.[20] Mahabharata talks about the best blankets (Kambalas) from Kambojas.[21] Harivamsa Purana mentioned that the Kambojas were formerly Kshatriyas.[22] Manu Samhita talks about the degradation of the Kshatriya of Kamboja. Kautilya's Arthashastra informs how the warriors from Kamboja used to live with their professions in trade, agriculture, and arms.

Panini further said, 'South of Kamboja lay Kapisi,[23] capital of the kingdom of Kapisa', which may be identified with modern Kafiristan, southeast of the Hindukush. South of Kapisi was situated Gandhara, comprising the valley of the Kabul River, with its frontier outpost at Takshasila.[24]

More than a thousand years later, in 629 CE, when the Chinese traveller Hiuen Tsang crossed through Salatura, he wrote that the tradition about Rishi Panini was current there, and his pupils erected a statue of him inside the village.[25]

The geographical extent of Gandhara, as per Herodotus' *Histories*, was comprised of 'the high tract extending from Cabool to Herat in one direction, and from Sir-pool to the banks of the Helmond in another'.[26] The inscriptions even seem to extend eastward to Margiana or the district of Merv of present-day Turkmenistan. Claudius Ptolemy (100–170 CE), the Egyptian geographer of Greek descent, places Gandhara between Bactria (Central Asia) and Arachosia (Arghandab Valley).[27] Their name is said to have signified 'the possessors of a hundred cows'.[28] Herodotus describes the Gandharians as 'a very remarkable people, and held in ancient times a very prominent position among the tribes dwelling between India and Persia'. However, all the early Sanskrit authorities gave the name Sindhu Gandhara to the country lying upon the banks of the upper Indus and its tributaries from where they issued from the mountains.[29] The term Gandhara continues to be applied to the Cabool country in the writings of the Arabian geographers.[30] When pressed upon by the Yue-Chi (Kushan),[31] a Tatar race, the Gandharians of Sindhu Gandhara relinquished their ancient abodes and migrated westward in the 5th or 6th century CE, carrying with them their sacred vessel – the water-pot of Fo – regarded as the most holy relic of Buddhism, which they transported from the upper Indus to the vicinity of the Arghandab. To this new country, they carried also their name, and here it remains in the modern Kandahar.[32]

Greek historian Hecataeus of Miletus (560–576 BC) explained that 'the Gandharians seem to be more properly regarded as an Indian than as an Iranian tribe'[33] while Persian King Darius, who spent the winter of 515–516 BC in Gandhara, attached the region to India in his list.[34] Greek geographer Strabo (64 BC–24 CE) regards the Gandharis as part of India[35] and Ptolemy includes Gandhara among his Indian nations.[36] Herodotus calls them 'a warlike race'.[37] They were retained by Mardonius, the general of of Xerxes I. But, curiously, they do not appear among the opponents of Alexander when the Greek King marched through their country on his way to the Indus.[38] While describing India, Herodotus said,

> They seem to have been enclosed upon the north by the Gandarians,[39] on the west by the Pactyans (Pashtun), Arachosians, and Gedrosians, on the

east by the great Indian desert, and on the south by the sea.[40] They were a warlike race in the time of Darius,[41] who forcibly brought them under the Persian sway;[42] and they maintained the same character down to the invasion of Alexander, who found in the native prince of these parts (Porus) and his men, the enemy whom he had the most difficulty in conquering.[43]

Economic exchanges between the people of the two territories were a common component of daily life.[44] The transportation of Indian goods, including grain and other food items, and the flamboyant import of beads from Shortugai and lapis lazuli from Badakhshan, which were an essential part of Harappan life because of their fondness for the fine workmanship of beads and lapis lazuli during 3500 BC, was well established.[45] Farming, trade and animal husbandry were common activities in the economic realm of the two territories.[46] The Chinese traveller, pious Hiuen Tsang (who visited India during 629–645 CE), mentioned the economic contact between the people of River Vakshu (Po-tsu) and Sindhu (Si-to).[47]

So many cultural commonalities existed between the two countries that the very names – India and Afghanistan – were attributed to Persian and Greek philological-colloquial expressions. Greeks, mostly the learned ones, were the first set of scholars to become overawed and overwhelmed by the astonishing civilizational wisdom of India. There was a deadly curiosity among the Greek scholars to understand the immense wonderland of India. They breathlessly admired the sheer concentration of philosophers, learned men, and knowledgeable persons. They were also amazed by the tradition of learning science, mathematics, and philosophy in India.[48] The Grecians were awed by India's wealth, flora and fauna, fabulous creatures, and the surprising sophistication of its common citizens. For nearly a millennium starting in 500 BC, there was also a cut-throat competition among Greek scholars to undertake field visits and make scholarly inquiries before writing and decoding the high culture of India.

The Chinese, mostly monks, were the second set of celebrated scholars who set foot in India with the explicit intention of augmenting wisdom and sharpening philosophical inquiry. The Chinese were amazed by the sociocultural set-up and stayed for decades to study religion and philosophy in India. While doing so, they left behind a wealth of 'on-field historical records' and volumes of 'original religious-philosophical interpretation and information about plainly practised daily life of Indians'.[49]

Since all the Grecian and Chinese scholars either crossed through Gandhara to reach India or visited Gandhara during their stay in India, their writings inform us about the history of Afghanistan and testify to historical linkages between India and Afghanistan. These scholars also discuss the Persian interpretation of India's and Afghanistan's historical past.

In continuation of their shared historical interpretation by outsiders, India and Afghanistan inherited their names from common Greek-Persian sources. The Persians called the river Sapta Sindhu *'Hapta Hindu'*[50] while the Grecians named the river Sindhu as 'Indus'[51]. The word *'Hindu'* was never used in any of India's ancient literature. The religious denomination, as understood by Indians, was *'Sanatana'*. The word *'Hindu'* was allegedly used for the first time in the travelogue of the famous Chinese Buddhist monk I-tsing, who set foot in India in the year 673 CE and stayed until 692 CE. 'Hindu (Hsin-tu)', he says, 'is the name used only by the northern tribes, and the people of India themselves do not know it'.[52] I-tsing clarified that 'The northern tribes (Hu-Mongols or Turks) alone call the Noble Land (*Aryadesha*) *'Hindu'*, but this is not at all a common name'. It is only a vernacular name and has no special significance. The people of India do not often know this designation, and the most suitable name for India is the 'Noble Land' (*Aryadesha*). Jawaharlal Nehru, in his *Discovery of India* explained that the first reference to *'Hindu'* found in any Indian book was in a *Tantrik* work of the 8th century CE, where *'Hindu'* means people and not a religion.[53] Nehru never named the text that used the term *'Hindu'* for the first time. The *Sacred Avesta* had been using the word *'Hindu'* since its recollection in the 9th century CE. The Persians and Central Asians used to call the people on the other side of the Sindhu River *'Hindu'*. The Sanskrit word Sindhu (सिंधु) is pronounced by the old Persian as 'Hindus', while the Greeks call it *'Indos'* (plural *Indoi*).[54] Later, the Latins called Sindhu 'Indus' and hence the name 'India' derived from the original word Sindhu.

Hiuen Tsang, the pious Chinese monk, wrote

> On examination, we find that the name of India (T'ien-chu) are various and perplexing as to their authority. It was anciently called Shin-tu, also Hien-tau; but now, according to the right pronunciation, it is called In-tu. The people of In-tu call their country by different names according to their district. The people generally speak of India as the country of Brahmans (Po-lo-men).[55]

Hiuen Tsang further said that 'the country embraced under this term of India are generally spoken of as the five Indies'.[56] I-tsing, the illustrious Chinese monk, calls India in general the West (Si-fang), the Five Countries of India (Wu-t'ien). But he named three only – Aryadesa (A-li-ya-t'i-sha or Noble Region), Madhyadesa (Mo't'i-t'i-sha or Middle Region), and Brahmarashtra (Po-lo-men-kuo or Region of Brahmanas).[57] Further, he explained that we ought to note that the whole country comprising the five parts of India is called the kingdom of the Brahmans (Brahmarashtra) or Jambudvipa (Chan-pu-chou). However, throughout his book, I-tsing wrote liberally about the 'five' kinds of everything – customs, lifestyles, vices, living, scriptures, and many more such things present in India.

Similarly, when Persian King Darius sent an intelligence mission under the able mariner Scylax to India sometime around 520 BC to inquire about the strength of the King and topography of the region, the Greek historian called the region Pactyïke.[58] Herodotus wrote that the mission of Scylax started from 'the city of Caspatyros and the land of Pactyïke, sailed down the river towards the East and the sun rising to the sea'.[59] Although the city of Caspatyros is never identified and scholars suspect four possible cities – Peshawar, Multan, Kabul and Kashmir – as Caspatyros, the word Pactyïke is identified with Pashtun.[60]

The sacred *Rig Veda* in classical Sanskrit names the 'Afghan' people as 'Pakthas'.[61] The word 'Afghan' comes from the Sanskrit root of *ashv* meaning 'horse', which becomes *asp* in ancient times. The Persian term for a horse is *Asb* or *Aspa*.[62] The genetic term for these horsemen was Ashvaka in Sanskrit and Aspagon[63] in Persian. Their country was where the usual mode of transportation was the horse, perhaps more so than in ancient India, thus the ancient land of the Pactyïke became Aspagonistan in Persian and then Afghanistan.[64]

Some Afghan experts, mostly led by British historians of the 19th century,[65] believed that it was not until the reign of Sultan Abouseid, of the race of Genghis Khan, that certain eastern writers spoke of them using the name Afghan. They believe Afghan is the plural of the Arabic word *Feghan*, meaning noise or tumult. However, the problem with this explanation is that there is no mention of the name Abouseid in the family tree or lineage of Genghis Khan, nor are the British historians able to locate his reign in their references. Citing a Persian manuscript of one Abdullah Khan of Herat, the British historian further proclaimed that the word Afghan was applied to them because they were always in a disunited state amongst themselves, continually addressing their complaints to the sovereigns on whom they were dependent. Nevertheless, British writers argue that the name was little used until the reign of Shah Abbas the Great (ruling during 1588–1629 CE), who, tired of their incessant lamentations, ordered them henceforth to be called by that designation – Afghan only. The British chroniclers probably did not pronounce the word's front from the rear. *Feghan* – the *n* ending being nasal – is Persian and not Arabic. This colloquial and philological interpretation is not supported by adequate evidence.[66] This lamentation theory is a figment of imagination without proper citation or academic scrutiny.

The British authors did not check the veracity of their citation, and they blindly enlisted the fictitious claim of a Persian scholar, Abdullah Khan. The translation of Abdullah Khan's manuscript, as cited by the British scholars, told us that, 'Malek Thalut Saul, King of the Jews, had two sons,

Afghan and Djalut – the first was the father of the Afghan nation and gave his name to it'. Abdullah Khan said, 'the word Afghan is derived from the Arab, that of *aoughan* from the Persian, and both one and the other are used in Hebrew'.[67] However, in reality, King Malek Thalut Saul had four sons (Jonathan, Abinadab, Malchishua, and Ish-Bosheth) and two daughters (Merab and Michal); none of their names was either Afghan or Djalut.[68]

Same Land, Similar People, and Homogeneity of Religion

That India and Afghanistan used to share the same landmass,[69] same kings,[70] similar population,[71] and homogeneity of religion[72] is proven beyond doubt. The ancient epic *Ramayana*, which is archaeologically dated to the 17th century BC[73] informs us that Pushkalavati and Taxila[74] were named after the two sons of Bharata, the brother of Lord Rama.[75] Charsada, which is situated on the confluence of the Kabul and Swat rivers in present-day Pakistan, is ancient Pushakalavati. Taxila is the garbled word for the original Sanskrit name Takšašila (Takshasila). The two cities were established simultaneously, and Charsada's 'early history thus runs parallel to that of Taxila in Punjab, and the assertion of the Ramayana that Taxila and Pushkalavati were found at the same time accords with the archaeological evidence'.[76]

The administrative influence of both cities, now in Pakistan, during the Gandhara era, stretched until Iran.[77] Mythical literature informs us that Bharata, the brother of Lord Rama, defeated King Nagnajit, who was a contemporary of Lord Rama and ruler of Gandhara.[78] After defeating his adversary, Bharata's first son Taksha established Takshasila, while his second son Pushkala built Pushkalavati.[79] The story of Pushkalavati is essentially the story of Taxila. 'In affirming that the two cities were founded at the same time, the Ramayana has more semblance of historical authority than is commonly credited in detail to the Indian epics'.[80] Literature and archaeology conform to each other about the common ancient destiny of India and Afghanistan.

Mahabharata, another ancient epic archaeologically dated to the 9th century BC,[81] is liberal in describing India's intense engagement with Gandhara.[82] The picturesque Bamiyan valley was a precious yet mysterious backyard of Indian kings. In the Bamiyan hill range, many noble images and statues were made by Hindu Rajas, especially by the five brothers or Pandavas of Mahabharata fame. When the Pandavas mortgaged the whole of their empire to Durjodhan, their uncle's son, to pay him their gambling debts, he immediately banished them from Hastinapur (near present-day Delhi) for 12 years. The poor Pandavas chose their ground in Bamiyan and spent their unhappy days making magnificent statues on the Bamiyan hill, which they and their followers worshipped for a long time.[83]

Archaeological evidence[84] as well as religious texts[85] leave no doubt about the fact that India and Afghanistan belonged to a common state boundary and homogeneous religion during the ancient era. The Grecians were overwhelmingly intrigued by the highly developed knowledge culture of ancient India, including Afghanistan. Similarly, the Chinese rushed to every nook and corner of ancient India in search of sacred texts and original religious codes. Collectively, these two sets of scholars provided the most expansive reference about the 'same land, similar people, and homogeneity of religion'[86] narrative.

Homer, the legendary Greek poet of circa 700 BC,[87] did not mention the name India or its affiliates in his masterpiece, the Odyssey. However, in lines 23–24, he wrote, 'the Ethiopians, the most distant of people, who are divided in two: those who live where the sun sets and those where it rises'.[88] Later scholars erroneously relate Homer's Ethiopian expression to his vague knowledge and reference to India.[89] Herodotus, a resident of Halicarnassus (modern Bodrum in southwestern Turkey), who lived during 484–424 BC, never visited India. Although he lived under Persian rule, by 443 BC he was granted Greek citizenship after he migrated to Thurium (Thurii, Italy).[90] He compiled the massive 'Histories'

> in the hope of preserving from decay the remembrance of what me have done, and of preventing the great and wonderful actions of the Greeks and the Barbarians from losing their due meed of glory, and withal to put on record what were their grounds of feud.[91]

His source of information about India includes an intelligence report of Scylax, who commenced an expedition to the Indus Valley at the instruction of Persian King Darius I (who ruled during 521–486 BC) before the Persian King undertook conquests and annexed India to his empire.[92] The original report of Scylax never survived. Scylax, after finishing his intelligence mission, sent a report to the King and wrote a book about his mission as well. His work was copied by Hecataeus, another Greek from Miletus (Aydin Province, Turkey), around 510–500 BC when he wrote a chapter about India in his geographical book. Herodotus used Hecataeus' work 70 years later for his masterpiece *Histories*. He also gained an understanding of India from his inquiry into the countless Indian visitors to the Persian and Greek empires.

Scylax put himself in a boat near Peshawar and sailed down the Kabul River and into the Sindhu, which took him all the way down to the ocean. Upon returning home to the Persian King, Scylax wrote a detailed report about what he saw for royal perusal. Hecataeus says that the 'Gandarae' is an Indian race. Their area is also called 'Gandari', and their land is 'Gandarian'. A peek into Scylax's intelligence report can be found in the work of another

Greek historian, Athenaeus (end of 2nd century–early 3rd century CE) of Naucratis (a city of Ancient Egypt). In his work *Deipnosophists*, quoting Scylax, Athenaeus wrote,

> that the land is well watered with fountains and with canals, and on the mountains, there grow artichokes and many other plants. From that point, a mountain stretches on both sides of the river Indus, very loft, and very thickly overgrown with wild wood and the prickly artichoke.[93]

Herodotus wrote strange things about the Indians who are called Callatians. His bizarre description includes that,

> the Indians consent to consume with fire the bodies of their fathers when they died; eat raw flesh; the sexual intercourse of Indians was open like cattle; their colour of the skin is like Ethiopians; the size of their ants is smaller than dogs but larger than foxes; all animals, both quadrupeds and birds, are much larger than they are in other countries, with the exception of horses.[94]

He wrote some exciting things as well. He said,

> There are many tribes of Indians; they speak many languages; Indians are greatest of any among men; there is abundance of gold there; they were a warlike race in the time of Darius; and the Indian population is the greatest of all nations.

What Herodotus talked about Afghanistan is as follows: 'The Gandarians are a very remarkable people, and held in ancient times a very prominent position among the tribes dwelling between India and Persia'.[95] Herodotus further mentioned the Gandarians as Indian when he wrote, like the other hill tribes of these parts, they seem to have been a warlike race, and it is not improbable that they were included among the Indians whose services were retained by Mardonius, the great general of Xerxes I (Persian King). The Indians rushed to the battlefield on behalf of Mardonius with their war equipment, like a Median-like head-dress, bows made of reed, short spears, and chariots.

Nearly 40 years after Herodotus, about 397 BC, Ctesias of Cnidos (southwest of Turkey) wrote a monograph on India in the name of *Indika*. Ctesias, a physician by training, was brought to Persia at some point towards the end of the 5th century to serve King Artaxerxes II Mnemon (404–358 BC).[96] The original *Indika* of Ctesias does not survive but fragments of his works compiled by Photius, the 9th-century CE Byzantine scholar, became the main source. Ctesias never visited India and therefore he was forced to rely on what he heard from travellers and Indian visitors to the Persian court, where he had the unique opportunity, especially for a Greek, to encounter many travellers from distant lands.[97]

Like Herodotus, Ctesias also wrote that

> the population of the Indians is nearly greater than the rest of the world combined; it does not rain but India is irrigated by the river; there is the wall-destroying elephants; the small monkeys with tails four cubits in length; roosters of enormous size; there lives in India a beast called the Martichora which has a human face, is the size of a lion; and in India live men who have the head of a dog.[98]

Ctesias claims that

> the Indians are very just people; there is a river of honey which flows from a rock; they do not suffer from headaches, ophthalmia, toothaches, cold sores, or putrefaction; and they live for 120, 130, and 150 years and some live to be as old as 200 years old.

Ctesias added that Bokhara was part of India and 'the Indians make very good wine and cheese and he had tasted them'. Throughout history, the wine of Bokhara has been highly praised by kings and commoners. Ctesias must have tasted wine from Bokhara. He compared Punjab, Balkh, and Bokhara when he talked about cultivation and how these regions depend more on the supply of water from rivers and canals than from rain.

Megasthenes (350–290 BC) was the next in the line of Greek philosophers who wrote about India and Afghanistan.[99] He was a great traveller and Greek Ambassador at the court of the illustrious Mauryan Empire.[100] The exact time of Megasthenes' stay at the Mauryan capital Pataliputra (Patna, Bihar) is not known, but he must have left the city before 297 BC when Mauryan King Chandragupta died.[101] *Indika*, the account of India written by Megasthenes from his knowledge of the country, is justly held to be almost invaluable for the light it throws upon the obscurity of early Indian history.[102] Though, unfortunately, not extant in its original form, Megasthenes' *Indika* has nevertheless been partially preserved through epitomes and quotations to be found scattered up and down the writings of various ancient authors, both Greek and Roman, such as the writings of Strabo, Diodorus Siculus, Pliny, and Arrian.[103]

In recorded history, Megasthenes was an eyewitness to the first-ever strong and widespread empire in India under Chandragupta Maurya. After the death of Alexander in 322 BC, the Greek empire collapsed. The brilliant Chandragupta (ruled 321–297) rose to power and established the flamboyantly powerful Mauryan dynasty at Pataliputra. Alexander's empire was divided into three principal empires: 1) Western Asia, Persia, and Mesopotamia, under Seleucus; 2) Egypt under Ptolemy; and 3) Macedonia, under Antigonus.

There is no record of contemporary writers when Alexander attacked India. Arrian wrote his *Indica* – an account of India and the history of Alexander's campaign 300 years later.[104] He said Alexander subdued many Indian tribes before reaching the River Indus. Arrian added that Eratosthenes (276–196 BC) and Dionysus (270–236 BC) mentioned that there were tutelary relations between the viceroy of Arachosia and Sandrakotus (Chandragupta). According to Arrian, the northern boundaries of India as defined are formed by Mount Taurus, though the range does not retain that name in these parts, which is called Parapamisus. The Hindukush Mountain range is known to the Greeks as Parapamisus.

Seleukus Nikator, the able general of Alexander, inherited Babylonia and the entire enormous eastern part up to India of Alexander's empire. When Chandragupta asserted his authority, 'Seleukos crossed the Indus and waged war on Chandragupta'.[105] The well-prepared and brave Chandragupta defeated his Greek adversary, and 'Seleukos Nikator gave to Sandrokotus a large part of Ariana'.[106] Ariana is the Latin name[107] for the geographical limit between Central Asia and the Indus River, covering the entire Afghanistan of present-day[108] and a portion of eastern Iran.[109] 'The Indians afterwards held a large part of Ariana, which they had received from the Macedonians'.[110] 'Seleukos entered into marriage relations with Chandragupta and received in return five hundred elephants'.[111] Greek sources mentioned that Chandragupta possessed an army of 600,000 men and he won all over India.[112] The Greek geographer Strabo explained 'India is bounded on the north by the extremities of Tauros, and from Ariana to the Eastern Sea'.[113]

It was for the first time that foreign historians provided authentic and graphic details, which reiterate the fact that the entire Ariana was under Chandragupta Maurya.[114] The province was ruled from Mauryan headquarters at Pataliputra for at least three generations down the line. After the demise of Chandragupta, his son Bindusara received another illustrious Greek ambassador, Deimachus, during the period 281 to 273 BC.[115] Deimachus was the ambassador of Antiochus Soter (reigned 281–262 BC). Deimachus wrote a work on India, but nothing more is known of it than that it consisted of two books and grossly exaggerated the dimensions of the country.[116] Bindusara received another ambassador from the Egyptian court in the name of Athenseus, who wrote the great treatise called

'Deipnosophists'.[117] All these works support the 'same land, similar people' history of India and Afghanistan.

After Bindusara, his son, Ashoka (269–236 BC) became the King of Pataliputra.[118] As a Mauryan Governor of Ujjain under Bindusara, Ashoka was deputed twice to quell revolts in Taxila and beyond. Ashoka outshone his grandsire and extended his rule to most of Afghanistan, even wresting bits of that country from its Greek masters.[119] Fortunately, Ashoka is the first emperor to leave behind evidence of his presence and domination in Afghanistan in his own words. Written in original classical Greek and hewn in stone, the end of the 12th Rock Edict and the beginning of the 13th Rock Edict commissioned by Emperor Ashoka at Kandahar is a living example of Mauryan rule in Afghanistan.[120] The 12th Rock Edict is all about moral conduct, and the 13th Edict is about Ashoka's repentance after the chillingly violent Kalinga War.[121] Kalinga is modern-day Odisha, situated in the eastern part of India. In his own words, the Mauryan King codified that

> Beloved-of-the-Gods, King Priyadarsi, conquered the Kalinga eight years after his coronation. One hundred and fifty thousand were deported, one hundred thousand were killed and many more died (from other causes). After Kalinga had been conquered, Beloved-of-the-Gods came to feel a strong inclination towards the Dharma, a love for the Dharma and for instruction in Dharma. Now Beloved-of-the-Gods feels deep remorse for having conquered the Kalinga.[122]

Emperor Ashoka overruns the kingdom of Kalinga after his decisive victory in the infamous Kalinga War in 261 BC. He was ruling his newly conquered province from his headquarters at Pataliputra. However, he inscribed his Kalinga exploits in stone in the city of Kandahar, deep inside Afghanistan. Geographically, Kalinga is situated in the Eastern corner of India, while Kandahar is in the North-Western part of India. The distance between Daya River near Dhauligiri where Kalinga War took place and Kandahar, which is in Afghan-Persia border, is 2300 kilometres. In other words, the stone inscription of Emperor Ashoka, which described about the gruesome nature of Kalinga War, is at a great distance from the battleground where Emperor Ashoka waged the Kalinga War. Codifying the Kalinga exploit in rock at Kandahar is mystifying. The emperor wanted to send the message that his entire empire was close knit and that events at a distant Kalinga were equally important for the residents of Kandahar. The other Ashokan Edict in Kandahar is known as Minor 4th Rock Edict which is written in a multi-language format using Greek and Aramaic.[123] The Minor 4th Rock Edict talks about abstaining from killings and other such vices.

The use of the Greek language and the choice of location for the 12th and 13th Rock Edicts signify the high level of philosophical refinement as well as the comprehensive presence of highly cultured Greeks in and around Kandahar. Ashoka maintained contacts with the Greek world during his reign. He received ambassadors from the court of Ptolemy of Egypt, which was part of the ancient Greek empire. He also hosted Antiochus, a Greek king, whose name was mentioned in Ashoka's 2nd Major Rock Edict. The 2nd Major Rock Edict talks about providing medical services and planting medicinal herbs for both humans and animals in his kingdom and bordering regions, including those of the Greek king Antiochus. This Antiochus is generally identified as Antiochus II Theos, the ruler of the Seleucid Empire. .[124] Nevertheless, the use of Greeks in his Rock Edicts is a plain reiteration of his Hellenic wisdom and matured application of political language.[125] Ptolemy Philadelphus, Ashoka's contemporary, dispatched an envoy called Dionysios to the Mauryan court.[126]

Megasthenes and Deimachus wrote a lot about India's strange creatures. However, all who have written about India have proved themselves, for the most part, fabricators, but pre-eminently so Megasthenes.

Some Greek authors and historians never visited India, but they still wrote about occurrences in India. It was natural for them to make mistakes. Onesicritus was the pilot of Alexander the Great, and hence he had accompanied Alexander during the latter's Indian campaign. Since Alexander's stay in India was short and full of fights and battles, Onesicritus might not have had enough time to understand India's historical character and verify facts. Therefore, errors from him are not unexpected. The same was the case with Nearchus, Alexander's general. Nearchus, although fully exposed to India, did not stay during peacetime, and his exposure was limited to the area where the Grecian waged war with Indian princes. It was understood and, to some extent, possible when these authors/narrators believed the erroneous explanations of Ctesias' writing and copied and pasted his stories about India.[127] Their writing was taken lightly and considered facetious and unreliable even at the time it appeared. But mistakes from famous historical characters like Meghasthenis and Deimachus were confabulating. Meghasthenis was sent to the court of Chandragupta Maurya by Seleucus I Nicator. He stayed in India for several years, specifically in the Mauryan capital of Pataliputra, during the reign of Chandragupta Maurya. While the exact duration isn't pinpointed, it was not less than 8 years and long enough for him to observe and write his account, 'Indica', in around 280 BC. Similarly, Deimachus succeeded Meghasthenis and became an ambassador to the court of Mauryan ruler Bindusara 'Amitragatha' in Pataliputra. Deimachus was sent by Antiochus I Soter and stayed in the Mauryan court for many years. Strangely, Meghasthenis and Deimachus also copied

Ctesias' erroneous information. Since we don't have the original copy of Meghasthenis' 'Indica', we don't know if a later author inserted that information into his work. They both repeated Ctesias' tale about the 'men that sleep in their ears'; the 'men without mouths'; the 'men without noses'; and about the 'men with one eye'; the 'men with long legs'; and the 'men with fingers turned backwards'. They revived, also, the Homeric story of the battle between the 'cranes' and the 'pygmies', who, they said, were three spans tall. These men also talk about the ants that mine gold and Pans with wedge-shaped heads; and about snakes that swallow oxen and stags, horns and all. It is difficult to decipher why they wrote such a fictitious tale despite the fact that they were on an ambassadorial mission and lived in Pataliputra for years as ambassadors. Megasthenes, during his posting in the court of Chandragupta, and Deimachus, while working in the court of Bindusara, travelled widely around the country. They should have known that Ctesias was writing fiction.[128]! Strabo wondered why the Greecians wrote such impractical things in their memoirs, which capture their experience about their stay in India. He was perplexed when he tried to find out the causes that prompted them to write such things.

The Greek writers must have been exposed to India's oral tradition and acquired folk stories to be translated in their numerous Indikas narrating those fictions as realities.[129] Indian folklore, bedtime stories of elders, and religious legends are full of impractical animal characters, unrealistic fictional human species, and unimaginable plant behaviours.[130] These legends and stories have delighted children of all ages in all places at all times, and continue to do so. These stories are mostly popular folklore and fairytales.[131] India has a highly sophisticated and clinically accurate oral tradition.[132] *Vedas* are the primary sources of knowledge, also known as Shruti literature. Shruti means hearing, and the entire Vedic texts were orally composed, without the use of script and without altering even a comma, full stop, or tonal or accentual style of pronunciation, transmitted in an unbroken structure from generation to generation.[133] It was Adi Shankara, the 8th-century philosopher and theologian, who created these scriptures in written format. UNESCO inscribed the Vedic Chanting as a 'Heritage of Humanity' in 2003.[134]

The impossible description of the monstrous life of Indians and their animals by the Greek writers was motivated by other factors too. The Hindu religion encompasses a great variety of gods, goddesses, worshippers, and animals, who possess far more body parts than a common mortal can sustain. For example, the Hindu God 'Brahma has four heads'; 'Siva has three eyes'; 'Goddess Lakshmi and Saraswati have four hands each while Durga has 10 hands'. 'Vishnu in his Avatars, has the tail of a fish, the body of a tortoise, the head of a boar, and talons of a lion'. 'Ganesa had the head of an elephant'. Among the Danavas, or children of Danu, the Titanic foes of the gods, we have one with the head of a tiger, one with the head of a goat, another with two heads and a fourth with ears like sharp spikes.[135]

These non-existent characters must have reached the eyes or ears of the Greek travellers and ambassadors through oral description or sculptured representation. This, in turn, must have borne the character of existing realities to ill-informed foreigners. Other than that, some of those strange descriptions have existed in India. Some of the favourite Yogic postures in India involve a person performing tapas, or penance, standing on one foot or standing on one's head. Representations of ascetics in these postures were probably frequent. The Kumbh Melas, which are held every 12 years in the cities of Allahabad, Haridwar, Nashik, and Ujjain, occur in such a fashion that there is a four-year rotational gap in the celebration in each city. In these Melas, ascetics, sages, and seers descend from their impregnable caves and forest abodes. These saints look like strange humans. Inscribed by UNESCO in its Representative List of Intangible Cultural Heritage of Humanity in 2017, Kumbh Mela is a mass Hindu gathering with the explicit purpose of bathing in a sacred or holy river at any of the four rivers – the Ganges (at Haridwar); at the confluence of the Ganges and Yamuna (at Allahabad/Prayag); the Godavari (Nashik); and the Shipra (at Ujjain). The Greek ambassadors must have had experiences of these Melas, and they must have got their stories of strange humans from these gatherings only.

All these daily life events of Indians intrigued the Western mind. From about the year 550 BC, Greek thinkers exhibited enormous interest in the affairs of India because of the reports of high culture and learning emanating from this great land of the Maha Sapta Sindhu, Ganga, and Yamuna.[136] Afghanistan was indistinguishably covered within the description of India.

Reiteration of Chinese Scholars

As mentioned above, the next wave of travellers to India started from the other part of the world – China. India received a stream of great scholars from China starting in 399 CE, who wrote great details about everything they had witnessed during their travels to India. Their descriptions of India include present-day Afghanistan as well.

After the introduction of Buddhism into China in 67 CE,[137] Fa-Hien was the first to make a pilgrimage to India. The date 67 CE marked the time of arrival of the first Indian Sramanas (Buddhist monks), Kasyapa Matanga, and Bharana (or Dharmaraksha), who were invited by the Chinese Emperor Ming-ti (CE 58–75). It was the historical beginning of Buddhism in China, though there are some traces of it in earlier literature.[138] *Chu Sanzcing Ji Ji*, a 515 CE Chinese publication by Sengyou (445–515 CE),[139] provides the legend behind how Buddhism was officially introduced in China. Emperor Ming-ti, inspired by a dream,[140] in 64 CE, sent a mission of learned Chinese envoys headed by Zhang Qian to the Yue-Che rulers (Kushans) to procure sacred texts. In a fantastic reciprocation, the mission returned three years later accompanied by an Indian group of monks headed by Kasyapa Matanga and Dharmaraksha, along with the translation of the sacred text *Sutra in Forty-two Sections*.[141] Overwhelmed by the Indian gesture, the Chinese Emperor built the first monastery in their memory, the Baimasi at Luoyang (at the confluence of the Luo River and Yellow River in Henan province).

Foguo ji, also known as Fo-Kue-Ki, translated into 'Records of the Buddhist Kingdoms', is the book written by Fa-hien after the completion of his 15-year-long momentous journey to India in 414 CE. Fa-hien started his journey in 399 CE and returned to China in 414 CE.[142] At the age of 25, to collect sacred books, Fa-hien, along with four other monks – Kwuy-king, Tao-ching, Hwuy-ying, and Hwuy-wei – embarked on a journey to India.

The region Khotan, where Fa-hien crossed, was practicing Hinduism.[143] Even today the language of Khotanese is Gandhari Prakrit, a branch of Sanskrit. Panini in his description of Kapisa informed that Badakhshan was under the 16 Mahajanapadas. At Khotan, Fa-hien witnessed 'an image procession', and after that 'Sang-shau, one of the companies, set out with a Tartar (Hu) pilgrim towards Ki-pin (Kabul). Fa-hien and the others pressed towards the Tseu-ho (Yarkand district) country'.[144] Before arriving at Gandhara, Fa-hien

> arrived at the country of Udyana, which lies due north of India. The language of Central India is universally used here, central India being what they call the 'Middle Kingdom'. The clothes and food of the people also resemble those of our Middle Kingdom, and the religion of Buddha is extremely flourishing. There are five hundred priests, all belonging to the Lesser Vehicle (Hinayana).[145]

After that, 'descending eastward for five days, the pilgrims arrived at the country of Gandhara'. This means Fa-hien was very much inside present-day Afghanistan before arriving at Gandhara. At 'Gandhara, where Dharma-vivardhana, the son of Ashoka, ruled', the people of the country were mostly students of the Hinayana. Travelling from Gandhara southward for seven days, the pilgrims arrived at the country of Peshawar.

Linking present-day Afghanistan with Buddhism, Fa-hien wrote that 'having got across the south of the range (Little Snowy Mountain or Safed Koh), they arrived at the country of Afghanistan, where approximately 3000 priests belonged to both the Greater Vehicle (Mahayana) and Lesser Vehicle (Hinayana)'.

Next followed the travels of Sun-yun and Hwui-seng in the year 518 CE. Sung-Yun (a native of Tun-wang, in Little Tibet) was sent by the Queen of the Wei country from Loyang to India in search of Buddhist books. He was accompanied by Hwui-Seng. He returned after three years with 175 volumes of the Great Development Series.[146] Unfortunately, their narrative is very short and cannot be compared with that of the other travellers.[147] The Ye-tha (Ephtalites or White Hun) were now in possession of the old country of the Yue-Chi and had recently conquered Gandhara. Sung-yun, after reaching as far as Peshawar and Nangarahara, returned to China in the year 521 CE.[148]

During the rule of the T'ang dynasty, the celebrated Chinese traveller Hiuen Tsang, who is a household name in India, landed in India. The pious Hiuen Tsang reached India overland through the modern Afghanistan and Uzbekistan route. He followed the same route during his return journey as well. His account *Si-Yu-Ki* or *The Record of the Western Kingdom*, which he completed after his travels, covering the period 629 CE to 645 CE is the all-embracing encyclopaedia of India's interface with Afghanistan. He recorded the comprehensive history of India for 17 years starting from 629 CE. An impeccable observer, Hiuen Tsang wrote about every single aspect of Indian life he noticed. He included the geographical dimension of the region immaculately. The intricate detail provided by Hiuen Tsang made the book an indispensable textbook for Indian history and geography.

Hiuen Tsang visited Fei-han (Ferghana); Sa-mo-kien (Samarkand); Pu-ho (Bokhara); Ta-Mi (Termed or Termiz, on the north bank of the Amu-Daria in present-day Uzbekistan). He came upon numerous Buddhist texts and religious institutions in those cities. There were hundreds of Buddhists in Sangharamas with thousands of monks residing in those Sangharamas.[149] The stupas and the images of the honoured Buddha are noted for various spiritual manifestations. Of all the countries named between the Oxus and the Hindukush, Hiuen Tsang visited Hwo (Kunduz), Po-ho (Balkh), Kie-chi (Gaz), and Fan-yen-na (Bamiyan).

During the 7th century, Hiuen Tsang witnessed the density of Buddhism in Balkh. So great was the concentration of Buddhist influence in Po-Ho (Balkh) that, owing to the numerous Buddhist sites in its neighbourhood, it 'is called generally the Little Rajagriha'.[150] Balkh used to imitate the Buddhist Magadhan city of 'Rajagriha' in the heart of India. The local ruler or Khan informed Hiuen Tsang, 'It is called the Little Rajagriha: its sacred relics are exceedingly numerous'.[151] 'Khan' is a title for the 'ruler' or 'head' of the region, and it has nothing to do with any religious denomination or surname of any person. Balkh was abuzz with about 100 convents and 3000 monks, who all studied the religious teachings of the Little Vehicle (Hinayana).

The people of Balkh were intimately affiliated with Buddhism and practised the religion with far more seriousness than the birthplace of Buddhism, i.e. Bodhgaya. Hiuen Tsang explained how the residents of Balkh used to revere Buddhist relics like the washing basin which Buddha used, a tooth of Buddha about an inch long, and the sweeping brush of Buddha, made of the plant Kasa. The covenants of Balkh were full of monks and commoners, and the number of priests stood at 100. So irregular are the morning and night in their duties that it is hard to tell saints from sinners.

The most important Buddhist abode in Afghanistan, as witnessed by Hiuen Tsang, was Bamiyan. He was overwhelmed by the religious fervour among the people of Bamiyan, situated in the northwest of Kabul. The people of Bamiyan were committed to Buddhist ideas and the Three Jewels, i.e. Buddha, Dharma, and Sangha. The residents were pure devotees of Buddha, and the merchants of Bamiyan used to arrange the prices of their commodities according to the signs afforded by the spirits of Buddhist monks. Hiuen Tsang was amazed by the existence of ten convents and about 1000 priests who belonged to the Little Vehicle (Hinayana) and the school of the Lokottaravadins.

The most important edifices in Bamiyan that stunned Hiuen Tsang were the colossal Buddha statues of Bamiyan. He noted that "the height of the statue in the declivity of the mountain range of Bamiyan was about 140 or 150 feet. Its golden hues sparkle on every side, and its precious ornaments dazzle the eyes with their brightness." He noticed a convent adjacent to the colossal Buddha statue and also a standing figure of Sakya Buddha about 100 feet in height, made of metallic stone. It had been cast in different parts and joined together, and thus placed in a completed form as it stands. A sleeping Buddha lying to the east of the city of Bamiyan, about a mammoth 1000 feet, also mesmerised Hiuen Tsang.[152]

We got to know from the record of Hiuen Tsang that the King of Kapisa was a Kshatriya by Varna.[153] He noticed that people were cruel, but the Kshatriya King was distinguished for wisdom and tact. A brave warrior, the King had brought the neighbouring countries under his power. Every year he made a silver figure of Buddha about 18 feet high, and at the same time he convoked an assembly called the Moksha Mahaparishad, during which he gave alms to those in need and relieved the bereaved. There were about 100 convents in this country and some 6000 priests. They mostly studied the rules of the Great Vehicle (Mahayana).

Hiuen Tsang noticed the presence of Tantrik forms of Hinduism, Jainism, and Shaivism. It is surprising to note that there were some ten temples of the Devas and 1000 or so of heretics (different ways of religion). There were naked ascetics, others who covered themselves with ashes, and some who made chaplets of bones, which they wore as crowns on their heads.[154] The three sects here enumerated are known as i) The Nirgranthas or Digambara Jainas; ii) Pasupatas; and iii) Kapiladharinas.

When we read Hiuen Tsang's travel record, especially about Afghanistan, it subscribes to the 'same land, similar people' narrative. In the olden days, particularly during Kanishka's era, during the cold season, the kings used to send people from Kapisa, Gandhara, and adjacent areas to India to avoid extreme cold and then receive them back in summer when the weather was pleasant in that area.[155]

Kanishka of Gandhara is often referred to in Chinese Buddhist texts as 'the Chandan Kanika'.[156] This simply means Kanishka of Gandhara, the use of '*Chandana*' (sandal) for '*gandha*' (fragrance) being common. The mountains of Gandhara are often described as the 'perfume mountains', as though from *gandha*. However, on an old Buddhist map, the Gandhara mountains are referred to as the earth holding (ti chi), as though *gan* were from an old root and *dhri*, to hold. Kanishka was King of the Yuei-chi, and the rise of his dynasty was placed by Chinese authors in the 1st century BC. On his coins, he is styled in the corrupt Greek legends kopavo, and in the Bactrian-Pali legends and Manikyala inscription, he is called Kanishka the Kushana, or 'of the Gushana family', connecting him with the tribe called the Chinese Kwei-shwang.[157] According to Hiuen Tsang, Kanishka ruled 400 years after Buddha's nirvana. Recent writers argue that Kanishka lived in the latter part of the 1st century and that the Saka era, which was fixed in 78 CE, originated with his reign.[158]

In Lamgham, Hiuen Tsang heard about feuds in the royal family and since they could not decide on a chief, they succumbed to the supremacy of Kapisa. In Lamgham and Nangarahar, he witnessed numerous Sangharamas and an overflowing number of monks and priests within those institutions. We found references to five Deva temples in Nangarahar and about three Buddhist stupas where relics of Tathagata, especially some of the hair and the nail-pairing, were preserved with great reverence. Not far from this is a stupa where Tathagata, making manifest the secret principles of his true doctrine, declared the *Skandha-dhatu-ayatanas* (*Skandha* means 'constituents of a being'; *Dhatus* constitutes 'earth, water, fire, air, space'; and *Ayatanas* means 'spheres of the organs of sense').[159]

Hiuen Tsang provided detailed topographical information along with the administrative system that prevailed in the region which later became Afghanistan. While writing about the kingdom of Gandhara, he said the Gandhara bordered the river Sind (Sindh) in the east and it was about 500 kilometres in length and 400 kilometres in breadth. This means that Gandhara was spread up to Bamiyan. Its capital was Po-lu-sha-pu-lo (Purushapura or Peshawar). The country of Gandhara is the lower Kabul Valley, along the Kabul River between the Khoaspes (Kunar) and the Indus. During his rule, Raja Kanishka built a stupa at Purushapura.

Soon after Hiuen Tsang's death, the illustrious Chinese Buddhist monk I-tsing set out for India in 671 CE via a marine route. Two years later, in 673 CE, he arrived in Tamralipti at the mouth of the River Hooghly. He studied at Nalanda and collected 400 Sanskrit texts, amounting to 500,000 slokas. On his way home, he stayed in Sribhoga (Palembang, in Sumatra), where he further studied and translated Buddhist books, either in Sanskrit or Pali. From Sribhoga, I-tsing sent his work through another Chinese priest, Ta-tsin, who was then returning to China. I-tsing's materials were translated into Chinese in 692 CE. The book is therefore called *Nan-hai-chi-kuei-nai-fa-ch'uan*, a *Record of the Inner Law Sent Home from the Southern Sea*.[160] The islands that lie off the Malay peninsula are known as the islands of the Southern Sea. I-tsing returned home in 695 CE and was well received by the ruling empress, Wu-hou of Chou (as the period of her reign was called). After 695, he was engaged at interpreting Buddhist texts with nine Indian priests, Sikshananda, Isvara, and others. During the period 700–712 CE, he completed 56 translations in 230 volumes. In addition, he compiled five works as well.

I-tsing never visited the land beyond Gandhara. However, he said that a Kshatriya was ruling Kambodja (Kamboja) and at that time when Buddhism was flourishing in Poh-nan (Siam), 'a wicked king (from Kambodja) expelled and exterminated them all, and there were no members of the Buddhist Brotherhood at all'.[161] In 626 CE, the King of Kambodja was Ishnavarman, and in perfect continuity with this, the *History of Tang* states that the King of Kambodja, Isana, a Kshatriya, at the beginning of the Cheng-kuan period (627–649 CE) conquered Fu-nan (East Siam) and took the territory. I-tsing may be referring to this King when he says that the wicked King destroyed Buddhism in Fu-nan.[162]

The discovery of a fragmentary manuscript of the Korean monk Hye Ch'o by Paul Pelliot at Tun-huang in 1908 shed new light on the state of affairs regarding Afghanistan's relations with India in the 8th century CE. Kye Ch'o's diary, known as *Wang Ocheonchukguk Jeon*, is translated as *Memoir of a Pilgrimage to the Five Regions of India*. The Korean monk, who was educated by an Indian Buddhist scholar, Vajrabodhi, at Kuang-chou (Canton) in South China in 719 CE, left China shortly before 724 CE and, through the waterway, reached India, probably at Tamralipti. He took his return journey to China overland through Afghanistan and reached An-hsi in China in 727 CE.

Hye Ch'o, in his diary, noted, 'From Kashmir travelling further north-west, after one month's journey, I arrived at the country of Gandhara. The King and military personnel are all Turks. The natives are Hu people; there are also Brahmins'. Surprisingly, Hye Ch'o noticed that 'Though the king is of Turkish origin, he greatly believes and respects the Three Jewels. The king, the royal consort, the prince, and the chiefs build monasteries separately and worship the Three Jewels'. He further noted a strange practice.

> The king institutes the great feast of the Wu-che assembly twice a year. Whatever he likes and uses like his wife, elephants, and horses, he donates to the Sangha. The king asks only that the monks fix the price of his wife and elephants so that he can redeem them. As for the rest, all were sold by the monks. The amount is shared by the monks for their expenditures.[163]

From Gandhara, Hye Ch'o entered 'the country of Udyana', where 'the king of this country greatly reveres the Three Jewels'.[164] The story was the same at Chitral and Lampaka (Lamgham). The King of Gandhara donated numerous villages for the upkeep of the monasteries. As noted by Hye, 'there are slightly more monks than laymen' in Gandhara.

Like Hiuen Tsang, Hye Ch'o also noted that Kapisa was under the authority of the King of Gandhara, and during summer the King came to Kapisa and resided there because of the cool temperature. During the winter, 'he goes to Gandhara and resides in that warm place'. He noted that at Zabulistan, though the King and the chiefs are Turks, they highly revere the Three Jewels. There are many monasteries and monks. Mahayana Buddhism is practised. Hye Ch'o, after leaving Zabulistan, reached Bamiyan. In Bamiyan, he noted, 'The King here is a Hu, and is independent of other countries. The King, the Chiefs, and the common people highly revere the Three Jewels. There are many monasteries and monks. Both Mahayana and Hinayana are practised'.[165]

From Bamiyan, Hye Ch'o travelled to Tokharistan. He wrote that 'the capital city is called Pectra. The King, the chiefs, and the common people respect the Three Jewels. There are many monasteries and monks. Hinayana Buddhism is practised. They do not profess any other religions. However, Hye Ch'o hinted at the presence of Arabs at the door of India'.

This means that Buddhism was abuzz in Afghanistan during the end of the 8th century. However, he noted that 'At present, the place is guarded and oppressed by Arab forces. The original King was compelled to leave the capital, and he resided at Badakhshan. It is also under the authority of the Arabs'.[166]

Finally, Hye Ch'o went to Persia and then to Arabia, and after that he went to six Central Asian countries – 'these are the countries of Bukhara, Kaputana, Kish, Shih-lo, Maimarg, and Samarkand'. Hye Ch'o noticed the changes in these countries and wrote, 'These countries are small, their armies are very limited, and they are unable to protect themselves. All these six countries serve the Fire Religion'. Surprisingly, in Bukhara and Baku, the fire religion is still in practice. He further noted, 'They have no knowledge of

Buddhism. Only in Samarkand is there one monastery and monk, who does not know how to revere the Three Jewels'.[167]

Greek, Chinese, and Sanskrit sources conform to the fact that there was complete synchronism between the people of heartland India and the far-flung population of Afghanistan. Starting from the Indus Valley population to the Vedic people and then also during the epic period to the Buddhist era, the two countries remained under the description of the 'same King, same population' theory.

The first sight of Arab domination and the Turk presence was witnessed at the end of the 8th century CE. Even then, those rulers, chieftains, and commanders were honouring the Three Jewels and funding Buddhist monasteries.

Notes

1. Herodotus, *The Histories of Herodotus*, Vol. IV. Translated by George Rawlinson (London: John Murrey, 1860), p. 216; Jawaharlal Nehru. *The Glimpses of World History* (New Delhi: Penguin, 2004), p. 905.
2. Herodotus, *The Histories of Herodotus*, Vol. IV, p. 214.
3. P. Bernard et al. *Fouilles d'Ai Khanoum I (Campagnes 1965–68): Memoires de la Delegation archeologique francaise en Afghanistqn, XXI* (Paris: Klincksieck Publisher, 1973), pp. 21–34; H.P. Francfort. *Second campagne de fouilles sur le sit.e proto-historique de Shortugai (Afghanistan du N.E.): 10 avril–2 juin 1978, mss., Kabul, 1978* (Paris: Klincksieck Publisher, 1978), p. 3.
4. M. Sharif and B.K. Thapar, *Food-producing Communities in Pakistan and Northern India*, in Vadim Mikhaïlovich Masson (ed.), *History of Civilizations of Central Asia* (New Delhi: Motilal Banarsidass Publications, 1999), pp. 128–137.
5. A. Sarkar et al. Oxygen Isotope in Archaeological Bioapatites from India: Implications To Climate Change and Decline Of Bronze Age Harappan Civilization, *Science Report 6*, Article No. 26555 (2016), pp. 1–9.
6. E.J.H. Mackay, *Further Excavations at Mohenjo-daro*, Vol. 2 (Delhi: Government of India), pp. 568–569; Madhu Sarup Vats, *Excavations at Harappa: Being an Account of Archaeological Excavations Carried Out at Harappa Between the Years 1920-1 and 1933-4* (Delhi: Manager of Publications, 1940), pp. 451–452; S.R. Rao, *Lothal: A Harappan Port Town, 1955–62*, Vol. II (New Delhi: Archaeological Survey of India, 1985), p. 225; J.P. Joshi, *Excavation at Surkotada and Exploration in Kutch. Memoirs of the Archaeological Survey of India No. 87* (New Delhi: Archaeological Survey of India, 1990), p. 282; B.K. Thapar. *New Traits of the Indus Civilization at Kalibangan: An Appraisal* in N. Hammond (ed.), *South Asian Archaeology* (London: Duckworth, 1973), pp. 85–104; H.P. Francfort, Excavations at Shortugai in Northeast Afghanistan, *American Journal of Archaeology*, Vol. 87, No. 4 (1983), pp. 518–519.
7. *Rig Veda*, Mandala 10, Hymn 126, No. 7 (Hoshiarpur: VVRI Publication, 1963).
8. Gandharibhyo mujabattahyah ...; *Rig Veda*, Mandala 10, Hymn 126, No. 7 (Hoshiarpur: VVRI Publication, 1963).
9. Atharva Veda, Mandala 5, Hymn 22, No. 14 (Hoshiarpur: VVRI Publication, 1961).

10 Max Muller (ed.) *The Zenda Avesta: The Sacred Books of the East* (New York: The Christian Literature Company, 1898), p. 2.
11 V.S. Agrawala. *India As Known to Panini: A Study of the Cultural Material in the Ashtadhyayi*, Vol. VI (Allahabad: Law Journal Press, 1953), p. 1106.
12 Sten Konow. The Copper Plate Grant of the Valabhi King Siladitya in *Epigraphia Indica XI* (New Delhi: Manager of Publications, 1911), p. 175.
13 Alexander Cunningham, *The Ancient Geography of India*, Vol. I (London: Trubner and Co., 1871), pp. 66–67.
14 Richard Salomon, Five Kharosthi Inscriptions, *Bulletin of the Asia Institute*, Vol. 10 (1996), pp. 233–246.
15 Panini, *The Ashtadhyayi of Panini*, Vol. VI, Chapter 1, Hymn 153, Trans. Srisa Chandra Vasu (Benares: Sindhu Charan Bose Publication, 1896), pp. 1107–1108.
16 Panini, *The Ashtadhyayi of Panini*, Vol. VI, pp. 1107–1108.
17 Panini, *The Ashtadhyayi of Panini*, Vol. VI, p. 694.
18 George Grierson, *Linguistic Survey of India*, Vol. X (Calcutta: Government Press, 1922), pp. 468, 473, 474, 476, 500.
19 Satya Shrava, *A Comparative History of Vedic Literature* (New Delhi: Pranava Prakashan, 1977), pp.37.
20 Rig Veda, Mandala – I, Hymn 102, No 9 (Hoshiarpur: VVRI Publication, 1963).
21 Vyasadev, *The Mahabharata*, Sabha Parvan, Chapter 51, No. 3. Translated by G.C. Vaidya. Bombay: Ramchandra Govind & Son, 1980.
22 Parashuram Lakshman Vaidya, *The Harivamsa* (Poona: Bhandarkar Research Institute Publication, 1971), p. 14.
23 Panini, *The Ashtadhyayi of Panini*, Vol. IV, Chapter 2, Hymn 99. Translated by Srisa Chandra Vasu (Benares: Sindhu Charan Bose Publication, 1896), p. 663.
24 Panini. *The Ashtadhyayi of Panini*, Vol. IV, pp. 691–692.
25 Hiuen Tsang. *Si-Yu-Ki: Buddhist Records of the Western World*, Vol. I. Translated by Samuel Beal (London: Kegan Paul, Trench, Trubner & Co., 1884), p. 114.
26 Herodotus, *The Histories of Herodotus*, Vol. IV. Translated by George Rawlinson (London: John Murrey, 1860), p. 216.
27 Claudius Ptolemy, *The Geography*, Vol. VI. Translated by E.L. Stevenson (New York: New York Public Library, 1932), p. 18.
28 H. C. Rawlinson, Notes on a March from Zoháb, at the foot of Zagros, along the mountains to Khúzistán (Susiana), and from thence through the province of Luristan to Kirmánsháh, in the year 1836, *Royal Geographic Society Journal*, Vol. IX, No. 26 (1839), p. 125.
29 H.H. Wilson, *Ariana Antiqua: A Descriptive Account of the Antiquities and Coins of Afghanistan* (London: East India Company, 1841), p. 131.
30 H.C. Rawlinson, Notes on a March from Zoháb, at the foot of Zagros, along the mountains to Khúzistán (Susiana), and from thence through the province of Luristan to Kirmánsháh, in the year 1836, *Royal Geographic Society Journal*, Vol. IX, No. 26 (1839), p. 126.
31 Yue-Chi is a Central Asiatic tribe that ruled in Bactria and India and is also known as the Kushans.
32 Herodotus, *The Histories of Herodotus*, Vol. III. Translated by George Rawlinson (London: John Murrey, 1860), p. 216.
33 Hecataeus, *Hecataei Milesii Fragmenta: Scylacis Caryandensis Periplus*. Rud Henr Klausen (ed.) (Berolini: Impensis G. Reimeri, MDCCCXXXI), p. 178.
34 Herodotus, *The Histories of Herodotus*, Vol. II. Translated by George Rawlinson (London: John Murrey, 1860), p. 485.

35 Strabo, *The Geography of Strabo*, Vol. VII. Translated by Horace Leonard Jones (London: William Heinemann, 1917), pp. 992–995.
36 Claudius Ptolemy, *The Geography*, Vol. VII. Translated by E.L. Stevenson (New York: New York Public Library, 1932), p. 1.
37 Herodotus, *The Histories of Herodotus*, Vol. IV. Translated by George Rawlinson (London: John Murrey, 1860), p. 117.
38 Herodotus, *The Histories of Herodotus*, Vol. IV, p. 218.
39 This, again, is not expressed on the map. The Gandharas, however, of the Hindu writers extend across the Upper Punjab to Kashmir; H.H. Wilson, *Ariana Antiqua: A Descriptive Account of the Antiquities and Coins of Afghanistan* (London: East India Company, 1841), p. 131.
40 For a description of the Punjab and the Indus Valley, see Herodotus, *The Histories of Herodotus*, Vol. I. Translated by George Rawlinson (London: John Murrey, 1860), pp. 540–541.
41 Herodotus, *The Histories of Herodotus*, Vol. IV. Translated by George Rawlinson (London: John Murrey, 1860), p. 113.
42 Herodotus, *The Histories of Herodotus*, Vol. IV, p. 44.
43 Arrian, *The Anabasis of Alexander or, the History of the Wars and Conquests of Alexander the Great*, Vol. V. Translated by E.J. Chinnock (London: Hodder and Stoughton, 1884), pp. 13–19.
44 Strabo, *The Geography of Strabo*, Vol. I. Translated by Horace Leonard Jones (London: William Heinemann, 1917), p. 274.
45 P. Bernard et al. *Fouilles d'Ai Khanoum I (Campagnes 1965–68): Memoires de la Delegation archeologique francaise en Afghanistqn, XXI* (Paris: Klincksieck Publisher, 1973), pp. 21–34; H.P. Francfort, *Second campagne de fouilles sur le sit.e proto-historique de Shortugai (Afghanistan du N.E.): 10 avril–2 juin 1978, mss., Kabul, 1978* (Paris: Klincksieck Publisher, 1978), p. 3.
46 H.P. Francfort, The Harappan Settlement of Shortugai. B.B. Lal, and S.P. Gupta (eds), *in Frontiers of the Indus Civilization* (New Delhi: Books and Books, 1984), pp. 301–310.
47 Hiuen Tsang, *Si-Yu-Ki: Buddhist Records of the Western World*, Vol. I. Translated by Samuel Beal (London: Kegan Paul, Trench, Trubner & Co., 1884), p. 12.
48 Salman Rashid, email communication with the author on 12 July 2013.
49 Emphasis by the author.
50 Max Muller (ed.) *The Zenda Avesta: The Sacred Books of the East* (New York: The Christian Literature Company, 1898), p. 9.
51 Herodotus. *The Histories of Herodotus*, Vol. I. Translated by George Rawlinson (London: John Murrey, 1860), p. 304.
52 I-Tsing, *A Record of the Buddhist Religion As Practiced in India and the Malay Archipelago, 671–695 AD*. Translated by J. Takakusu, Oxford: The Clarendon Press, 1896, p. lii.
53 Jawaharlal Nehru, *The Discovery of India* (New Delhi: Penguin Publications, 2004), p. 69.
54 Jawaharlal Nehru, *The Discovery of India* (New Delhi: Penguin Publication, 2004), p. 70.
55 Hiuen Tsang, *Si-Yu-Ki: Buddhist Records of the Western World*, Vol. I. Translated by Samuel Beal (London: Kegan Paul, Trench, Trubner & Co., 1884), p. 69.
56 Tsang. *Si-Yu-Ki*, p. 69.
57 I-Tsing, *A Record of the Buddhist Religion As Practiced in India and the Malay Archipelago, 671.–695 AD* Translated by J. Takakusu (Oxford: The Clarendon Press, 1896), p. lii.

58 Herodotus, *The Histories of Herodotus*, Vol. IV. Translated by George Rawlinson (London: John Murrey, 1860), pp. 220–225.
59 Herodotus, *The Histories of Herodotus*, pp. 220–225.
60 Olaf Caroe, *The Pathans: 550 BC–AD 1957* (London: Macmillan and Co., Ltd., 1958), pp. 32–33.
61 Together came the Pakthas, the Bhalanas, the Alinas, the Sivas, the Visanins. Yet to the Trtsus came the Ārya's Comrade, through love of spoil and heroes' war, to lead them; *Rig Veda*, Book – 7, Hymn – 18, Verse – 7 (Hoshiarpur: VVRI Publication, 1961).
62 *Encyclopedia Iranica*, ASB, 'horse' (*equus* caballus, Av. *aspa*-, Old PerS. *asa-* and *aspa-*, Mid. and NPers. *asp/b*), http://www.iranicaonline.org/articles/asb-horse-equus-caballus-av
63 Which is written in Persian as follows: اسپاگان
64 Salman Rashid. Pakhtun, *Express Tribune*, 11 November 2011.
65 Jean Pierre Ferrier, *History of the Afghans*, Trans. *Original Unpublished Manuscript by Captain William Jesse* (London: John Murrey, 1858), p. 6.
66 Email conversation with the Pakistani author and historian Salman Rashid, 29 March 2013.
67 Jean Pierre Ferrier, *History of the Afghans*, Trans. *Original Unpublished Manuscript by Captain William Jesse* (London: John Murrey, 1858), p. 6.
68 1 Samuel 14:51 lists three sons – Jonathan, Ishvi, and Malchi-shua – and the two daughters. But see also 2 Samuel 2:8 and 1 Chronicles 8:33.
69 Other than mountains and rivers, which were effortlessly crossed by people, there is no physical dissociation between India and Afghanistan; see Edward Thornton, *A Gazetteer of Countries Adjacent to India on the North-West*, Vol. I (London: W.M.H. Allen and Co., 1844), pp. 4–27.
70 Starting from Bharat of the Ramayana era until King Asoka, we find strong evidence of a common King; Valmiki. *Ramayana, Uttarakhand*. Translated by M.N. Dutt (Calcutta: Girish Chandra Chakravarty, 1891); Vyasadev. *The Mahabharata*, Trans. G.C. Vaidya (Bombay: Ramchandra Govind & Son, 1980); Herodotus, *The Histories of Herodotus*, Vol. IV. Translated by George Rawlinson (London: John Murrey, 1860); Hiuen Tsang, *Si-Yu-Ki: Buddhist Records of the Western World*, Vol. I. Translated by Samuel Beal (London: Kegan Paul, Trench, Trubner & Co., 1884), p. 69.
71 Herodotus, *The Histories of Herodotus*, Vol. IV. Translated by George Rawlinson (London: John Murrey, 1860), p. 218.
72 Valmiki, *Ramayana,. Uttarakhand* Translated by M.N. Dutt (Calcutta: Girish Chandra Chakravarty, 1891); Vyasadev, *The Mahabharata*. Translated by G.C. Vaidya (Bombay: Ramchandra Govind & Son); Herodotus, *The Histories of Herodotus*, Vol. IV. Translated by George Rawlinson (London: John Murrey, 1860); Hiuen Tsang, *Si-Yu-Ki: Buddhist Records of the Western World*, Vol. I. Translated by Samuel Beal (London: Kegan Paul, Trench, Trubner & Co., 1884), p. 69.
73 B.B. Lal, *Indian Archaeology 1969–70 – A Review* (New Delhi: Indian Archaeological Survey of India, 1970), p. 40; B.K. Thapar, *Indian Archaeology 1976–77 – A Review* (New Delhi: Indian Archaeological Survey of India, 1977), p. 52–53.
74 Kalidasa, *Raghuvamsa* (Bombay: Gopal Narayan & Co., 1952, Hymns 89–91), p. 102.
75 Romesh C. Dutt, *The Ramayana and Mahabharata* (Whitefield: Kessinger Publications, 2012), p. 153.
76 Sir Mortimer Wheeler, *Charsada: A Metropolis of the North-West Frontier* (London: Oxford University Press, 1962), p. xi.

77 Arrian, *The Anabasis of Alexander or, the History of the Wars and Conquests of Alexander the Great* Vol. VI. Translated by E.J. Chinnock (London: Hodder and Stoughton, 1884), p. 19.
78 Valmiki, *Ramayana,. Uttarakhand* Translated by M.N. Dutt (Calcutta: Girish Chandra Chakravarty, 1891).
79 Kalidasa, *Raghuvamsa* (Bombay: Gopal Narayan & Co., 1952), Hymns 89–91, p. 102.
80 Sir Mortimer Wheeler, *Charsada: A Metropolis of the North-West Frontier* (London: Oxford University Press, 1962), p. xi.
81 B.B. Lal, Mahabharata and Archaeology, in S. P. Gupta and K. S. Ramachandran (eds) *Mahabharata: Myth and Reality* (New Delhi: Agam Prakashan, 1976), pp. 57–58.
82 Vyasadev, *The Mahabharata* Translated by G.C. Vaidya (Bombay: Ramchandra Govind & Son), Hymns – 257, 326, 503, 691, 1110 and 1188.
83 Mohan Lal, *Travels in the Punjab and Afghanistan and Turistan to Balkh, Bikhara and Herat and a Visit to Great Britain, Germany* (London: Murry and Co., 1946), p. 50.
84 Herbert Cushing Tolman, *A Guide to the Old Persian Inscription* (New York: American Book Company, 1893) p. 146; H.P. Francfort, *Second campagne de fouilles sur le sit.e proto-historique de Shortugai (Afghanistan du N.E.): 10 avril–2 juin 1978, mss., Kabul, 1978* (Paris: Klincksieck Publisher, 1978), p. 3.
85 As explained in detail in *Rig Veda* and the *Atharva Veda*.
86 Emphasis by the author.
87 There is no consensus on the age of Homer; Barbara Graziosi, *Inventing Homer: The Early Reception of Epic* (Cambridge: Cambridge University Press, 2002), pp. 90–92.
88 Homer, *The Odyssey*. Translated by W. Lucas Collins (London: William Blackwood and Sons, 1879), p. 13; Homer, *The Odyssey*. Translated by E.V. Rieu (London: Clays Ltd, 1946), p. 3.
89 H.G. Rawlinson, 'Early Contacts Between India and Europe', in A.L. Basham (ed.) *A Cultural History of India* (Oxford: Oxford University Press, 1997), pp. 425–441; Jean W. Sedlar. *India and the Greek World: A Study in the Transmission of Culture* (New Jersey: Rowman and Littlefield publication, 1980), pp. xxi–381.
90 Aristotle, *Politics* Translated by Ingram Bywater (Oxford: Claredon Press, 1920), p. 7; Aristotle. *The Metaphysics of Aristotle*, Trans. Thomas Taylor (London: David, Wilks, and Taylon, 1801).
91 Herodotus, *The Histories of Herodotus*, Vol. I. Translated by George Rawlinson (London: John Murrey, 1860), p. I.
92 Hecataeus, 'Fragment 294a', in Jacoby (ed.) *Fragmente der Griechischen Historiker*, Vol. 1 (Berlin: Weidmann, 1923), p. 142.
93 Athenaeus, 'The Deipnosophists: Banquet of the Leashed Athneaeus', Vol. I. Translated by C.D. Yonge (London: Henry G. Bohn, 1853–1854), p. 82.
94 Herodotus, *The Histories of Herodotus*, Vol. IV. Translated by George Rawlinson (London: John Murrey, 1860), pp. 220–225.
95 Herodotus, *The Histories of Herodotus*, pp. 216–217.
96 Hecataeus, 'Fragment 294a', in Jacoby (ed.) *Fragmente der Griechischen Historiker*, Vol. 1 (Berlin: Weidmann, 1923), p. 688.
97 Ctésias, *Histoires de l' Orient*. Translated by Janick Auberget. Paris: Les Belles Letters, 1991), p. 87.
98 Ctésias, *Histoires of the Orient*, p. 30.
99 Diodorus Siculus, *Library of History*. Translated by C. H. Oldfather (Cambridge: Harvard University Press, 1933), p. VII.

100 Arrian, *Indica of Arrian* Translated by Watson McCrindle (Bombay: Education Society Press, 1896), pp. 8, 10, 14, 18.
101 Strabo, *The Geography of Strabo*, Vol. I. Translated by Horace Leonard Jones (London: William Heinemann, 1917), p. 70.
102 Pliny, *Natural History*, Vol. VI. Translated by H Rackham (London: William Heinemann, 1942), p. 58.
103 Those who have recorded portions of Megasthenis' *Indika* include Diodorus Siculus, Strabo, Pliny, and Arrian; Megasthenes, *Indica. Translated by* E.A. Schwanbeck (Bonn: Sumptibus, 1846), p. 8.
104 Arrian, *The Anabasis of Alexander*. Translated by E.J. Chinnock (London: Butler and Tanner, 1884), p. 340.
105 Strabo, *The Geography of Strabo*, Vol. XV. Translated by Horace Leonard Jones (London: William Heinemann, 1917), p. 724.
106 Arrian, *The Anabasis of Alexander*, Vol. VI, Trans. E.J. Chinnock (London: Butler and Tanner, 1884); Pliny. *Natural History*, Vol. VI. Translated by H Rackham (London: William Heinemann, 1942), p. 21.
107 Pliny, *Natural History*, Vol. VI. Translated by H Rackham (London: William Heinemann, 1942), p. 23.
108 William Smith, *Dictionary of Greek and Roman Geography* (Boston: Little, Brown, and Co., 1980), pp. 210–211.
109 Krishna Chandra Sagar, *Foreign Influence on Ancient India* (New Delhi: Northern Book Centre, 1992), p. 91.
110 Pliny, *Natural History*, Vol. VI. Translated by H Rackham (London: William Heinemann, 1942), pp. 22–25; Phylarchus. 'Historiarum Reliquiae', A. Brueckner (ed.) (Vratislaviae: Apud Georgium Philippum Aderholz, MDCCXXXIX), p. 31; Athenaeus. *The Deipnosophists: Banquet of the Leashed Athneaeus*, Vol. I. Translated by C.D. Yonge (London: Henry G. Bohn, 1930), p. xii.
111 Plutarch, *The Life of Alexander* (New York: Philips and Hung, 1883), p. 62.
112 Megasthenis, *Indica*. Translated by E.A. Schwanbeck (Bonn: Sumptibus, 1846), p. 9.
113 Strabo, *The Geography of Strabo*, Vol. XV. Translated by Horace Leonard Jones (London: William Heinemann, 1917), pp. 10–11.
114 Pliny, *Natural History*, Vol. VI, Trans. H Rackham (London: William Heinemann, 1942), p. 23.
115 W.M. Crindle, *Ancient India: As Described in Classical Literature – A Collection of Greek and Latin Texts Relating to India* (London: The Hakluyt Society, 1897), p. xv.
116 Strabo. *The Geography of Strabo*, Vol. XV. Translated by Horace Leonard Jones (London: William Heinemann, 1917), p. 256.
117 Athenaeus. *The Deipnosophists: Banquet of the Leashed Athneaeus*, Vol. I, Trans. C.D. Yonge (London: Henry G. Bohn, 1930), p. 30.
118 Athenaeus, *Mahavamsa*, Trans. Wilhelm Geiger (London: Oxford University Press, 1912), p. xxxi.
119 King Ashoka mentions the Greek kings Antiochus, Ptolemy, Antigonus, Magas, and Alexander by name as recipients of his teachings; E. Hultzsch, *Inscription of Asoka*, Pliny. *Natural History*, Vol. VI. Translated by H Rackham (London: William Heinemann, 1942), Vol. I (Oxford: Clarendon Press, 1925), p. 71.
120 E. Hultzsch. *Inscription of Asoka*, Pliny. *Natural History*, Vol. VI, Trans. H Rackham (London: William Heinemann, 1942), Vol. I (Oxford: Clarendon Press, 1925), p. 71.
121 Vincent A. Smith, *Rulers of India: Asoka, The Buddhist Emperor of India* (Oxford: Clarendon Press, 1901), pp. 15–17.

122 E. Hultzsch, *Inscription of Asoka*, Pliny. *Natural History*, Vol. VI. Translated by H Rackham (London: William Heinemann, 1942), Vol. I (Oxford: Clarendon Press, 1925), p. 71; Vincent A. Smith, *Rulers of India: Asoka, The Buddhist Emperor of India* (Oxford: Clarendon Press, 1901), p. 16.
123 D.D. Kosambi, 'Notes on the Kandahar Edict of Asoka', *Journal of the Economic and Social History of the Orient*, Vol. 2, No. 2, May 1959, pp. 204–206.
124 Jawaharlal Nehru, *Glimpses of World History* (New Delhi: Penguin Publication, 2004), p. 74.
125 E. Hultzsch. *Inscription of Asoka*, Pliny. *Natural History*, Vol. VI. Translated by H Rackham (London: William Heinemann, 1942), Vol. I (Oxford: Clarendon Press, 1925), p. 71.
126 Pliny, *Natural History*, Vol. VI. Translated by H Rackham (London: William Heinemann, 1942), pp. 22–25.
127 Strabo, *The Geography of Strabo*, Vol. I. Translated by Horace Leonard Jones (London: William Heinemann, 1917), pp. 8–11.
128 Strabo, *The Geography of Strabo*, Vol. I. Translated by Horace Leonard Jones (London: William Heinemann, 1917), pp. 8–11.
129 Vishnu Sarma, *Panchatantra*. Translated by Chandra Rajan (New Delhi: Penguin Publication, 1993), p. xii.
130 Emphasis by the author.
131 Nārāyaṇa, *The Hitopadeśa*, Trans. A.N.D. Haksar (New Delhi: Penguin Publication, 1998), p. 1.
132 Adi Shankara, *Complete Works of Sri Sankaracharya* (Srirangam: Vani Vilas Press, 1910).
133 M Witzel, 'Vedas and Upaniṣads', in Gavin Flood (ed.) *The Blackwell Companion to Hinduism* (Blackwell Publishing Ltd., 2003), pp. 68–71.
134 Koichiro Matsuura, 'Chanting of Vedas in India: An Outstanding Example of Heritage and Form of Cultural Expressions', Paris: UNESCO, 7 November 2003.
135 Koichiro Matsuura, *Vishnu Puran: A System of Hindu Mythology and Tradition* Translated by H.H. Wilson (London: Trubner & Co., 1864), p. 1.
136 Salman Rashid, travel writer of Pakistan and Fellow of the Royal Geographic Society, email communication with the author on 'Classic Travels', 13 July 2013.
137 Original Source: T.2145.4c.20ff, 辭之質文繁於執筆。或善胡義，而不了漢旨，或明漢文，而不曉胡意。雖有偏解，終隔圓通。… 豈經礙哉？譯之失耳！; also see Erik Zurcher. *The Buddhist Conquest of China: The Spread and Adaptation of Buddhism in Early Medieval China*, Vol. I (Leiden: Brill Publication, 1972), p. 23.
138 Fa-hien, '*FoéKouéKi, ou, Relations des royaumesbouddhiques: voyage dans la Tartarie, dansl'Afghanistan et dansl'Inde, exécuté, à la fin du IVe siècle, par ChyFaHian*'. Translated by Jean Pierre Abel Rémusat (Paris: l'Imprimerie Royale, 1836), pp. 40.
139 Original Source: T.2145.4c.20ff, 辭之質文繁於執筆。或善胡義，而不了漢旨，或明漢文，而不曉胡意。雖有偏解，終隔圓通。… 豈經礙哉？譯之失耳！; also Erik Zurcher, The Buddhist Conquest of China: The Spread and Adaptation of Buddhism in Early Medieval China, Vol. I (Leiden: Brill Publication, 1972), pp. 20–24.
140 This theme has been developed much later into the story of a magical contest between the first Buddhist missionaries and a number of Daoist masters, supposed to have been held at the court in 69 CE under imperial auspices, and followed by the conversion of the emperor, the ordination of several hundred

Chinese monks and the foundation of ten monasteries in and around Luoyang. This fantastic tale was set forth in great detail in a (now lost) apocryphal work, the 'Han Faben Neizhuan', passages from which have been preserved in later Buddhist treatises. The text probably dates from the early 6th century.
141 Original Source: T.2145.4c.20ff, 辭之質文繫於執筆。或善胡義，而不了漢旨，或明漢文，而不曉胡意。雖有偏解，終隔圓通。... 豈經礙哉？譯之失耳！; Erik Zurcher. *The Buddhist Conquest of China: The Spread and Adaptation of Buddhism in Early Medieval China*, Vol. I (Leiden: Brill Publication, 1972), p. 22.
142 In the book *Biographies of Eminent Monks*, also known as the *Liang Gaoseng Zhuan*, written in 519 CE, Fa-hien's journey to India is described in detail by its author Huijiao (497–554). It is a collection of biographies of famous and/or archetypal monks compiled by the monk Huijiao (497–554) of the Liang dynasty. The Gaoseng zhuan contains the biographies of nearly 500 monks (253 full biographies and 243 miscellaneous figures) who were active in China from 67 to 519 CE.
143 Fa-hien, '*FoéKouéKi, ou, Relations des royaumesbouddhiques: voyage dans la Tartarie, dansl'Afghanistan et dansl'nde, exécuté, à la fin du IVe siècle, par ChyFaHian*'. Translated by Jean Pierre Abel Rémusat (Paris: l'Imprimerie Royale, 1836), p. 12.
144 Fa-hien, '*FoéKouéKi, ou, Relations des royaumesbouddhiques: voyage dans la Tartarie, dansl'Afghanistan et dansl'nde, exécuté, à la fin du IVe siècle, par ChyFaHian*'. Translated by Jean Pierre Abel Rémusat, Paris: l'Imprimerie Royale, 1836), p. 11; also see: Fa-hien, *Fo-Kwo-Ki*. Translated by Samuel Beal (London: Trubnet and Co., 1884), pp. XXVII–XXIX.
145 Fa-hien, '*FoéKouéKi, ou, Relations des royaumesbouddhiques: voyage dans la Tartarie, dansl'Afghanistan et dansl'Inde, exécuté, à la fin du IVe siècle, par ChyFaHian*'. Translated by Jean Pierre Abel Rémusat (Paris: l'Imprimerie Royale, 1836), p. 11.
146 Hiuen Tsang, *Si-Yu-Ki: Buddhist Records of the Western World*, Vol. I, Trans. Samuel Beal (London: Kegan Paul, Trench, Trubner & Co., 1884), p. xxxi.
147 A translation by Samuel Beal, *Travel of Fah-hien and Sung Yun: Buddhist Pilgrims From China to India* (London: Trubner and Co, 1869), pp. 174–208.
148 Hiuen Tsang, *Si-Yu-Ki: Buddhist Records of the Western World*, Vol. I. Translated by Samuel Beal (London: Kegan Paul, Trench, Trubner & Co., 1884), pp. XVII–XVIII.
149 Hiuen Tsang, *Si-Yu-Ki: Buddhist Records of the Western World*, Vol. I. Translated by Samuel Beal (London: Kegan Paul, Trench, Trubner & Co., 1884), p. 31.
150 Stanislas Aignan Julien, Histoire de la vie de Hiouen-Thsang et de ses voyages dans l'Inde: depuis l'an 629 jusqu'en 645 / par Hoeï-li et Yen-thsong; suivi de documents et d'éclaircissements géographiques tirés de la relation originale de Hiouen-Thsang, Translation from original Chinese (Paris: Print Imperial, 1853), p. 64.
151 Hiuen Tsang, *Si-Yu-Ki: Buddhist Records of the Western World*, Vol. I. Translated by Samuel Beal (London: Kegan Paul, Trench, Trubner & Co., 1884), p. 44.
152 Hiuen Tsang, *Si-Yu-Ki*, pp. 50–53.
153 In colloquial English, the word 'Caste' is adapted from the Spanish-Portuguese origin word '*casta*' or '*kaest*'. As per John Minsheu's Spanish dictionary, which he compiled in 1569 CE, '*Kaest*' means 'race, lineage, tribe or breed'. Unlike the Spanish-Portuguese term '*karst*', '*Varna*' in the Indian context is a set of people who profess the same kind of profession or work culture. They need not

belong to the same race, lineage, tribe or breed. In other words, in one family, there might be members of different '*Varna*'. Lord Krishna, in the *Bhagavad Gita*, explained: 'The four varna of human society are my creation according to their Virtue and Character and also as per one's professed professional ability/performance and not associated by birth'.
Chatur varnam maya srishtam,
Guna karma vibhagasah;
Tasya kartaram api mam,
Viddhi akartaram avyam (*Bhagavad Gita*, Chapter 4, Sloka 13).

154 A resemblance to present-day Himalayas or any Kumbh Mela where tantriks perform their skills under broad daylight (opinion mine).
155 Hiuen Tsang, *Si-Yu-Ki: Buddhist Records of the Western World*, Vol. I, Trans. Samuel Beal (London: Kegan Paul, Trench, Trubner & Co., 1884), p. 58.
156 Fa-hien, 'FoéKouéKi, ou, Relations des royaumesbouddhiques: voyage dans la Tartarie, dansl'Afghanistan et dansl'Inde, exécuté, à la fin du IVe siècle, par ChyFaHian', Trans. Jean Pierre Abel Rémusat (Paris: l'Imprimerie Royale, 1836), pp. xxviii, xxix
157 James Prinsep, *Essay on Indian Antiquities, Historic, Numismatic and Palaeographic*, Vol. I (London: John Murrey, 1858), p. 145.
158 D.C. Sircar, *Indian Epigraphy* (New Delhi: Motilal Banarsidass, 1965), pp. 262–266.
159 Hiuen Tsang, *Si-Yu-Ki: Buddhist Records of the Western World*, Vol. I, Trans. Samuel Beal (London: Kegan Paul, Trench, Trubner & Co., 1884), p. 91.
160 Nanjio's Catalogue of the Chinese Buddhist Books, No. 1492; Nanjio Bunyiu. *A Catalogue of the Chinese Translation of the Buddhist Tripitaka the Sacred Canon of the Buddhists in China and Japan Compiled by Order of the Secretary of State for India* (Oxford: At the Clarendon Press, 1883).
161 I-Tsing, *A Record of the Buddhist Religion As Practiced in India and the Malay Archipelago, 671–695 AD*, Trans. J. Takakusu (Oxford: The Clarendon Press, 1896), p. 12.
162 John Crawford, *Journal of the Embassy of the Governor General of India of Ava in the Year 1827 to the Court of Siam* (London: Henry Colburn, 1830), p. 615.
163 Paul Pelliot, *Un Bibliotheque Medieval Retrouvee au Kan-sou* (Annee: Bulletin de l'Ecole Francaise d'Extreme-Orient, 1908), pp. 501–529; Han-sung Yang et al. *The Hye Cho's Diary: Memoir of the Pilgrimage to the Five Regions of India*, Trans. Han-sung Yang et al. (Berkeley: California University Press, 1984), p. 49.
164 Paul Pelliot, *Un Bibliotheque Medieval Retrouvee au Kan-sou*, pp. 501–529; Han-sung Yang et al., *The Hye Cho's Diary*, p. 49.
165 Paul Pelliot, *Un Bibliotheque Medieval Retrouvee au Kan-sou*, pp. 501–529; Han-sung Yang et al., *The Hye Cho's Diary*, pp. 52.
166 Paul Pelliot, *Un Bibliotheque Medieval Retrouvee au Kan-sou*, pp. 501–529; Han-sung Yang et al., *The Hye Cho's Diary*, pp. 52.
167 Paul Pelliot, *Un Bibliotheque Medieval Retrouvee au Kan-sou* (Annee: Bulletin de l'Ecole Francaise d'Extreme-Orient, 1908), pp. 501–529; Han-sung Yang et al. *The Hye Cho's Diary: Memoir of the Pilgrimage to the Five Regions of India*, Trans. Han-sung Yang et al. (Berkeley: California University Press, 1984), pp. 54.

2
THE CONTESTED HISTORIES
Journeying Through the Ages

Not far from Afghanistan, a new religion – Islam – was born in Arabia. This new religion was introduced by Prophet Mohammad, who was born in Mecca in 570 CE. Before the emergence of Mohammad, Arab's Bedouins tribe, who used to live in the deserts for generations, remained the same without much change. Some of their residents became Christians while some became Jews, but mostly the Arabs remained worshippers of the 360 idols – chiefly of animals – and the far-famed Black Stone in Mecca until Prophet Mohammad started this new religion.[1] Therefore, when Mohammad began preaching against those idols, he was driven away from Mecca by his people in 622 CE. He was forced to take refuge in Yethrib and this flight was called *Hijrat*. Islam, although it had emerged a little earlier, may be said to have commenced with the flight in 622 CE. The residents of Yethrib received Mohammad with honour and changed the name of the city to 'Madinat-un-Nabi' – the city of the Prophet or Madina.

Prophet Mohammad died in 632 CE, a mere ten years after the *Hijrat*, but before his death in 629 CE he returned to Mecca, where he established himself as its master. He sent out emissaries to rulers and kings as far away as Constantinople, Persia, and China to acknowledge the new religion's idea of one God and Mohammad as God's Prophet.[2] Mohammad had supreme confidence in himself and his mission, which inspired his followers in the desert to spread his religion and conquer far-flung places. After his death, Mohammad was succeeded by Abu Bakr, a member of his family, as Khalifa, Caliph, or Chief. After the death of Abu Bakr, within two years of becoming Caliph, Omar succeeded him for ten years.

DOI: 10.4324/9781003627678-2

In 636 CE, during the reign of Omar, a naval expedition was sent to the coast of Bombay, which failed terribly. A few years later, in 644 CE under Caliph Osman, Abdullah bin-Amar led an intelligence mission by land through Persia and Afghanistan to Hind and Sindh. After his return, he reported back to Damascus, the headquarters of the Caliph, that in Hind, 'Its water is dark (and dirty); its fruit is bitter and poisonous; its land is stony, and its earth is saltish. A small army will soon be annihilated there, and a large army will soon die of hunger'.[3]

Throughout these periods, Afghanistan used to be the western exterior of India and the western wall against the sword of Islam. Numerous attempts to subdue India and overrun Afghanistan ended in the loss of men, materials, and resources before imminent failures. In 710 CE, Caliph Al-Walid ibn's representative of the Eastern provinces, Hijjaj, sought approval to send a fresh expedition to conquer Hind. But a distraught Caliph wrote in reply, 'This affair will be a source of great anxiety, and so we must put it off; for every time the army goes on such an expedition, vast numbers of Mussalmans are killed. So, think no more of such a design'.[4]

However, using his guileful persuasion, Hijjaj was able to assure the Caliph about the unimaginable material riches awaiting after the success of such a mission. Hijjaj sent his 17-year-old son-in-law Muhammad Qasim to conquer Sindh. Raja Dahir, the valiant King of Debal from the Brahmin dynasty, offered stiff resistance. However, Dahir suffered defeat before being killed in 712 CE. His Queen Ranibai put up an equally heroic defence only to be vanquished by the invading army, forcing her to commit *Jauhar* – the mass self-immolation by women to avoid capture by an enemy.[5] The Brahmin dynasty was abolished with the death of the royal couple Raja Dahir and Queen Ranibai. The Hindu Shahi dynasty was built on the edifice of the extinct Brahmin dynasty.

Al Beruni, the Uzbek historian and court poet of Mahmud of Ghazni, in his work *Kitab al-Hind* originally written in Arabic around 1030 CE, explained that during the 8th century CE, Kabul was ruled by the Hindu Shahi kings. They replaced the Turks of Tibetan origin.[6] The last ruler of Turk lineage named Lagaturman lost his empire to his Vazir named Kallar, a Brahman. Kalhana Pandit, in his *Rajatarangini*, stated that King Lalliya of the Hindu Shahi dynasty was ruling Udbhandapura during the same time.[7] Modern historians recognize the fact that Lalliya was the same person as Al Beruni's Kallar.[8]

This is a reiteration of the assertion made by Sir H. Elliot in his book *India as Known to the Arabs during the first four centuries of the Hijri Era* that the Arab occupation of Sindh was but temporary and native princes regained power immediately.[9] Both Kalhana and Al Beruni agree with the fact that Lalliya was a King of repute and the great founder of the Hindu

Shahi dynasty, which ruled the vast kingdom from its capital Kabul. The capital was later shifted to Udbhandapura or Und. Kalhana further elaborated that Lalliya's lineage was continued by his son Kamaluka. Al Beruni provided the chronology of Hindu Shahi rulers after Lalliya. The list of rulers is as follows – Samand (Samanta), Kamalu, Bhim (Bhima), Jaipal (Jayapala), Anandapala, and Trilocanapala. Trilocanapala was killed in 1021 and his son Bhimapala five years later in 1026 CE.[10] This Hindu Shahi dynasty gradually shifted its capital from Kabul to Und to Lahore to finally Bhatinda before extinction.

The Brahmin kingdom of Kabul under Raja Dahir was taken over by the Turks of Tibetan origin for a brief interregnum before it was again retaken by another Brahmin dynasty, i.e. the Hindu Shahi dynasty. The Brahmin dynasty of Raja Dahir, followed by another Brahmin dynasty the Hindu Shahi dynasty, together not only resisted the marauding advance of Islamic expansion for an amazing 400 years but also extended their sway from Chenab in Kashmir to Kabul, Kandahar, and Parwan in Afghanistan. They raised magnificent buildings and ruled their kingdom well.

Gradually, the Hindu Shahi kingdom was overrun by the Turks in the closing years of the 10th century. Subuktigin, the Islamic general of Turkic origin, and the predatory army of his son Mahmud settled in Ghazni, Afghanistan. Although they were Turkic in race from the Tibetan plateau, they settled in Afghanistan and started their campaign against India from Ghazni. Chinese and Korean travellers, who travelled through Afghanistan during the 7th century, noticed Turkic rule in a portion of Afghanistan. But they reiterated the fact that those Turkic rulers were adherents of Buddhism, and they used to worship the 'Three Jewels' and fund Buddhist monasteries in their kingdom. The early Turkic migrants from Tibet to Afghanistan never subscribed to Islam in their initial days. They followed Buddhist precepts and worshipped Buddhist ideals.

Over time, Islam overwhelmed the Turkic population of Afghanistan. They became the adherents of the new religion, and Islam's entry into Afghanistan stood in contrast with Buddhist ideals. Islam vanquished Afghanistan's Buddhism, and this led to the delinking of Afghanistan from mainland India. Buddhism, which used to be a great binder for the people of Afghanistan and India, and which used to serve as a bond among the people of Magadh and Kalinga with Balkh and Kandahar, is no longer the state religion of Afghanistan.

By the time of Subuktigin, who ruled from 977 CE, and his son Mahmud, who ruled from 997 CE, the Turkic race of Afghanistan was completely converted to Islamic ideals. Mahmud conducted 17 expeditions between 1000 and 1024 CE against India.[11] He went as far as Pataliputra, Mathura, and Kanauj. Other than Al Beruni, Mahmud's court was endowed with another poet of great repute, Firdausi. He was the author of Shahnama. Firdausi lamented Mahmud for not honouring his promise to pay 60,000 mishkals of gold because the Turkic general promised Firdausi to pay one gold dinar for each verse in the Shahnama. Firdausi left Ghazni for the city of Mazandaran, where Sepahbad Shahreyar from the lineage of the Zoroastrian–Sasanian era was ruling. Firdausi wrote a satire against Mahmud, which read as follows:

> Long years this Shahnama I toiled to complete,
> That the king might award me some recompense meet,
> But naught save a heart writhing with grief and despair,
> Did I get from those promises empty as air!
> Had the sire of the king been some price of renown,
> My forehead had surely been graced by a crown,
> Were his mother a lady of high pedigree,
> In silver and gold had I stood to knee!
> But, being by birth not a price but a boor,
> To praise of the noble he could not endure![12]

Afghanistan became the springboard for the Turks to start the campaign against India. During the 11th and 12th centuries, India was under the rule of the Chauhan, Sena, Gurjara-Pratiharas, Palas, Rashtrakutas, Chalukyas, Chola, Chera, and Pandya dynasties. Until the time of Muhammad Ghori, the Indian empire remained under the strict control of Indian princes. During this period, Islam consolidated its position in Afghanistan while India's grip reduced considerably. Finally, the Turks, who were now adherents of Islam, marshalled attacks against India and established Sultanate rule in the country.

The five dynasties that ruled Delhi during the Sultanate period, starting from 1206 until 1526, either came through Afghanistan or belonged to Afghanistan. Muhammad Ghori, the Turkic general from Ghor, Afghanistan, after vanquishing Sindh and Multan, proceeded to Delhi in 1191. He tasted a scathing defeat. Delhi's King, Prithviraj Chauhan, crushed Ghori's ambition on the battlefield of Tarain. The next year Muhammad Ghori returned to wage war against Prithviraj Chauhan on the same battlefield, where he was able to defeat the Chauhan King. He established a Muslim empire in India. Unlike the Greeks or the Scythians, who gave fine arts, culture, and town planning to India, these Islamic armies from Arabia belonged to an impoverished region, and they used savagery and brutal tactics to plunder India and seek wealth in the name of their newly acquired belief: Islam.[13]

The loot of various Muslim tribes needs no audio visualization. It is well-documented even by the contemporary historians employed by the Islamic invaders themselves.[14] Mahmud of Ghazni sustained pillage and plunder on an unimaginable scale in India. 'India was to him just a place from which he could carry off treasure and material to his homeland'.[15] Mahmud's historian Al Beruni wrote, 'He utterly ruined the prosperity of the country (of India), and performed those wonderful exploits by which the Hindus became like atoms of dust scattered in all directions'.[16] Mahmud's looting spree was aptly captured during his attacks on India. Al Beruni wrote that

> To Mahmud the Hindus were infidels, to be dispatched to hell as soon as they refused to be plundered. To go on expeditions and to fill the treasury with gold, not to make lasting conquests of territories, was the real object of his famous expeditions; and it was with this view that he cut his way through enormous distances to the rich temples of India at Taneshar, Mathura, Kanoj, and Somanath.[17]

The savagery unleashed by Sultanate rulers from time to time is no secret. Moroccan traveller Ibn Battuta explained the fiendish fashion of killings and gory deaths as adopted by his employer Muhammad bin Tughluq.[18] Khushwant Singh, in his novel *Delhi*, provided a long list of graphic details about mass killings in Delhi many times by different Islamic rulers including Taimur Lang and Nadir Shah. He wrote about Nadir Shah's order of 22 March 1739 in the following words: 'While passing the gateway of Dariba we ordered our men to level every home in that accursed street inhibited by infidels. Our soldiers slew every man, woman, and child in Dariba and then set fire to the bazaar'.[19] Mughal attacker Babur's ruthlessness is recorded by Ahmad Yadgar in his *Tarikh-i-Salatin-I Afghana*. He wrote, 'The slaughter was great, and there was a heap of severed heads'.[20] One cannot disagree with undisputed historical facts. The plunder and savagery of Turkic attackers as well as Mughal marauders do not require a critical examination, as it may lead to a different narrative. The purpose of this manuscript is to unearth the hitherto untold history of India–Afghanistan relations.

Of the five dynasties of the Delhi Sultanate, the Mamluk or Slave dynasty, which was founded after the assassination of Muhammad Ghori in 1206, was of Turkic origin with its roots in Ghor, Afghanistan. The Khalji dynasty belonged to the Turkic cradle as well. They started their campaign from the Afghan village Qalat-e-Khalji situated in present-day Zabul province. The Tughlaq dynasty traced its lineage to Turko-Indian origin, as the founder of the dynasty Ghyasuddin Tughlaq, had a Turkic father and a Hindu mother. The Sayyid dynasty inherited Turkic natives as well. The Lodi dynasty was the only one that belonged to the Pashtun stock of the Afghan tribe.

It is often believed that the Ghaznavids, Ghorids, Tughlaq, and Sultanate kings were all Pashtuns. However, this claim does not withstand historical scrutiny, and as previously explained, they all belonged to a Turkic ethnic background. Pakistani historian and travel writer Salman Rashid refers to Abul Qasim Ferishta's *Tarikh-e-Ferishta*, which was completed during the early years of the 17th century during the Mughal period, as the originator of this misconception. He asserted that Ferishta mistakenly referred to the Turks as Afghans, and once this error occurred it gradually became accepted.[21] But a thorough reading of Ferishta's volumes tells a different story. Ferishta mentioned the name Afghans abundantly, but while explaining the racial background of all five dynasties, he was extremely careful and applied all his intelligence to speak the truth. He was categorical when he wrote that Subuktigin, Mahmud's father was a Turk by descent[22] while his mother was from Zublistan. While explaining about Ghyasuddin Balban, he stated that Balban was a Turk of Kurra Khutta and of the tribe of Albery.[23] About the racial origin of the Khilji tribe, he said the Khiljis were descended from Khulich Khan, a son-in-law of Ghengis Khan. But he elaborated the fact that he suspected the Khiljis were an Afghan clan.[24] About Ghyasuddin Tughlaq, he said that Tughlaq was a Turkic slave of Balban who married a Jat farmer woman from Lahore.[25] He asserted that Khizr Khan of the Syed dynasty was a descendant of Prophet Mohammed, and hence he was a Syed, and Bahllol Lodi belonged to an Afghan tribe.[26]

Since most of the Sultanate rulers who successfully established dynastic rules in India were slaves, it was difficult for Ferishta to trace their racial lineage properly. However, as he explained in his book, he consulted scholarly texts and met with scholars and locals to find out their racial descents.[27] Despite his clinical writings, later historians picked up his vague explanation about the racial origin of Sultanate dynasties in India and labelled them as Afghan Pashtuns.

In the winter of 2014, I was conducting a tour of the Mughal-era Zafar Mahal at Mehrauli in New Delhi for a group of Pashtu-speaking visitors from Afghanistan. When I noted that the 'Mughals' were originally 'Mongols' and the Sultanate rulers had 'Turkic' origins, they appeared surprised. As they were not completely aware of the ethnic details surrounding the Sultanate rulers and Mughals, they requested to me to explain the ethnic background of each dynasty. After clarifying their ethnic backgrounds, the Afghan visitors ceased to express concerns.[28]

Another enduring myth about Afghanistan is the 'invincibility of Afghans'. No group in human history has ever been truly invincible. From Cyrus the Great to the countless waves of invaders – such as the Achaemenians, Greeks, Scythians, Parthians, Kushans, Sasanians, Turks, Mongols, and ultimately the Mughals – the Afghans/Pashtuns either submitted to or were defeated by every external force. Historical records do not indicate any significant resistance or victories by the Afghans against these invaders.[29]

The only notable instance of Afghan resistance to an invader took place during the First Anglo-Afghan War against the British forces from 1839 to 1842. Some British historians wrote extremely good and honest analytical books on the folly of British Governor-General in India Lord Ellenborough and the defeat of the British Army in the First Anglo-Afghan War.[30] William Dalrymple fantastically cites British Commander-in-Chief Sir Jasper Nicholls's report:

> After all the waste and destruction of an expensive and unnecessary war of dubious legality, with the honour and reputation of British army tarnished and British authority undermined; after spending £15 million (well over £50 billion in modern currency), exhausting the Indian treasury; pushing the Indian credit networks to the brink of collapse and permanently wrecking the solvency of the East India Company; after losing maybe 40,000 lives, as well as those of around 50,000 camels, and after alienating much of the Bengal army, leaving it ripe for mutiny, the British had left Afghanistan much as they found it.[31]

However, following the British debacle in the First Anglo-Afghan War, another set of historians created the myth of the 'invincible Afghan' without rigorous historical scrutiny.[32] Often, such historians have referred to Afghanistan as the 'graveyard of empires'[33] without proper citation or historical verification. This label is primarily rooted in the Anglo-Afghan Wars of the 19th century and the Soviet experiences in the 1980s.

The term 'graveyard of empires' is not a historical phrase coined by a single individual but rather a collective representation of the repeated failures of various empires in Afghanistan, most notably the British and the Soviet Union, followed by the Americans.[34] While the label 'graveyard of empires' has been used to describe Afghanistan due to the challenges faced by invaders, it does not reflect the full historical picture. Although Afghanistan has experienced numerous foreign invasions throughout history, the notion that Afghans are invincible is overly simplistic and misleading, particularly considering that Afghanistan itself was often part of, or under the control of, many of these empires. The Achaemenid Empire, founded by Cyrus the Great, controlled parts of Afghanistan (such as Bactria) for centuries. There is no evidence to suggest that the Achaemenians were defeated in Afghanistan; rather, it became integrated into their empire. After Alexander the Great's invasion in the 4th century BC, Afghanistan was incorporated into the Greek Empire (Greek Bactria). Alexander's troops did face challenges, but his forces did not fail to establish a lasting Greek presence in the region. The area was later governed by the Greco-Bactrian Kingdom.[35]

Invaders such as the Scythians, Parthians, Kushans, and Sasanians exercised control over parts of Afghanistan at various points in history and expanded their influence into the region. The Kushans, who succeeded the Parthians, ruled over much of Afghanistan, reaching the pinnacle of their empire under Kanishka in the first century CE. The Ghaznavids and Ghurids, both of Turkic origin, governed extensive regions of Afghanistan during the medieval period. The Mongols, led by Genghis Khan, invaded Afghanistan; although their invasion was brutal, they ultimately established control over the region. In 1222, Genghis Khan spearheaded a scathing attack against the Afghan province of Herat and spared only 40 inhabitants of the province out of its 160,000 total populations.[36] The Timurid Empire, a Turkic–Mongol empire, also held sway over Afghanistan for several centuries. The Mughals, who were the descendants of the Mongols, eventually established control over Afghanistan, despite periods of conflict.[37] They successfully brought the region under their sway. If the myth were true, and if the Afghans had indeed defeated all invaders, these empires would never have reached India. These empires not only reached India but also exerted control over Afghanistan during their conquests.

When Ziauddin Babur, the founder of the Mughal empire, established his rule in India in 1526 after defeating the Lodi Sultan, he came from Fergana in Northern Afghanistan.[38] Babur's victory over the feeble and contemptible Afghan Sultan of Delhi in 1526 was due to the introduction of 'artillery' fire, which had hitherto never used in India. Although the name 'Mughal' is borrowed from the term 'Mongol', which refers to his ancestors, Babur had a special fascination for Kabul. Babur died in Agra and was buried there, but later his burial was exhumed and taken back to Kabul as his final resting place.[39]

Babur ruled for barely four years in India. A brief interval apart, Mughal rule lasted for 181 years. Babur stated that 'There are two trade-marts on the land route between Hindustan and Khurasan; one is Kabul, the other, Kandahar'.[40] When Islam dominated India, Afghanistan itself was under the control of Arabs, Persians, Turks, and Mongols.[41] The domination of Islam continued in India for more than 730 years. Hinduism was subdued for some time only to survive foreign rule and rise again later. But Afghanistan succumbed to the sword of Islam forever. Buddhism and Hinduism waned during this time in Afghanistan and have all but vanished in subsequent times.

'Islam' and 'artillery' acted as catalysts of change for the new developments in both countries. Although the 'loot of treasure' and 'plunder of everything' came their way and not 'religion' was the motivating thrust behind their invasion of India,[42] it was an ascending 'Islam' through its Caliphate that provided guidance, scaffold, and legitimacy to keep the invaders moving despite centuries of failures. Therefore, Islam acted as a catalyst until the Mughal period when Babur introduced artillery, another catalyst. Accompanying these invasions came a new experience for India: the conversion of the unbelievers into Islam, until a time arrived when, finally, Islam itself was transformed by India, intermeshing with it and ultimately being absorbed by it as an integer.[43]

Afghanistan is a strange admixture of complex groups of tribes and races. Since time immemorial, the country has been divided into four or five power centres mostly centred around – Herat, Balkh (Mazar-e-Sharif), Kabul, Kandahar, and, to some extent, Badakhshan. This is true even today. There was a virtual absence of centralized government in Afghanistan until 1750.

In 1747, the great King of Afghanistan Ahmad Shah brought all these provinces under one rule and tried to make Afghanistan one entity. However, his measures were not to encourage the centralization of power. Local tribal heads were allowed to rule provinces – and although there was only one sovereign King, there were many powerful governors, generals, and tribal chiefs.

Afghanistan used to dominate and rule most parts of South Asia. The invaders of Afghanistan widened the land route towards India. Afghanistan is a region of caravan routes joining Central Asia to the plains of India, with cities such as Kabul and Kandahar, which are frequently designated as the keys to India. Therefore, being in the midst of land routes between Central Asia and oriental countries, Afghanistan's neighbouring countries, as well as contemporary great powers of the world, have always taken a keen interest in controlling the country. This has kept the state in turmoil for a long time. The Sunni sect of Islam has taken deep root in Afghanistan, although there is a wide presence of the Shia sect and paganism. Apart from that, a small presence of the Hindu population has also continued. Afghans are accustomed to hard-pressed and poverty-stricken primitive lives.

The stabilization of various races in Afghanistan occurred primarily after the 16th century. Before the onset of Islam, Afghanistan hosted people of various hues. For 600 years, Islam tried to establish its foothold, but that was disturbed by the Mongol invasion led by Genghis Khan during 1219 and 1222 CE. The hordes of Genghis Khan beat down the ill-concerted and desultory opposition offered by the world of Islam, and for a time the fabric of society and civilization was overthrown by the onslaught of the Mongols. For more than 300 years and more, wandering hordes of Mongols, Turks, and later Uzbeks rendered life in Afghanistan too strenuous for the Afghans, who were pushed about the country or forced into India. It was not until the 16th century and the early part of the following century that the Uzbeks were forced beyond the Hindukush and the vacant lands that existed in all districts were available for the Afghans to occupy. These conditions, which lasted for nearly 300 years, have left their impression on the population, which is now composed of three races,[44] each of which differs from its neighbours in many very important respects: in physiognomy, in character, and in their mode of life.

As per the British explorer G.P. Tate, the three races were 'the Hazara, the Tajik, and the Afghans'. However, later it was proved that his classifications were faulty. During the 19th century, when Tate classified the races of Afghanistan into three races, the reality was different. Afghans, as defined by Tate, were not a race but a vague geographical/linguistic term. Tate himself quoted Veda and called the Afghans 'Pakhtas', and citing locals he referred to the Afghans as Pathans. Out of the three races, Tate was unsure about the Afghans. While he entirely missed the Uzbek race, Tate used geography (Afghan) interchangeably with race (Pashtun). By the 18th century, Afghanistan was divided into four races, which were Pashtun, Tajik, Hazara, and Uzbek.[45] Sub-classifications of races, if any, ran from these four prime races.

The Hazaras are Mongols – relics of the invasion of Genghis Khan, reinforced afterwards by later arrivals from the banks of the Oxus and the country beyond. More precisely they are found around the south of the Hindukush, in the mountains between Bamiyan and the Herat Valley. The physical traits of the Hazaras have rendered them easily distinguishable. They adhere to the heretical form of belief of the Ali Ilahi of the Shia sect and are consequently despised and oppressed by the fanatical Pashtuns.[46] They do not coalesce socially or politically with either Tajik, Uzbek, or Pashtun. They are located to the west of the road from Kandahar to Kabul, and they occupy that tract today in which the Huns settled and where they had their centres of government in the 6th century CE. The Hazaras are hardy and industrious cultivators. They are strongly built and industrious, and the ranks of servants and labourers throughout the country are recruited from them. As a consequence of this, they are to be found all over Afghanistan and have even provided the Indian Army with soldiers.[47]

The Tajiks today display all those qualities which distinguished the agricultural population in the valley of the Oxus, known to the Chinese as the Ta-hia. They live in houses and form orderly village communities. They are appreciative of the benefits of education and the amenities of civilized existence; and in their households they maintain a higher standard of comfort than that which prevails among the Pashtuns or Hazaras. They are everywhere regarded as the people of the soil; descendants of the ancient race that owned the land. Despite centuries of misgovernment and oppression at the hands of predatory barbarians, they have clung tenaciously to agriculture and engaged in commerce as well. Wherever there is arable soil and water to irrigate it, there is always to be found a remnant of this ancient race.

Called by different names in different localities, they are one people and, in all probability, they represent the original Iranian or Aryan race among whom Zoroaster published his doctrine; among whom the Greek colonists of Alexander settled, and to whom a thousand years later the soldiers of Islam offered the alternatives of the Koran, the poll-tax, or the sword.[48]

If the Pashtuns are, generally speaking, nomads, the Persian element, the oldest established inhabitants of the country, known as Tajiks, are village dwellers, as are their kinsmen in Persia and Central Asia. They probably occupied all the fertile areas of the country before the Afghans from the eastern mountains surged westwards. Organized, as a rule, in village communities, as in neighbouring Persia, of which, generally speaking, they formed a part until the middle of the 18th century, they supplied the traders and artisans of the towns. Although they do not possess the outstanding martial qualities of the Pashtun tribesmen, the Tajiks did not lack courage and fought well. It remains to be added that where the Pashtuns have seized lands, the Tajiks almost invariably remain their tenants. Fortunately for them, they have adopted the Sunni tenets.[49] While the Mongol Hazara remain aloof, the Tajiks and Pashtuns are drawn together by common interests; and the former first call themselves Afghans, being Tajiks afterwards.

Considerable intermixture has taken place, yet each race possesses outstanding features. Today, the Turks, chief of whom are the Uzbeks, occupy the provinces once famous as Afghan Turkistan. These Uzbeks are closely related to their kinsmen in Central Asia, where Bokhara was a powerful Uzbek state.

The choice of the language of Afghanistan is also based on the social conditions of the Afghan people. The rugged character of its (Pashtu) sound suits the nature of the speakers and of the mountains that form their home; however, it is most inharmonious to the somewhat fastidious oriental ear. Tradition tells us of the earliest linguistic survey on record, in which a Grand Wazir brought to his King specimens of all the languages spoken on the earth; however, the specimen of Pashtu consisted of the rattling of a stone in a pot. According to a well-known proverb, Arabic is science, Turkish is accomplishment, Persian is sugar, Hindustani is salt, but Pashtu is the braying of an ass! Despite these unfavourable remarks, though harsh sounding, it is a strong, virile language that is capable of expressing any idea with neatness and accuracy. It is much less archaic in its general characteristics than Baluch and has borrowed not only a good deal of its vocabulary but even part of its grammar from Indian sources.[50] Pashtu is written in a modification of the Arabic-Persian alphabet. It has received considerable attention from scholars both in India and in Europe.

Afghanistan as the Key to India

Kandahar and Kabul have rightly been recognized as the keys to India by the Mughal Emperors.[51] It is discernible even from a cursory look into the medieval history of India that the ruler who held Kabul and Kandahar also controlled Delhi. Afghanistan was intrinsically integrated with the heartland of India. The natives of India have known the Afghans for centuries under the name of Pathans and Rohillas. The Afghans, who came to India as military recruits, settled in India and married Indian women, were subsequently known as *Rohillas*. 'Roh' in the Pashtu language signifies mountain, and Rohilla is the inhabitant of mountains. Rohilla seems to be an Indian term, and the less honourable Afghans identified themselves as Rohilla or Hillmen.[52] Many Afghan adventurers stayed back in India in or around the erstwhile Rajputana, Central India, and in the fertile lands on the left bank of the Ganges. In these regions, there was a very strong Afghan element in the population. The country in which they settled became known as Rohilkand, the country of the Rohillas, the geographical area comprising half a dozen districts of north-western Uttar Pradesh.[53] Linguistically as well, Hindi and Persian are spoken interchangeably in both countries. Abul Fazl, the eminent scholar in the court of Mughal Emperor Akbar, noted Hindi as one of the 11 languages spoken in Kabul.[54]

From the time of the Mughals, successive emperors in Delhi realized the necessity of maintaining Afghanistan as a buffer against attacks from the Shahs of Persia to the West, and from the Uzbek rulers of Bokhara to the North. The British, who succeeded the Mughals, faced the same problem during their time in India. For the British, Russia became the successor of Bokhara. This buffer state premise had hardened the Afghans, who started viewing every foreign power, including India, with suspicion. A by-product of this suspicion is radical ideology and intolerant behaviour towards outsiders.

Emperor Akbar had much trouble with the turbulent tribes who lived in the vicinity of the Khyber Pass. To strengthen the Mughal position along the vital highway, the Khyber Pass was made fit for wheeled transport, and forts were constructed to guard the route. But the predicament continued until the reign of Akbar's great-grandson, Aurangzeb. The Afghan clans, unable to gain a living from their barren lands and aided by the advantageous terrain, had always considered highway robbery an honourable profession.[55] Mughal emperors paid subsidies to various border chiefs that, under Aurangzeb, amounted to an annual expenditure of 600,000 rupees to guard the all-important route between Peshawar and Kabul.[56] The British followed the same system. This allowance system continued even until the Taliban takeover in 2021. It was well documented how former Afghan President Hamid Karzai paid allowances to tribal chiefs on the Afghanistan–Pakistan border.⁵⁷ Since robbery and raid are part of Afghan life and are never considered a crime, foreigners or persons of foreign origin automatically became the first targets of such forays.

Most of Afghanistan is barren and desolate. Only 10 per cent of the whole country is cultivable. This was owing to a variety of causes, of which 'the varying quality of the soil, the precarious supply of moisture by nature, and the nomadic proclivities of the population are the more important'.⁵⁸ After the unification of Afghanistan, Ahmad Shah Durrani clearly and rightly recognized that constant attacks on surrounding states, especially India, were most desirable for the safekeeping of his empire. It was necessary because such expeditions provided plunder and food for his poor, turbulent subjects whose rivalries and feuds, unless they were occupied abroad, would have constituted a danger to the stability of his kingdom. Therefore, the Afghans had undertaken regular and precise incursions against India. Even now, the supply–demand condition in the country is almost identical to the medieval era. As a result of this, the behaviours of Afghans always remained that of an insecure lot who have always been struggling for survival.

A Dithering Afghanistan

Afghanistan started dithering from mainland India after 1739 when Nadir Shah made himself the ruler of Persia. Suddenly he swooped down from the northwest of India and after much killing and plundering, walked off with enormous treasure. Nadir Shah brought his dominions right up to the Indus. Thus, Afghanistan was cut off from India. From the days of the Mahabharata and Gandhara, right through Indian history, Afghanistan was intimately connected with India.⁵⁹ It is now cut adrift.

After this drifting apart, Afghanistan never remained the same. It has developed its empire and established its own rule. Upon the assassination of Nadir Shah in 1747, the Afghan tribes decided to repel Persian rulers and elected Ahmad Shah as monarch, who assumed the title of '*Dur-i-Durran*' or 'Pearl of Pearls'. The Abdali tribe, to which Ahmad Shah belonged, consequently became known as the Durrani.⁶⁰ When Ahmad Shah ascended to the throne of Kandahar, Afghanistan in those days was a fragment of land pieces divided among the rulers of Persia, India, and other Central Asian countries. He made every attempt to unify Afghanistan by way of conquest. With strong determination, he won and merged the territories of Kabul, Ghazni, Khurasan, Herat, Mashhad, Seistan, Nishapur, Balkh, Badakhshan, and other provinces north of the Hindukush, thereby completing the new kingdom as it is today. The Durranis are also known as the Sadozai clan. Later, the Sodozais were succeeded by the Barakzai clan, who ruled the country for some time.

Peshawar, or ancient Gandhara, also fell into the hands of the Afghans. The Barakzai clan gradually removed inhabitants alien to their faith. During the 19th century, the Sikhs of India wrested Peshawar from the Afghans, but although Gandhara again became part of India, it was all too late to revive the past. In the presence of the inscriptions of Ashoka, cows are slaughtered, and it is Pashtu that is spoken in the birthplace of Panini![61]

After establishing his power at home, Ahmad Shah led several expeditions into India from 1748 to 1767. Those attacks were not mere predatory raids.[62] The Durranis utterly defeated a great host of Marathas at the old battlefield of Panipat in 1761 to become the master of the North of India. But in the moment of their triumph, Ahmad Shah had to face trouble and revolt among his people, and he returned home.[63]

After that, the British occupied India after the much-touted Battle of Plassey and the Battle of Buxar. From then onwards, India's Afghan relations were guided by British imperial interests. The British policy in Afghanistan was overshadowed by the Great Game struggle. India's age-old contact with Afghanistan was again hijacked by a foreign ruler. Britain redefined India's relations with Afghanistan.

The famous traveller William Moorcroft was the first person of English descent to travel to Afghanistan in May 1824. Moorcroft wrote extensively about the many Hindu localities, Hindu officers, and Hindu ministers in Northern Afghanistan, even under Afghan rulers.[64] He met Atma Ram, the Hindu Chief Minister under Mir Muhammad Murad Beg of Kunduz. Five years later, another British officer, Sir Alexander Burnes, travelled to Afghanistan along with his Persian interpreter, Mohan Lal Kashmiri, of Kashmiri descent. Both of them tell us about the rich presence of Hindu edifices as well as the Hindu population in Afghanistan. Mohan Lal observed that the 2000 Hindu population of Kabul had large families, and they are known by their robes and by their painted foreheads, which are marks of pious Hindus. Their shops are spread over all the streets and bazaars, while their Mohammedan neighbours, though they are prejudiced against them, treat them very tolerantly.[65]

The Catalyst of Change in India–Afghanistan Relations

The spread of the Russian Empire in Central Asia upset the nerves of the British, and as early as 1839, the British in India made an entirely unprovoked attack on Afghanistan. However, the Afghans resisted the attack. As stated earlier, many western as well as eastern historians tried to portray the Afghans as freedom lovers and invincible.[66] Jawaharlal Nehru also fell into those historians' trap and stated that Afghanistan has always been a 'hornets' nest' for any foreign army that invaded it. A whole British army suffered destruction and defeat. Nearly 40 years later, in the 1878 Second

Anglo-Afghan War, history repeated itself to a large extent. The British took some measures of retribution and again withdrew from Afghanistan.[67] But for many years afterwards, the position of Afghanistan was peculiar. The British would not allow the Amir of Afghanistan to have any direct relations with other foreign countries as per the Treaty of Gandamak of 26 May 1879, and at the same time they gave him a large sum of money annually. In 1919, there was a Third Anglo-Afghan War which resulted in Afghanistan becoming fully independent with full control of its foreign relations with other countries.[68]

Afghanistan had to depend on the British rulers of India essentially because of the position of the country. Landlocked and resource-poor, Afghanistan's easiest way to communicate with the outside world was through India. There was no proper communication in those days in the Russian territory to the north of Afghanistan. Later, when the Soviet government developed communications, both by building railways and encouraging air and motor services, dependency on India was reduced.[69] From ancient times until the Soviet intervention in Afghanistan, the region was thinly connected through narrow trails with Central Asian empires. Although there was direct contact with the Persian empires, Afghanistan was heavily tilted towards India. Its communication network, mountain passes, and roadways, with India playing a major role in keeping the two regions' civilizational contact intact. So communication network and the development of supply arteries in the northward and westward directions reduced Afghanistan's dependence and proximity with India. In other words, the development of modern communication systems snapped the civilizational contact between India and Afghanistan to a considerable extent. The development of communication links with other countries acted as a positive catalyst in delinking the two countries.

Persian was the language of the learned in northern India until the onset of the 20th century, and even now it is popular, especially among Muslims. In Afghanistan Dari Persian[70] is still the official language along with Pashtu. For political reasons, Persian in Afghanistan is known as Dari. In the mid-20th century, the Pashtu language was promoted to replace Persian as the court language. As a compromise in 1958 the term 'Dari' was adopted officially for the Afghan version of Persi. Persian, the *lingua franca* of the two countries, binds them together for a considerable period. For five centuries before British rule, Persian was the second language of India and the sole 'official language' during the time of the Mughals.[71] The British introduced English, which replaced Persian, providing the final death blow to the age-old India–Afghanistan contact. Therefore, language, in this case the removal of Persian as the official language, acted as the final catalyst to dislodge India–Afghanistan people-to-people relations.

After the treaty of Gandamak in 1879, the British Government of India controlled the foreign policy of Afghanistan until 1919. During that time Britain wanted to draw a boundary line with Afghanistan for the safekeeping of their jewel in the crown, 'India', from the predatory lurch of Russia. There was another reason that lay behind the necessity of drawing an urgent boundary with Afghanistan. The ungovernable tribes of Afghanistan, especially the Pashtun, were a considerable headache for the British, as the tribes were opposing British sway in and around Afghanistan. Therefore, to get rid of the troublesome tribes Britain devised a devious tactic and divided the region by erecting a border in the midst of Afghanistan, separating families, clans, and tribes from each other. Considering his precarious condition, Amir Abdur Rehman was also anxious for such a demarcation of Afghanistan's boundary with British India. This effort ended with the instatement of the Durand Line, the boundary line between Afghanistan and British India, which became a dispute encyclopaedia from the outset.

To draw the borderline, Amir Abdur Rehman suggested three joint commissions: one for the Khyber Pass area, one for the Kurram Valley area, and one for Baluchistan. The British Government agreed to his request and employed numerous commissions for this purpose. Earlier, in 1854, Britain entered into a treaty with the Khan, the ruler of Baluchistan, to defend its territories against external invasion from Central Asia and Iran. Baluchistan was bordered by Persia and Afghanistan on one side and British India on the other. The Seistan (Iran)–Baluchistan boundary was demarcated by British officer Major General Sir Frederick John Goldsmid in 1871–1872.[72] However, the boundary was not entirely accepted by either party. In 1895–1896, to resolve the dispute, the British Government appointed the Perso-Baluch Boundary Commission with Colonel T.H. Holdich as its chair. Holdich's job was to demarcate the line between the seas to the Iran–Afghan border.[73]

At the same time, in 1895–1896, another Boundary Commission was running its course – that was the Afghan–Baluch Boundary Commission under Captain A.H. McMahon. The Afghan–Baluch or McMahon Line covers the area from New Chaman to the Persian–Baluch border. The British Crown and its administrative apparatus sought a definitive and enduring resolution to the longstanding boundary dispute with Afghanistan. However, in the course of pursuing this objective, the proliferation of numerous commissions and the resultant inconsistencies and disarray in their reports significantly complicated the matter. In response to these increasingly untenable circumstances, Viceroy Lord Elgin appointed Sir Mortimer H. Durand with the mandate to bring the issue to a conclusive settlement. By this time, Baluchistan was fully integrated into British India. The Durand agreement was signed on 12 November 1893 and the Boundary Commission concluded its work in May 1896.[74] The boundary demarcation started from Chitral to the Iranian border. After the conclusion of the treaty, the Viceroy allowed many small changes to the boundary line to appease the Amir. This commission superseded all previous commissions' demarcation lines on the Afghan–British India border issue. The Durand Line remained unchallenged until 1947 when India gained independence and Pakistan was born after the partition of India.

Afghanistan was intrigued by the change as its boundary is now totally cut off from its old civilizational partner India, which is full of wealth and wisdom. The newborn Islamic Pakistan became the new neighbour of Afghanistan. Crestfallen with the development, Afghanistan rejected the Durand Line as an internationally accepted boundary between Afghanistan and Pakistan. The western terminus of the line is the junction of the Iran–Afghanistan–Pakistan borders. The eastern terminus is the junction of the Afghanistan–Pakistan–India borders. From the eastern terminus of the line eastward to the junction of the Afghanistan–China–India – borders the boundary is undefined by any agreement. The entire stretch between the western terminus of the line and a point northwest of Parachinar, as well as a small sector in the vicinity of the Khyber Pass, is demarcated; the remainder is un-demarcated.[75] This line was the last nail in the coffin of India–Afghanistan dissociation.

Under the division, while India was absolved from the disputed legacy of the Durand Line, Pakistan automatically inherited a complex and potentially troubling boundary line with Afghanistan. The Durand Line, which was drawn against great geographical odds and local tribal wishes, was meant to shield the British Government from the predatory designs of Russia and to divide the intransigent Pashtun tribes. Since the prime motto of the boundary line was to divide the tribes, it never followed geographical or natural features but was rather drawn artificially amid settlements and provinces by constructing border pillars. Pakistan accepted the line, but Afghanistan believed that the agreement was a vestige of colonial domination and that the terms were agreed under unequal authority, and coincided with the departure of the British.[76]

Out of the total 2640-kilometre-long Durand Line, the Pashtuns inhabit both sides of around 1600-kilometres of the borderlands. It is estimated that nearly 12 million Pashtuns live on the Afghan side and 27 million on the Pakistani side. They speak Pashtu and follow the traditional code of legal and moral conduct, popularly known as *Pashtunwali* customs. The customs are based on three principles: '*Melmastia*' means hospitality; '*Badal*' signifies the right to seek revenge; and '*Nanawatai*' implies an offer of sanctuary even to an enemy. The border was considered by the British and subsequently by Pakistan as binding, while successive Afghan governments thought that it was imposed on them.⁷⁷ The Pashtuns, who live on both sides of the line, view it as 'a line drawn on water'. Unable to comprehend the change of status, the Pashtuns started evoking an independent homeland called Pashtunistan, an aspirational name coined by the Pashtuns of the region.⁷⁸ Based on its objections to the Durand border,⁷⁹ Afghanistan cast the sole vote against Pakistan's entry into the United Nations. From 1893 onwards, British India's and later Pakistan's policies toward Afghanistan have been greatly influenced by anxiety over the Afghans' claim to a 'Pashtunistan' that would unite the Pashtuns of both countries and give Afghanistan easier access to the Indian Ocean.⁸⁰

The medieval era was a time when Afghanistan was forced to accept a new religion. During the ancient era, it used to be the heartland of the Vedas and Puranas, where Hinduism and Buddhism flourished for millennia. After a few centuries of tumult, the country gave way to Islam. The hoard of Turks from the Tibetan plateau entered Afghanistan, where they acquired reign over the province. The new migrants were not serious about their religious beliefs, and when they reached Afghanistan, they adopted the local religious system, which was Buddhism. They practised Buddhism like their Afghan predecessors. However, the rise of a new religion in the neighbourhood exposed them to new ideas. Being outsiders and unaware of the ancient character of Afghanistan, the Turks were prone to accepting the militant character of Islam. As time progressed, the Turk rulers started soliciting Islamic ideas in their kingdoms in Afghanistan. Over many centuries, as the Turks started following Islam in their kingdoms, the original character of Afghanistan, which stood on Hindu–Buddhist ideas, faced tremendous challenges. Although the region was steeped in Hindu–Buddhist architecture and belief systems, the new religion gradually eclipsed the impact of the old twin religions. The Arabs overwhelmed Afghan – militarily and morally.

They tried the same in India as well, but their experiment, despite a mammoth 750 years in India, failed terribly. India stood against the moral superiority of Arabic ideas. The Arabs were amazed by the philosophical and scientific vigour of India. They could not convert the military victory into a moral-religious triumph. Consequently, while Afghanistan changed its character, India remained the same. Earlier, Afghanistan used to be a part of India and Indian rulers used to rule the country from cities like Patliputra, Pushkalavati, Purushapura, and Kabul. The Afghans used to look towards India for moral and philosophical guidance. But the new rulers of Afghanistan – the Turks – who were imbued with the ideas of Islam, viewed India as a storehouse of resources and a wealthy kingdom to loot and plunder. They made India a hunting ground for wealth, riches, and resources. Therefore, every new ruler of Afghanistan and their Sardars also took this view. Starting from the onset of Islam until the British colonization, the adherents of the new religion, Islam, in Afghanistan continued their attacks against India, and some royal dynasties of Turkic–Mongol lineage established their kingdoms in India.

The British colonizers who won India from the clutches of Islamic rulers had turned the clock backwards. They waged three giant battles against Afghanistan on its very own soil. The British army with their Indian recruits, mounted their attacks from the soil of India. The hunter becomes the hunted.

Notes

1. E. Maxon, *Agathonia: A Romance, 1844*, New York Public Library, p. 161.
2. Jawaharlal Nehru, *Glimpses of World History* (New Delhi: Penguin Publication, 2004), p. 167.
3. Mirza Kalichbeg, *The Chachnamah* (Karachi: Commissioners Press, 1900), p. 43.
4. Mirza Kalichbeg, *The Chachnamah* (Karachi: Commissioners Press, 1900), p. 51.
5. V.D. Mahajan, *History of Medieval India* (New Delhi: S. Chand Publication, 1988), p. 17.
6. Al-Biruni, *Al-Beruin.'s India, Vol. 2* Translated by Edward C. Sachau (Kigan Paul, Trench, Trubner & Co. Ltd. London, 1910), p. 13.
7. M.A. Stein, *Kalhana's Rajatarangini, Vol. 2* (Srinagar: Gulshan Publisher, 2007), p. 336.
8. M.A. Stein, Professor C. H. Seybold, and General Cunningham subscribe to this assertion.
9. John Dowson ed., Op. cit., p. 44.
10. Al-Biruni, *Al-Beruin's India, Vol. 2*, Translated by Edward C. Sachau (Kigan Paul, Trench, Trubner & Co. Ltd. London, 1910), p. 13.
11. A.B.M. Habibullah, *The Foundation of Muslim Rule in India* (Calcutta: Calcutta University, 1945), p. 98.
12. Edward G. Browne, *A Literary History of Persia From Firdousi to Sa'di, Vol. II* (London: T. Fisher Unwin, 1906), p. 81.
13. Salman Rashid, Foreign Invaders Through Afghanistan, 5 August 2013, http://odysseuslahori.blogspot.com/2013/08/pakistanhistory.html
14. *Alberuni's India*. Translated by Edward C. Sachau, Vol. I (London: Kegan Paul, Trench, Trubner & Co. Ltd, 1910), p. XVII.
15. Jawaharlal Nehru, *Discovery of India* (New Delhi: Penguin, 2004), pp. 250–254
16. Alberuni, Op. cit., p. XI.
17. Alberuni, Op. cit., p. XVII.
18. Ibn Battuta, *Travels in Asia and Africa 1325 to 1354*. Translated and selected by H.A.R. Gibb (London: George Routledge and Sons Ltd, 1929), pp. 219–254.
19. Khuswant Singh, *Delhi A Novel* (New Delhi: Penguin, 1990), p. 186.
20. John Dowson ed., *History of India as Told By Its Own Historians: The Muhammadan Period, Vol. I* (Lucknow: Kitab Mahal, 1869), p. 42.
21. Salman Rashid, Foreign Invaders Through Afghanistan, 5 August 2013, http://odysseuslahori.blogspot.com/2013/08/pakistanhistory.html
22. Mohamed Kasim Ferishta, *History of the Rise of the Mohamedan Power in India Till the Year AD 1612*, Translated from the original Persian by John Briggs, Vol. I (London: Oriental Translation Fund, 1829), p. 7.
23. Mohamed Kasim Ferishta, *History of the Rise of the Mohamedan Power in India Till the Year AD 1612*, Translated from the original Persian by John Briggs, Vol. I (London: Oriental Translation Fund, 1829), p. 137.

24 Mohamed Kasim Ferishta, *History of the Rise of the Mohamedan Power in India Till the Year AD 1612*, Translated from the original Persian by John Briggs, Vol. I (London: Oriental Translation Fund, 1829), p. 160.
25 Mohamed Kasim Ferishta, *History of the Rise of the Mohamedan Power in India Till the Year AD 1612*, Translated from the original Persian by John Briggs, Vol. I (London: Oriental Translation Fund, 1829), p. 229.
26 Mohamed Kasim Ferishta, *History of the Rise of the Mohamedan Power in India Till the Year AD 1612*, Translated from the original Persian by John Briggs, Vol. I (London: Oriental Translation Fund, 1829), pp. 294, 317.
27 Mohamed Kasim Ferishta, *History of the Rise of the Mohamedan Power in India Till the Year AD 1612*, Translated from the original Persian by John Briggs, Vol. I (London: Oriental Translation Fund, 1829), p. 317.
28 Author's interaction with a group of Afghans from Jalalabad, Afghanistan, 3 January 2014.
29 Salman Rashid, Foreign Invaders Through Afghanistan, 5 August 2013, http://odysseuslahori.blogspot.com/2013/08/pakistanhistory.html; Pierre Briant, *Histoire de l'Empire Perse*. Translated by Peter T. Daniels titled *From Cyrus to Alexander: A History of the Persian Empire* (Winona Lake: Indiana Eisenbrauns Publication, 2002), pp. 3–9.
30 George Pottinger, *The Afghan Connection: The Extraordinary Adventures of Major Eldred Pottinger* (Edinburgh: Scottish Academic Press, 1983), p. ix.
31 William Dalrymple, *Return of a King: The Battle for Afghanistan 1839–1842* (London: Bloomsbury Publishing, 2013).
32 Seth G. Jones, *In the Graveyard of Empires: America's War in Afghanistan* (New York: W W Norton & Co, 2009).
33 Scott Mariani, *Graveyard of Empires* (New York: HarperCollins, 2023); Imran Firoz, *Graveyard Empire* (Northampton: Interlink Books, 2024); Milton Bearden, Afghanistan, Graveyard of Empires, *Foreign Affairs*, November/December 2001; Salman Rashid, Foreign Invaders Through Afghanistan, 5 August 2013,
http://odysseuslahori.blogspot.com/2013/08/pakistanhistory.html
34 Seth G. Jones, *In the Graveyard of Empires: America's War in Afghanistan* (New York: W W Norton & Co, 2009).
35 Pierre Briant, *Histoire de l'Empire Perse*. Translated by Peter T. Daniels titled *From Cyrus to Alexander: A History of the Persian Empire* (Winona Lake: Indiana Eisenbrauns Publications, 2002).
36 Ahmed Rashid, *Taliban: The Story of Afghan Warlords* (Oxford: Pan Macmillan Publications, 2001), p. 37.
37 Muhammad Babur, *Babarnama, Vol. I*. Translated from original Turkic text by Annette Susannah Beveridge (London: Luzac & Co, 1922), pp. 198–202.
38 Muhammad Babur, *Babarnama, Vol. I*. Translated from original Turkic text by Annette Susannah Beveridge (London: Luzac & Co, 1922), p. 1.
39 Muhammad Babur, *Babarnama, Vol. I*. Translated from original Turkic text by Annette Susannah Beveridge (London: Luzac & Co, 1922), p. 246.
40 Babur, p. 202.
41 G.P. Tate, *The Kingdom of Afghanistan: A Historical Sketch* (Bombay: Bennett Coleman and Co., 1911), pp. 14–15.
42 Percy Sykes, *A History of Afghanistan* (London: MacMillan and Co., 1940), p. 188.
43 Jaswant Singh, *Jinnah: India-Partition Independence* (New Delhi: Rupa Publications, 2009), pp. 4–5.
44 G. P. Tate, *The Kingdom of Afghanistan: A Historical Sketch* (Bombay: Bennett Coleman and Co., 1911), pp. 14–15.

45 Olaf Caroe, *The Pathans: 550 B.C.–A.D. 1957* (London: Macmillan & Co Ltd, 1958).
46 Percy Sykes, *A History of Afghanistan* (London: MacMillan and Co., 1940), p. 13.
47 G.P. Tate, *The Kingdom of Afghanistan: A Historical Sketch* (Bombay: Bennett Coleman and Co., 1911), pp. 14–15.
48 G.P. Tate, *The Kingdom of Afghanistan: A Historical Sketch* (Bombay: Bennett Coleman and Co., 1911), pp. 14–15.
49 Percy Sykes, *A History of Afghanistan* (London: MacMillan and Co., 1940), p. 13.
50 H.H. Risley and E.A. Gait, *Report on the Census of India, 1900, Languages* (Calcutta: Superintendent of Government Printing, 1903).
51 Percy Sykes, *A History of Afghanistan* (London: MacMillan and Co., 1940), pp. vii, 5.
52 G.P. Tate, *The Kingdom of Afghanistan: A Historical Sketch* (Bombay: Bennett Coleman and Co., 1911), p. 23.
53 G.P. Tate, *The Kingdom of Afghanistan: A Historical Sketch*, Bombay: Bennett Coleman and Co., 1911, p. 23.
54 Abul Fazl Allami, *Ain-i-Akbari*. Translated by Col. H. S. Jarrett (Calcutta: Asiatic Society of Bengal, 1938), pp. 399–400.
55 Percy Sykes, *A History of Afghanistan* (London: MacMillan and Co., 1940), pp. 306–307.
56 Farah Abidin, *Suba of Kabul Under the Mughals: 1585–1739* (New Delhi: Partridge India Publication, 2014), p. 36.
57 Dexter Filkins, Iran Is Said to Give Top Karzai Aide Cash by the Bagful, *New York Times*, 23 October 2010.
58 G.P. Tate, *The Kingdom of Afghanistan: A Historical Sketch* (Bombay: Bennett Coleman and Co., 1911), p. 8.
59 Jawaharlal Nehru, *Glimpses of World History* (New Delhi: Penguin Publication, 2004), p. 373.
60 Percy Sykes, *A History of Afghanistan* (London: MacMillan and Co., 1940), p. 353.
61 A. Foucher, *Notes on the Ancient Geography of Gandhara*. Translated by H. Hargreaves. (Calcutta: Superintendent Government Printing, 1915), p. 2.
62 R.C. Majumdar, *An Advanced History of India. Part 2* (New Delhi: Macmillan, 1967), pp. 527–529.
63 Jawaharlal Nehru, *Glimpses of World History* (New Delhi: Penguin Publication, 2004), p. 373.
64 William Moorcroft and George Trebeck, Travels in the Himalayan Provinces of Hindustan and the Punjab in Ladakh and Kashmir. In *Peshawar, Kabul, Kunduz, and Bokhara, 1819–1825* (New Delhi: Asian Education Service, 2004), p. 419.
65 To Balk, *Bokhara and Herat* (New Delhi: National Archives of India and Three Rivers Press, New Delhi, 2011), p. 42.
66 William Darlymple, *Return of a King: The Battle for Afghanistan 1829–1842* (London: Bloomsbury Publishing, 2013), p. 3.
67 Jawaharlal Nehru, *Glimpses of World History* (New Delhi: Penguin Publication, 2004), p. 478.
68 Jawaharlal Nehru, *Glimpses of World History* (New Delhi: Penguin Publication, 2004), p. 907.
69 Nehru, *Glimpses of World History*, p. 906.
70 Asta Olesen, *Islam and Politics in Afghanistan, Volume 3* (Oxford: Psychology Press, 1995), p. 205.

71 Patrick Clawson, *Eternal Iran* (London: Palgrave Macmillan Publication, 2004), p. 6.
72 F.J. Goldsmid, *Eastern Persia: An Account of the Journeys of the Persian Boundary Commission 1870–72, Vol. 2* (London: Macmillan and Co., 1876).
73 T.H. Holdich, *The Indian Borderland, 1880–1900* (London: Cambridge University Press, 2012), p. 314.
74 Durand Line Agreement, Agreement between Amir Abdur Rehman Khan, G.C.S.I., and Sir Henry Mortimer Durand, K.C.I.E., C.S.I., 12 November 1893, Kabul.
75 Central Intelligence Agency, Durand Line, Office of Research and Reports, Confidential, July 1961, p. 2.
76 W.K. Fraser Tytler, *Afghanistan: A Study of Political Developments in Central and Southern Asia* (London: Oxford University Press, 1967), pp. 308–311.
77 Research Department, Foreign Office, UK (1947) *A Survey of Anglo-Afghan Relations, Part I, 1747–1919, Part II, 1919–1947* (London: Foreign Office, IOR/L/P&S/12/1321).
78 Scott Shane, The War in Pashtunistan, *New York Times*, 5 December 2009.
79 Selig S. Harrison, Drawn and Quartered, *New York Times*, 1 February 2008.
80 Vartan Gregorian, The Yearnings of the Pashtuns, *New York Times*, 15 November 2001.

3
SPECIAL SYMMETRY IN THE MODERN ERA

On a foggy wintry afternoon on 4 January 1950 at 3:25 pm, Prime Minister of India Pandit Jawaharlal Nehru, who was also the Minister for External Affairs, and Afghan Ambassador to India Sardar Najibullah Khan, arrived at the External Affairs Ministry, New Delhi, and inked a treaty of 'perpetual friendship'.[1] The signing ceremony was the formalization of diplomatic relations between the two independent sovereign states in modern times. As per the agreed understanding, the

> Treaty shall continue in force for five years after coming into force and shall thereafter continue in force: Provided that after the said period of five years either Government may give to the other not less than six months' notice of its intention to terminate the Treaty, and on the expiry of the period of such notice the Treaty shall cease to be in force.[2]

While the treaty affirms everlasting peace and friendship between the two countries, it also provides for the establishment of diplomatic and consular posts in each other's territory and grants their representatives diplomatic and consular privileges. Four copies of the treaty, which were written in English and Persian, were signed by the Prime Minister and Afghan Ambassador. As the Indian Prime Minister and Afghan Ambassador warmly shook hands after the treaty was signed, affirming friendship between India and Afghanistan, the historic occasion was filmed. Two copies of the treaty remain in India, and two were sent to Afghanistan to exchange the instruments of ratification.[3]

DOI: 10.4324/9781003627678-3

Although the formal signing of the friendship treaty happened in January 1950, Wing Commander Rup Chand was appointed Ambassador of India to Afghanistan in June 1948.[4] On 2 June 1948, the Indian Mission in Kabul held a reception in honour of Wing Commander Rup Chand, and the function began with the singing of the National Anthem – 'Jana Gana Mana', with all the invitees standing. Wing Commander Rup Chand delivered his speech by praising Mahatma Gandhi's leadership.[5] A few months later, on 11 February 1949, answering a question from Lala Raj Kanwar, Pandit Jawaharlal Nehru informed the Constituent Assembly of India that His Excellency Sardar Najibullah Khan was the Ambassador of Afghanistan to India and His Excellency Wing Commander Rup Chand was the Ambassador of India to Afghanistan.[6]

The relations between the two countries continued to expand even before the signing of a formal treaty of friendship, as both countries allowed the exchange of Ambassadors in each other's countries. The formal agreement between Afghanistan and India 'Regarding Radio-Telegraphic Communication' was signed in Kabul on 14 December 1949.[7] It was inaugurated officially by the Communications Ministers of the two governments.

Writing about India–Afghanistan relations, Ambassador Rup Chand in his report stated that the treaty of 4 January 1950 'brought these two countries nearer to each other and opened a new chapter of close cooperation in trade, commerce and cultural sphere. It had its political significance and has cemented relations between India and Afghanistan'.[8]

Immediately after the signing of the Treaty of Friendship, the two countries resumed flamboyant bilateral relations and never missed any occasion to join each other's national programmes. India participated in the Afghan *Jashan*, the annual cultural extravaganza, in August 1950. Every year the freedom-loving Afghans celebrate the last week of August as their Independence Week, popularly known as *Jashan*. The military music played by Afghan bands echoes through the decorated streets of the city of Kabul. The bands attract hundreds of handsome, red-cheeked young Afghan boys from their homes, and thousands of tribesmen from their farmlands, who carry their guns as a sign of honour. All those Afghans gather to show respect to the memory of the martyrs who gave their lives so that Afghanistan could survive. Liberty-loving Afghans cherish their national freedom above everything else. The monument commemorating the martyrdom of the great mujahid, the late King Ahmad Shah, the father of modern Afghanistan, reminds them of the heroic sacrifices of generations of their countrymen in the cause of national independence.

As part of the *Jashan* celebration, the Afghan Government gladly invited Indian hockey and football teams. Both teams arrived under the captaincy of Nawab of Pataudi from India on 22 August and returned to India on 30

August 1950. Their visit was warmly welcomed by the Afghans and contributed immensely towards cementing the friendly relations between the two countries. Sri Prakasa, the Commerce Minister, represented the Government of India at the *Jashan* from 23 to 28 August 1950. Pandit Hriday Nath Kunzru, an Indian freedom fighter and eminent public figure, visited Kabul as a distinguished non-official visitor from 16 August to 4 September 1950.[9]

Dr B.V. Keskar, Indian Deputy Minister for Foreign Affairs, represented India during the *Jashan* celebration of 1951. From the beginning, the India–Afghanistan friendship was regulated by the two countries' common dislike towards Pakistan. From the early days of independence, India's congenital conflict with Pakistan was a matter of great interest for the Afghan people and government. The Afghan official circles and the intelligentsia in general always take a keen interest in India–Pakistan relations. The Minority Agreement signed between India and Pakistan, which was not received well in the tribal belt of Pakistan adjacent to Afghanistan, was a matter of interest for the Afghans.[10] This is because the Afghans wanted to know how India intended to treat its minorities, especially Muslims.

As per the Minority Agreement, also known as the Nehru–Liaqat Agreement, the Governments of India and Pakistan solemnly agreed that each shall ensure, to the minorities throughout its territory, complete equality of citizenship, irrespective of religion, a full sense of security in respect of life, culture, property, and personal honour, freedom of movement within each country, and freedom of occupation, speech, and worship, subject to law and morality. Members of the minorities shall have equal opportunity with members of the majority community to participate in the public life of their country, to hold political or other office, and to serve in their country's civil and armed forces.[11]

But the India–Pakistan dispute over Kashmir always gives the Afghans consolation and relief.[12] From the early days, India's stand on the Kashmir issue found general sympathy and support in the Afghan press. Afghanistan's support for India's stand was especially important for Afghanistan because of the Pashtunistan issue. It was stated that 'Pakistan's territorial ambitions were the root cause of the Kashmir problem … It aimed to kill two birds with one stone; to exterminate the Pashtuns and thereby crush their freedom movement; and second, to grab Kashmir'. Describing Pakistan as 'an aggressive imperialist wearing the mask of Islam', the press repeatedly declared that the Kashmir issue 'has nothing to do with any such thing as a Jihad'.[13]

Another important event of the year 1950 was the signing of the 'Indo-Afghan Trade Treaty' on 4 April i1950, in Kabul, which further consolidated the friendly relations between the two countries. India is an important importer of Afghan dry and fresh fruits, while Indian clothes and tea continue to be extremely popular in the Afghan market. While there were immense possibilities of building up a market for goods of Indian manufacture, the difficulties which Pakistan from time to time created to hinder the free flow of goods between the two countries acted as a very great deterrent.[14] Moreover, the Afghan merchants lack information regarding the industrial developments in India.

As per the record of the Indian Embassy in Kabul, in the year 1950 there were about 150 Indian nationals residing in Kabul. These consisted of 19 Indian firms doing business in Kabul. Some of them had their head offices in India. As no foreigner in Afghanistan can carry on business without obtaining a '*Jawaz Nama*' (Trade permit), the Afghan Government granted about 42 Trade permits to Indian traders, their partners and agents, and in some cases to their '*Munshis*' (Clerks). In comparison, there are only four or five Pakistani firms and one Swiss firm. Generally, Indian businessmen in Afghanistan were in an advantageous position and played an important role in the economic life of the country during the 1950s. The treatment of the Afghan Government towards Indians, as per the consular report, was generally good and helpful. None of the Indians was reported to be taking part in the political affairs of the country. One Mr Radha Krishan Seth, a businessman, became bankrupt during 1950. He was said to be under a debt of more than a lakh Afghanis. The Indian cloth merchants' association tried its best to clear his outstanding debts by raising subscriptions, and the matter was resolved.[15]

Diplomatic cables as far back as 1951 reported that 'full possibilities of trade between the two countries cannot perhaps be developed till relations between India and Pakistan on the one hand and Pakistan and Afghanistan on the other become cordial'.[16] The same is true even today in the year 2025. The Afghans have, however, completely despaired of such a development since 1950. According to the understanding of Indian officials in Kabul, the Afghans felt that only the creation of the independent state of Pakhtoonistan from Chitral to Baluchistan, with a contiguous border with India at one end and an outlet to the sea at the other, could remove the thorn from the sides of the Indo-Afghan trade and provide the conditions for its development to the maximum heights.[17] Even during the early days of independence, Indian diplomats showed a desire 'to play [a] legitimate and well-deserved role in the reconstruction and development of the economic life of both Pakhtoonistan (shattered by over a 100 year[s] of war which the British waged there) and Afghanistan'.[18] Indian diplomats believed that Russia would not have the same objection if India took a leading role in the development of the Afghan national resources as it had when Afghanistan showed signs of leaning towards the Anglo-American bloc. Indian diplomatic correspondence further stated that apart from political reasons, the economic interests of India demand that the independent state of Pakhtoonistan should come into being as early as possible and thus provide a free and unhampered trade route to India to get her requirements of agricultural and raw produce on one hand and to supply her industrial products to Afghanistan and Pakhtoonistan on the other hand.[19]

There was a marked desire in the Afghan financial circles to invite Indian capital to develop its resources in cooperation with Afghan capital. But for the limitations that transport difficulties through Pakistan have created, Indo-Afghan cooperation in the economic field could have been significantly strengthened and the volume of India–Afghanistan trade considerably increased.[20] Bribery and corruption were rampant in Government offices and the higher classes continued to evade the payment of income tax, etc. Sardar Shah Mahmood Khan's Government lacked the necessary drive and talent to initiate new measures to bring about an improvement in the economic field. Shah Mahmood Khan was Prime Minister of Afghanistan from 9 May 1946 to 7 September 1953 under King Mohammad Zahir Shah's monarchy. To improve the Afghan economy, Dr L.C. Jain, a noted Gandhian and economist, was appointed as the UNO Economic Adviser to the Afghan Government in January 1953. He returned to India in November 1953. Though high hopes were raised at the creation of this post, Dr Jain was disappointed with the results achieved. The Afghan Government took months to provide him with the necessary facilities for the efficient prosecution of his work. The response to the recommendations he made was poor. His reports met with the usual fate of being pigeonholed in some departments.[21]

As Shah Mahmood's Government had failed to arrest the growing deterioration in the economic situation, Daoud Khan was appointed Prime Minister on 7 September 1953 and asked to form a new Cabinet.[22] Sardar Daoud Khan's new Government initiated new measures to check bribery, corruption, and evasion of income tax, and to attract foreign capital. However, its new policies were taking time to implement, and it was difficult for him to produce a turnaround quickly and bring substantial improvement. Daoud Khan remained as Prime Minister until 10 March 1963 and became the first president of Afghanistan after a bloodless coup on 17 July 1973, continuing until 28 April 1978.

Although one of the prerequisites of India–Afghanistan trade for many years was to achieve a balance of trade between the two countries, the experience has repeatedly proved that India was always faced with an unfavourable balance of trade. Various reasons could be attributed to this decline, e.g. the withdrawal of foreign exchange convertibility facilities for Afghans; keen competition from Russia, Japan, Germany, Pakistan, and China to capture markets for their manufactured products in Afghanistan. The general attitude of the Afghans to improve their relations with other countries and the high cost of production in India also contributed to the unfavourable balance of trade. By the year 1960, the entire India–Afghanistan trade was Rs 5 crores annually.[23]

Apart from neutrality in the Cold War, Afghan foreign policy was characterized by anti-colonialism and support for all measures designed to relax international tensions and promote world peace.[24] A common cultural heritage, similarity of views on important world problems, especially the rejection of military pacts and the common hostility to Pakistan, are some of the factors which mark a natural friendship between Afghanistan and India. The bonds of friendship were further strengthened by an official visit paid by Daoud, the Prime Minister of Afghanistan, to India in the early part of the year 1959 and the return visit by Pandit Jawaharlal Nehru, the Indian Prime Minister, to Afghanistan in September 1959.[25]

Indian Embassy records conform to the fact that in the matter of India's border dispute with China, the Afghan Government, while refraining from taking sides, displayed much friendly interest and expressed, though not without understandable diffidence, her readiness to do what she could to help in a settlement. When the Afghan Foreign Minister Naim paid a state visit to China in 1959, his talks with the Chinese leaders were mostly concerned with the India–Chinese dispute; very little time was devoted to matters of direct interest between Afghanistan and China.[26]

The independent stand taken by India at the United Nations and the efforts of the Prime Minister of India to save the world from disaster raised India's standing in the estimation of Afghans. The Afghan Government recognized the new China and believed, like India, that the solution to the Korean conflict lay in the entry of the new Chinese Republic into the United Nations. Afghanistan looked towards India as a friend and expected help to improve its economic condition.[27].

His Majesty King Ali Zahir Shah visited India on 11 February 1958 and he was greeted by Prime Minister Nehru, President Rajendra Prasad, and Vice President Dr Sarvapalli Radhakrishnan. A year later, the Prime Minister of Afghanistan, His Royal Highness Limer Ali Sardar Mohmad Daoud, visited New Delhi on 5 February 1959 for an eight-day tour. Reciprocating the visits of the Afghan King and Afghan Prime Ministers, Indian Prime Minister Jawaharlal Nehru embarked on a five-day visit to Afghanistan on 14 September 1959. Far-reaching social reforms were introduced in Afghanistan in the year 1959. Purdah, the age-old custom of Afghanistan, was abolished by the Government of Mohamad Daoud. It was particularly gratifying for India to find that 'the official banquet at which Afghan ladies attended for the first time was the one given in honour of Prime Minister

Jawaharlal Nehru' in September 1959.²⁸ This was too good an opportunity for the Pakistan press to let go unnoticed. Some Urdu papers deeply mourned the fact that the ladies of the Royal Family should have been allowed to appear before the Prime Minister of India by the Government of the very country which had produced Mahmud Ghazni, the bearer of the torch of Islam into India. The boldness of such a measure in a backward country, dominated by reactionary Mullahs, can be judged from the fact that when Amanullah Khan tried the same experiment some 30 years ago, he had to pay for his zeal by losing his throne. The fact that the then Government led by Prime Minister Daoud felt strong enough to make this revolutionary change is evidence of its stability.²⁹

The press and the radio gave wide publicity to Prime Minister Nehru's visit to Kabul from 14 September to 18 September 1959. Nehru, along with his daughter Indira Gandhi, visited Kabul on the invitation made by the Afghan Government. A civic reception was accorded to Nehru on 16 September 1959 at the Ghazi Stadium. Prime Minister Daoud Khan reiterated, 'I am very happy to welcome on behalf of the government and people of Afghanistan a distinguished and outstanding personality like the Prime Minister of India'.³⁰ Prime Minister Nehru responded to the Afghan prime minister's remark by saying that India and Afghanistan have been 'good friends and neighbours' not only in the past but in the present as well. The joint communique issued by Prime Minister Nehru and Sardar Mohamad Daoud promised 'increased cultural cooperation and promotion of mutual trade'.³¹

Kandahar and Jalalabad, the erstwhile keys to entering India, had been cities of great significance for India–Afghanistan relations. Kandahar, in the year 1960, was an important trade centre in Afghanistan. The local Afghan traders used to visit India in quite large numbers to sell fresh dried fruits and import cloth, tea, and other general merchandise including bicycles and sewing machines. According to the Embassy records, in the year 1960, there were about 38 Indians, including Vice Consulate staff and six families, living in Kandahar. The Indian population fluctuated from time to time and a few Indians also visited Kandahar in connection with business and other interests.³² Reporting on Jalalabad, the Indian Embassy record states that 'even though several development schemes have been taken up in this province, no attention has so far been paid to the prevailing sanitary conditions'.³³ In 1960, there was no Indian student in Jalalabad, and there was only one Indian teacher who was teaching English at the local Government College.³⁴

The number of Indians, as recorded by the Indian Embassy for various cities, is not the total number of persons of Indian origin. Rather, they were the visa-holding Indians who entered Afghanistan and registered with the

Indian Embassy. Many other persons of Indian origin had been living in Afghanistan.

India has not been on good terms with Pakistan since the partition of the subcontinent, and their mutual relations have not witnessed any improvement for many years after independence. In addition to being inimical to India, Pakistan was also on unfriendly terms with Afghanistan. Thus, its defence forces are deployed not only along the India–Pakistan frontiers but also to protect the Pakistan–Afghanistan border. Following the age-old Kautilya's adage that enemy's enemy is friend, the Indian Foreign Ministry used to receive suggestions from the Embassy staff that 'it will be in India's interest to cultivate greater friendship with Afghanistan'.[35]

In fact, since India's independence, Afghanistan has looked up to India for guidance and help in many fields – political, military, economic, and cultural. There was, however, an impression amongst quite a few Afghan high-ups that its advances towards cultivating greater friendship with India were fully reciprocated.[36] Despite this, there was no doubt that because of historical and cultural affinity, Afghans continued to bear genuine goodwill towards India. Such a feeling was greatly increased with the assumption of office by Ambassador J.N. Dhamija, who was much admired, respected, and loved amongst the Afghan ruling hierarchy. The Afghan Government was the first to voice open support for India on the Goa action. Then again, whereas previously they favoured the settlement of the Kashmir dispute by holding a plebiscite, by 1962 their stand was that it should be resolved by negotiations between the two contending parties.[37]

Suddenly, the question of the Durand Line came to the fore.[38] This was due to a statement by Prime Minister Nehru at a press conference on 7 September 1961. Pakistan protested Nehru's statement, and the Pakistani Foreign Ministry sent a protest note to India on 26 September. After the statement from the Prime Minister, the Indian Ambassador J.N. Dhamija met Sardar Naim, the Afghan Foreign Minister, and among other things, they discussed the issue of the Durand Line with his usual frankness.[39] J.N. Dhamija stated that 'hitherto India's views on [the] Durand Line have been mostly conditioned by drawing a parallel with [the] McMahon Line'. Ambassador Dhamija reiterated that 'this has not been wholly a correct approach and as the Prime Minister remarked in his press interview, it is a complicated matter and many new factors have come in'.

Unlike the McMahon Line, which is the traditional boundary along the main watersheds of the mountainous region, the Durand Agreement of 12 November 1893 did not describe the line as the boundary of India, but as the frontier of the Amir's dominions and the line beyond which neither side would exercise interference. Therefore, the Indian Embassy explained to their Afghan counterpart that 'It is a historical fact that the Durand Line was not calculated to demarcate the boundary between India and Afghanistan but to delimit the sphere of influence of the Amir's authority in the tribal area'. This fact has been patently admitted even by a pro-Pakistani person like Sir Olaf Caroe in his book *The Pathans*.[40] Therefore, India claimed that 'it is wrong for Pakistan to assert in their protest note of 26 September 1961 that the Durand Line constituted an international frontier between pre-partition India and Afghanistan'. Similarly, India refused to accept 'the Pakistan Government's assertion in the note that the Afghanistan Government have since recognized that Pathans living on the eastern side are British Indian nationals'[41] because it had no basis.

Ambassador J.N. Dhamija was working with the erstwhile Indian Political Service, which was shuffling between the Foreign Department and the Political Department of the East India Company and Her Majesty's Government. The recruits were from the Indian Civil Service and the Indian Army, and, considering the inefficiency of the service, the adage about the Indian Political Service was, 'the civil servants who did not want to work and the soldiers who did not want to fight'. Its primary job was to deal with the princely states and foreign affairs.

In a secret note sent to the Foreign Office in New Delhi, Dhamija opined that

> having served in these regions during the old Indian Political Services days,[42] it may be well to state the recognized fact that there were actually two western frontiers of the pre-partition India – one running along the settled areas of NWFP, the other being the Durand Line.

He was explaining the nature of the Afghanistan–Pakistan border and the demarcation of the international boundary. The area between these two frontiers was vicariously called by the British themselves 'independent territory', 'no man's land', and 'unsettled and unadministered areas'. The British had various treaties and arrangements with the independent tribes such as the Afridis, Mahmods, and Masuds, who never paid any revenue or otherwise admitted the suzerainty of the British. J.N. Dhamija categorically stated that 'Why Durand Line was not specifically mentioned as the international line between pre-partition India and Afghanistan is because the British Government had no intention whatsoever to absorb the tribes in between into their administrative system'.

It is also amazing that, unlike the McMahon Line which runs along watersheds and uninhabited areas, the Durand Line runs through the thick of populated tribal areas, cutting across families of the same tribes living on both sides. Afghanistan's idea of Pashtunistan was based on the thesis of self-determination of all these tribes, which were free and independent, and despite the Durand Line, they never formed a settled part of India.[43]

Afghanistan has long supported and followed India's policies and has been a deterrent influence over Pakistani recruitment in tribal areas for Jihad in Kashmir. The Prime Minister of Afghanistan was the first to support India on Goa, and they changed their attitude in 1962, shifting their views in India's favour over the plebiscite question in Kashmir. The Foreign Minister of Afghanistan informed the Indian Ambassador and wished it to be conveyed to the Indian Prime Minister that their view was that Kashmir was India's domestic affair, and Afghanistan would like to see this problem resolved by mutual negotiations without UN interference.[44] This was quite a shift in India's favour from Afghanistan's previous stance, as it is recalled that on 14 April 1957 Prime Minister Daoud expressed his views on Kashmir for the first time by publicly upholding the plea for a plebiscite. Describing Kashmir's annexation as an error of 'British judgment', Sardar Daoud then voiced the feeling that the 'error' should be rectified by taking into consideration the desires and aspirations of the people concerned. This statement of Sardar Daoud was followed up by editorials in the officially controlled local press urging the Government of India to hold an impartial plebiscite in Kashmir. As aforementioned, there has been a reversal of the Afghan view in India's favour on this issue.[45]

India's foreign ministry declassified some top-secret files, which dealt with some of the vexed foreign policy issues that related to the US policy towards Pakistan and vice versa. In those days, India's foreign relations with Afghanistan were regulated by United States–Pakistan relations. The secret US policy towards Pakistan was stoically noted by India's Ambassador during the visit of Chester Bowles, the Special Adviser to President John F. Kennedy. On 27 February 1962, Ambassador Chester Bowles came to Kabul on an official visit. During this visit, J.N. Dhamija met the US President's Special Advisor and broached the important subject of the 'US continuing military aid to Pakistan'. This issue seriously concerned both India and Afghanistan, and Sardar Naim discussed it with Chester Bowles with some emphasis. J.N. Dhamija clarified to Chester Bowles that 'Geographically, the USSR was far too near and had an overwhelming superiority in arms and manoeuvrability over Pakistan. Therefore, US arms aid to Pakistan could hardly serve the avowed purpose for which it was intended'. He said, 'On the contrary, such a situation meant an invitation to trouble. It was a source of potential danger and in the event of a major flare-up [the] USSR could easily and conveniently occupy Pakistan within a matter of hours'. Furthermore, such arms aid created natural apprehensions from Afghanistan and India regarding their being used against them, and this had been made quite obvious by Pakistani President Ayub Khan's statement of 20 January 1962 in Mardan, Pakistan.

The result was that such a situation would start an arms race with the dangers of an eventual clash. For obvious reasons, Afghanistan turned to the USSR for arms aid to counterbalance US aid to Pakistan.[46]

The briefing of J.N. Dhamija went well, and Mr Chester Bowles said that he completely understood the position, as actually he had to bear the main brunt of India's protests when the US decided to give military aid to Pakistan. In response 'the USA not only gave an assurance to India that these arms would never be used against [it] but went further that in the event of Pakistani attack, the USA would come to the aid of India'.

He then disclosed, as he had already informed Prime Minister Nehru, that contrary to what had appeared in the press reports, his Government had only given 12 supersonic jets to Pakistan. 'President Kennedy had reluctantly taken this decision', Mr Bowles said, 'and [it] was more in the nature of honouring the commitment of his predecessor'.[47] The important issue about United States–Pakistan relations was that the

> US had a system of 'communications' in Pakistan. When asked to explain Mr. William R. Polk, Member, State Department (a professor at Harvard University before taking up his position at the State Department), said that they had their satellite observation posts and other missile bases.[48]

The India–Afghanistan relations were also guided by Afghanistan's dealings with superpowers like the USSR, the US and Britain. Soon after his accession to the Afghan throne in 1919, King Amanullah started to modernize the country in different fields, particularly in the military field. He bought military equipment from France, Germany, and Italy. The military development during the few years of his reign was quite significant. In other areas, Afghanistan progressed at a good pace. On 22 February 1921, Afghanistan concluded a 'Treaty of Friendship' with the new revolutionary Government of Russia. The British, who were still all-powerful in this region, could not naturally be expected to be a silent spectator to all these changes. They reacted sharply and did not rest until they caused Amanullah's downfall in 1929. After a couple of years of turmoil in the country, the first ruler of the new dynasty, King Nadir Shah, started off from where Amanullah had left off. Nadir Shah was born on 9 April 1883 in Dehradun, India. He belonged to the Musahiban branch of the Royal dynasty of Afghanistan of the Mohammadzai section of Barakzai Pashtuns. He assumed the throne on 15 October 1929 and began modernizing the Army and equipping it with the latest weapons. But before he could achieve much, he was shot dead in 1933, and progress was impeded. Before fresh efforts could bear fruit, the Second World War broke out.[49]

After the war, Afghanistan once more started on the path of development. Again, they wanted to modernize their armed forces and replace obsolete weapons with the latest models. They looked for the possible sources of supply of arms. They had no intention of going to go and buy from England and France; Afghanistan had seen enough of them. Germany and Italy, who in the past had supplied certain arms to them, were not in a position to do so any more. The US, Russia, and India were the only countries left. India did her bit but could do no more.[50] They then went to the US and, after much haggling, the Americans refused (which refusal they now so deeply regret!), unless, of course, the Afghans fulfilled certain conditions. The latter did not feel like doing so at that moment. It may be recalled that this was the time when the Cold War was precipitating and the system of defensive alliances was formed.

The situation existing at the time left no option for Afghanistan but to turn to the USSR. The Russians did not lay down many conditions and agreed to do the needful. Thus, in 1954, a considerable quantity of small arms and ammunition was imported from Czechoslovakia. The Afghan authorities made part payment and wanted to pay the rest when certain other developments took place. One of these important developments was the provision of significant arms aid to Pakistan and Iran by the US. This upset the balance of power in this region, and Afghanistan naturally felt afraid. This country could not possibly have pursued bigger and heavier armament if it had not been beaten in a show of force by Pakistan during a few small clashes that took place on the Pakistan–Afghanistan border when Pakistan brought its latest arms and aircraft to threaten Afghanistan with its might. The latter felt very perturbed and alarmed and thought that not only could Pakistan do this, but also Iran could do the same one day. It was under these circumstances that, in order to defend against the two powerful neighbours, Afghanistan approached Russia for heavier arms and aircraft. The USSR willingly agreed to oblige its neighbour and without any strings.

In December 1955, Nikolai Alexandrovich Bulganin, Prime Minister and Georgy Zhukov, Defence Minister of the USSR, visited Afghanistan along with President Nikita Khrushchev. During this visit, a Russian loan of $100 million, at a nominal interest of 2 per cent, was announced. The leanings of Afghanistan towards the USSR increased not only due to geopolitical considerations but were also aided by inept actions on the part of the US. The Americans engaged with Afghanistan long before Russia did. They started pouring financial aid into Afghanistan from 1946 onwards. When the Russians also entered the field in a big way in 1955, a keen competition between the two major powers ensued. The shrewd Afghans played one against the other and acquired maximum benefit from both.[51]

The Russian interests in Afghanistan were vital, especially because Russia was aware of the fact that the Western bloc had created a chain of bases around her in the form of interlinked North Atlantic Treaty Organization (NATO), Central Treaty Organization (CENTO), and South East Asia Treaty Organization (SEATO) alliances with the alleged purpose of containment of communism. In this context, the geographical area of Afghanistan, sympathetic to Russia, or at least unaligned, is strategically vital to the USSR.[52]

As given out to the outside world by the Afghan authorities, Afghanistan was non-aligned and had followed a neutral policy since its independence in 1919. Given the massive Russian aid and her complete dependence in military affairs on the USSR, some foreign circles doubted whether Afghanistan was really non-aligned.[53] There was also doubt in some quarters that a secret bilateral defence pact exists between Russia and Afghanistan. Whether or not such a written agreement was there, the diplomatic circle in Kabul gossiped that it was unbelievable that the USSR was doing so much in such a generous fashion for her neighbour without any consideration or expectation. The Military Attaché of the USSR in Kabul told Indian Defence Attaché Colonel Deewan Singh in a confidential meeting that during their visit to Afghanistan in 1955, Bulganin and Khrushchev were entertained at a lunch at the Afghan Military Academy. On this occasion, Daoud, the Afghan Premier, made a speech wherein he mentioned that in case its enemies started a war, Afghanistan would side with the USSR. The authenticity of this statement was confirmed by the Russian Military Attaché because he was himself present at the function and heard Daoud saying this. The text of the speech in question was not made public. Thus, if there was an understanding on the part of Afghanistan to go to the help of Russia in an emergency, the same obligation should be there on the part of the latter.[54]

The Indian Embassy was privy to such secret information; therefore, India's position was very high in the annals of Afghan history. As a matter of reiteration of the excellent friendly relationship with India, Afghanistan displayed extraordinary support during the India–China war.

In its September 1962 report, one month before the India–China war, the Indian Ambassador in Kabul, J.N. Dhamija, reported back that India's relations with Afghanistan continue to be as good as ever. Afghanistan needs India as much as India needs Afghanistan. They have always considered India as their elder brother, followed India's policies, and invariably collaborated and sided with India's approach in the councils of the world.[55] In addition, Afghanistan has been a great balancing factor in India's favour. They continued to restrain and thwart Pakistani efforts to recruit tribals for the invasion of Kashmir and, to India's relief, were holding quite a few divisions of Ayub's Army on the western front.[56]

Not since 1939 had the world has been so near the brink of an abysmal chasm as during October 1962. The massive and premeditated attack by China launched on India's North Eastern Frontier Agency (NEFA) front on 20 October 1962, which seemed a prelude to the wholesale invasion of India and a precursor to a prolonged and devastating war between the two great countries of Asia, was to some extent overshadowed by the Cuban crisis.[57] It was Napoleon who, referring to China, remarked that *when this giant wakes up, the world would tremble*. Indian Ambassador J.N. Dhamija quoted Napoleon Bonaparte and also concluded that 'The giant is awakened stirring out of the dreams to new conquests and achievements of crimson glory and tutelage of ancient past'.[58] However, determined research proved that this is an unverifiable quote wrongly attributed to Napoleon Bonaparte.[59]

When the war broke out at the India–China border at the North East Frontier Agency, for about a week there was a stony silence in the press and the radio in Kabul. It was on 27 October when, for the first time, the officially controlled *Kabul Times* reported the declaration of a state of emergency in India and the steps India was taking for total mobilization to face the aggressor. This outward silence on their part was certainly not due to the lack of interest of the Royal Afghan Government, who well realized that the disturbing events in India would affect the whole of the region and South East Asia. During his meetings with the Prime Minister, Marshal Shah Wali Khan, First Deputy Prime Minister, Foreign Minister, and all those who make up the Afghan hierarchy, the Indian Ambassador J.N. Dhamija was made to feel that their sympathies and support were entirely on the side of India and that they were themselves afraid of this 'yellow monster' (China) sitting on their doorsteps, who one day might try to gobble up part of the adjoining territory, regarding which there had been ominous indications from the Chinese side.[60]

At the same time, geographically situated as Afghanistan is, it was difficult for it to come out with an open condemnation of the Chinese naked and unabashed aggression. Afghans also had an eye on the attitude of the USSR, their most powerful neighbour, who had maintained a sphinx-like silence on this issue.[61] Since the Afghan Foreign Office shared all the propaganda materials they had received from the Chinese – materials asserting the legitimacy of China's stance against India – the Indian Embassy in Kabul came to realize that China had not only launched a sudden and unexpected war but had also meticulously prepared for it through a comprehensive propaganda campaign. China wrote to the whole world explaining its position on how the war was necessitated and how India was the culprit.

Sardar Naim met J.N. Dhamija and placed before the Ambassador the six maps which formed part of Chinese Prime Minister Chou En-lai's letter of 15 November 1962 to the heads of all the states. Naim remarked that even with understanding and appreciation of India's case, one was likely to be confused by such original and clever propaganda. Although this did not affect his Government's point of view or understanding of India's case, Naim suggested on a personal basis that India might take urgent steps to put its case before the other governments in a more effective way than has hitherto been done.[62]

On 14 November 1962, Sardar Naim, the Afghan Foreign Minister, called Indian Ambassador J.N. Dhamija again in the presence of Nur Ahmed Etemadi, Director General (Political). Etemadi was equivalent to India's Foreign Secretary. Naim handed J.N. Dhamija the reply of King Zahir Shah to India's Prime Minister's message of 26 October 1962. This was unsigned, without even any initials or a cover letter. At the request of India's Ambassador, this was done.[63] The King's letter originally in Pashtu translated as follows:

[Translation]

Your Excellency,

I acknowledge receipt of your message of October 26 which was communicated through His Excellency the Indian Ambassador. I thank Your Excellency for the explanation of the situation on the borderlands of India and China. Strains between the two friendly countries has been closely followed here with genuine concern.

The unfortunate situation between our two friends, the Republic of India and the People's Republic of China, is causing deep sorrow and frustration to us. Continuation of this state of affairs between the two great Asian countries is not only detrimental to the cause of the Asian solidarity and the principles of Bandung Conference which are the guiding principles of our policies to serve the cause of peace, but it also definitely jeopardizes world peace and security of the region, to the dissatisfaction of all your friends.

Because of this general concern, several friendly states have already expressed their readiness to exert every peaceful effort to end the existing conflict between India and China. It is our sincere desire to participate in such efforts.

We believe that peaceful ways and means can be sought for the solution of any understanding issue.

I send you my best wishes for a speedy and peaceful solution of this problem as well as for the preservation and consolidation of Asian solidarity and Your Excellency's personal well-being.

Sd/–

Mohammed Zaher

There was nothing special or extraordinary about the king's message. Naim, however, verbally stated that the Afghan Government was convinced about the fact of Chinese aggression and that their wholehearted sympathies were entirely with India. At the same time, for obvious reasons and to avoid any embarrassment, it would be best not to give an open expression of their feelings, which in addition may have detracted from the Afghan Government's usefulness in playing its active role along with other friendly nations in bringing about a rapprochement. It was even suggested to Dhamija that, as far as possible, India may for the time being, avoid publication of the king's reply.

Geographically situated as to be surrounded by both China and Russia, towards whom they were gradually drifting, Afghanistan, in spite of their professed policy of independence and non-alignment, had to be overcautious in its approach to this matter. Furthermore, the Royal Afghan Government feared that China, which loomed over the Wakhan Corridor, appeared like threatening encroachment of the region. This fear was evident in the recorded conversations between Amir Abdul Rahman and Sir Mortimer Durand in October–November 1893, during which the Amir disclosed that he had nearly ceded the Wakhan territory to China. However, taking in view its strategic position *vis-à-vis* Russia, Sir Mortimer with great difficulty prevailed in convincing the Amir to retain it.[64] On Naim mentioning that the Afghan border with China was well marked along the watersheds, the Indian Ambassador replied that the same was true for position of India's border with China!

Before handing over the King's reply, Sardar Naim told the Indian Ambassador that he had called the Ambassador to discuss the India–China position further to enable him to understand the basis of common points of agreement on which peaceful negotiations could start.

In the meanwhile, President Gamal Abdel Nasser has suggested a four-point plan for a peaceful settlement of the Chinese–Indian border dispute, the authoritative newspaper *Al Ahram* reported on 1 November 1962.[65] As per Nasser's plan, he suggested the return of soldiers of both countries to the pre-8 September 1962 position. The Chinese side immediately rejected the proposal while India agreed to this suggestion.[66]

'President Nasser's proposal having been turned down', Naim said, 'we must look for a different basis'. The reason why China rejected Nasser's proposal is, Naim said, because in the Ladakh region, the position of 8 September 1962, was more advantageous to India than that of 7 November 1959. This has been conveyed to Naim by the Chinese Charge d'Affaires.[67]

In reply, the Indian Ambassador said that the fact remained that there had been an open, unabashed and premeditated attack on India, that fighting was going on on Indian soil, and whatever the position in the Ladakh area in 1959 or 1962, the line to be delineated would remain on Indian territory.

The first step, therefore, the Ambassador told Naim, for all freedom-loving countries was to condemn the Chinese aggression and impress upon Chou En-lai, directly or indirectly, that India's was the correct stance and the least Chinese could do was to get back to the line of 8 September 1962 before commencing their wholesale attack.

Sardar Naim admitted that, in spite of their professed principles of Panchsheel, the Chinese did not believe in co-existence and had openly proclaimed the inevitability of a total war between the two worlds. Chou En-lai had, in fact, declared that 'he was not afraid of atomic war as he knew that even when practically the whole world is destroyed, a few Chinese would be left over to populate the rest'.[68]

The Indian Ambassador categorically wrote in his note, 'From my talk with Naim, I gained a distinct impression that although Afghanistan's sympathies and support are entirely with India they wish, because of the geographical position and other considerations of security and strategy, to play a cautious role'. Mr Nur Ahmed Etemadi reiterated that compared with China, Afghanistan's friendly relations with India were centuries old, 'both having common heritage and culture'. Mr Etemadi told an interesting anecdote. He said that while Naim had seen the Indian Ambassador three times since his arrival on 1 November from his foreign visit, he made the Chinese Charge d'Affaires wait for five days when a request for a meeting was made. The Afghan camp was trying to convince their Indian friends that 'since President Nasser's suggestion had been rejected by Chou En-lai, the Indian Prime Minister might possibly consider a compromise approach on the basis of which Afghanistan could play an effective role'.[69]

Throughout the war, Afghanistan stood with Indian strategic thinking and continued to play a vital role in mobilizing other non-aligned countries. Similarly, India's action towards the liberation of Goa, Daman and Diu brought quick support from the government and people of Afghanistan. The Afghan Premier promptly sent a cable to the Prime Minister endorsing the action taken by India. The message of reciprocation from the Indian Prime Minister was widely acclaimed in Afghanistan.[70]

The way the Afghan Royal Family behaved showed that they recognized India's influence at the Royal Palace from the very beginning of their diplomatic ties. Diplomatic cables disclosed that every year the King and Queen specially invite Indian artists to the Palace for a performance. This has never been done in the case of Russians or artists from any other country. At this function, since 1961, only the Indian Ambassador and his wife, together with the leader of the Indian delegation were asked to join the Royal family with their wives, prince, and princess. It is a family affair, and no other diplomat is invited. It also became a feature that the Indian Ambassador hosted a special and private dinner for some members of the Royal family, who are entertained by Indian artists. The Afghan Royalty has made this the only exception in favour of the Indian Embassy.

In 1962, the Indian Ambassador expressed the desire to build India's own Embassy and Chancery in Kabul. Afghan Foreign Minister Sardar Naim, in a meeting with the Ambassador on 11 August 1962, informed the Ambassador that the Royal Afghan Government would provide all possible support. India used to spend nearly Rs 2 lakhs every year on rentals alone, which was a great drain on India's foreign exchange. However, in a strange proposition, India's Foreign Office informed the Indian Ambassador during his visit to New Delhi that the amount for the construction of the Embassy and Chancery would be forthcoming if the Ambassador managed to create foreign exchange in Afghanistan to the extent of Rs 30 lakhs through additional exports.[71] Otherwise, the Indian Government would not support the construction of the Embassy and Chancery.

This was a difficult proposition. However, the learned J.N. Dhamija spoke to the Afghan Commerce Minister in this regard and then approached Sardar Naim. The Afghan Foreign Minister stoically said that as a good gesture to the Ambassador personally and as a representative of a great and friendly country, the Afghan Government would agree to the Ambassador's suggestion. He also said that the Afghan Government would very much like India to build a good Embassy and Chancery of its own design and architecture to decorate the city of Kabul. The Indian Ambassador was 'overwhelmed with this gracious gesture'. Immediately, the Indian Ambassador officially received the intimation from the Royal Afghan Government of his understanding with Sardar Naim. This was a very big concession for a country like Afghanistan to give, as her limited financial position was not very sound.

India has been one of the biggest trade partners of Afghanistan. During the trade negotiation process of 1962, Commerce Minister Mr Manubhai Shah arrived in Kabul on 9 September 1962 with an Indian trade delegation. Since this was the first time in the history of India's trade negotiations with Afghanistan that an Indian Minister paid a visit, it greatly impressed the sensitivities of Afghans. The Afghan Commerce Minister Mr G. M. Sherzad cancelled his visit to Czechoslovakia so as to enable him to be in Kabul to receive the Indian Commerce Minister.[72] The Afghan hierarchy was highly impressed by the wisdom and approach of the Indian Commerce Minister. Both countries showed great interest in the European common market and were glad to hear the views of the Indian Commerce Minister. Views were also expressed on the possibility of the formation of the Asian common market.[73]

India–Afghanistan friendship was at its peak during the early 1960s. The Indian diplomatic cable speaks volumes about how India–Afghanistan relations were at work. It hardly took both sides two or three days to finalize commerce agreement when the USSR ordinarily had been taking nearly two arduous months of haggling to conclude such an agreement with the Royal Afghan Government.[74] Afghanistan appreciated India's approach, realizing as they did that although the US and the USSR may have their interests and axes to grind, India at any rate had no concealed purpose or design and was always there to help Afghanistan grow into a strong and independent nation.[75] According to the local press, India's trade agreement with Afghanistan, in addition to being another step towards the further consolidation of friendship, was described as a vivid example of cooperation and goodwill between the people and governments of the two countries.[76]

The Indian Embassy was keeping an eye on the functioning of the royal family and their attitude *vis-à-vis* the Afghan people. Commenting on the Afghan royalty, the Indian Embassy note stated that 'King Zahir Shah who has been on the throne for 29 years is perhaps the only King of Afghanistan who has given much long stability to his reign'. About his personal belief, the note states,

> He is God-fearing and one of the most popular kings of Afghanistan. His influence over the tribes and his ministers is considerable. He travels, mixing freely with the tribals and his people without any escort or a protective guard. Although possessing unlimited power he has used it wisely and benevolently, always bearing the welfare of his country foremost in his mind.[77]

The King along with Sardar Daoud, Prime Minister, and Sardar Naim, Foreign Minister, both brothers and sons of the uncle of the King, was, in fact, the real ruler of Afghanistan and unlimited power was concentrated in their hands. They had done extremely well, and although the Afghan hierarchy was honest and above reproach, corruption was widespread even among ministers. There was an unwritten convention, always taken for granted, which fixed the quantum of the 'fee' which the minister must receive upon making a particular appointment in their department. To curtail corruption, Prime Minister Daoud ordered all the ministers and officials of the Government to provide statements about their assets and how they managed to amass so much wealth and property with salaries that, even by Indian standards, must be regarded as meagre.

Yet this was the way in which successive governments have been run in the past. Although there was stability and otherwise sure signs of progress in Afghanistan, there was an unknown fear and apprehension as to what may happen after the demise of the King. Events as of 1957 were fairly fresh when a powerful Finance Minister, Mr Abdul Malik Abdul-Rahimzay, had treacherously laid a plot to usurp the throne by assassinating the King and all the members of the royal family. Because of this and Afghanistan's past history, the country nurtured the most efficient and powerful intelligence system.

While commenting on Afghan intelligence, the Indian diplomatic notes stated that Ambassador Dhamija had been plainly told that 'At the ministerial level ... they were ... suspicious of Indian Muslims who, according to them, have natural pro-Pakistani leanings and therefore, does not inspire confidence'. Royal Afghan Government thus avoided Indian Muslims being employed in service, especially as doctors, in Afghanistan, and preferred other Indians instead! However, this sentiment was an unspoken diplomatic preference aired privately by the Afghans. India continued to send Muslim officials including Muslim Ambassadors like Mr Mohammad Hamid Ansari to Kabul to work at the Indian Mission. It is also most extraordinary that Afghanistan's intelligence system knew much more about some of the high officials at the Indian Embassy and their activities than the Indian Embassy could have ever imagined. Most of the official secrets were relayed to the Ambassador by Mr Sherzad, the Commerce Minister, who was related to the king and was otherwise fairly high up in the hierarchy. He confided that 'he even did not know as to who amongst them may be a secret agent. The system is most dangerous and acts as a double-edged weapon cutting both ways'.[78]

In May 1963, President S. Radhakrishnan visited Kabul. On 13 May 1963, during his speech at the Indo-Afghan Society meeting, the President remarked:

> We are all the children of God; so we have a claim to help one another as belonging to one great family. And it is my hope and desire that the relations which are so cordial and happy between our two countries – there is not one problem which is dividing us or giving us concern – will continue to be in the same state and will grow as the years pass and make us faster friends.[79]

Two days later at Kandahar, the Indian President said,

> Now a thing that occurred to me today was that at the time when transport and communications were difficult Afghanistan had been the meeting place of so many different cultures – the Brahmanical, the Buddhistic, the Greek, the Islamic cultures met here. Here when I went around the city, I found people of European origin or nationality, Indians, and others, working together with the one object of helping the Afghan people to raise their living standards.[80]

Ambassador J.N. Dhamija, the illustrious diplomat and most popular Indian in Kabul, left the Indian Embassy in August 1964. He was replaced by General P.N. Thapar, who continued as Indian Ambassador until January 1969.

In 1966, India proposed to build a 100-bed children's hospital in Kabul. To finalize the plans for the proposed hospital, a two-man Afghan delegation consisting of architect Abdullah Breschna and Dr Abdul Ghaffar Aziz, Adviser to the Afghan Health Ministry on Maternity and Child Welfare, arrived in India on 27 February 1967.[81] The Indian delegation, comprising Shri J. Mukund, Additional Chief Engineer, Shri P.C. Jaitley, Architect, and Shri V.G. Ramdasi, Surveyor, arrived in Kabul on 11 November 1967. Noticing the delay in the implementation of the hospital, an Indian Embassy note stated that 'With the arrival of this delegation, the hopes of the Afghan Government that the Government of India is really serious about building this hospital have once again been revived'.[82] The construction work was completed in 1971, and its Director, Dr S.S. Manchanda, and one doctor had arrived to take up their duties. This was India's largest project abroad under the ITEC Programme. Over 30 Indian medical staff joined it.[83]

Indian expertise was sought by the Afghan Royal Government to preserve the heritage sites at Bamiyan, and a bilateral agreement on this was inked in 1969. A team of Indian experts started working immediately after the agreement, and the work progressed tremendously under the Superintending Engineer in charge, Mr B.R. Chopra, when he arrived at Bamiyan in the summer of 1971.

In January 1967, the King and Queen of Afghanistan, along with their phalanx of courtiers, arrived in India at the invitation of the President of India, Dr S. Radhakrishnan.[84] Afghan press reported liberally about the prospect of success of the King's visit. According to the *Kabul Times*, 'Their majesties trip to India, a neighbouring and friendly country bound to Afghanistan by strong ties of history and culture, will surely contribute towards the further strengthening of these bonds and reorientation of views on subjects of common interest'.[85]

At the end of their visit to India, the King and his party flew directly to Pakistan for an unofficial visit from 7 to 13 February 1967. There were rumours in the business circles in Kabul that the opening of the land route was expected, and according to these businessmen an announcement was anticipated during King's visit to Pakistan. This question was taken up by the Afghans with the Pakistani authorities during the King's visit, but Pakistan's reply was that due to the present relations existing between India and Pakistan, it was difficult for them to open land routes for Indo-Afghan trade.

The general, though wrong, impression in commercial circles was that the unfortunate incident of the shooting down of a Pakistani plane stood in the way of the opening of this land route. There was no doubt that the Afghans had very much resented this attitude of Pakistan.[86] As per the Indian Defence Ministry, an Indian Air Force plane shot down a Pakistani military aircraft on 2 February 1967 when it crossed into India. The plane intruded near Ferozepur, at 12:50 pm. It had penetrated 30 miles into India 'in clear weather and good visibility', about which the Defence Ministry lodged a formal protest. The pilot had ignored orders to land in India and tried to take 'violent evasive action' to escape to Pakistan.[87] Indian Air Force shot down the plane, which was destroyed.

During his visit to Pakistan, the King held informal talks with Pakistan on the issue of the Pakhtoon problem. The Afghans presented two alternatives, namely the creation of an independent Pakhtoonistan or the creation of a Pakhtoon province linked with Pakistan. The proposal was turned down by President Ayub, who observed that there was hardly anything in the tribal area that could be termed a Pakhtoon movement, so there was no reason for a change in the status quo.[88] The King and Queen arrived in Kabul on 13 February, and according to a report the King on the return made a comparison between the reception accorded to him in India and Pakistan, stating that there was genuine and sincere warmth shown to him in India; in Pakistan it was stage managed.[89]

The Pakhtoon issue had been boiling for some time in Pakistan as well as in Afghanistan. During this period Pakhtoon leaders from the Bajaur area apprised Khan Abdul Gaffar Khan, the great Gandhian and former Indian freedom fighter, about Pakistan's efforts to enrol tribals from their area for Jihad in Kashmir. They asked for Khan Abdul Gaffar Khan's permission to attack the Pakistani establishment in Khar and Jindol to counteract these efforts. The Khan advised patience and asked them to continue their efforts to forge unity among themselves.[90] Khan Abdul Gaffar Khan is also reported to be disappointed with the attitude of the Afghan Government. He maintains that if Afghanistan and India gave moral and material assistance to the Pakhtoonistan movement, Pakistan was bound to come to terms with them. He was further of the view that since the US and the USSR would not allow the situation to escalate into a conflagration, India and Afghanistan should not apprehend an open confrontation with Pakistan.[91]

Khan Abdul Gaffar Khan went to Kabul on 11 March 1967 and met the King to find out the result of talks that had taken place in Pakistan on the Pakhtoonistan issue. The King evaded giving him an idea of what had transpired on the Pakhtoon issue. He told him that Prime Minister Mainwandwal would discuss the issue with the Pakistani authorities during his impending visit to Pakistan.[92]

The Afghan people, particularly the residents of Jalalabad, evinced keen interest in the May 1967 Presidential election of India and hailed the election of Dr Zakir Hussain as a triumph for secularism in India. There was a feeling of satisfaction at the election of Dr Zakir Hussain as President. The tribals in particular felt elated over the elevation of a Muslim to the highest office in the country. They thought that it would deal a stunning blow to the mischievous propaganda of Pakistan regarding the alleged maltreatment of Muslims in India.[93] As is well known, Pakistan exploits to the fullest the religious susceptibilities of Muslim nations to bring them into its fold. This equally applies to the Muslims of Afghanistan. The people living in this region of Afghanistan are orthodox in their belief system. They have little exposure to modern education and literacy, and maintain a traditional way of life. Therefore, they are vulnerable to the propaganda carried out by Pakistani radio. In this connection, the regular flow of traffic between Peshawar and Jalalabad also proves useful to Pakistan. The effect of this propaganda on the local populace is being discerned by the Afghan Hindus and Sikhs residing at Jalalabad.[94]

A message of congratulations was sent by His Majesty the King to Dr Zakir Hussain. The editorial in Pushtu daily *Ishla*, while congratulating the President described him as 'one of the famous scholars and politicians of the country' and 'originally Dr Zakir Hussain is Afridi and is an able and enlightened descendant of famous Pashtoons'.[95] Recalling Dr Zakir Hussain's visit to Afghanistan in the year 1966, the *Kabul Times* wrote, 'The speeches he made here – some in Dari – on various occasions were a manifestation of his profound thinking and unbiased reasoning. He impressed Afghans with his sense of scholarship and his humility'.[96]

In response to the message of goodwill and greetings from the Indian President to His Majesty the King, which was radioed by the Air-India plane while flying over Afghanistan, an invitation was immediately extended on behalf of His Majesty to the Indian President to make a brief stop at Kabul Airport on his return journey from Montreal to India.[97] However, due to the Air-India pilots' strike and the lack of landing facilities for Boeing planes at Kabul Airport, the invitation could not be accepted.[98]

Ambassador Thapar, before bidding farewell to Kabul, made a courtesy call to the King. During this meeting, the King went into detail regarding Afghan–Pakistan relations. His Majesty remarked that their relations with Pakistan were improving, but with the publication of Ayub's book *Friends Not Masters* they have now come to a standstill. His Majesty was fairly critical of the President of Pakistan and termed the egoism exhibited by him as a sign of immaturity.[99]

In his book, the Pakistani dictator wrote that 'relations with Afghanistan have not followed the friendly and fraternal lines which should have been expected of two neighbouring Muslim states'. Ayub mentioned two misconceptions in the minds of Afghans. The first, he wrote, was arising from constant Indian propaganda, that Pakistan could not survive as a separate State. The Afghan rulers believed this to be true and decided to stake a claim to our territory before Pakistan disintegrated. Ayub made a scathing remark when he said that the Afghans consequently laid claim to part of Pakistan's northern areas where the Pathans or Pashtuns live. In this way, the idea of an artificial State of Pakhtoonistan inside Pakistan's borders was made an issue by the Afghan rulers, he said. He reiterated that 'this was unacceptable to us'. Ayub reiterated that

> In this claim, the Afghans were backed by India whose interest lay in ensuring that in the event of a war with us over Kashmir, the Afghans should open a second front against Pakistan on the North-West Frontier. They also reasoned that if they had this understanding with Afghanistan, we would not be able to use the Pathan tribesmen against them.[100]

The second misconception, as per Ayub, lay in the attitude of the Afghan rulers themselves. If their first premise proved wrong and Pakistan did survive, they realized that it would have a democratic government. This would naturally undermine the position of the rulers in Afghanistan. So, they made these claims to our lands and also carried out raids over the Durand Line, which divides the two countries, and they hired agents and dissident tribesmen to create incidents in these areas. All this helped them to divert the attention of their people from internal difficulties.[101]

Ayub added, 'We were disappointed that Afghanistan adopted an attitude of open hostility from the very day of our independence. Ironically enough, Afghanistan was the only country that opposed our admission to the United Nations'.[102]

In this toxic background and the King's difficult visit to Pakistan, Khan Abdul Gaffar Khan met Prime Minister Mohammad Nur Ahmad Etemadi to felicitate him on his assumption of office in November 1967. Although Etemadi promised that his Government would make all-out efforts to find a solution to the Pakhtoon problem, he did not pledge any material support. The Khan also met the King and impressed upon him the need for activating the Pakhtoon movement. He pointed out to the King that in view of what had been stated in *Friends Not Masters*, there was hardly any scope left for the settlement of the issue at the diplomatic level. The Khan did not receive any encouraging response from the King who, on the other hand, disapproved of some of the activities and statements of the Khan, which, according to the King, caused embarrassment to the Afghan Government. The Afghan Government was reported to have taken exception to a broadcast on

All India Radio in which the Khan appealed to India to extend aid for the achievement of Pakhtoonistan. They further suspected that the Khan was receiving material assistance from the Indian Ambassador in Kabul for the promotion of Pakhtoon activities.[103]

Before 1947, the only outlet to the sea for Afghanistan was through India. All her imports and exports were mainly routed through the Karachi Port. With the partition of this subcontinent and the birth of a newly born baby in the guise of Pakistan, which, with her first breath, claimed that she was the most powerful and advanced Islamic country in the world, Afghanistan started entertaining doubts and fears about her security as well as free flow of Afghan trade.[104] In this context, one might remember that Afghanistan was the only country to vote against the admission of Pakistan into the UN.[105]

Afghans are a proud and sensitive nation. They have not forgotten their glorious past when their forefathers ruled India. They proudly claim that the whole of the old NWFP and Baluchistan at one time formed part of the Afghan empire. They profess an emotional and cultural affinity with Pashtuns living on the Pakistan side of the border. In a rising crescendo, Afghanistan has demanded self-determination for all Pathans in Pakistan and the creation of a homeland called Pashtunistan for them.[106] The Afghan authorities have had some ulterior motives in this agitation. Pakistan does not admit any justification for the so-called Pashtunistan issue, and this forms the main bone of contention between the two countries. Another contributory cause is the stoppage through Pakistan of the flow of goods to and from this landlocked country.[107]

India's relations with Afghanistan continued to soar at an unimaginable scale. By the year 1971, the number of Indian families in Afghanistan was nearly 370. The total population of Indians and their families was estimated to be 1600. Almost all of them are well off financially. Although no official census was carried out by the Royal Afghan Government, the approximate number of Afghan Hindus and Sikhs of Indian origin was said to be 20,000.[108] They were mostly residing in Kabul, Kandahar, Jalalabad, and Ghazni. While the majority of them had been settled there for generations, some of them migrated from the NWFP in 1947, at the time of the partition of India and have since acquired Afghan nationality. Their financial position as a whole is satisfactory and many of them own immovable property. The Afghan Sikhs and Hindus maintained close social, cultural, and business links with India and often visited India for purposes of business, pilgrimage, and meeting their relatives. They too were subjected to all the restrictions which Pakistan imposed on Indians for travel through Pakistan by the overland route since 1965, though they are allowed to visit Pakistan for business purposes. Restrictions for travelling through Pakistan were, however, relaxed for Sikhs during their pilgrimage to Pakistan on important occasions like Guru Nanak's birthday and Baisakhi.[109]

Afghanistan was an important transit centre for tourists to India via the land route. A good number of them did not come equipped with Indian visas from the country of their origin. Every effort was made by Indian Embassy to weed out undesirable tourists of the hippie type. Afghanistan used to receive a good number of hippie tourists who in turn used to travel to India through the Khyber Pass and Bolan Pass. Hippie type means tourists who follow the hippie lifestyle that started in the 1960s and 1970s. The hippie travellers generally behaved in ways the authorities or local people found inappropriate or disruptive, such as being disrespectful or rebellious. The Indian authorities tried to prevent these tourists from different countries who arrived in Afghanistan and wanted to visit India.

The Afghan Parliament, at one stage, showing signs of increasing assertiveness, came out against the Government of Prime Minister Etemadi and was instrumental in his downfall. Dr Abdul Zahir, who replaced him as Prime Minister on 9 June 1971, initially seemed to be heading an administration that was both more dynamic and more responsive to public demands than his predecessor. Yet when the dust had settled, it was apparent that no basic changes would take place; the new Government was more active in some fields, but it did not wield any more real political power. The long political crisis connected with the overthrow of Etemadi's Government and his replacement by Dr Abdul Zahir did little to disturb Afghanistan's tranquillity; thus, it was demonstrated once again that stability and continuity in Afghanistan rest with the Monarchy and not with the Government.

Afghanistan was adept at following a policy of balance in its relationship with the major powers. The independence-loving Afghans did not permit themselves to be used as an instrument of one or the other superpowers, and the superpowers, in turn, came to avoid any real struggle for ascendancy in Afghanistan.[110]

In foreign affairs, there was no departure from the traditional Afghan policy of neutralism. Indo-Afghan relations continued to be cordial. The India–Pakistan War of 1971 saw Afghanistan taking a genuinely independent and neutral position, in contrast to most of the countries at the UN. The Indian Minister for Industrial Development, Mr Moinul Haque Choudhury, visited Afghanistan in June 1971 to clarify to the Afghans the issues involving the crisis of East Bengal.[111] During the testing events of the year, it was confirmed once again that the close relations between India and Afghanistan have a firm and stable base.[112]

Although Afghanistan did not overtly support the emergence of Bangladesh, or condemn Pakistan for its acts of aggression against its own population and against India, it gave sufficient evidence of understanding and sincerity in its approaches to India and made clear where its sympathies lay. The Afghans were close observers of the Indian political scene, and they showed genuine pleasure at the massive victory of the Indian Prime Minister Mrs Indira Gandhi, in the mid-term poll. Among other things, they regarded this as a guarantee for secularism in India, about which they were certainly concerned. The crackdown in Pakistan, which came almost immediately after the Indian elections, subsequently dominated thinking about the subcontinent. From the start, the Afghan Foreign Office demonstrated that its assessment of the reasons for the Pakistani action coincided on almost every point with the Indian assessment. The Afghans, however, did not feel themselves strong enough to issue any outright condemnation of Pakistan. This was the position as explained to Mr Moinul Haq Choudhury, Minister of Industrial Development, who visited Kabul in the middle 1971 as a special emissary of the Prime Minister.[113] As the year progressed and no sign of an end to the crisis could be seen, Afghan statements took on a slightly stronger tone. In September 1971, the King visited Moscow, where the joint communique represented a definite advance in the Afghan position. About the same time, the Foreign Minister, in his address to the UN General Assembly, once again showed that the Afghans were then prepared to be a little bit more outspoken in public about the realities in the subcontinent.

When hostility broke out between India and Pakistan, a distinct Afghan position was evident. To begin with, the Afghan Prime Minister spoke to Parliament about the war and implied very clearly that it had been started as a result of Pakistani air strikes against India. The rights of the Bengalis were recognized, while Afghanistan took a neutral position on the conflict as a whole. Most important was Afghanistan's abstention at the UN General Assembly on the resolution which was supported by an overwhelming majority of other countries.[114] This showed that it has a distinct and independent viewpoint on the affairs of the subcontinent and would not permit itself to be stamped against its own judgement.

Another notable feature of the Afghan stand during the war was its condemnation of the Indian bombing of Peshawar. .The action was carried out largely as a formality rather than with genuine intent or seriousness. Moreover, it was not pursued vigorously enough to become a source of significant annoyance or tension. In 1965, also, a similar protest had been issued by the Afghan Foreign Office.[115] Although Afghanistan did not issue any official statement after the Tripartite Agreement between Pakistan, Bangladesh, and India was signed, the Agreement was generally welcomed both by the local press and in Government circles. President Daoud told Mr Jamil-ur-Rehman, Editor of the *New Times* (Pakistan), that although the Tripartite Agreement did not concern his country directly, as a peace-loving nation, Afghanistan welcomed it.[116]

The official English daily, *The Kabul Times*, reflected the Government's opinion in an editorial entitled: 'Return of Peace to Sub-Continent'. It said, 'All Peace-loving countries of the world, especially countries of the region, have warmly welcomed this forgetting and forgiving by the peoples and leaders in the subcontinent'.[117]

On 17 July 1973, the mountainous kingdom of Afghanistan was proclaimed a republic in a bloodless coup d'etat led by Mohammad Daoud, a brother-in-law of King Mohammad Zahir Shah, who was on a visit to Italy. Lieutenant General Mohammad Daoud Khan said in a broadcast that he had led the coup to replace the 'corrupt and effete' rule of the King with a 'genuine democracy' and to save the country from ruin. Within an hour, the country of 15 million people – largely farmers and herdsmen – was placed under martial law. Between periods of martial music, Kabul radio proclaimed the loyalty of the Army and asked the people to cooperate with the 'military Government'. Zahir Shah, who had been on the island of Ischia near Naples since 8 July 1973 for a vacation and mineral water digestive treatments, went to Rome after hearing of the coup. In his broadcast, General Daoud, who was 64 years old and a cousin as well as brother-in-law of the King, pledged that Afghanistan would continue her policy of non-alignment and would not join any military pact.

The deposed King, who was 59 years old at that time, had occupied the throne of his landlocked Central Asian country since 1933 when his father was assassinated. Zahir Shah was 19 at the time, and for many years thereafter he was a near prisoner of his uncles and cousins. General Daoud was Prime Minister from 1953 to 1963, the last decade of the King's reign as a figurehead. The nation, which depends heavily on foreign aid, had received substantial assistance under Zahir Shah from its neighbours, the Soviet Union, China, and the United States. Its armed forces were equipped mostly by the Soviet Union.[118]

The July 1973 coup d'etat in Afghanistan had neither eroded the country's traditional neutralism nor brought about any drastic change in its economic system. The fears of a tilt towards the Soviet Union and of sweeping socialist reforms proved unfounded. The shadowy central committee which assumed power after deposing King Zahir Shah remained as shadowy as ever, while Mohammad Daoud, President and Prime Minister, ran the country in much the same authoritarian style as when he was the King's Prime Minister between 1953 and 1963.[119] Daoud's mention of the Pashtunistan dispute with Pakistan in his broadcast proclaiming the republic also contributed to misgivings, the suspicion being that he had done so to win favour with Moscow and New Delhi. But anyone familiar with his record as Prime Minister should have known that he had very strong feelings on this issue. Western dignitaries who had talked to Daoud since his return to power had come away convinced that he had a deep emotional commitment to the cause of Pashtunistan. This may have something to do with the fact that Daoud's great-great-grandfather, Sultan Muhammad Khan, was the last Afghan governor of Peshawar – i.e. until the Sikhs under Ranjit Singh elbowed him out in 1823. There is Sir Olaf Caroe's testimony that, for the descendants of the Sultan, 'the lure of Peshawar is a passion, deep in their hearts'.

The Indian–Afghanistan bilateral relations acquired a new dimension with the highly successful visit of the first-ever military delegation led by the Defence Secretary, Govind Narain, in March 1974. The Afghans went all out to honour the Indian team, and the President himself, in an unusual gesture of appreciation and gratitude, hosted a dinner at which all members of his cabinet, all senior Generals of the Afghan Army, the Air Force, and the entire diplomatic staff of the Indian Embassy were invited.[120] The delegation had three meetings with President Daoud. India offered to provide more facilities for training Afghan military personnel in India. As a token of friendship, the Defence Secretary announced the gift of a Sainik School to Afghanistan.[121]

The explosion of a nuclear device by India at Pokhran in the desert of Rajasthan on 18 May 1974 was reported in the press without comment, and no official statement was issued by the Afghan Government. However, as diplomatic correspondence indicated, 'satisfaction with the test was indicated at the highest level' and India's assertion that the test was for peaceful purposes was accepted. There is an implied feeling that this will act as a deterrent to Pakistan in pursuing its policies in this region.[122]

The election of Mr Fakruddin Ali Ahmed as the fifth President of India on 17 August 1974 received wide coverage in the English as well as the Pashtu language press. Like the election of Mr Zakir Hussain, the election of Fakruddin Ali Ahmed also received an equal degree of appreciation in the Afghan circle.[123]

Commenting on relations with Pakistan on 16 November 1974, President Daoud said that while Afghanistan wanted to live in peace with Pakistan, ever since the establishment of the Republican regime, Pakistan had been trying to undermine the new order and create problems inside Afghanistan. He alleged that 'the Pakistani propaganda had reached as low a level of crudity and falsehood as can be imagined'. President Daoud spoke warmly about the relations with India, which have become closer since the advent of the Republican regime.[124]

President Daoud visited India from 10 to 14 March 1975. Indian Prime Minister Mrs Indira Gandhi reciprocated the visit when she made an official tour of Afghanistan from 4 to 7 July 1976. The peculiarity of Mrs Gandhi's visit was the high-decibel announcement made by the Afghans just a few days before Pakistani Prime Minister Mrs Benazir Bhutto arrived in Kabul.

The Afghans were really too keen that the visit should take place as soon as possible, and they literally rushed to announce it a couple of days before Prime Minister Bhutto's visit, which was precisely what the Afghans desired. The reception accorded to Mrs Gandhi was in sharp contrast to that given to Mrs Bhutto, a difference that was not lost upon the diplomatic observers.[125] A couple of years later, President Daoud visited India in March 1978 and helped further improve Indo-Afghan relations.[126]

It was during these years that the Indian Embassy in Kabul noticed that there was a large influx of Indian nationals coming to Afghanistan from Punjab every year. Many of them were brought by unscrupulous travel agents on the promise of taking them on to Iran, Turkey, Greece, and other European countries to get them jobs. The travel agents, after spending some time with them in Afghanistan, on some pretext or another disappeared leaving their 'clients' stranded. Most of these Indians did not have any money and eventually approached the Indian Embassy for repatriation. During 1976, the number of Indian nationals stranded in Afghanistan stood at 80 while 131 faced the same fate during 1975. All those Indian nationals were repatriated from Kabul.

Pakistan does not issue transit visas to Indian nationals travelling from India to Kabul. Afghanistan, however, grants Indian nationals a one-month tourist visa upon arrival at any Afghan immigration point. Taking advantage of this relatively easy access, fraudulent travel agents deceive unsuspecting Indians by promising to help them reach Turkey or Iran through Afghanistan. These agents typically arrange for Indian travellers to fly from Amritsar to Kabul, where they obtain the one-month tourist visa at the airport. Many of these travellers, often illiterate villagers, are misled by the agents and unaware of the challenges they will face when applying for visas to Iran and Turkey in Kabul. The Iranian Embassy and Turkish Embassy in Kabul refused to grant any visas to any Indian nationals falling into this category.[127] The Indian Embassy suggested that 'We strongly recommend that more stringent checking is done before our passport issuing authorities, especially RPO Chandigarh, RPO Delhi, issue passports. Also, strict action must be taken against unscrupulous travel agents'.[128]

During the year 1977, the Indian Embassy in Kabul estimated there were about 20,000 to 25,000 Afghan nationals of Indian origin, who were largely Hindus and Sikhs residing in Afghanistan. They were mostly residing in Kabul, Kandahar, Jalalabad, and Ghazni. A majority of them were petty traders. A few had been serving in Government Departments, mainly in unimportant jobs. There was, however, freedom of worship for these communities, and they were permitted to maintain their temples and gurdwaras. They continue to have close social, cultural, and trade links with India and often visit India to meet their relatives or for business.[129]

Notes

1 Treaty of Friendship Between the Govt. of India and the Royal Govt. of Afghanistan, Ministry of External Affairs, Government of India, New Delhi, File No. 1-I/2/Afghanistan/50,1950, 4 January 1950, National Archives of India (NAI hereafter).
2 See Article 9; Treaty of Friendship Between the Govt. of India and the Royal Govt. of Afghanistan, Ministry of External Affairs, Government of India, New Delhi, File No. 1-I/2/Afghanistan/50, 1950, 4 January 1950, NAI.
3 Special Correspondent, 'Indo-Afghan Friendship Treaty Signed', *Indian Express*, 5 January 1950.
4 Letter of Evidence & Commission of Appointment in Favour of Wing Commander Rup Chand as Indian Ambassador to Afghanistan, Ministry of External Affairs, Government of India, File No: 1(6)-PT, 1948, NAI.
5 Letter of Evidence & Commission of Appointment in Favour of Wing Commander Rup Chand as Indian Ambassador to Afghanistan, Ministry of External Affairs, Government of India, File No: 1(6)-PT, 1948, NAI.
6 Jawaharlal Nehru, *Constituent Assembly of India (Legislative) Debates*, Vol. 1, Part 1 (New Delhi: Government of India Press, 1949), pp. 643–644.
7 Agreement between Afghanistan and India Regarding Radio-Telegraphic Communication between Their Respective Countries, Certificate of Registration No. 2005, Signed at Kabul on 14 December 1949, Ministry of External Affairs, Government of India, File No. 1-I/1/Afghanistan/49, 1949, NAI.
8 Rup Chand, Ambassador of India, Embassy of India, Kabul, Secret, Note No. A-21/51, File No. 3(13)-R&I/51, 1951, NAI, 1 February 1951, NAI.
9 Annual Report from Afghanistan (Kabul), Research and Intelligence Branch, MEA, GoI, File No. 3(13)-R&I/51, 1951, NAI.
10 Agreement Between the Governments of India and Pakistan Regarding Security and Rights of Minorities, Signed by Jawaharlal Nehru and Liaqat Ali Khan, Ministry of External Affairs, Government of India, New Delhi, File No. PA50B1228, 8 April 1950, NAI.
11 Agreement Between the Governments of India and Pakistan Regarding Security and Rights of Minorities, Signed by Jawaharlal Nehru and Liaqat Ali Khan, Ministry of External Affairs, Government of India, New Delhi, File No. PA50B1228, 8 April 1950, NAI.
12 Annual Report from Afghanistan (Kabul), Research and Intelligence Branch, MEA, GoI, File No. 3(13)-R&I/51, 1951, NAI.
13 M. Sahai, Press Attaché, Main Trend of Afghan Press During January to June 1951, Secret, Publicity Wing, Embassy of India, Kabul, Annual Report from Afghanistan (Kabul), Research and Intelligence Branch, 1 October 1951, Ref. No. 3(13)-R&I/51, 1951, MEA, GoI, NAI.
14 Cultural Relations Officer, Embassy of India, Kabul, Annual Commercial Report of the Embassy of India, No. 5/23, 2 November 1951, NAI.
15 K.D. Bhasin, Charge d'Affaires, Annual General Report of the Indian Embassy Kabul, D. O. No. 5/23, 24 January 1951, NAI.
16 Cultural Relations Officer, Embassy of India, Kabul, Annual Commercial Report of the Embassy of India, No. 5/23, 2 November 1951, NAI.
17 Annual Report from Afghanistan (Kabul), Research and Intelligence Branch, MEA, GoI, File No. 3(13)-R&I/51, 1951, NAI.
18 Annual Report from Afghanistan (Kabul), Research and Intelligence Branch, MEA, GoI, File No. 3(13)-R&I/51, 1951, NAI.
19 Cultural Relations Officer, Embassy of India, Kabul, Annual Commercial Report of the Embassy of India, No. 5/23, 2 November 1951, NAI.

20 G.L. Puri, Cultural Relations Officer, Embassy of India, Kabul, The Economic Report for Afghanistan for the Period From 1 April 1952 up to 31 March 1954, No. G. 27/Muscat/55, MEA, GoI, 19 June 1955 (by the time G.L. Puri prepared the report he had been transferred to Muscat), NAI.
21 Copy of Letter from Shri Mehr Singh, Ministry of External Affairs, New Delhi to Shri G.L. Puri, No. F.1/54/1327/17, 17 September 1955, NAI.
22 Annual Report on Afghanistan (Kabul) for 1954, Research and Intelligence Branch, MEA, GoI, File No. 3(14)-R&I/55, I, II, & II, 1955, NAI.
23 D. Murugusan, Charge d'Affaires, Annual General Report, No. F. 2/25/60, 28 June 1960, NAI.
24 Annual Report for 1959 from Kabul, Research and Intelligence Branch, MEA, GoI, File No. 3(14) R&I/60-I, 1960, NAI.
25 Annual Report for 1959 from Kabul, Research and Intelligence Branch, MEA, GoI, File No. 3(14) R&I/60-I, 1960, NAI.
26 Annual Report for 1959 from Kabul, Research and Intelligence Branch, MEA, GoI, File No. 3(14) R&I/60-I, 1960, NAI.
27 Rup Chand, Ambassador of India, Embassy of India, Kabul, Secret, No. A-21/51, 1 February 1951, NAI.
28 H.N. Haksar, Ambassador of India, Embassy of India, Kabul, Annual Political Report for the year 1959, No. 1/SES/59, 22 December 1959, NAI.
29 H.N. Haksar, Ambassador of India, Embassy of India, Kabul, Annual Political Report for the year 1959, No. 1/SES/59, 22 December 1959, NAI.
30 Mr Nehru's Visit, 'Asian Recorder', Vol. V, No. 40, 3–9 October 1959, p. 2923.
31 D. Murugusan, Charge d'Affairs, Annual General Report, No. F. 2/25/60, June 1960, NAI.
32 A.K. Bakshi, Vice Consul, Vice Consulate of India, Kandahar, Annual Consulate Report from the Vice Consulate of India, Kandahar, No. F. 1-S/60, 26 April 1960, NAI.
33 Annual Report from Jalalabad, File No. 3(14)-R&I/60-II, 1960, MEA, GoI, NAI.
34 Annual Report from Jalalabad, File No. 3(14)-R&I/60-II, 1960, MEA, GoI, NAI.
35 Colonel Deewan Singh, Special Intelligence Report Number 2/6/63, Strained Pak-Afghan Relations and their likely Effects, No. 192(a)/MAK/62, 28 February 1962, NAI.
36 Colonel Deewan Singh, Special Intelligence Report Number 2/6/63, Strained Pak-Afghan Relations and their likely Effects, No. 192(a)/MAK/62, 28 February 1962, NAI.
37 Colonel Deewan Singh, Special Intelligence Report Number 2/6/63, Strained Pak-Afghan Relations and their likely Effects, No. 192(a)/MAK/62, 28 February 1962, NAI.
38 J.N. Dhamija, Ambassador of India, Kabul, Secret Note on Durand Line, No. 1/PS/62/3, 4 February 1962, NAI.
39 J.N. Dhamija, Ambassador of India, Kabul.
40 Olaf Caroe, The Pathans: 550 BC-AD 1957, London: Macmillan & Co Ltd, 1958, p. 382.
41 J.N. Dhamija, Ambassador of India, Kabul, Secret Note on Durand Line, No. 1/PS/62/3, 4 February 1962, NAI.
42 Political and Secret Department Records, IOR/L/PS Political and Secret Department Records
43 J.N. Dhamija, Ambassador of India, Kabul, Secret Note on Durand Line, to Mr B.F.H.B. Tyabji, Special Secretary, MEA, New Delhi, No. 1/PS/62/3, 4 February 1962, NAI.

44 J.N. Dhamija, Ambassador of India, Kabul.
45 J.N. Dhamija, Ambassador of India, Kabul.
46 J.N. Dhamija, Ambassador of India, Kabul, Secret Note on Chester Bowles Visit to Afghanistan, sent to Mr B.F.H.B. Tyabji, Special Secretary, MEA, New Delhi, No. 1/PS/62/J, 3 March 1962, NAI.
47 J.N. Dhamija, Ambassador of India, Kabul, Secret Note on Durand Line, to Mr B.F.H.B. Tyabji, Special Secretary, MEA, New Delhi, No. 1/PS/62/3, 4 February 1962, NAI.
48 J.N. Dhamija, Ambassador of India, Kabul, Secret Note on Chester Bowles Visit to Afghanistan, sent to Mr B.F.H.B. Tyabji, Special Secretary, MEA, New Delhi, No. 1/PS/62/J, 3 March 1962, NAI.
49 Political Reports (Other than Annual) from Kabul, Historical, Research and Intelligence Section, MEA, GoI, File No. 6(1)-HI/62, 1962, NAI.
50 Colonel Deewan Singh, Special Intelligence Report Number 2/6/63, Strained Pak-Afghan Relations and their likely Effects, No. 192(a)/MAK/62, 28 February 1962, NAI.
51 Colonel Deewan Singh, Special Intelligence Report Number 2/6/63, Strained Pak-Afghan Relations and their likely Effects, No. 192(a)/MAK/62, 28 February 1962, NAI.
52 Political Reports (Other than Annual) from Kabul, Historical, Research and Intelligence Section, MEA, GoI, File No. 6(1)-HI/62, 1962, NAI.
53 Political Reports (Other than Annual) from Kabul, Historical, Research and Intelligence Section, MEA, GoI, File No. 6(1)-HI/62, 1962, NAI.
54 Colonel Deewan Singh, Special Intelligence Report Number 2/6/63, Strained Pak-Afghan Relations and their likely Effects, No. 192(a)/MAK/62, 28 February 1962, NAI.
55 J.N. Dhamija, Ambassador of India, Kabul, Political Report for the Month of August 1962, Secret, No. 1/PS/62, 18 September 1962, NAI.
56 J.N. Dhamija, Ambassador of India, Kabul, Political Report for the Month of August 1962, Secret, No. 1/PS/62, 18 September 1962, NAI.
57 J.N. Dhamija, Ambassador of India, Kabul, 'Political Report for the Month of October 1962', Secret, No. 1/PS/62, 8 November 1962, NAI.
58 J.N. Dhamija, Ambassador of India, Kabul, 'Political Report for the Month of October 1962', Secret, No. 1/PS/62, 8 November 1962, NAI.
59 Saroj Kumar Rath, China's Belt Loses Its Charm, Fountain Ink, October 2018.
60 J.N. Dhamija, Ambassador of India, Kabul, 'Political Report for the Month of October 1962', Secret, No. 1/PS/62, 8 November 1962, NAI.
61 J.N. Dhamija, Ambassador of India, Kabul, 'Political Report for the Month of October 1962', Secret, No. 1/PS/62, 8 November 1962, NAI.
62 J.N. Dhamija, Ambassador of India, Kabul, 'Note of the Ambassador to MEA', Secret, No. C-22/PC, 12 December 1962, NAI.
63 J.N. Dhamija, Ambassador of India, Kabul, Note on Chinese Aggression and Afghan Policy, Secret, No. C-22/PC, 15 November 1962, NAI.
64 J.N. Dhamija, Ambassador of India, Kabul, Note on Chinese Aggression and Afghan Policy, Secret, No. C-22/PC, 15 November 1962, NAI.
65 Reuters, Nasser Is Said to Offer India-China Peace Plan, *New York Times*, 1 November 1962.
66 Prime Minister on Sino-Indian Relations, Vol. I, Part II, External Publicity Division, Ministry of External Affairs, New Delhi, 1963, p. 150.
67 J.N. Dhamija, Ambassador of India, Kabul, Note on Chinese Aggression and Afghan Policy, Secret, No. C-22/PC, 15 November 1962, NAI.
68 J.N. Dhamija, Ambassador of India, Kabul, Note on Chinese Aggression and Afghan Policy, Secret, No. C-22/PC, 15 November 1962, NAI.

69 J.N. Dhamija, Ambassador of India, Kabul, Note on Chinese Aggression and Afghan Policy, Secret, No. C-22/PC, 15 November 1962.
70 Military and Air Attaché, Embassy of India, Kabul, Monthly Intelligence Report Number 10/61 for the Month of December 1961, N.150/MAK/62, 11 January 1962, NAI.
71 J.N. Dhamija, Ambassador of India, Kabul, Political Report for the Month of August 1962, Secret, No. 1/PS/62, 18 September 1962, NAI.
72 J.N. Dhamija, Ambassador of India, Kabul, 'Monthly Political Report for September 1962', Secret, No. 1/PS/62, 18 September 1962, NAI.
73 J.N. Dhamija, Ambassador of India, Kabul, Political Report for the Month of August 1962, Secret, No. 1/PS/62, 18 September 1962, NAI.
74 Extension of Trade Arrangement Exchange of Letters, Kabul, 12 September 1962, Government of India, Ministry of Commerce and Industry, Kabul, 12 September 1962.
75 J.N. Dhamija, Ambassador of India, Kabul, 'Monthly Political Report for September 1962', Secret, No. 1/PS/62, 8 October 1962, NAI.
76 J.N. Dhamija, Ambassador of India, Kabul, Political Report for the Month of August 1962, Secret, No. 1/PS/62, 18 September 1962, NAI.
77 J.N. Dhamija, Ambassador of India, Kabul, 'Monthlty Political Report for September 1962', Secret, No. 1/PS/62, 8 October 1962, NAI.
78 J.N. Dhamija, Ambassador of India, Kabul, 'Monthly Political Report for September 1962', Secret, No. 1/PS/62, 8 October 1962, NAI.
79 S. Radhakrishnan, Speech at the Indo-Afghan Society, Kabul, 13 May 1963, 'President Radhakrishnan's Speeches and Writings; May 1962–May 1964', Publication Division, Government of India, February 1965.
80 S. Radhakrishnan, Speech at the Indo-Afghan Society, Kandahar, 15 May 1963, 'President Radhakrishnan's Speeches and Writings; May 1962–May 1964', Publication Division, Government of India, February 1965.
81 Brij Kumar, Monthly Political Report for February 1967, Secret, Embassy of India, Kabul, MEA, GoI, No. Kab/101/67, 7 March 1967, NAI.
82 Brij Kumar, Monthly Political Report for November 1967, Secret, Embassy of India, Kabul, MEA, GoI, No. KAB/101/67, 9 December 1967, NAI.
83 Annual Report for 1971 from Kabul, MEA, GOI, File No. HI/1011 (14)/72-I, 1972, NAI.
84 Monthly Political Report, Historical, Research and Intelligence Section, MEA, GoI, File No. HI/1012(I)/67, 1967, NAI.
85 Editorial, King Zahir Shah Commenced His Eight Day Visit to India, *Kabul Times*, 28 January 1967
86 Brij Kumar, Charge d'Affaires, Monthly Political Report for January 1967, Secret, Embassy of India, Kabul, MEA, GoI, No. KAB/101/67, 8 February 1967, NAI.
87 Indian Air Force Plane Downs Pakistani Craft, *New York Times*, 3 February 1967.
88 H.A.K. Barathi, Monthly note on Pakhtoonistan Activities, Secret, No. MII/503(4)/67, 16 June 1967, NAI.
89 Brij Kumar, Charge d'Affaires, Monthly Political Report for January 1967, Secret, Embassy of India, Kabul, MEA, GoI, No. KAB/101/67, 8 February 1967, NAI.
90 I.S. Hassanwalia, Note on Pakhtoonistan Activities 1967, Intelligence Bureau, Ministry of Home Affairs, DIB U.O.No.1/PTS(FP)/67(1), 6 March 1967, NAI.
91 H.A.K. Barathi, Note on Pakhtoonistan Activities for the Month of December 1967, Secret, Historical, Research and Intelligence Section, MEA, GoI, No.2702/68, 10 May 1967, NAI.

92 H.A.K. Barathi, Monthly note on Pakhtoonistan Activities, Secret, No. MII/503(4)/67, 16 June 1967, NAI.
 93 M.L. Choudhary, Consul, Consulate of India, Jalalabad, Monthly Political Report for the Month of May 1967, No. JAL/101(1)/66, 1 June 1967, NAI.
 94 M.L. Choudhary, Consul, Consulate of India, Jalalabad, Monthly Political Report for the Month of July 1967, No. JAL/101(1)/66, 3 August 1967, NAI.
 95 Brij Kumar, 'Monthly Political Report for May 1967', No. KAB/101/67, MEA, GoI, 10 June 1967, NAI.
 96 Brij Kumar, 'Monthly Political Report for May 1967', No. KAB/101/67, MEA, GoI, 10 June 1967, NAI.
 97 Monthly Political Report for June 1967, Embassy of India, Kabul, Secret, MEA, GoI, No. KAB/101/67, 13 July 1967, NAI.
 98 Monthly Political Report for June 1967, Embassy of India, Kabul, Secret, MEA, GoI, No. KAB/101/67, 13 July 1967, NAI.
 99 Brij Kumar, Monthly Political Report for December 1967, Secret, Embassy of India, Kabul, MEA, GoI, No. KAB/101/67, 4 February 1968, NAI.
100 Mohammad Ayub Khan, Friends Not Masters: A Political Autobiography (London: Oxford University Press, 1967), pp. 174–176.
101 Mohammad Ayub Khan, Friends Not Masters: A Political Autobiography (London: Oxford University Press, 1967), pp. 174–176.
102 Mohammad Ayub Khan, Friends Not Masters: A Political Autobiography (London: Oxford University Press, 1967), pp. 174–176.
103 H.A.K. Barathi, Note on Pakhtoonistan Activities for the Month of November, 1967, Secret, No. MII/503(4)/67, MEA, GoI, 15 January 1967, NAI.
104 Colonel Deewan Singh, Special Intelligence Report Number 2/6/63, Strained Pak-Afghan Relations and their likely Effects, No. 192(a)/MAK/62, 28 February 1962, NAI.
105 Political Reports (Other than Annual) from Kabul, Historical, Research and Intelligence Section, MEA, GoI, File No. 6(1)-HI/62, 1962, NAI.
106 Political Reports (Other than Annual) from Kabul, Historical, Research and Intelligence Section, MEA, GoI, File No. 6(1)-HI/62, 1962, NAI.
107 Colonel Deewan Singh, Special Intelligence Report Number 2/6/63, Strained Pak-Afghan Relations and their likely Effects, No. 192(a)/MAK/62, 28 February 1962, NAI.
108 Annual Report for 1971 from Kabul, MEA, GOI, File No. HI/1011 (14)/72-I, 1972, NAI.
109 Annual Consular Report, 1971, Embassy of India Kabul, No. KAB/PV/414/1/72, 29 February 1972, NAI.
110 S. Haider, First Secretary, Embassy of India, Kabul, 'Annual Political Report for the Year 1971', No. KAB/101/1/71, 15 May 1972, NAI; Annual Consular Report, 1971, Embassy of India Kabul, No. KAB/PV/414/1/72, 29 February 1972, NAI.
111 Annual Report for 1971 from Kabul, MEA, GOI, File No. HI/1011 (14)/72-I, 1972, NAI.
112 S. Haider, First Secretary, Embassy of India, Kabul, 'Annual Political Report for the Year 1971', No. KAB/101/1/71, 15 May 1972, NAI; Annual Consular Report, 1971, Embassy of India Kabul, No. KAB/PV/414/1/72, 29 February 1972, NAI.
113 S. Haider, First Secretary, Embassy of India, Kabul, 'Annual Political Report for the Year 1971', No. KAB/101/1/71, 15 May 1972, NAI; Annual Consular Report, 1971, Embassy of India Kabul, No. KAB/PV/414/1/72, 29 February 1972, NAI.

114 Annual Consular Report, 1971, Embassy of India Kabul, No. KAB/PV/414/1/72, 29 February 1972, NAI.
115 S. Haider, First Secretary, Embassy of India, Kabul, 'Annual Political Report for the Year 1971', No. KAB/101/1/71, 15 May 1972, NAI; Annual Consular Report, 1971, Embassy of India Kabul, No. KAB/PV/414/1/72, 29 February 1972, NAI.
116 Political Report for the Month of March 1974 (Part I), No. KAB/101/1/74, 10 April 1974, NAI.
117 L. Mansingh, First Secretary, Embassy of India, Kabul, Political Report for the Month of April 1974 – Part I, No. KAB/101/1/74, MEA, GoI, 8 May 1974, NAI.
118 L. Mansingh, Afghan King Overthrown; A Republic Is Proclaimed, *New York Times*, 18 July 1973.
119 Dilip Mukerjee, Asian Survey, Vol. 15, No. 4 (April 1975), pp. 301–312.
120 Political Reports Etc. (Other than Annual Reports) From Kabul/Pakhtoonistan, MEA, GoI, File No. HI/1012(1)/74, 1974, NAI.
121 K.L. Mehta, Ambassador, Embassy of India, Kabul, 'Political Report for the Month of March 1974 (Part I)', No. KAB/101/1/74, April 1974, NAI.
122 R.C. Shukla, Counsellor, Embassy of India, Kabul, Political Report for the Month of May 1974 – Part I, No. KAB/101/1/74, 5 June 1974, NAI.
123 R.C. Shukla, Counsellor, Embassy of India, Kabul, Political Report for the Month of August 1974 – Part I, No. KAB/101/1/74, 9 September 1974, NAI.
124 R.C. Shukla, Counsellor, Embassy of India, Kabul, Political Report for the Month of November 1974 – Part I, No. KAB/101/1/74, 7 December 1974, NAI.
125 Annual Reports from Kabul for the year 1976, MEA, GoI, File No. HI/1011 (13)/77-I, 1977, Part I, NAI.
126 P.K. Thakkar, Consulate of India, Kandahar, Monthly Record of Events of the Month of March 1978, No. KAN/101/1/77, 4 April 1978, NAI.
127 Annual Reports from Kabul for the year 1976, File No. HI/1011 (13)/77-I, Part I, MEA, GoI, 1977, NAI.
128 Annual Reports from Kabul for the year 1976, File No. HI/1011 (13)/77-I, Part I, MEA, GoI, 1977, NAI.
129 Chancery, Embassy of India, Kabul, 'Annual Consular Report of Indian Missions/Post Abroad – 1976', No. KAB/PV/414(3)/77, 16 March 1977, NAI.

4
TESTING TIME FOR PERPETUAL FRIENDSHIP

The year 1978 was a watershed in the India–Afghanistan relationship. Afghanistan was about to enter into a new phase, an era of predatory foreign intervention, internal civil disorder, and chaos. For the next 11 years, up to 1989, it witnessed unprecedented power struggles, involvement of foreign fighters, and civil strife. India was caught unprepared for the unprecedented change that was about to take place. Although diplomatic cables sent from the Indian Embassy and Consulates vividly explained possible changes with captivating details, unlike the pre-1978 era, a convincing bilateral relationship was absent. Added to that, there was a frequent change in New Delhi's position *vis-à-vis* the Afghan Government.

A coup was in the offing in Kabul. The Indian Consulate at Kandahar detected unusual changes in the city and reported back to the home Government in New Delhi about the trajectory of the intricate development. In those days, the Kandahar Consulate used to exercise consular jurisdiction over the provinces of Zabul, Kandahar, Helmand, Nimroz, Farah, and Herat in Southern Afghanistan. The Kandahar region is known for its traditionally close trade contacts with India. In 1978, there were approximately 2000–2500 people of Indian descent settled in Kandahar town. All of them, without exception, were traders, both big and petty.[1]

Abrupt disruption in telephone communication and radio broadcasts on 27 April 1978 aroused suspicion in Kandahar about abnormal happenings in Kabul.[2] Residents of the city expected immense change in the functioning of the Government, and Afghans were curious to know what was in store for them. News about the coup, however, came to be known in the evening.

A military mutiny started at Jalalabad a week before the coup in Kabul. The mutiny on the night of 20/21 April 1978 in the Army garrison at Jalalabad was started by dissenting troops of an artillery unit. The Commander, Captain Islam Gul, refused to obey the orders of the Garrison Commander for the movement of his unit to Kunar to take part in the operations there. The commander said he was unwilling to be a party to the killing of his 'own Muslim brethren'. Rather than proceeding on the order of his superior, the rebel officers opened fire at the General Officer Commanding Major Behramuddin. Disillusioned and antipathetic like the troops of some units in the Jalalabad garrison, they rose in revolt, and in the fighting that ensued between the loyalists and rebels about 180 officers and men were killed on both sides, including two Soviet Military Advisors. Some sources put the figures of the dead at over 300. Among the large number of wounded was the 7th Artillery Brigade Commander Major Abdul Rahim, who was hit in the temple and removed to Kabul in a coma. Following the commencement of fighting in the garrison, armoured vehicles of the 81st Mechanized Brigade, Hadda, were ordered to besiege the embattled garrison, and para-commando units were also subsequently flown to Jalalabad. Following heavy bloodshed and Government warnings, the besieged rebels, mostly soldiers, surrendered on 21 April.[3]

Before starting any action in Jalalabad, the revolutionary army officers disconnected all telecommunications with Kabul and took into custody the Governor of Nangarhar and all Heads of Provincial Departments, including the Director of Intelligence, Police Chief, Financial Commissioner, Chief Judge, etc. These officers were identified by the Chief Organizer, Dr Khudaidad Basharmal, who accompanied the young officers. While Governor Rafiqi was sent to Kabul, all civilian officers were later released and allowed to function in their offices following the extension of allegiance to the new military regime.[4]

For India and Indian communities living in Afghanistan, Jalalabad was an important centre of commerce and culture. Jalalabad is the provincial headquarters of Nangarhar province and is situated on the Kabul–Peshawar highway at a distance of 150 km east of Kabul and 140 km northwest of Peshawar. The actual border of Pakistan at Torkham is at a distance of 76 km from Jalalabad, an eastern gateway of Afghanistan, through which not only tourists but also the bulk of goods from India and Pakistan have to pass. Sultanpur, a small town located at a distance of about 15 km from Jalalabad, is associated with Guru Nanak Dev Ji, who is believed to have rested there during his journey towards Mecca. The Afghan Hindus and Sikhs assemble and perform mass marriages there during the Baisakhi festival and camp there for a few days.[5]

On 27 April, young officers at the middle and low levels, mostly trained in the Soviet Union, of the Afghan Armed Forces had leanings towards the pro-Moscow Khalq Democratic Party (KDP) that overthrew the Government of President Mohammad Daoud.[6] According to the Afghanistan Government radio, President Daoud was shot dead when he refused to surrender to rebel troops at the presidential palace. His brother Mohammad Naim, members of his cabinet, and family lost their lives. The rebels, led by a high-ranking military officer named Colonel Abdul Qadir, employed tanks and artillery in Kabul's streets before taking over the Government with a military Revolutionary Council. With a poor economy and a population of 15 million population, Afghanistan had traditionally maintained closer ties with the Soviet Union and received aid from the United States.[7] On 1 May 1978, Noor Mohammad Taraki, the General Secretary of the Khalq Party, became the new Prime Minister and chairman of the ruling Revolutionary Council.[8] The Khalq Democratic Party of Afghanistan constituted a 35-member Central Revolutionary Council (CRC) to organize and direct the affairs of the Government.

As the battle for the throne engulfed Kabul, American Ambassador Mr Theodore Eliot issued an order asking 1,300 Americans residing in Kabul to remain inside and maintain absolute caution.[9] Three months later, on 23 July 1978, Mr Hodding Carter, a Department of State official, announced the withdrawal of 100 American Embassy staff and their dependants, leaving only 48 people in the Embassy. Outside government service, it was believed that 100 other Americans were living in the country, who were also asked to vacate Afghanistan as the civil war was intensifying.[10]

Reports from the Indian Embassy in Kabul stated that President Daoud's family had approached the French Embassy, which was situated closer to the Presidential Palace, for political asylum. Day-long fighting involving tanks, MIG fighters, and guns ended with nightfall. The radio broadcast announced that 'The power of the family has been put to an end. Now, for the first time, power has come into the hands of the people'. The radio announcement pledged to maintain friendly relations with all countries.

Frustration among these rebel officers over the Government's policy of promotion of its favourites and poor wages enraged the rank and file. Further discontent caused by the Government's failure to eradicate poverty, illiteracy, and backwardness had been growing, and these officers felt that a change of Government was essential. With this end in view, the rebels had been working on a plan of action to overthrow the Government. Diplomatic correspondence from Kabul stated that 'the way the Government of President Daoud has been overthrown and the change of Government successfully executed, the involvement of the USSR in preparing a plan of action cannot be ruled out'. The revolutionaries were led by their Soviet-trained leaders, Colonel Abdul Qadir and Colonel Aslam Watanyar. Colonel Qadir and Colonel Watanyar were pilot and tank commanders, respectively. On 27 April 1978, Colonel Qadir announced over Radio Afghanistan that a Revolutionary Council of the Armed Forces had been established and he was the head of the council.

The Jalalabad Garrison was captured by Lieutenant Colonel Ghulam Nabi and Capt. Sirajuddin, supported by young leftist officers. The GOC of the Garrison, Lieutenant General Yunus Khan, who had surrendered at gunpoint, was being held in custody by the new military rulers. Several men supporting the former Daoud Government were killed at Jalalabad when they refused to surrender to the new Military Administration. Former Agriculture Minister Azizullah Wasifi, who was trying to escape to Pakistan with Qadir Shah, a known smuggler, was arrested by a contingent of the leftist officers.[11]

In Kandahar, more or less, normalcy prevailed as there was no untoward incident even after the news about the coup was public. Shops remained open as usual and even late open-air cinema shows were not cancelled. There was no let-up in holiday crowds on 28 April 1978 at the popular picnic resorts in and around Southern Afghanistan, especially in Kandahar. Bus services from Kandahar to Herat and Lashkargah remained normal. Service to Kabul was disrupted for a day only, i.e. on 28 April, and telephone communication remained suspended from the afternoon of 27 April afternoon to 30 April 1978 and was resumed on 1 May 1978.[12] On 30 April 1978, the leader of the People's Democratic Party of Afghanistan (PDPA), Nur Mohammad Taraki, assumed power. The PDPA was formed on 1 January 1965 with Nur Mohammad Taraki and Babrak Karmal as leader and deputy leader, respectively.

By 5 May 1978, in Kabul, the rebel leaders pulled the tanks off the streets of the city. Almost the entire corps of soldiers in the revolution returned to their barracks. Gradually, the routine of Afghan life returned to the city within a week of the coup. Weeks after the coup, Noor Mohammad Taraki announced that 'the revolution has come. The people of Afghanistan are supreme, finally, after generations of oppression'. Government radio regularly proclaimed after the coup d'état, 'Come and see the way the oppressors lived on the wealth of the people'. Responding to the Government's call, tens of thousands of Afghan men and women queued through the elegant palace grounds never before opened to the public. Residents of Kabul and adjacent areas looked on in awe at the old royal family's luxurious lifestyle. Inside the palace, visitors longingly gazed at the 'delicate French furniture, the marble hallways, the gold picture frames and the heavy purple velvet draperies, symbols of wealth that contrast so sharply with their own mean lives'.

The coup in Kabul made the Indian Consulate staff in Kandahar anxious and uneasy. Security measures adopted by the Afghan Government included posting guards at the Indian Consulate as well as the Pakistani Consulate. Governor Mohammad Ayub Aiz was dismissed and placed under detention in Kandahar. He was replaced by Brigadier General Tohmas Rouf, who was designated as Governor-cum-Corps Commander. Rouf was earlier Chief of Staff in III Corps at Pakhtia.[13]

Immediately after the installation of the Noor Mohammad Taraki-led Communist government in Kabul, the 'Democratic Republic of Afghanistan' requested the Indian Embassy in Kabul to recognize the regime. The Soviet Union was the first country to afford it recognition, followed by Bulgaria and Cuba. On 1 May 1978, India recognized the new regime.

Taraki, in his radio address, refused to admit that his Government was communist, stating, 'technically there has never been a party under the name of the Communist Party in Afghanistan'. He accused the Western press of 'false propaganda' as he pointed out that many of the articles in the Government-controlled news media began 'In the name of Allah'.

Afghanistan is predominantly a Muslim country, where a significant portion of the population continues to adhere strictly to traditional interpretations of Islam. Unlike some other Islamic nations that have embraced modernization and contemporary lifestyles, Afghanistan has largely retained conservative and traditional social structures. Therefore, to appease Afghanistan's predominantly orthodox population, the communist-led Democratic Republic of Afghanistan deliberately declared that it would be guided by the principles of Islam. The strategy has been adopted by the party to delude the illiterate and conservative sections of society, mostly living in rural areas. To counterbalance the propaganda that the new Communist government was a threat to Islam, the KDP initiated several measures which, among others, included the increase in the salary of the Khatibs in the mosques and prompted statements at congregations in the mosques from some spiritual leaders in the country that the new Government led by the KDP was a Government of the oppressed and downtrodden and further that it would work for their betterment and progress.[14] To enlist the support of the minority Hindu and Sikh communities and also to give a secular look to it, the new Khalq Government accommodated some persons from the said communities when it gave them high positions in the administration. Such new appointees were further learnt to be members of the party.[15]

The Indian Consul General at Kandahar, P.K. Thakkar, had a meeting with the new Governor on 2 May 1978 after India had recognized Afghanistan. On the same day, the Indian Ambassador in Kabul, S.K. Singh, met the new Afghan President.[16] The new Governor at Kandahar was full of confidence about his capability to control the situation and informed the

Consul that a large number of public men had been calling on him to express their loyalties.

Capturing the palpable fear and volatility of the environment, a diplomatic cable from Kandahar explained that

> notwithstanding near normalcy in Kandahar, public, however, was afraid to talk even among themselves, leave aside their broaching the subject with foreigners. It was difficult to draw them out. They rather offered the impression of indifference and apathy on their part.[17]

The public, however, had shown reluctance to develop confidence in the new incumbents. The law-and-order situation in Kandahar town deteriorated during the last week of May 1978. There were two cases of murder and a number of robberies and thefts. India's assessment on the ground at Kandahar was different from what the protagonists of the April Revolution claimed. It stated that 'a large number of people at [the] lower level expressed satisfaction with the change but these feelings appeared to be born more out of their disenchantment with the previous regime rather than any spectacular expectations from the present set-up'.

As per the Indian Consul General's report, the new Government remained busy consolidating its position. There was a complete overwhelming of the civil administration in Kandahar. All of the members were committed members of the Khalq Democratic Party. The new Government started propaganda in the press and radio, which began affecting the general public. The man in the street, influenced by the promises of the new Government, was in the post-coup days pinning hopes on proper employment, reduction in prices, and the allotment of land for the construction of houses. The public also began to believe, to a great extent, the reports about the atrocities committed during Daoud's regime, rampant corruption, expatriation of capital, nepotism, and indifference towards the general welfare. The Khalq workers were endeavouring to convince the backward and orthodox Muslims that the new Government was not irreligious and would not go against Islamic tenets.[18]

The coup had impacted the non-resident Afghans the most. Afghan nationals, particularly Hindus and Sikhs, whose families were in India or other countries or whose children were studying in foreign countries, were reluctant to call them to Afghanistan. The main reason was that the Afghans feared that their families might face difficulties regarding passports, etc., which may hamper their return. There were very few tourists coming to Afghanistan.[19]

The opposition to the new regime from the rightist elements persisted. Restrictions were placed upon speeches by a prominent Mullah of Kandahar

Abdur Rab Akhundzadeh, who happened to be the Pesh Imam. While all the prominent Mullahs in Kandahar were in position, a few middle-ranking individuals did go underground or even crossed over to Pakistan. Reports also indicated that several religious teachers affiliated with the Tablighi Jamaat, a proselytizing group based in Pakistan, had entered Kandahar and were engaging in anti-regime propaganda within Afghanistan. They were particularly active in disseminating disinformation about the government among the traditionally conservative, orthodox, and rural populations in the tribal regions, who were more susceptible to such messaging.[20] According to some reports, the military Government in Pakistan had sent several Mullahs from Baluchistan and gave them Rs 10,000 each asking them to write articles against the Afghan Government, branding it pro-communist and irreligious, and appealing to the Muslims to oppose such a set-up. These reports further stated that these articles would ultimately be printed in book form and smuggled into Afghanistan at a later stage.[21]

Achakzais in Kandahar and Spin Boldak (Pakistan–Afghanistan border) areas were visibly displeased with the new Government. The Achakzai tribe claims closeness to the Mohamedzai tribe. In addition to clan loyalty, Achakzais resent restrictions imposed by the Taraki Government on trans-border smuggling, which had become their mainstay in the past. The new Government has also asked them to obtain Afghan identity cards. This step restricted their movements to Pakistan. Earlier, Achakzais enjoyed the best of both worlds by claiming Afghan and Pakistani nationalities depending on their convenience. Achakzais also formed a sizeable portion of the presidential guard during Daoud's time. A large number of them were killed on the eve of the coup. The families found it difficult to overcome the deprivation.[22]

A few Achakzai leaders organized a Fateha Ehawni for the late President Daoud and others killed during the coup in Chaman town on 14 July 1978. They also sacrificed two dozen cows and sheep on the occasion. The function was attended by nearly 1000 persons, including a large number of Pakistani officials and army officers located in Chaman. The Political Agent of Pishin was also reported to have attended the function. The Achakzais in Chaman also approached the Commercial Agent of Afghanistan and handed a letter to him addressed to Noor Mohammad Taraki, demanding *inter alia* that the dead bodies of Daoud and his family members should be handed over to them as they were the real heirs.[23]

The new Government faced formidable opposition from other sections of Afghan society as well. The Government faced partial opposition from the tribal belt of the Afghanistan–Pakistan border, and a large number of tribesmen belonging to Laghman, Kunar, Nangarhar, and Paktia provinces had refused to extend their allegiance to the new Government. A large number of these tribesmen, reportedly at the instigation of Mullah elements, had instead taken up arms against the regime. In several incidents in Kunar and Paktia provinces, scores of people, including security troops, were stated to have died, and following trouble in the Shigal, Shurtan, and Marwara areas of Kunar province, the Afghan Air Force used planes to shoot the rebels.[24]

India–Afghanistan Outreach in Troubled Times

The year 1978 witnessed dramatic changes not only in Afghanistan but also in Iran. Since these changes were internal, India continued with its policy of non-interference in any country's internal matters and recognized the new regimes in both Afghanistan and Iran with due alacrity. India's policy of beneficial bilateralism, meaningful cooperation, non-interference in internal affairs, and goodwill has created a general atmosphere of confidence and trust in the region.[25]

In this troubled time, the Government of India decided to send its Foreign Minister Atal Bihari Vajpayee to Kabul to strengthen India–Afghanistan relations. On 18 September 1978, Hafizullah Amin, Deputy Prime Minister and Minister of Foreign Affairs, welcomed his honourable guest Atal Bihari Vajpayee at Kabul Airport. Vajpayee made this official and friendly visit at the invitation of Amin.[26] The visit to Kabul by Foreign Minister Atal Bihari Vajpayee between 18 and 20 September 1978[27] was considered successful by the Afghan authorities. The visit went a long way in providing respectability and acceptability to the new Government. This was because the Government was in a 'weak' situation, considering the discovery of alleged anti-government plots and large-scale arrests and dismissals of civilian and military personnel.[28]

Strangely enough, although Vajpayee's visit was considered a success, a day later, on 21 September, Prime Minister Taraki clarified Afghanistan's disagreements with India on three pertinent issues. In a meeting with a group of Indian and Afghan journalists (the latter presumably included intentionally for posing questions on the role of India and Afghanistan in the Non-Aligned Countries' Group) on 21 September, Mr Taraki spelt out his Government's three main differences with India. Those were a) India's stance on Russian and Cuban support to Angola and Ethiopia was not in line with the thinking of Afghanistan, which justified the two countries' intervention as necessary; b) Afghanistan considered all socialist countries which were members of the non-aligned group as natural allies, while India presently did not; and c) Afghanistan did not favour the membership of such countries which were members of defence pacts (meaning Pakistan) in the Non-Aligned Nations, but India, according to Taraki, should not have recommended/sponsored the names of a member of a defence pact country for attending the meetings of the Non-Aligned Bureau.[29] India's reply to these scathing remarks is not known as it decided to keep quiet on these issues.

It was reported by diplomats in Afghanistan that the Afghan perception of Indian politics received a bit of a shock from the electoral defeat of the Indian National Congress in the general election of March 1977. Their 'normalization' process with Pakistan could, they felt, be affected by the unexpected removal of leaders of a political party whom Afghans thought they understood and could rely upon. The new leaders of India were to them a question mark. A few months after the defeat of the Indian National Congress in the Indian general elections, Atal Bihari Vajpayee visited Afghanistan in September 1977 before the military coup. He visited Kabul from 3 to 6 September 1977, accompanied by the Foreign Secretary and other officials.[30] Their doubts, even bewilderment, dissipated after the September 1977 visit to Kabul by Vajpayee. The candour and eloquence of Vajpayee made a deep and positive impact on the consciousness of Afghans.[31] Vajpayee maintained regular contact with the Afghan Government.

A couple of months after Vajpayee's Kabul visit, the fifth meeting of the Indo-Afghan Joint Commission, which was held in New Delhi from 8 to 13 December 1977, was attended by the Foreign Minister of India, while the Afghan delegation was led by M.K. Jalalar, Minister of Commerce.[32]

Vajpayee's September 1977 visit to Afghanistan, as well as his visit again a year later in September 1978, although portrayed as stories of grand successes, does not reflect the reality on the ground. The bureaucratic claim stands in contrast to this. Nevertheless, even when Afghanistan was entering a phase of civil war, India sustained her friendly bilateral relations and continued support for the economic development of Afghanistan.

In 1979, diplomatic correspondences from Kabul explained the economic difficulties the Afghan Government was facing. The report stated that the Government of Afghanistan was experiencing serious economic difficulties and its revenues had reached an all-time low. The main source of income of the Afghan Government in the past was the income from the export of dried fruits, carpets, and customs duty levied on imports of goods from other countries, which generally were smuggled to Iran and Pakistan. These imports included synthetic textiles, tea, motor tyres and motor parts, electronic gadgets including radios and tape recorders, blades, and ammunition for shotguns, etc. Following the imposition of restrictions on individual trade and government directions to the traders for forming cooperatives and charging a fixed percentage on the proforma invoice value, along with the Government's decision to monopolize certain items of export, the private traders were discouraged and disheartened. The inception of the communist regime and the introduction of socialistic policies led big traders decide to first reduce exports to the extent of local consumption and seemed to gradually wind down their business and move to those countries where they could conveniently stay and engage in free trade. India was the country that suited the Hindus and Sikhs, and Pakistan the Muslims. Given the Government's policies and traders' fears, there was a drastic reduction in imports, thus affecting the revenue from customs duty. It was estimated that the revenue from customs duty had gone down from 10 million Afghani per day to only 1.5 million Afghani per day. With the drastic reduction in trade, the revenue from income tax automatically went down. Because of these setbacks, the Government was suffering acute economic problems and was unable to pay the salaries of its employees belonging to various departments.[33]

Even before the April Revolution of 1978, about 250 Ikhwan-ul-Musalmeen (IUM) guerrillas earlier stationed in Pakistan reportedly arrived in Kabul in batches during the first week of April 1978. These guerrillas, who had shaved off their beards, which they had grown while living in Pakistan, were reported to have been given shelter by the IUM party leaders and supporters like former Minister Rawan Farhadi and Deputy Attorney General in the Ministry of Justice Gazi Hidayat. The group was led by Inayatullah, hailing from Tootu in the Khugiani area of Nangarhar province and a former student of Kabul University. The purpose of the visit of these guerrillas was not known. The IUM, however, had earlier had a plan to indulge in terroristic activities and liquidate its opponents, especially Khalq leaders.[34]

The Mullahs belonging to the areas across the border in Pakistan were reported to have started a propaganda campaign against the new Khalq Government which they dubbed communist and '*Kafir*' (non-believers). The new Government, according to them, posed a threat to the very existence of Islam both in Afghanistan and Pakistan. In several Jirgas held in the tribal areas, these Mullahs stated that the Soviet Reds had occupied Afghanistan and urged all Muslims to be prepared for a 'Jihad' (holy war) against these communists. The developments in the Kunar province were the result of the Mullah campaign.[35]

A large number of tribesmen opposed to the new Government belonging to Nooristan, Darra Pech, Asmar, and Shinwar areas of the eastern provinces were reported to have fled to Pakistan and taken shelter with the Pakistani authorities who had set up refugee camps.[36] Pakistan got involved with the development of its western neighbour. The setting up in Pakistan of the National Front for the Liberation of Afghanistan (NFLA), comprising eight parties, with Dr Burhanuddin Rabbani, a former Professor of Theology at Kabul University and a prominent IUM leader, as its General Secretary was announced in the last week of May 1978.[37] The NFLA aimed at uniting and organizing all the forces opposed to the new Khalq Government with the object of overthrowing it through an uprising with the support of the officers of the armed forces aligned to the front. The IUM leaders, stationed in Pakistan during the formation of the NFLA, prominently including Dr Rabbani, Maulvi Fazal Hadi Shinwari, Maulvi Jandar, Maulvi Khalis, and

Gulbuddin Hekmatyar, had been actively engaged in mustering support for the contemplated plan of action. While the military rulers of Pakistan led by General Zia-ul Haq assured all moral and material support, the Government of Saudi Arabia, through its Embassy in Islamabad, released huge sums of money to the NFLA for its proposed action. Pro-Zia circles were propagating that General Zia had given up the idea of a National Government in Pakistan. He also refused to conduct early elections to appropriately face the new developments in Afghanistan. The Military Government was endeavouring to attract the religious leaders from Afghanistan to Pakistan and also to throw some bait for the rebel Pashtuns.[38]

A large number of Afghan Army officers loyal to the previous Daoud regime were reported to have escaped to Pakistan immediately after the coup and were further learnt to have joined the IUM guerrillas stationed there. The opposition forces thus were jointly planning to stage an uprising in Afghanistan to overthrow the KDP Government. The contemplated plan envisaged an internal uprising by the people (for which a campaign to malign the Government offering a threat of extermination of Islam had been initiated), assassination of top Khalq Party leaders, and attacks on military/air bases. It was also learnt that about 5000 IUM commandos were being imparted special training for an attack on Baghlan and Shindand air bases with the object of killing pro-KDP Air Force officers and paralysing the Afghan Air Force.[39]

An intelligence report received from the Indian Embassy in Kabul stated that 'The Ikhwan-ul-Musalmeen cadres in Afghanistan had received instructions from their leadership in Pakistan to keep themselves in readiness for executing their contemplated plan of action against the KDP-led Government sometime after *Eid-ul-Fitr* of the year 1978'. The IUM cadres had further been informed that identity cards would be sent and the task to be assigned to each member of the party would be intimated shortly before the implementation of the contemplated plan. Intensive training in guerrilla warfare for the Ikhwanis financed by Saudi Arabia, had been offered in some camps at Abbottabad, Mansehra, and Attocks. Indian intelligence further stated that 'One Col. Din Mohammad of 8 Inf Div. Kabul, an active member of IUM, was said to be directing and controlling a cell of the IUM army officers in Kabul'.[40]

This intelligence report was shared with the Afghan Government, and what happened after that was not known. However, no senior leader of Khalq was killed in 1978.

Burhanuddin Rabbani, a senior leader of the IUM, who was stationed in Pakistan, visited the United Nations Headquarters in early August 1978 to appraise the UN Secretary General of the inhuman atrocities being perpetrated by the KDP Government. He pleaded for the restoration of political and civil liberties in the country by holding free and fair elections under the aegis of the UN.[41] The opposition leaders fleeing to Pakistan, especially the rightist Ikhwan-ul-Musalmeen party, which enjoyed the support of the Muslim world as well as perhaps the United States, were reported to have decided to resort to a major insurgency plan by guerrillas trained in Pakistan. The training programme started immediately after the April coup when the weather improved. The contemplated plan envisaged the explosion of bombs at crowded places, setting fire public buildings, disruption of roads and telecommunications, and the assassination of ruling KDP leaders and Russian advisors.[42]

The Afghan National Liberation Front, comprising several opposition parties based in Pakistan, had formed a shadow government with Sibghatullah Mojaddedi as its President. Other prominent members were Professor Rabbani, Musa Tawans, Gulbuddin Hikmatyar, former MP Mohd. Akbar, former Governor Mohd. Gul Sulemankhel, former MP Sadaqat, Maulvi Fazal Hadi Shinwari, and Afandi Agha. Earlier differences between Mojaddedi and Hikmatyar were said to have been resolved through the intervention of Jamaat-e-Islami leaders of Pakistan. The Front had issued a call for a 'Jihad' against the Afghan Government.[43]

The Jamat-e-Islami of Pakistan was the main conduit to transfer funds, which it received from Saudi Arabia and other oil-rich countries meant for Afghan dissidents. Besides food and shelter, the Afghan exiles were being trained in guerrilla warfare at several camps. According to a prominent Afghan dissident leader, the Front was hopeful of achieving success in its aims as, besides the realization of the unity of purpose among leaders of various groups, several Muslim countries, the US and China had started giving material assistance with the object of dislodging the Marxist regime. Shipments of arms from the People's Republic of China (PRC) and the United States were also said to have been received. Former Afghan President Daoud's nephew Aziz Naim, son of Sardar Naim, earlier living in Tehran, had moved to Peshawar and joined the Revolutionary Council set up by the opposition groups.[44]

Nearly for a year after the April 1978 coup, Pakistan exercised restraint concerning the coverage of the rebels' activities. But after a year, precisely since March 1979, Pakistan decided to give publicity through its information media. Following demonstrations and accusations by the Afghan Government of Pakistani involvement in anti-regime activities, Pakistan rather stepped up propaganda against Afghanistan.[45]

Leaving the Jamaat-e-Islami aside, Pakistan's intelligence arm, the Inter Services Intelligence (ISI), was directly involved with the mujahideen parties. The ISI's Afghan Bureau, operating primarily from Quetta and Peshawar, was headed by Brigadier Syed Raza Ali.[46] The headquarters of the Afghan

Bureau was at Ojhri Camp in Rawalpindi. The Afghan Bureau used to distribute arms to the Afghan Mujahideen. Numerous Afghan parties had been clamouring for arms and financial support from the ISI. The new ISI Director Lieutenant General Akhtar Abdul Rehman, who was appointed by General Muhammad Zia-ul Haq in June 1979, was not happy with Brigadier Raza Ali's opaque functioning.

Meanwhile, the Afghan Mujahideen parties resisting Soviet occupation had been creating havoc within the Afghan Bureau of the ISI, staking claim for more and more funds and weapons. They made it extremely difficult for the Pakistan Army to deal with myriad groups of Mujahideen. Field Commanders used to get arms and funds directly from the ISI. But as evident from the infamous 'Quetta Scandal' of 1983, the opportunities for corruption were so great, and with commanders being so numerous, together with a multiplicity of small parties, the system had become a nightmare.[47] In August 1983, the ISI's Afghan Bureau was hit with a shocking arms-selling scandal, later famous as the 'Quetta Scandal'. Three senior army officers of the Afghan Bureau, along with the Bureau Chief Brigadier Syed Raza Ali, were charged with selling arms on the open market and accepting bribes from Mujahideen Commanders in exchange for the issue of extra weapons, well above their allocations. The price of those weapons was higher on the open market in the Afghanistan–Pakistan frontier areas. The involved officers were arrested, court-martialed, and received jail terms, while the Bureau Chief Brigadier Raza Ali was reprimanded for his act of dereliction.[48] Raza Ali was dismissed from his position in September 1983 and demoted to a junior post within the bureau.[49] Brigadier Muhammad Yousaf, who was a Brigade Commander at Quetta, replaced Raza Ali to head the Afghan Bureau. The period starting from 1978, when the resistance began, up until 1983, the fighting in Afghanistan was chaotic and complicated by many issues. A formula was required to run the Afghan resistance.

After the takeover of the Afghan Bureau by Brigadier Muhammad Yousaf, the resistance strategy received a facelift. By October 1983, the Afghan Mujahideen were directed by General Zia-ul Haq and Prince Turkie, Head of Saudi Intelligence, to align with any of the 'Seven Parties' recognised by the Pakistan Army as the accredited Mujahideen eligible to receive funds and weapons. The ISI firmly informed the Mujahideen that every commander must belong to one of the seven parties; otherwise, he would not get any support from the ISI – 'no arms, no ammunition and no training'.[50] The heads of the seven parties were asked to be stationed in Peshawar. A party means one of the seven Afghan resistance political parties.[51] There was a complicated system of parties and leadership. The political heads of each party are different from Field Commanders, who fight on the ground. Rarely does a political leader venture into the battlefield. They resided in Pakistan but frequently visited Afghan battlefields to meet senior commanders at their bases. The Mujahideen commanders received their instructions, reinforcements, supplies and material support from their party bosses. During the Afghan resistance, some of the leaders were criticized and condemned by soldiers and resistance fighters for their soft living, smart cars, and well-furnished villas. However, it was part of the age-old cantankerous disdain of the soldiers who complained that they risked their lives to enable their countrymen to live a safe and peaceful life while the civil leaders of the country always enjoyed a life of comfort and luxury.

All these seven parties used to receive most of the total grant allocated by the ISI for Afghan Jihad. However, a small percentage of money and weapons was distributed to special recruits directly. The seven parties comprised the following groups:[52]

1. Hizb-i-Islami (Party of Islam): The Hizb-i-Islami is led by Gulbuddin Hekmatyar, who has been affiliated with the Egyptian Islamic organization the Muslim Brotherhood since the 1970s. Hekmatyar is a Pashtun, and most of his followers belong to the same ethnic group, the biggest in Afghanistan. He was strongly backed by Pakistan and also heavily funded by Saudi Arabia.
2. Jamiat-i-Islami (Islamic Society): The Jamiat-i-Islami is led by Burhanuddin Rabbani, a former professor and theologian at Kabul University, whose party consists primarily of ethnic Tajiks from the north of the country. Ahmad Shah Massoud, also of Tajik background, was his Defence Minister. Although Massoud refused to take the Defence Minister position officially, he was defending Rabbani's Government until 1996, when the Taliban entered Kabul.
3. Itehad Islami (Islamic Unity): Itehad Islami is led by former Professor Abdul Rasul Sayaf, who received most of his support from radical elements in Saudi Arabia, Iraq, and other Muslim countries.
4. Hezb-i-Islami (Party of Islam): The Hizb-i-Islami is led by Moulavi Younis Khalis, an Islamic scholar, former teacher, and journalist. Originally with Hekmatyar, Khalis, being a traditional Islamist, split from the former in 1979. His party was called Hezb-i-Islami (Party of Islam), the same as Gulbuddin Hekmatyar's party. The two are commonly differentiated as Hezb-i-Islami (Khalis) and Hezb-i-Islami (Gulbuddin).
5. Mahaz-i-Milli Islam (National Islamic Front of Afghanistan): The Mahaz-i-Milli Islam is led by Pir Sayed Ahmad Gilani, leader of the powerful Qadiri Sufi sect.
6. Jabha-i-Nijat-Milli (Afghan National Liberation Front): The Jabha-i-Nijat-Milli is led by Sibghatullah Mojadidi, a religious leader from Kabul and a royalist.

7. Harakat-i-Inquilab-i-Islami (Islamic Revolutionary Forces): The Harakat-i-Inquilab-i-Islami is led by clergyman Mohammad Nabi Mohammadi, whose party's membership was derived from the intellectuals of Afghanistan and Pakistan.⁵³

As per the authorized writings of former Afghan Bureau chief Brigadier Muhammad Yousaf, once the system was formalized and parties were established, the ISI's Afghan Bureau started providing training to the Mujahideen. From 1984 until 1987, the ISI's Afghan Bureau trained 80,000 Mujahideen. The Afghan Bureau, as per Brigadier Yousaf, was comprised of 300 Non-Commissioned Officers (NCOs), 100 Junior Commissioned Officers (JCOs), and 60 officers.

Cold War Politics and Afghanistan's Descent into Civil War

When the land of Afghanistan was getting prepared to embrace a long spell of civil war, on 14 February 1979, the United States Ambassador to Afghanistan, Adolph Dubs, was abducted in the street of Kabul by a group of Afghans. Mr Dubs's car was stopped by four armed men at about 8:45 am as he was going to the Embassy. The kidnappers were described as right-wing Muslim terrorists. They shot the Ambassador dead in broad daylight. There was a lot of confusion about the circumstances that led to Mr Dubs's death. Afghan radio reported that the abductors were wearing the uniform of Kabul traffic policemen and drove the Ambassador to the Hotel Kabul in the downtown section of the capital. A different report said the envoy was 'dragged from his car' and taken away. Mr Dubs was taken to a room in the hotel, which had been surrounded by the security men. The accounts said the abductors demanded the release of men described as Muslim 'religious figures' who they said were being held by the leftist Government of Prime Minister Noor Mohammad Taraki. The Government later denied that any such people were in custody. It was unclear whether 58-year-old Mr Dubs was killed by his abductors, as they had threatened, or was shot when Government Security aides rushed into the hotel where he was being held.⁵⁴ Immediately after the incident, the US responded with due urgency and urged the security forces to wait and not take any action against the abductors so that they might not endanger Dubs's life. But the Afghan police disregarded these pleas to negotiate and attacked on the advice of Soviet officers.

President Jimmy Carter's administration was outraged by the murder of the Ambassador and began immediate disengagement from Afghanistan. By July 1979, the US reduced its Embassy staff to 20, cancelled humanitarian and military aid, and started sympathizing with the rebels. It terminated all economic support by December 1979, when Soviet troops occupied Afghanistan.

Anti-regime activities of the rebels were on the increase during June and July of 1979 in Jadran, Khost, Tani, and Jaji Maidan areas of Paktia. The rebels adopted hit-and-run tactics in the skirmishes with the Government Security Forces during the night and thus caused loss of life and property. The civil administration virtually has very little or no control in the rural areas of the province. The Afghan Air Force has also failed to dislodge the rebels from their hideouts in the mountains along the Pak-Afghan border. Pakistani military personnel in civilian dress had been guiding the insurgency operations of the rebels and participating in the skirmishes against the Government Security Forces.[55]

The long-simmering rivalry between the two factions of the PDPA was exposed in June 1979. The PDPA was founded in 1965 but split into two factions – Parcham and Khalq – in 1967. They were reunited in 1977 at the Soviet's urging. The Parchamists, led by Babrak Karmal, drew support from a small segment of the educated upper classes in the Kabul area and advocated a gradualist approach to building socialism in Afghanistan. They participated in the free elections that were held in the late 1960s during the period of the monarchy and even won a few seats in parliament. The Khalqis, led by Taraki, drew their support from the newly emerging middle class in Afghanistan and favoured a more conspiratorial approach to seizing power. They concentrated on seeking clandestine recruits among the Afghan military.

In late June and July 1978, Taraki, relying on the support of the military, moved to exile most of the leaders of the Parcham faction; Babrak Karmal was named Ambassador to Prague. The Soviets acquiesced in his power play. The Soviets also acquiesced a month later when Taraki moved to eliminate potential rivals in the military as well as the few remaining Parchamists still in the Government. When Taraki ordered the exiled Parchamists to return home in early September 1978 to face certain imprisonment and possibly even a death sentence, the Soviets gave them safe haven in Eastern Europe.[56]

Since the leading actors in the Afghan Government indulged in infighting, the country was slipping into civil war mode. There was indiscipline and desertion in the army rank and file. As per the United States Government report as of 14 August 1979, the Afghan Army, which had 80,000 men when Noor Mohammad Taraki seized power in a coup on 27 April 1978, had been heavily hit by desertions, which stood as high as 40,000 defections.[57] In 1984, the Indian Military Attaché in Kabul prepared a report about the desertions in the Afghan Army. The report estimated that between 18,000 and 23,000 troops and paramilitary personnel deserted the armed forces during the year 1984.[58] As per Indian assessments, not all deserters joined forces with the Mujahideen. Many of them disappeared into the countryside with weapons owing to their disillusionment with the Government, while some of them acted as bandits to earn a living.

It was widely reported by international media that by mid-1979, Afghanistan was virtually in the midst of a civil war. There was widespread rebellion in the countryside. The Government forces were consolidated around the capital, where the civilian population was reportedly terrorized by frequent executions and random imprisonment.[59] The sustained military resistance had created a problem for the Soviet Union, which backed the Taraki regime but significantly with fewer men, accounting for no more than 4500 Soviet military and civilian advisers in Afghanistan. Although the Soviet intervention in Afghanistan was touted as 'their Vietnam', a reference to America's ill-fated war in Vietnam, nobody denied Afghanistan's strategic significance for the national security of the Soviet Union. Afghanistan used to share a border with Soviet Uzbekistan. The same peoples – Tajiks, Kalmuks, and Uzbeks – live on both sides of the border. For Russia, local insurrection with an element of Islamic holy war aroused fears of contagion. Beyond that, the birth rate in Soviet Central Asia was far greater than that in the Russian Republic and Ukraine. In these terms, turbulence in Afghanistan could be perceived as a matter of national security by the Soviet Union.

However, Afghan traditions for resistance increased the prospects of a long war. Added to this, the Americans were vowing to apply appropriate and equal force against the Soviet intervention. On 3 August 1978, President Jimmy Carter asked the Russians to refrain from Afghanistan. Zbigniew Brzezinski, his adviser for national security, cited 'prudent' American restraint during the Iranian crisis and said: 'We expect others similarly to abstain from intervention and from efforts to impose alien doctrines on deeply religious and nationally conscious peoples'.[60]

The Afghan Government led by Taraki had been split over the inability of the army to put down a rebellion by Muslim tribesmen, who are said to control about half the countryside. The split led to an internecine fight and a palace shootout at Arg Palace in Kabul. The gun battle began on 14 September 1979 after Prime Minister Hafizullah Amin had announced cabinet changes that removed supporters of Taraki. Supporters of Taraki were outgunned by followers of Amin, who then declared himself head of state and party.

Taraki, who was replaced by Hafizullah Amin on 16 September 1979, died on 18 September from gunshot wounds received during the gun battle on 14 September. According to Kabul Radio, President Amin met Ambassador Aleksandr M. Puzanov of the Soviet Union at his office on 17 September, the day after the violence.[61] Only a week before his ousting, Taraki was photographed with President Leonid I. Brezhnev during his stopover in Moscow on his way back from the non-aligned conference in Havana. President Brezhnev had promised 'all necessary help' to the Taraki Government to deal with the dozens of insurrections flaring throughout Afghanistan. It was speculated that Amin learnt that Taraki, with probable Soviet support, was planning to move against him. He acted first and emerged from the shootout in control of the state, the party, and the army.

Although the Soviets had been supporting Amin, there was evidence that the Soviet Government was dismayed when its Afghan friend, Taraki, was deposed. For Russia, the descent into a quagmire in Afghanistan began shortly after army units loyal to Taraki's Khalq Party toppled the Government of Mohammad Daoud in April 1978. Daoud, who was killed in the coup, had made some effort to weaken Soviet influence in his country by turning to Saudi Arabia and other Islamic states. Nonetheless, Russia insisted that the coup caught it by surprise. However, within a few months of seizing power, the Khalq Party cemented ties with Russia, and civilian and military advisers, up to 5000 in all, were sent to Afghanistan from the Soviet Union. On 5 December 1978, a 'Treaty of Friendship, Good Neighbourliness, and Cooperation between Afghanistan and the USSR' was concluded.[62]

On the surface, Russia maintained cordial relations, and the press spoke glowingly of Amin's efforts to rebuild Afghanistan and restore order. However, the Soviet leaders were understood to have been dissatisfied with his lack of popular support and his repressive ways. Soviet Russia was unhappy with President Hafizullah Amin, who received his degree from the United States; therefore, the Russians considered him an unpredictable partner. They wanted to remove him and install a more friendly leader instead. The Russian secret service, the KGB, reported that he was trying to ally with the United States. They reportedly felt that he should have pursued conciliation with the Muslim tribesmen who were rebelling against Soviet-backed rule. Amin's brutal methods to quell the revolt and crush rivals had generated large-scale public criticism against the communist rule. As Amin's policies contributed to the demoralization of the army and the strengthening of the insurgents, Soviet policymakers were believed to have turned their thoughts to another Afghan revolutionary leader, Babrak Karmal, who headed the party's Parcham wing. On 25 December, airborne Soviet troops landed at Bagram and Kabul. The Kremlin decided to remove Amin, and on 27 December, Soviet special forces or the Spetsnaz surrounded the President's residence, Tajbeg Palace. Codenamed 'Operation Storm 333', the Soviet special forces stormed the Tajbeg Palace.[63] Amin's food was poisoned, and hundreds of Soviet special forces stormed the palace to kill Amin and his family members. The Soviet forces killed President Hafizullah Amin, seized important Government installations in Kabul, and installed Babrak Karmal as his successor on 28 December. Since then, Soviet occupation became more obvious as thousands of troops and hundreds of planes and tanks crossed into Afghanistan in the following days. Resistance against the Soviet occupation started immediately by various groups and warlords in Afghanistan.

Before his rise to power, Babrak Karmal was living in exile in Czechoslovakia. He had gone to Prague as Afghanistan's Ambassador in June 1978 after having served less than two months as Vice President and Deputy Prime Minister in the revolutionary Government of President Noor Mohammad Taraki. Anahita Ratebzad, who married Karmal after having served for years as a political associate, was shunted off to Yugoslavia. She served as Ambassador to Yugoslavia until the September 1978 purge. But the purge of Government elements from Karmal's faction, Parcham, continued, and in September of 1978 he was dismissed as Ambassador and ordered home to face charges of plotting a coup against President Taraki. He ignored the order and stayed in Czechoslovakia as a private citizen. For years, Karmal's Parcham faction waged intensive political and ideological warfare against the Khalq, which became the People's Democratic Party, but by mid-1977 the two groups had come together and staged the 1978 coup against President Daoud.[64]

The Carter Administration decided to publicize Moscow's military role in the Afghan civil war and said that during early December 1979, the Soviet Union had significantly increased its support for the Marxist Government's drive against Muslim insurgents. On 22 December 1979, the Carter Administration announced that the Soviet Union had moved three army divisions to its border with Afghanistan and sent at least 1500 combat soldiers into the country. They said that more than 30,000 soldiers had been placed on alert near the Afghan border and that three battalions of armoured and airborne troops had been flown to an air base near Kabul and Bagram.[65] Since January 1979, Soviet military advisers had taken over virtual control of the Afghan Army, and by the end of 1979, Soviet pilots had reportedly flown helicopter gunships in missions against the insurgents.[66]

On 28 December 1979, President Jimmy Carter warned Soviet Union President Leonid I. Brezhnev on the hotline that the Soviet actions 'if not corrected, could have very serious consequences for United States-Soviet relations'. The message specifically called for a troop withdrawal.[67] In a public statement from the White House, President Carter stated that the Soviet military intervention in Afghanistan, which has now resulted in the overthrow of the established Government and the execution of the President of that country, has caused increased concern about peace and stability in the region. Such gross interference in the internal affairs of Afghanistan is in blatant violation of accepted international rules of behaviour. This is the third occasion since the Second World War that the Soviet Union has moved militarily to assert control over one of its neighbours, and this is the first such venture into a Muslim country since the Soviet occupation of Iranian Azerbaijan in the 1940s. The Soviet action was a major matter of concern to the entire international community.[68]

The Soviet Union responded on 28 December 1979, stating that its military intervention in Afghanistan was a response to a request for military assistance by the Government of Afghanistan against the provocations of external enemies. The statement issued by the Soviet Union stated:

> The Government of the Democratic Republic of Afghanistan, taking into account the continuing and broadening interference and provocations of external enemies of Afghanistan, and with a view to defending the gains of the April revolution, territorial integrity and national independence and maintaining peace and security, proceeding from the treaty of friendship, good neighbourliness and cooperation of 5 December 1978, has approached the USSR with an insistent request for urgent political, moral and economic aid, including military aid, which the Government of the Democratic Republic of Afghanistan repeatedly requested from the Government of the Soviet Union previously. The Government of the Soviet Union has met the request of the Afghan Government.[69]

Civil War in Afghanistan and India's Afghan Policy

The Soviet intervention placed India at odds so far as its Afghan policy was concerned. India's Afghan policy faced a strange dilemma, especially when America was openly espousing a pro-Pakistan tilt with an explicit intention to counter the Soviet Union in Afghanistan and take revenge for the Vietnam War.

President Carter displayed particular concern about the possibility of the Soviet troops continuing to Pakistan, and the US National Security Advisor Zbigniew Brzezinski went out of his way to affirm the American security agreement with Pakistan that dated from the 1950s. President Carter indicated that the United States was going to increase military aid to Pakistan. This announcement was significant because, except for minor training programmes, the United States had supplied no military assistance to Pakistan since the 1971 war with India until 1979. The United States stopped sending arms to Pakistan after the 1971 Indo-Pak war for several important reasons. First, Pakistan used American weapons – meant only for self-defense – against India and in violent actions during the crackdown in East Pakistan (now Bangladesh). This misuse caused anger in the U.S., especially among members of Congress and human rights groups. The Pakistani government's role in the mass killings during the Bangladesh Liberation War was widely condemned, and many in the U.S. called it genocide. As a result, there was strong pressure on the Nixon administration to stop military support to Pakistan. Later, in the mid-1970s, the U.S. Congress passed laws (like the Symington Amendment) that banned aid to countries working on nuclear weapons outside the Nuclear Non-Proliferation Treaty (NPT). Pakistan's secret nuclear programme triggered these restrictions and led to even tighter limits on U.S. arms. However, this changed in 1979 when the Soviet Union invaded Afghanistan. Pakistan became an important ally for the U.S. in stopping Soviet expansion in the region. This led the Carter administration to restart military aid and arms supplies to Pakistan to support its role in helping the Afghan Mujahideen. In 1975, the United States lifted an embargo imposed on military sales to Pakistan and India and said it would sell limited supplies on a case-by-case basis. This aid amounted to about $40 million to Pakistan in 1978. In April 1979, because of concern that Pakistan was developing nuclear weapons, the United States, as mandated under law, cut off all existing aid, which was only economic assistance and the small training mission.[70]

As the situation unfolded in Afghanistan, in New Delhi the then Soviet Ambassador Yuli Vorentsov rang up the joint secretary in charge of Eastern Europe, Arvind Deo, seeking an appointment with Prime Minister Charan Singh late at night on 27 December 1979. Charan Singh was not available, nor was then Foreign Minister Shyam Nandan Mishra. Ultimately, the Soviet Ambassador met with the Foreign Secretary, R.D. Sathe, around midnight. Vorentsov explained the rationale of the Soviet military intervention to Sathe verbally and said he had a message for the Prime Minister, Charan Singh, from Soviet General Secretary Leonid Brezhnev, which he would like to deliver as early as possible.[71]

Ambassador Vorentsov met Prime Minister Charan Singh on 28 December. General elections were scheduled in India by the end of January 1980 and, therefore, Charan Singh was in the last days of his tenure. However, unfazed by his lame duck stature, Charan Singh categorically told the Soviet Ambassador that the Soviet military intervention was unacceptable, particularly since the intervention had taken place against a close neighbour of India and a non-aligned country. He urged that Soviet troops should withdraw from Afghanistan as early as possible. Charan Singh also said that India would generally articulate the same views in Moscow and also at the UN. The Indian prime minister stood by his convictions, and India issued a statement regretting the Soviet intervention in Afghanistan and asking for the withdrawal of Russian troops. India's Permanent Representative to the UN, Brajesh Mishra, was instructed to inform all other UN delegations and the UN secretariat about the policy response of Prime Minister Charan Singh, which he did in the first half of January 1980.[72]

Indian and Soviet strategic interests began to diverge with the Soviet invasion of Afghanistan in 1979, which was undertaken without India's foreknowledge. From New Delhi's perspective, Pakistan replaced Afghanistan as India's western buffer, and its concern about Soviet intentions in Pakistan increased. From Moscow's perspective, Islamabad's support for the Afghan resistance gave Moscow an interest in neutralizing Pakistan that went beyond support for India's strategic concerns.[73]

However, political leadership changed rather swiftly in New Delhi. The Congress Party won the general elections, and Mrs Indira Gandhi was back as Prime Minister on 14 January 1980. Circumvented by India's dependence on the Soviet Union and the utility of the superpower to counter American and Chinese hegemony in South Asia, she reversed the policy of her predecessor. While she publicly supported the Afghan revolutionaries, Mrs Gandhi appealed to the Soviets to withdraw over a period of time. On 23 January 1980, in an interview with the *Daily Express*, Mrs Gandhi opined that the Soviets would leave Afghanistan as soon as possible. She said,

> Our problem here is not to take sides. We are only concerned with India. We are not in one bloc or the other. But Russia feels everyone is pressing them. They have told me that they will leave Afghanistan as soon as possible. They have definitely said they will go.

Asked how soon that might be, she was quoted: 'I do not know. But they say they will go'.[74]

She further added that the events in Afghanistan had to be viewed in an international context. 'If the Russians feel encircled – as they tell me they do – then they were bound to react, but their real obsession is with the Chinese'.[75] India did not oppose the Russian move publicly or ever indulge in diplomatic polemics against the Soviets.

Immediately after assuming the charge, Mrs Indira Gandhi summoned Mr Brajesh Mishra and directed him to change the earlier position as articulated by Mr Charan Singh. Mr Brajesh Mishra tried to convince the Prime Minister to continue with Mr Charan Singh's view, as a change of policy may affect India's reputation. Mrs Gandhi overruled him, and the Government of India sent him a statement prepared by Mr G. Parthasarathi, the Policy Planning Advisor to the Prime Minister, and Mr T.N. Kaul, Former Foreign Secretary, fully supporting the Soviet intervention, which Mr Brajesh Mishra was asked to make at the concerned UN fora. Mr Brajesh Mishra obliged with the Government of India's directive but noted his dissent. Unhappy with his protest, Mrs Indira Gandhi removed Mr Brajesh Mishra from his position and appointed Mr N. Krishnan as India's Permanent Representative to the UN. Mr Mishra was asked to take up another post, which he declined.

He joined the UN as the Secretary-General's Special Representative in Namibia and eventually retired from that post.[76]

But despite Mrs Gandhi's assertive support for the Soviets, India was moving cautiously on the Afghan issue. In March 1980, India refused to contemplate the idea of an international conference in which the United States, the Soviet Union, China, India, Pakistan, Afghanistan, and other countries could participate in the pattern of the earlier India–China conferences. The Government of India was aware that the US and the Soviet Union continued to keep in touch through various channels to make their strong feelings or views known on various developments in each other's actions. However, they were not ready to engage in any formal discussion on Afghanistan. There was no consensus yet within the non-aligned community on what could be done to bring about a peaceful settlement and how it should proceed to prevail upon the two superpowers to avoid the perils of further escalation. There was some satisfaction in Delhi that India had made some headway in trying to isolate the Afghan factor from India–Pakistan relations. The fact that India was strongly opposed to any large-scale rearming of Pakistan by the US in the name of preventing a spillover of Soviet influence from Afghanistan into the subcontinent had not proved to be an insuperable barrier to the moves for an early resumption of the Shimla process of normalization.[77]

The Indian strategy was to carry forward its diplomatic efforts to improve relations with Pakistan before engaging in any major initiative for settling the Afghan issue. India continued to explore the possibilities of a peaceful settlement to pave the way for Soviet withdrawal and the restoration of the independence and non-aligned status of Afghanistan. But at the same time, it had no intention of allowing itself to be pushed around by busybodies who wanted to stampede it into initiating any premature moves without assessing the consequences of failure.[78]

Prime Minister Mrs Gandhi, who returned from Belgrade on 10 May 1980, spoke rather cautiously about the possibility of India taking any fresh initiative to resolve the Afghan problem. Answering the newsmen's questions on arrival, she said everybody thinks that India can play an important role in this connection, but I do not think it is as simple as that, particularly when many world issues are involved. She said, before taking any initiative, 'we have to consider what results it will yield'. Mrs Gandhi said 'India had already taken some initiative but no new initiative was mooted at Belgrade. Everybody there was for a solution for various crises in the world. The question was how to make a breakthrough'.[79]

The Afghanistan crisis was giving sleepless nights to Indian policymakers. Foreign Secretary, R.D. Sathe, visited Kabul in May 1980 while Foreign Minister, Narasimha Rao, visited Moscow from 3 to 7 June 1980 to meet his Soviet counterpart Andrei Gromyko. During the visit, matters of mutual interest were discussed, leading to a clear understanding of each other's points of view.[80] Just before one of the sessions, the Indian delegation received news about Soviet troops and Afghan police having fired on a procession of schoolgirls in Kabul who were protesting against the Soviet military presence. Mr Narasimha Rao asked Mr Gromyko during the full delegation meeting how the Soviet Union could justify opening fire on schoolgirls. They were only taking part in a procession and they were not armed. Gromyko told Mr Narasimha Rao that the Afghans were the agents of the counter-revolutionary forces and religious fanatics, that these schoolgirls were trying to hinder the modernization of Afghanistan and that those who opposed the Afghan revolution and reforms deserved to die.[81] Such was the policy of Russian ruthlessness in Afghanistan.

India conveyed the message to the world that it is against the presence of foreign troops and bases in any country.[82] The traditionally friendly relations between India and Afghanistan continued through 1979–1980 and India considers the domestic political developments in Afghanistan during this period as the internal affairs of Afghanistan.

Making the best of what India considered a bad situation, the Indian leadership pressed the Soviets for more advanced military equipment at reduced prices to match the US support for Pakistan. The USSR and India signed a comprehensive arms agreement worth approximately $2.4 billion in May 1980. India had a key place in Moscow's Afghan policy. The USSR valued India as a potential threat to Pakistan and as the most important Third World country that had not condemned the Soviet occupation. New Delhi's refusal to condemn Moscow had helped keep the Soviets attentive to India's requirements. In dealing with New Delhi, Moscow had minimized the role of the Afghan War in stimulating Pakistan's military build-up, denied that it had regional ambitions, and encouraged the notion that the Soviet presence in Afghanistan keeps Pakistan from directing its full attention to India. The Soviets had sought to undermine improvements in India–Pakistan relations with a steady stream of articles in leftist Indian newspapers and magazines warning India of Pakistani duplicity.[83]

By August 1980, there was a marked slowdown of Indian diplomacy on Afghanistan because of the growing realization that nothing more could be done to break the ice until the two superpowers were ready to talk to each other about the wider ramifications of the crisis in the region. It has not deviated from the initial stand that while the Soviet intervention should not be viewed in isolation, the continued presence of Soviet forces rules out the possibility of any accord for restoring peace in Afghanistan or reducing the big power rivalries in the region.[84]

During 1980–1981, the Government of India was in touch with the countries working towards a solution.[85] R.D. Sathe, Foreign Secretary, and Shri S.K. Singh, Additional Secretary in the ministry, visited Kabul and met the Afghan leaders. The Minister of External Affairs, on more than one occasion, held talks with the Foreign Minister of Afghanistan in New York. India's stance on Afghanistan was guided by the principles that (i) There should be no interference or intervention in the affairs of one country by any other country by the use of armed force; (ii) There should be no effort to destabilize existing regimes by interference or subversion from outside; and (iii) There should be no destabilization of the South Asian region by excessive induction of arms, the entry of great power influence and resultant confrontation.[86] India's stance on the Soviet Union's intervention in Afghanistan was largely shaped by considerations of national interest. The three stated principles were broad in scope and expressed in highly diplomatic language. There was no explicit criticism of the Soviet action; in effect, India's so-called principled position amounted to an implicit endorsement of the Soviet intervention. India considered the situation in Afghanistan as a ripe and fit case for Soviet intervention because America and China used Pakistani militants and domestic insurgents to alter the nature of the Government in Afghanistan.

The Afghans were, however, disappointed with India's response to the Soviet intervention. Major General Samay Ram, who was India's Military Attaché in Kabul from May 1982 to March 1986, explained in plain language how Afghans felt let down by India for the lack of support when they most needed it, and always expressed their feelings, though in a guarded manner, so as to show no disrespect to India or to Indian staff in Afghanistan.[87]

Nevertheless, India continued its normal friendly ties with Afghanistan. The Foreign Minister of Afghanistan, Shah Mohammed Dost, arrived in Delhi on 7 September 1981 on his way back to Kabul from his visits to Algeria, Syria, and Ethiopia, for talks with the External Affairs Minister, P.V. Narasimha Rao. During his one-day stopover in New Delhi, he discussed the negative Pakistani response to the latest Afghan proposals for talks in the presence of the UN Secretary General or his representative to explore the possibilities of a political settlement. On 25 August 1981, Afghanistan sent a proposal suggesting bilateral or trilateral talks with Iran and Pakistan under UN auspices. The Afghan Minister briefed the Prime Minister, Mrs Indira Gandhi, and Mr Narasimha Rao on all aspects of the Afghan problem, which was to be addressed at the Commonwealth conference in Melbourne and during the UN General Assembly session. Foreign Minister Dost arrived with a letter from President Babrak Karmal to Mrs Gandhi explaining the scope of the latest proposals and seeking India's continued support in evolving a political settlement of the problem. The Indian view was that the latest Afghan offer could serve as a good starting point for talks with Pakistan under UN auspices as a prelude to a peaceful solution. The Secretary General, Dr Kurt Waldheim, has kept India informed of the outcome of the talks that his Special Representative, Mr Javier Perez de Cuellar, has had in Kabul and Islamabad on the subject.[88]

During the 1981 UN General Assembly (UNGA) Sessions, Dr Waldheim tried a joint meeting with the Foreign Ministers of Afghanistan and Pakistan, but it was not possible because the Pakistani dictator General Zia-ul Haq did not want his Foreign Minister, Mr Aga Shahi, to meet Mr Dost even informally at the UN while Pakistan was engaged in wide-ranging discussions with the US for the acquisition of American arms. At one stage during the 1980 UNGA, Mr Narasimha Rao tried to bring Mr Shahi and Mr Dost to a private dinner in his hotel suite in New York. However, the Pakistan Foreign Minister backed out at the last moment after first accepting the invitation.[89]

The UN General Assembly on 18 November 1981 adopted a resolution on 'the situation in Afghanistan and its implications for international peace and security', which had been tabled by members of the Islamic Conference. The resolution 'called for the immediate withdrawal of foreign troops from Afghanistan and a political solution in accordance with the provisions of the UNGA resolution' by a vote of 116 in favour, 23 against, and 12 abstentions. India abstained on the resolution. A similar resolution was adopted by the UNGA in August 1980, with 111 votes in favour, 22 against, and 12 abstentions.[90]

In January 1982, J.N. Dixit was appointed as the Ambassador of India in Kabul. In his book *An Afghan Diary*, Dixit stated that on 11 January 1982, referring to Afghanistan, Mrs Gandhi stated that

> The situation is static and will remain so. Russians will not move out. Americans and Pakistanis wish the Russians to stay on. It suits their purpose. India should be correct, should maintain and sustain long-term linkages with Afghan people, must not antagonize the Soviets or arouse their suspicion. We must try and increase Indian presence and influence in Afghanistan. Keep an eye on Pakistani and Iranian activities in Afghanistan.[91]

In an official document released by the Ministry of External Affairs in 1982, India noted her stance on the situation concerning Afghanistan as guided by the following principles: (i) Opposition to all forms of external interference or intervention in the domestic affairs of the countries of the region; (ii) Opposition to the extension of the quarrels of other countries and the induction of cold-war tensions into the region; (iii) Respect for the independence, sovereignty, territorial integrity and the non-aligned status of the countries of the region; and (iv) Preference for a negotiated political solution to problems through dialogue among the parties concerned.⁹²

If we compare what Mrs Gandhi stated to the Indian Ambassador privately and what the official policy was as stated by the MEA release and also by Mrs Gandhi during her various public interactions, the gap is visible. Publicly, India adopted the policy of seeking Soviet withdrawal from Afghanistan, but secretly and practically, its stance was different whereby it supported every Soviet move in Afghanistan. Because of this gap in India's response to the Afghan crisis, the Afghans were annoyed with India. Stoically, India had all the information about the Soviet plan. On 12 March 1982, the Russian Ambassador in Kabul, Mr F.A. Tabeev told the Indian Ambassador J.N. Dixit:

> We have come here to stay. We would not allow the Pashtoons to dominate the other tribes of Afghanistan who have linkages with the peoples of the Central Asian Republics of the Soviet Union. We want a Parcham-dominated ruling party; we will maintain the necessary force levels to keep this country under control.⁹³

Amrullah Saleh, former associate of Ahmed Shah Massoud and former Director of Afghanistan's National Directorate of Security, stated at a conference in Jaipur, India that

> India has been a darling friend of Afghanistan. India helps Afghanistan in every sphere of life. Except for the brief period of the Afghan War precisely during 1979–89, when India was going against the popular sentiments of Afghanistan, the country has always stood with Afghans.⁹⁴

Resultantly, Indian interests were attacked in Afghanistan at regular intervals. India had two Consulates, one at Kandahar and the other at Jalalabad, apart from the Indian Embassy in Kabul. The Indian Military Attaché posted in Kabul reported that in 1982, 'The Kandahar consulate was attacked by the Mujahideen with rockets forcing its closure'.⁹⁵ The Consul at Kandahar reported that the situation was bad in Kandahar and the surrounding areas during 1982. Russian troops were concentrated at the airport, 28 kilometres away from the city. The Afghan Corps never patrolled the city, and insurgents had access at will to the city and bazaar areas. Mr Kapoor, the Consul at Kandahar, reported that 'in December 1981, there were about 1500 Afghan Hindus and Sikhs in the Kandahar area who wish to go to India with refugee status'. But India refused to grant refugee status. The Indian strategists thought that if all Indians vacated Kandahar, India's strategic presence and people-to-people connection would be broken. Therefore, they refused to grant refugee visas.

The refusal resulted in attacks against the Indian Consulate. These Hindu Afghans went to the rebels and asked them to attack the Indian Consulate.[96] The staff shifted to Kabul and remained there for almost six months, reluctant to return to Kandahar.[97] The Military Attaché, Major General Samay Ram, noted that 'Mr. Dixit did not know how to send them back, and the functioning of this Consulate was vital to us'. In his memoir, Samay Ram stated

> I volunteered to go to Kandahar and spent three days there. I used my good offices with the Afghan Corps Commander at Kandahar and made all the arrangements for the security of the consulate. The staff was happy to get back and confident to function. We, thus, re-opened the consulate.[98]

But the disconnect between the Military Attaché and the Ambassador can be noticed easily if one reads both of their Afghan memoirs. J.N. Dixit did not mention the valorous act of his Military Attache; rather, he noted in his diary that 'Consul Kandahar had to call in the leaders of the Indian community and read them a tempered riot out, which seems to have made them desist somewhat, for how long, no one knows'.[99]

Nevertheless, the dual policy of India – supporting and opposing Soviet intervention in Afghanistan – continued. On 15 May 1982, during the Indo-Afghan Joint Commission meeting, which was taking place after a gap of nearly five years, Foreign Secretary Natwar Singh's opening statement about India's reservations regarding the Russian presence in Afghanistan was unexpected by the Afghan leadership. By 1983, it was evident that many countries were supporting the insurgency in Afghanistan while India was siding with the Soviets.

In 1983,

> a French national named Ogayar Fillip Jean Marriet was arrested by Afghan and Soviet forces in the Logar province. It was alleged that he was supporting an insurgent group belonging to the Harkat-e-Inqilab-e-Islami. However, the French government in Paris announced that he was a doctor providing medical and humanitarian assistance to the refugees.[100]

The arrest exposed foreign presence and interference in Afghanistan on a larger scale. However, Marriet was not the only foreign national supporting insurgents; individuals from Saudi Arabia, China, Egypt, and other countries arrived in Afghanistan to participate in the guerrilla war. In 1984, it was noted that the entire Pakistan mission in Kabul, from the Charge d'Affaires down to the junior-most official, belonged to the Pakistan intelligence service. There was no career foreign service officer of Pakistan in Kabul.[101]

In the summer of 1983, as the snow started melting in the high passes, civil war gripped Afghanistan, and refugees fled to Pakistan while arms shipments filtered to the waiting insurgents. A *New York Times* article captured the situation in vivid terms. It stated 'the Soviet army and air force established control of the major cities and towns, and they had built a number of major airfields capable of taking the most advanced jets, Mig-25's and Su-24's'.[102] But the article goes on to explain that the insurgency was also increasing at the same speed. The country was devastated by the firefights and internecine war. On 11 April 1983, Afghanistan's Prime Minister Sultan Ali Keshmand informed the world that half of the country's schools and hospitals had been destroyed by guerrilla action. Desertion in the Afghan Army was rampant. The army's strength was down to about 20,000 men in 1983 compared with 40,000 a year ago. The Army had become so unreliable that the Russians, worried about mutiny, disarm Afghan units at night and returned the weapons in the morning.

Back in India, an insurgency engulfed the western province of Punjab. Pakistani-trained Sikh militants wreaked havoc in the province, demanding a separate state for the Sikhs. The situation reached a stalemate when Mrs Gandhi issued an order in June 1984 to flush out Khalistani militants hiding at the Harmandir Sahib in the Golden Temple of Amritsar. The Indian army's action inside the revered and sacred Harmandir Sahib Temple in Amritsar enraged the feelings of Sikhs across the world. There was emotional tension and resentment in the Afghan Sikh community as well. To counter any deleterious effect in Afghanistan, the Indian Embassy and Consulates in Afghanistan stopped issuing visas to all foreigners from about 20 August 1984 to 4 September 1984. This was to prevent Afghan Sikhs from reaching Amritsar for the Sikh convention organized by the head priests of the Golden Temple. The Embassy did not wish to discriminate against the Sikhs alone, as it would have exacerbated tensions already existing between the Afghan Hindus and Afghan Sikhs since India's firm action against Sikh terrorists in Amritsar in June 1984. The issuing of visas restarted on 5 September 1984. However, representatives from the Gurdwara management committees in Kabul went to London around mid-June and participated in meetings and demonstrations against the Government of India as well as against the High Commission of India.[103]

To get a view of the Afghan Civil War, Nikhil Chakravarty, editor of *Mainstream*, met the top Afghan leadership during the period from 12 to 21 September 1984. He met with President Karmal, Prime Minister Keshmand, Foreign Minister Dost, and the Ministers of State for Defence and for

Tribes and Nationalities. He also had a meeting with Mrs Ratebzad. Mr Chakravarty was informed in all these meetings about the importance that Afghanistan attaches to its relations with India and to Mrs Gandhi's leadership of India and the non-aligned movement.[104]

When news about Prime Minister Indira Gandhi's assassination reached President Karmal, he immediately summoned the Indian Ambassador for an urgent meeting on 31 October 1984. The Afghan President delivered a moving condolence message to Ambassador Dixit in the presence of his Foreign Minister Dost.[105]

As explained in the previous chapter, India had developed excellent outreach even to the inner sanctum of Afghan political leadership and bureaucracy. An example of this outreach was provided by the Indian Military Attaché, Major General Samay Ram. In a report to the Ambassador, sent during December 1985, the military attaché stated that he gave the 'information about President Babrak Karmal's replacement by Najibullah six months before the deposition of President Babrak Karmal'.[106] On 4 May 1986, Babrak Karmal resigned and was replaced by Najibullah, the former chief of the Afghan secret police. Karmal was 57 years old when he resigned, while Najibullah was 39 years old when he took charge. Karmal was in Moscow during the period from 30 March to 1 May 1986. He even missed the celebration of the April 27 Sour Revolution. Karmal remained a member of the Politburo and the President of the Presidium of the Revolutionary Council, a largely ceremonial post while effective leadership of the country was passed to Najibullah, a former medical student who headed the Khad secret police until December 1985, when he was promoted to party secretary charged with overall security. Karmal, who was not a Pashtun, belonged to the Parcham faction. Najibullah was one of the few Pashtuns in the Parcham faction. As head of the secret police, Najibullah had worked closely with the Soviet Secret Service, the KGB.[107]

Ever since Mikhail Gorbachev became the General Secretary of the Soviet Communist Party on 11 March 1985, Moscow had been seeking to shape a more flexible image in regard to the Afghan War. Astonishingly, India's Military Attaché received intelligence about the Soviet withdrawal plan from Afghanistan as early as 1984. This was a bombshell and created ripples in the Indian Foreign Ministry.

> Prime Minister Indira Gandhi summoned Indian Ambassador J.N. Dixit to Delhi for consultations. Later, Mr. S.K. Singh, additional Secretary in the Ministry of External Affairs, was deputed to ascertain the veracity of this information. He had extensive discussions with the military attaché and came convinced that there appeared to be merit in this information.[108]

No one believed it then, but the Soviets started withdrawing troops two years later in 1986.

The change in Moscow precipitated cascading reciprocal moderation in Washington's Afghan policy. On 17 June 1986, President Ronald Reagan met a group of Afghan rebels at the White House for 35 minutes. Burhanuddin Rabbani led the Afghan rebel coalition. Although President Reagan met the rebels and turned down their request that the United States extend diplomatic recognition and sever relations with the Soviet-backed Afghan Government, he voiced an 'unshakable commitment' of support to the rebels. But despite America's support, the insurgents were unhappy with Americans' continued recognition of the Afghan Government, their backing for United Nations-sponsored peace talks without rebel participation, and Washington's failure to provide advanced weapons to the rebels, including Stinger shoulder-fired anti-aircraft missiles. The United States believed it was more important to maintain an Embassy in Kabul, which has been described as a listening post for American intelligence.[109] The US supported 'proximity talks' going on in Geneva between representatives of the Afghan and Pakistani Governments. The delegates did not meet face to face, but their views were conveyed by a United Nations official.[110]

Back in Pakistan, a rift surfaced as the Afghan rebel alliance split publicly on 17 June 1986 over the question of identification with the United States. Gulbuddin Hekmatyar, leader of the Hezb-i-Islami guerrilla group, and Rasul Sayaf, head of another small insurgent group, issued a statement saying the trip to Washington had not been approved by the rebel alliance. Mr Sayaf and Mr Hekmatyar insisted that insurgents should not be identified with the United States.[111]

The intelligence gathered by India in 1984 proved trustworthy when the General Secretary of the Soviet Communist Party, Gorbachev, announced at the party Congress in February 1986 that the Soviet Union would like to withdraw its forces from the country 'in the nearest future'. He said the Russians had agreed with the Afghans on a schedule for a phased withdrawal 'as soon as a political settlement is reached that will ensure an actual cessation and dependably guarantee the non-resumption of foreign armed interference in the internal affairs' of Afghanistan.[112] A few months later, on 29 July 1986, Mikhail Gorbachev made a speech in Vladivostok. In this speech, he announced that 'Six regiments will be returned home from Afghanistan before the end of 1986. These units will be returned to their areas of permanent deployment in the Soviet Union, in such a way that anyone interested can easily verify it'.[113]

The intelligence about the change in Soviet strategy necessitated a re-orientation of India's foreign policy in 1984. A prudent policy course correction was enacted, and the forging of an alliance with the rebel group that was the Northern Alliance was a consequence of that orientation.[114]

The war had created the world's largest refugee problem for one-third of Afghanistan's pre-war population of 15 million. About 3 million refugees landed in Pakistan and 2 million in Iran.[115] On 1 January 1987, President Najibullah announced a ceasefire effective from 15 January.[116] During a visit to New Delhi between 7 and 10 February 1987, the Afghan Foreign Minister Abdul Wakil said that 22,000 Afghan nationals had returned home from Iran and Pakistan since President Najibullah's proclamation of a ceasefire on 1 January 1987.[117] The Afghan Foreign Minister told newsmen in New Delhi that 'After the unilateral ceasefire took effect from January 15, as many as 81 Afghan resistance groups comprising 8000 armed persons had responded to the call for national reconciliation'. Appointed as Afghanistan's Foreign Minister in December 1986, the February 1987 visit was Mr Wakil's first visit to India. He was earlier Finance Minister in Mr Babrak Karmal's Government. The visit was primarily to brief the Government of India on the national reconciliation moves initiated in Afghanistan and to have a consultation with India before the next round of the 'Proximity Talks'.[118] The 'Proximity Talks' with Pakistan in Geneva for deciding on a timetable for the withdrawal of Soviet forces from Afghanistan were not a separate process from the effort at national reconciliation.[119]

India had naturally taken an active interest in developments concerning Afghanistan. The Soviet offer to withdraw troops from Afghanistan within a limited time frame and the steps taken by the People's Democratic Party of Afghanistan to seek national reconciliation have brought about a qualitative change in the situation. India maintained contact with various Afghan elements, including those opposed to the Government, to promote the objective of a peaceful, non-aligned and independent Afghanistan, free from external interference or intervention.[120] Both the Soviet Union and Afghanistan offered the withdrawal of Soviet troops from Afghanistan in a period of 12 months or less, provided this was accompanied by a cessation of external interference. India was deeply affected by the situation in Afghanistan. Accordingly, India initiated contacts with various Afghan opposition elements and the countries involved in the Afghan situation to help contribute towards a political solution. President Najibullah made brief halts in New Delhi in December 1987 while transiting through India en route to Vietnam and Kampuchea. This opportunity was utilized for an exchange of views on matters of bilateral and regional importance.[121]

Annually, the United Nations General Assembly, the Non-Aligned Movement, the Organization of Islamic Conference, etc., debated and voted on the issue. India consistently maintained abstention from UN voting. On 28 November 1987, Moscow decided to pull out its troops, even if that ended the Najibullah regime. Days later, on 10 December 1987, during the Washington Summit, Mr Gorbachev proposed to withdraw his 115,000 troops from Afghanistan over a 12-month period, which the Americans took as a small concession, but he refused to set a date for the pull-out to start. The Russian stand on not specifying the date of withdrawal disappointed the American President.[122]

But soon, on 8 February 1988, Michael Gorbachev announced that

> Seeking to facilitate a speedy and successful conclusion of the Geneva talks between Afghanistan and Pakistan, the Government of the USSR and the Republic of Afghanistan have agreed to set a specific date for beginning the withdrawal of Soviet troops – 15 May 1988 – and to complete their withdrawal within 10 months.[123]

On 14 April 1988, an accord on Soviet withdrawal was signed in Geneva. The two bilateral agreements were signed by Afghanistan and Pakistan. The agreement on interrelationships was signed by those two countries, with the Soviet Union and the United States signing as witnesses, and the Declaration on International Guarantees was signed by the United States and the Soviet Union. A bilateral agreement between the Republic of Afghanistan and the Islamic Republic of Pakistan on the principles of mutual relations, in particular on non-interference and non-intervention, was signed.

India welcomed these accords. Immediately after the Geneva Accord, President Najibullah made an official visit to India in May 1988. The visit was significant in the context of India's dialogue on the Afghan problem with different shades of opinion. Indian officials publicly welcomed Najibullah and other members of his Government for a three-day visit from 4 to 6 May 1988, including at least three meetings or official dinners with Prime Minister Rajiv Gandhi.[124]

The unusually full round of activities suggested that India rejected the view of many that Mr Najibullah's Government was bound to collapse under pressure from Afghan insurgents once the Soviet Union withdrew its 115,000 troops. Prime Minister Rajiv Gandhi sought to confer some legitimacy on Mr Najibullah to strengthen him in Afghanistan, hoping that he could serve as a counterweight to India's rival, Pakistan.[125] The Afghan President valiantly stated that if the insurgents chose to keep on fighting, Government forces would 'deal them a heavy and severe blow'.[126] Earlier, on 3 May 1988, Foreign Secretary Mr K.P.S. Menon visited Islamabad as the Prime Minister's special emissary for discussions on the Afghan situation with President Zia and other Pakistani leaders.

India maintained good bilateral relations with Afghanistan and pledged assistance worth Rs 10 crores for the relief and rehabilitation of the Afghan refugees.[127] Given its vital stakes in Afghanistan, India continued to take an active interest in the rapidly changing situation there. The Geneva Accords had not, however, been implemented by all the parties involved despite the complete withdrawal of Soviet troops by 15 February 1989.[128]

The last Soviet soldier in Afghanistan, Lieutenant General Boris Gromov of the Red Army contingent, crossed the Afghan–Soviet border on 16 February 1989 and returned home, marking the completion of the Soviet pull-out from Afghanistan after nine years of military intervention. The 45-year-old General, who was Commander-in-Chief of the Soviet troops in Afghanistan, crossed the bridge across the Amu Darya River at 9:55 am Moscow time. While stepping over to the Soviet side, Lieutenant General Gromov stood for a minute on the red line separating the two countries on the nearly 1-kilometre-long bridge, uttered a few words, and then moved towards the welcoming party from the Soviet Union without looking back. General Gromov, whose 14-year-old son Maxim was in the welcoming party, headed nearly 125,000 Soviet troops following a military intervention that did not produce any positive results. Only the General with his staff had remained behind to complete the pull-out on the last day under the Geneva Accords.[129]

On 15 February 1989, Russian Deputy Foreign Minister Yuli Vorontsov met Prime Minister Rajiv Gandhi, Foreign Minister P.V. Narsimha Rao and Foreign Secretary S.K. Singh in New Delhi. On 17 February 1989, addressing a news conference in New Delhi, Mr Vorontsov observed, 'Americans appeared to be in favour of a military solution to Afghanistan by continuing the internecine warfare. But wishful thinking that the Government in Kabul will crumble was not going to settle issues'. He disclosed that intelligence reports and space-based surveillance systems had established the presence of artillery and military equipment maintained by Pakistan. Army personnel were deployed within striking distance of Jalalabad. They had not been brought into use yet. Mr Yuli Vorontsov cautioned that 'Anyone who tries to take that city (Kabul) of 2 million people will suffer heavy casualties'.[130]

On 30 March 1989, Professor Sibghatullah Mojaddedi, President of the Afghan rebels' so-called Interim Government, warned India against what he alleged was sending its air force pilots to help the Afghan forces in the 24-day-old stalemated battle for Jalalabad city. He said the alleged involvement of Indian pilots and military advisors was 'an open interference in our country'. It was alleged that Indian pilots were bombing rebel positions in Afghanistan and that Indian military advisers were helping the Afghan Army. New Delhi had denied such allegations in the past. Three days before the allegation, Professor Mojaddedi had denied knowledge of Indian military advisers or air force pilots taking part in the Afghan conflict. He had told newsmen that he had no proof to substantiate the claim made by a field commander in the Kabul area.[131]

India's policy on Afghanistan, though a target of criticism by Pakistan and some Western countries, proved to be a success in the long run. India was in a better position than ever before as far as Afghanistan was concerned. It was acceptable to Iran-based Afghan Mujahideen as well as to both Khalq and Parcham factions of the ruling People's Democratic Party of Afghanistan.[132] On 2 December 1989, there was a change of guard in New Delhi. Vishwanath Pratap Singh was elected as the Prime Minister of India. The new Government, which was made up of coalition partners, needed time to grasp Afghan affairs and spell out a policy. New Delhi's Afghan policy again entered a new phase of uncertainty.

Notes

1. Annual Reports Etc – 1977 From Kandahar, MEA, GoI, File No. HI/1011/13/78-III, 1977, NAI.
2. P.K. Thakkar, Consulate of India, Kandahar, Monthly Record of Events of the Month of May, 1978 – Coup d'etat in Afghanistan, No. KAN/101/1/77, 7 May 1978, NAI.
3. M.K. Malik, Monthly Report for April 1979, No. JAL/101/1/78, Consulate of India, Jalalabad, 1 May 1979, NAI.
4. M.K. Malik, Consul General, Monthly Report for April 1978, Consulate of India, Jalalabad, No. JAL/101/1/78, 2 May 1978, NAI.
5. M.K. Malik, Consul of India, Annual Consular Report for the Year 1977, Jalalabad, No. JAL/414/2/78, 7 March 1978, NAI.
6. Political Reports for the year 1978 from Jalalabad, MEA, GoI, File No. HI/1012/2/78, 1978, NAI.
7. National Archives and Record Administration (NARA hereafter), Afghanistan Report: Moving Images Relating to International Development Programs and Activities, 1979–1991, 1980, National Archives Identifier: 2733355.
8. NARA, Moving Images Relating to Intelligence and International Relations, 1947–1984, National Archives Identifier: 652980. Central Intelligence Agency, 12 April 1981.
9. US Department of State, 28 April 1978.
10. Department of State, 23 July 1978.
11. M.K. Malik, Consulate of India, Jalalabad, Monthly Report for April 1978, No. JAL/101/1/78, 2 May 1978, NAI.
12. P.K. Thakkar, Consulate of India, Kandahar, Monthly Record of Events of the Month of May, 1978 – Coup d'etat in Afghanistan, No. KAN/101/1/77, 7 May 1978, NAI.
13. P.K. Thakkar, Consulate of India, Kandahar, Monthly Record of Events of the Month of May, 1978 – Coup d'etat in Afghanistan, No. KAN/101/1/77, 7 May 1978, NAI.
14. M.K. Malik, Consul General, Monthly Report for May 1978, Consulate of India, Jalalabad, No. JAL/101/1/78, 4 June 1978, NAI.
15. M.K. Malik, Consul General, Monthly Report for May 1978, Consulate of India, Jalalabad, No. JAL/101/1/78, 4 June 1978, NAI.

16 P.K. Thakkar, Consulate of India, Kandahar, Monthly Record of Events of the Month of May, 1978 – Coup d'etat in Afghanistan, No. KAN/101/1/77, 7 May 1978, NAI.
17 P.K. Thakkar, Consulate of India, Kandahar, Monthly Record of Events of the Month of April 1978, No. KAN/101/1/77, 7 May 1978, NAI.
18 P.K. Thakkar, Consulate of India, Kandahar, Monthly Record of Events of the Month of May, 1978 – Coup d'etat in Afghanistan, No. KAN/101/1/77, 7 May 1978, NAI.
19 P.K. Thakkar, Consulate of India, Kandahar, Monthly Record of Events of the Month of June 1978, No. KAN/101/1/77, 6 June 1978, NAI.
20 P.K. Thakkar, Consulate of India, Kandahar, Monthly Record of Events of the Month of July 1978, No. KAN/101/1/77, 2 July 1978, NAI.
21 P.K. Thakkar, Consulate of India, Kandahar, Monthly Record of Events of the Month of July 1978, No. KAN/101/1/77, 2 July 1978, NAI.
22 P.K. Thakkar, Consulate of India, Kandahar, Monthly Record of Events of the Month of July 1978, No. KAN/101/1/77, 2 July 1978, NAI.
23 P.K. Thakkar, Consulate of India, Kandahar, Monthly Record of Events of the Month of August 1978, No. KAN/101/1/77, 3 August 1978, NAI.
24 M.K. Malik, Consul General, Monthly Report for May 1978, Consulate of India, Jalalabad, No. JAL/101/1/78, 4 June 1978, NAI.
25 Ministry of External Affairs, Government of India, Annual Report 1978–79, p. 1.
26 *Kabul Times*, Vajpayee Arrives Here on Official, Friendly Visit, 18 September 1978.
27 Walter K. Anderson, India in Asia: Walking on a Tightrope, Asian Survey, December 1979.
28 M.K. Malik, Consul General, Monthly Report for September, 1978, Consulate of India, Jalalabad, No. JAL/101/1/78, 3 October 1978, NAI.
29 M.K. Malik, Consul General, Monthly Report for September, 1978, Consulate of India, Jalalabad, No. JAL/101/1/78, 3 October 1978, NAI.
30 Dwarka Dheesh, Second Secretary, Annual Consular Report of Indian Missions/Posts Abroad for the Year – 1977, No. KAB/PV/414(3)/78, 2 February 1978, NAI.
31 S.K. Singh, Ambassador of India, Kabul, Annual Political Report, Kab/101/1/77, 26 March 1978, NAI.
32 Dwarka Dheesh, Second Secretary, Annual Consular Report of Indian Missions/Posts Abroad for the Year – 1977, No. KAB/PV/414(3)/78, 2 February 1978, NAI.
33 M.K. Malik, Monthly Report for March 1979, No. JAL/101/1/78, Consulate of India, Jalalabad, 8 April 1979, NAI.
34 M.K. Malik, Consulate of India, Jalalabad, Monthly Report for April 1978, No. JAL/101/1/78, 2 May 1978, NAI.
35 M.K. Malik, Consul General, Monthly Report for May 1978, Consulate of India, Jalalabad, No. JAL/101/1/78, 4 June 1978, NAI.
36 M.K. Malik, Consul General, Monthly Report for 4 July 1978, Consulate of India, Jalalabad, No. JAL/101/1/78, 4 July 1978, NAI.
37 M.K. Malik, Consul General, Monthly Report for 4 July 1978, Consulate of India, Jalalabad, No. JAL/101/1/78, 4 July 1978, NAI.
38 P.K. Thakkar, Consulate of India, Kandahar, Monthly Record of Events of the Month of August 1978, No. KAN/101/1/77, 3 August 1978, NAI.
39 M.K. Malik, Consul General, Monthly Report for 4 July 1978, Consulate of India, Jalalabad, No. JAL/101/1/78, 4 July 1978, NAI.

40 M.K. Malik, Consul General, Monthly Report for August 1978, Consulate of India, Jalalabad, No. JAL/101/1/78, 5 September 1978, NAI.
41 M.K. Malik, Consul General, Monthly Report for August 1978, Consulate of India, Jalalabad, No. JAL/101/1/78, 5 September 1978, NAI.
42 M.K. Malik, Monthly Report for February 1979, No. JAL/101/1/78, Consulate of India, Jalalabad, 5 March 1979, NAI.
43 M.K. Malik, Monthly Report for February 1979, No. JAL/101/1/78, Consulate of India, Jalalabad, 5 March 1979, NAI.
44 M.K. Malik, Monthly Report for February 1979, No. JAL/101/1/78, Consulate of India, Jalalabad, 5 March 1979, NAI.
45 M.K. Malik, Monthly Report for April 1979, No. JAL/101/1/78, Consulate of India, Jalalabad, 1 May 1979, NAI.
46 Raza Ali, 'The Shadow War' (unpublished manuscript), p. 1.
47 Mohammad Yousaf and Mark Adkin, *Afghanistan the Bear Trap* (New Delhi: Bookwise Pvt. Ltd, 2007), p. 38.
48 Mohammad Yousaf and Mark Adkin, *Afghanistan the Bear Trap* (New Delhi: Bookwise Pvt. Ltd, 2007), p. 20.
49 Hein G. Kiessling, *Faith, Unity, Discipline: The ISI of Pakistan*. (New Delhi: Harper Collins, 2016, p. 53.
50 Mohammad Yousaf and Mark Adkin, *Afghanistan the Bear Trap* (New Delhi: Bookwise Pvt. Ltd, 2007), p. 40.
51 Mohammad Yousaf and Mark Adkin, *Afghanistan the Bear Trap* (New Delhi: Bookwise Pvt. Ltd, 2007), p. 38.
52 Mark Adkin, *Afghanistan the Bear Trap*, pp. 101, 104; in 1987 the broad percentages allocated to the parties were Hikmetyar 18–20 per cent, Rabbani 18–19 per cent, Sayyaf 17–18 per cent, Khalis 13–15 per cent, Nabi 13–15 per cent, Gailani 10–11 per cent, and Muhaddadi trailing with 3–5 per cent.
53 Adam K. East, 'Afghani Groups: the Peshawar Seven', *Executive Intelligence Review*, 13 October 1995.
54 Robert Trumbull, US Asserts Afghans Ignored Pleas Not to Attack Abductors of Envoy, *New York Times*, 15 February 1979.
55 K.C. Bhardwaj, Monthly Report for July 1979, No. JAL/101/1/78, Consulate of India, Jalalabad, 11 August 1979, NAI.
56 Director of Central Intelligence, The Soviet Invasion of Afghanistan: Implications for Warning, Interagency Intelligence Memorandum, October 1980, Department of Defence, NARA, Washington DC, p. 6.
57 NARA, Moving Images Relating to UK Domestic and International Activities, 1982–1999, UK Information Agency, 24 August 1982, National Archives Identifier: 54188.
58 J.N. Dixit, *An Afghan Diary: Zahir Shah to Taliban* (New Delhi: Konark Publishers, 2000), p. 421.
59 Michael T. Kaufman, Afghan Guerrillas Boast of Success in Struggle Against Soviet-Backed Regime, *New York Times*, 14 August 1979, p. 1.
60 Hedrick Smith, US is Indirectly Pressing Russians to Halt Afghanistan, *New York Times*, 3 August 1979, p. 1.
61 Associated Press, Ex-Afghan Leader is Reported Killed, *New York Times*, 19 September 1979, p. 4.
62 Michael T. Kaufman, Taraki's Downfall Came Immediately After a Visit to Moscow, *New York Times*, 23 September 1979, p. 1.
63 Aleksandr Antonovich Lyakhovskiy, 'Inside the Soviet Invasion of Afghanistan and the Seizure of Kabul, December 1979', Working Paper 51, Woodrow Wilson International Centre, January 2007, p. 48.

64 Graham Hovey, From Exile to Afghan Rule, *New York Times*, 28 December 1979, p. 3.
65 Hodding Carter III, Spokesperson, State Department, Government of United States, NARA, 22 December 1979, National Archives Identifier: 54495.
66 Richard Burt, Soviet Build-up Seen at Afghan Frontier, *New York Times*, 22 December 1979, p. 14.
67 Jimmy Carter, Soviet Invasion of Afghanistan and US President Jimmy Carter's Imposed Peacetime Reprisals, White House, Government of United States, NARA, 28 December 1979, National Archives Identifier: 652980.
68 Jimmy Carter, Soviet Invasion of Afghanistan and US President Jimmy Carter's Imposed Peacetime Reprisals, White House, Government of United States, NARA, 28 December 1979, National Archives Identifier: 652980.
69 Anthony Austin, Soviet Says Afghans Asked for Its Help, *New York Times*, 29 December 1979, p. 2.
70 Bernard Gwertzman, Brzezinski Increases UK Estimate of Soviet Soldiers in Afghanistan, *New York Times*, 31 December 1979, p. 3.
71 J.N. Dixit, *An Afghan Diary: Zahir Shah to Taliban* (New Delhi: Konark Publishers, 2000), pp. 21–24.
72 J.N. Dixit, *An Afghan Diary: Zahir Shah to Taliban* (New Delhi: Konark Publishers, 2000), pp. 21–24.
73 J.N. Dixit, India-USSR: Strains in Relations, Director of Intelligence Report, Department of Defence, November 1986, p. 1.
74 J.N. Dixit, Soviets not in Afghanistan Forever: PM, *The Indian Express*, 23 January 1980.
75 J.N. Dixit, Soviets not in Afghanistan Forever: PM, *The Indian Express*, 23 January 1980.
76 J.N. Dixit, *An Afghan Diary: Zahir Shah to Taliban* (New Delhi: Konark Publishers, 2000), pp. 21–24.
77 G.K. Reddy, India Proceeding with Caution on Afghan Issue, *The Hindu*, 28 March 1980.
78 G.K. Reddy, India Proceeding with Caution on Afghan Issue, *The Hindu*, 28 March 1980.
79 Initiative on Afghan Issue Not Simple: PM, *The Indian Express*, 10 May 1980.
80 Ministry of External Affairs, Supplement to the Report of the Ministry of External Affairs 1979–80, Annual Report 1979–1980 Supplement, p. 2.
81 J.N. Dixit, *An Afghan Diary: Zahir Shah to Taliban* (New Delhi: Konark Publishers, 2000), pp. 21–24.
82 Annual Report of Ministry of External Affairs for 1979–80, New Delhi, India, p. ii.
83 India-USSR: Strains in Relations, Director of Intelligence Report, Department of Defence, November 1986, pp. 3–4.
84 G.K. Reddy, Afghanistan: India will keep talking to Russia, *The Hindu*, 9 August 1980.
85 Annual Report of Ministry of External Affairs 1980–1981, MEA, New Delhi, India, pp. iv–v.
86 Annual Report of Ministry of External Affairs 1980–1981, MEA, New Delhi, India, p. 1.
87 Major General Samay Ram, *The New Afghanistan Pawn of America* (New Delhi: Manas Publication, 2004), p. 18.
88 Major General Samay Ram, Afghan Minister to brief P.M., *The Hindu*, 7 September 1981.
89 Major General Samay Ram, Afghan Minister to brief P.M., *The Hindu*, 7 September 1981.

90 Annual Report of Ministry of External Affairs 1981–82, MEA, New Delhi, India, p. 38.
91 J.N. Dixit, *An Afghan Diary: Zahir Shah to Taliban* (New Delhi: Konark Publishers, 2000), p. 32.
92 Annual Report of Ministry of External Affairs 1981–82, MEA, New Delhi, India, p. v.
93 J.N. Dixit, *An Afghan Diary: Zahir Shah to Taliban* (New Delhi: Konark Publishers, 2000), p. 67.
94 Interview with the Author, 14 March 2015, Jaipur, India.
95 Major General Samay Ram, *The New Afghanistan Pawn of America* (New Delhi: Manas Publication, 2004), p. 20.
96 J.N. Dixit, *An Afghan Diary*, p. 37.
97 Major General Samay Ram, *The New Afghanistan Pawn of America* (New Delhi: Manas Publication, 2004), p. 20.
98 Major General Samay Ram, *The New Afghanistan Pawn of America* (New Delhi: Manas Publication, 2004), p. 20.
99 J.N. Dixit, *An Afghan Diary: Zahir Shah to Taliban* (New Delhi: Konark Publishers, 2000), p. 37.
100 J.N. Dixit, *An Afghan Diary: Zahir Shah to Taliban* (New Delhi: Konark Publishers, 2000), p. 37.
101 J.N. Dixit, *An Afghan Diary: Zahir Shah to Taliban* (New Delhi: Konark Publishers, 2000), p. 296.
102 Afghan War Isn't Over But Soviet Seems to be Winning, *New York Times*, 1 May 1983, p. 3.
103 J.N. Dixit, *An Afghan Diary: Zahir Shah to Taliban* (New Delhi: Konark Publishers, 2000), p. 381.
104 J.N. Dixit, *An Afghan Diary*, p. 388.
105 J.N. Dixit, *An Afghan Diary*, 405.
106 Major General Samay Ram, *The New Afghanistan Pawn of America* (New Delhi: Manas Publication, 2004), p. 19.
107 Serge Schmemann, Afghan Leader Quits Top Post, Moscow Reports, *New York Times*, 5 May 1986.
108 Major General Samay Ram, *The New Afghanistan Pawn of America* (New Delhi: Manas Publication, 2004), p. 19.
109 Bernard Gwetzman, Reagan Bars Ties to Afghan Rebels, *New York Times*, 17 June 1986, p. 5.
110 Richard Halloran, US May Establish Afghan Rebel Ties, *New York Times*, 18 June 1986, p. 1.
111 Associated Press, Rift in the Rebel Alliance, *New York Times*, 17 June 1986, p. 12.
112 Serge Schmemann, Afghan Leader Quits Top Post, Moscow Reports, *New York Times*, 5 May 1986, p. 1.
113 Special Correspondence, Excerpts from Gorbachev's Speech, *New York Times*, 29 July 1986, p. 2.
114 Major General Samay Ram, *The New Afghanistan Pawn of America* (New Delhi: Manas Publication, 2004), p. 20.
115 Louis Dupree, On Afghanistan: Repercussions of Soviet Invasion, *New York Times*, 9 November 1987, p. 5.
116 Bernard Gwertzman, Afghanistan to Observe a Ceasefire, *New York Times*, 2 January 1987, p. 1.
117 Refugees Returning Home: Afghan Minister, *The Hindustan Times*, 8 February 1987.

118 Annual Report of Ministry of External Affairs 1986–87, New Delhi, India, p. vii.
119 Refugees Returning Home: Afghan Minister, *The Hindustan Times*, 8 February 1987.
120 Annual Report of Ministry of External Affairs 1987–88, New Delhi, India, p. vi.
121 Annual Report of Ministry of External Affairs 1987–88, p. 6.
122 R.W. Apple Jr., The Summit: 2 Leaders Discuss Long-Range Arms and Afghan War; An Air of Optimism, *New York Times*, 10 December 1987, p. 1.
123 Michael Gorbachev, Text of Gorbachev Statement Setting Forth Soviet Position on Afghan War, *New York Times*, 9 February 1988, p. 5.
124 Richard M. Weintraub, India Embraces Najibullah in Bid for Role in Afghanistan, *Washington Post*, 7 May 1988, p. 1.
125 Steven R. Weisman, Afghanistan Chief Visits India Today, *New York Times*, 4 May 1988, p. 3.
126 Najibullah in New Delhi, *New York Times*, 8 May 1988, p. 1.
127 Annual Report of Ministry of External Affairs 1988–89, New Delhi, India, p. vi.
128 Annual Report of Ministry of External Affairs 1988–89, p. vi.
129 Soviet Pullout Complete, *The Hindustan Times*, 16 February 1989.
130 Let us leave Afghans alone: Vorontsov, *The Hindustan Times*, 18 February 1989.
131 Afghan Rebel Chief Warning to India, *The Hindustan Times*, 31 March 1989.
132 Year of Bittersweet Foreign Ties, *The Hindustan Times*, 25 December 1989.

5
THE DIMENSIONS OF CHOICES IN BILATERAL RELATIONS

The long war resulted in the death of 15,000 Soviet lives and undisclosed billions of Rubles. But the withdrawal was never meant to switch off the light and leave the room. Vadim Perfilyev, a Soviet Foreign Ministry spokesman, described the situation in Kabul after the withdrawal as 'relatively calm and 160 Soviet trucks bearing food and fuel reached Kabul safely on 16 February 1989 to relieve shortages in time for an expected siege'.[1] He also made it clear that aircraft were still ferrying supplies into airports at Kabul, Kandahar, and Mazar-i-Sharif, while an estimated 250 Soviet civilians stayed on at the Soviet Embassy in Kabul after the troops left.

The international community and even some Soviet observers expected that after Moscow's withdrawal, President Najibullah's days would be numbered. Contrary to everyone's estimation, President Najibullah's forces proved sturdier than expected. They had vast arsenals of Soviet-supplied weapons. Najibullah's air force, while dependent on Moscow for supply and maintenance, was still operationally effective, and the large stocks of Scud-B missiles, short-range missiles, tanks, and trucks provided critical protection to the capital.[2] They had also been motivated by the fear of rebel reprisals if they lost. They were assured by the Soviet leadership that support and reinforcement would continue unabated. In other words, the Soviets withdrew from Afghanistan but they never abandoned the country. All these factors motivated Najibullah's troops to sustain the pressure from the insurgents even after the withdrawal of Soviet troops.

While the Najibullah Government appeared confident in its ability to stay the course even after Moscow's withdrawal, the view in Pakistan was upbeat. On 5 March 1989, Ms. Benazir Bhutto convened a meeting where

DOI: 10.4324/9781003627678-5

US Ambassador Robert B. Oakley was also present. In this meeting, it was decided that the assault by Afghan guerrillas on the eastern city of Jalalabad must be convened immediately. The Bhutto Government in Pakistan had been told for many months by its intelligence directorate, as well as by Washington, that the two Afghan cities, Jalalabad and Kandahar, would fall to the rebels within weeks of the Soviet military withdrawal, paving the way for the capture of Kabul shortly thereafter.[3]

ISI Director General Lieutenant General Hamid Gul cautioned against an assault, stating that the mutually antagonistic guerrilla groups were incapable of conducting such a large-scale act of conventional warfare as seizing a major city by storm. However, Bhutto's aide, Major General Nasirullah Babar, overruled the ISI Director, and Ms Bhutto ordered the intelligence directorate to set in motion the attack against which it had counselled. The meeting on 5 March 1989 came shortly after the transformation of the seven-party alliance into an Interim Afghan Government.

No Afghan leader was present during the meeting where the decision to storm Jalalabad was taken. This decision illustrates how the war of the Mujahideen was managed where major decisions were made by Pakistan. Such decisions were made in the absence of the Afghans but with the presence of the Americans. Intelligence estimates of a quick success were belied, both by the attackers' military ineffectiveness and the defenders' combat morale and use of air power. The siege entered a stalemate even after seven weeks of fighting. The attack had bogged down into a costly siege and brought into question the ability of the guerrillas to achieve an early victory, or any victory, over the Soviet-backed Government in Kabul.[4] Once the Russians were gone, many Afghans began to see the United States in a new guise, as a distant power that sanctioned the routine killing of civilians.[5]

President Najibullah declared that the successful defence of Jalalabad by his forces, 'can be considered a strong blow to those who were speaking of the immediate collapse of our revolution'.[6] By September 1989, a Mujahideen victory proved elusive and tensions within the rebel coalition made it ever less likely.[7] Amid Mujahideen disarray, after criticism in Congress and elsewhere, the United States had sharply cut arms supplies to Gulbuddin Hekmatyar's Hizb-i-Islami, which had been accused of attacking other factions in the seven-member rebel coalition.[8] Despite these failures, Mujahideen commanders competed among themselves to capture Kabul and dethrone Najibullah at the first opportunity.

India established contact with the leaders of the Resistance Movement against the Soviet Union. It was not impossible to establish such contact with individuals who were operating from their bases in Pakistan.[9] As mentioned in the previous chapter, after the secret report from Brigadier General Samay Ram in 1984 that the Soviet Union would leave Afghanistan, India established contact with Northern Alliance leaders, especially with Ahmad Shah Massoud of Hizb-e-Islami. After February 1989, India maintained contact with the leaders of all the groups, including Sibghatullah Mojaddedi, Burhanuddin Rabbani, Gulbuddin Hekmatyar, Abdul Rashid Dostum, and Ahmed Shah Massoud so that it could deal with whosoever came to power in Kabul.[10]

Soviet military and economic assistance, estimated at $250 million to $300 million a month or $3 billion to $3.6 billion a year, enabled Najibullah to remain in power.[11] Najibullah managed to gain the support of many Afghan militia, including prominent Uzbek Commander General Abdul Rashid Dostum. The withdrawal of Soviet troops robbed the motives of militias who were waging war to 'save their country from foreign occupation' and responding to the call to save 'Islam in danger'. Many of them wanted to enter into a peace deal with the Government in exchange for pelf and position. Both Najibullah and the tribal commanders proved adaptive to the traditional Afghan behaviour of give and take that characterized Afghan tribal history.

On 6 March 1990, as Mr Najibullah sat at a conference table in the Gul Kharna Palace with civilian members of the ruling Politburo, a 1100-pound bomb was dropped on the palace by a MIG-21 fighter-bomber. It was the opening blow in another coup attempt, this time by Lieutenant General Shahnawaz Tanai, who was then Defence Minister and had made a bizarre compact with Gulbuddin Hekmatyar. As the bomb exploded less than 100 feet away, the ceiling of the conference room collapsed, along with a chandelier, and its windows shattered. But somehow the ruling elite remained alive. Mohammed Aslam Watanjar, then Interior Minister who was later promoted to Defence Minister, saved the day and General Tanai's 24-hour coup attempt ended with his fleeing by helicopter to Pakistan.[12]

India continued its traditional friendly policy towards the Najibullah Government. In May 1990, Najibullah organized a Loya Jirga (Grand Assembly) and decided to rename his party Watan or Homeland Party. A month later, Afghan Foreign Minister Mr Abdul Wakil came to New Delhi on 11 June 1990 for the meeting of the Indo-Afghan Joint Commission, which was held on 12 and 13 June.[13] Thereafter, President Najibullah visited India on a 'State Visit' from 28 to 31 August 1990.

During his visit to India, Najibullah looked very confident as he successfully maintained control over the country. The Afghan President wanted to reduce his fledgling reliance on Russia for material support; therefore, he wanted India to contribute to the sustenance of his Government. Although cooperation in various fields was promised during the Indo-Afghan Joint Commission sessions at the Foreign Minister level, Najibullah wanted quick and practical support. At that time, India was in the midst of whirlwind political changes. Rajiv Gandhi was replaced by Vishwanath Pratap Singh, the leader of a coalition of rightist parties; therefore, even mere political support from India to a communist regime was not sufficient. During this visit, non-essential agreements like the Prevention of Trafficking in Narcotic Drugs and Psychotropic Substances, cooperation between agricultural institutions, and cultural exchanges were signed.[14] Afghanistan was not on the minds of the top leadership in India, as the V.P. Singh Government's Prime Minister's Office was embroiled in domestic issues like 'Other Backward Classes' reservations in the grant of Government jobs and seats in educational institutions. The V.P. Singh government (December 1989–November 1990) faced intense internal turmoil, especially after implementing the Mandal Commission recommendations in August 1990, granting 27% reservations to OBCs in jobs and education. This sparked widespread protests and political polarization and ultimately led to the BJP withdrawing support, causing the government's fall. Amidst this domestic upheaval, foreign policy took a backseat. The Afghan conflict, critical after the Soviet withdrawal in 1989, was neglected. Unlike earlier governments, India under V.P. Singh played a minimal role, allowing Pakistan to expand its influence in Afghanistan. It was during this time in Jammu and Kashmir that Home Minister Mufti Muhammad Sayyid's daughter Rubaiya Sayyid was kidnapped, exposing weaknesses within the ruling coalition.

Vijay K. Nambiar was appointed as Indian Ambassador in Kabul in October 1990, replacing Ambassador Hamid Ansari. Both the Afghan President Najibullah and his closest advisor and chef-de-cabinet Mohammad Ishaq Tokhi were cordial and open to the Indian Ambassador. Amid violent war, the small Indian community remained upbeat when the Indian Ambassador visited the Asa Mai temple as well as three Sikh Gurdwaras in Kabul 'whose simple hearts were warmed by the presence of the official representative of the mother country'.[15] Owing to the security situation, the Indian Mission, like most others in Kabul, was formally declared a non-family station, but occasionally the families of Mission staff did visit Kabul. These were challenging years for the Indian staff. They were in the midst of war. Death used to lurk on the doorstep. The heightened physical insecurity around the Mission, as well as the continuous bombardment of the city, had contributed to severe hypertension and a variety of post-traumatic stress disorder symptoms. These illnesses were neither officially diagnosed nor locally curable. Therefore, Mission staff members had been stoically working with great courage.[16]

Kabul had no more than 20 resident Missions at best, and several premises were looked after by local caretakers with no personnel of diplomatic status. The US Embassy was shut down on 31 January 1989, and the United Kingdom Embassy closed immediately after that.

On 10 November 1990, the V.P. Singh Government lost the confidence of the Indian Parliament. He was replaced by another coalition Government led by Chandra Shekhar. The new Government's view was not yet made public when the Minister for Commerce, Law and Justice, Mr Subramaniam Swamy, visited Kabul from 30 December 1990 to 1 January 1991.[17] The Afghans wanted economic assistance from India in a range of areas, including food and agricultural supplies, equipment and essential spares covering the transport industry and civil aviation sector, medical supplies, and hospital equipment connected with the upkeep and expansion of the Indira Gandhi Institute of Child Health in Kabul. India, although obliged to the request, can provide a very small amount against the desirable volume of requests. The Indian-made 'Jaipur foot', which adorned numerous limbless Afghan legs, was high in demand. Indian doctors were also very much in demand. India used to organize health camps by Indian doctors from time to time to meet the unending needs of the civilian population disabled and maimed by mine explosions throughout the length and breadth of the country. The 'Jaipur foot', more than any other item, roused the lasting gratitude of the Afghan people towards the Government and people of India.[18]

Despite India's commitment to the welfare of Afghans, logistic issues in the face of Pakistan's steadfast refusal to allow the transit of Indian goods made the supply of materials nearly impossible. India used to send materials through Dubai or the circuitous route of Mumbai port to Odesa port to Termez to Hairatan to Kabul. As explained by Indian Ambassador V.K. Nambiar, as the travel route is unbearably lengthy, the consignment used to spend more than a year in transit.

Foreign Minister Abdul Wakil, during his visit to India in February 1991, requested help for the starving Afghans.[19] Later in September 1991, when the Afghan Vice President Mr Abdul Hamid Mohtat came to India, along with many agreements, the Government of India agreed to supply 50,000 tonnes of wheat to Afghanistan on a grant basis.[20] However, the shipment was lost in transit and never reached its destination during the rule of Najibullah, who was removed from power in April 1992.

Meanwhile, India welcomed the UN Secretary General Perez de Cuellar's Five-Point Peace Proposals announced in May 1991.[21] Benon Sevan, the head of the Office of Secretary General in Afghanistan and Pakistan (OSGAP), had explained the contours of the five-point plan to the Indian Ambassador in Kabul in April 1991.

On 21 May 1991, when news reached Kabul that Rajiv Gandhi was killed in a terrorist attack at an election rally in Sri Perumbudur in the province of Tamil Nadu, President Najibullah personally telephoned the Indian Ambassador seeking confirmation of the reports. 'Najibullah was distraught and wept on the phone. He spoke in moving terms of his friendship and deep personal loyalty towards Rajiv Gandhi and the debt he and his party owed to the Gandhi family'. The President himself flew to Delhi to attend the funeral and stayed on for several brief meetings with the caretaker Government and with the senior Congress leadership and returned to Kabul within two days.[22]

On 21 June 1991, P.V. Narasimha Rao of the Congress Party became the Prime Minister with a strong mandate. He rechristened India's Afghan policy and gave much-needed direction to bilateral relations and strategic objectives.

During this melee, in 1991, *Bollywood* superstar Amitabh Bachchan, along with his crew members, embarked on an 18-day shoot of his film *Khuda Gawah* in Mazar-e-Sharif and Kabul. This proposal for filming was first made to the Afghan Government by Rajiv Gandhi when he was the Prime Minister. Rajiv Gandhi was a friend of Amitabh Bachchan, and the Afghan Government agreed to the proposal at the highest level. But sadly, the shooting was to take place after the tragic death of Rajiv Gandhi.[23] The Indian Mission organized a dinner for the *Khuda Gawah* team. Nearly 100 persons, including one Vice President, several ministers, and the two brothers of President Najibullah (Roushan and Ahmedzai), as well as a large number of youngsters from the families of the senior leadership, were present at very short notice. Amitabh and his fellow actor colleagues were generous to a fault, both with their time and their enthusiastic appreciation of the warmth and support of the Afghan hosts towards the film crew.[24] This is an example of Afghanistan's fascination for *Bollywood*, which generated tremendous goodwill for India.

Reflecting on the film shoot in Afghanistan, Amitabh Bachchan recounted, 'Following the Soviet withdrawal, power transitioned to Najibullah Ahmadzai, a devoted admirer of Hindi cinema. He expressed a desire to meet me, and we were accorded exceptional treatment'. The entire film crew was received as VIP state guests in Mazar-e-Sharif and toured the stunningly beautiful country extensively by aeroplane, accompanied by armed escorts. Bachchan noted, 'We experienced the characteristic warmth of the local people, who are renowned for their generous hospitality. We were not permitted to stay in a hotel; instead, a family vacated their own residence for us, relocating to a smaller dwelling'. He added, 'Despite the evident security concerns, with tanks and armed soldiers present throughout the streets, it remains the most unforgettable journey of my life'.[25]

Amitabh Bachchan's reminiscence is a living testimony of the Afghan landscape in those days. The megastar's diary note-type description captured every aspect of Afghan lives, which provides a rare glimpse into the contrasting lives of Kabul where fighting and feasting go on side by side. Amitabh recalled that their film unit was invited by a group of warlords.

It was surprising to see that the *Bollywood* megastar was not perturbed by the security situation and accepted the invitation of dreaded warlords whose hands were still soaked in blood. Film stars Danny Dengzongpa, Biloo, Amitabh, and producer Mukul boarded a chopper gunship, flanked by five other helicopters. He recalled how it was an unforgettable ride for the whole crew as the aerial view offered them the 'vista of purple mountains turning pink and red because of poppies growing there'. In a poetical recollection of the experience, Amitabh stated that 'Time seemed to have stood absolutely still in the valley where the chopper landed, and they could see a medieval castle-like structure in the distance'. Much to the surprise of the whole crew, they all were 'bodily lifted by the warlords and carried there because traditionally, the feet of guests aren't supposed to touch the ground'. From the castle, the crew were taken to the grounds where the Buzkashi tournament had been organized for the guests. Buzkashi is a popular sport in Afghanistan and a traditional equestrian game prevalent in Central Asia. The name literally translates from Persian as goat pulling. The primary goal is for horse-mounted players (called *chapandaz*) to seize a headless body of a goat or calf, carry it around a designated marker or across a goal line, and deposit it in a specific scoring area (often a circle). The game is often chaotic and physically demanding, requiring immense skill in horsemanship and strength. Riders jostle, pull, and manoeuvre to gain control of the goat's body.

Such games are organized to honour very special guests or to prove skill, courage, and display strength, as it is called the sport of Kings. Amitabh and his fellow companions were amazed by the colourful tents, which had been erected for them to enjoy the game, which hypnotized the megastar who thought he was in Ivanhoe land. In a flamboyant display of traditional treatment of revered guests, the warlords insisted that the four film crew members must spend the night there, and to their surprise, the palace was emptied for their stay. He recalled 'the four of us kept eating and drinking and looking as if we'd wandered into an unbelievable fairy tale. We were smothered with gifts. In Kabul, the night before we flew back to India, Najab called us to the President's residence and decorated all of us with the "Order of Afghanistan". That evening, his uncle sang an Indian raga for us with impeccable ease'.[26]

The film was shot in 1991, and Amitabh Bachchan wrote his fantastic reminiscence 22 years later, in 2013, when much had changed in Afghanistan and American troops had replaced Russians in guarding the country. Najibullah was killed, and his family took asylum in New Delhi while Abdul Rashid Dostum, one of the hosts of Amitabh, became a powerful shareholder in the Afghan Government. In a melancholic voice, he finished his reminiscence, 'I don't know where our hosts are; I often wonder where they are today'.

Such were India–Afghanistan relations at the people-to-people level, even during the time of duress.

Najibullah Lost Power: End of an Era in India–Afghanistan Relations?

Meanwhile, General Secretary Mikhail Gorbachev of Russia was caught up in a coup attempt by the military and KGB in August 1991, which eventually failed. On 25 December 1991, Gorbachev resigned from his position after the coup and finally resigned from the newly created Russian Federation. On 26 December 1991, the Soviet Union was formally dissolved, and nine independent states were created other than Russia. Boris Yeltsin formally became the Russian President. There was a sudden change in the Afghan policy of the Russian Government. A month after the coup attempt, Gorbachev signed the Joint US–USSR announcement in September 1991. As per the announcement, the two superpowers stopped arms deliveries to Afghanistan with effect from 1 January 1992. Boris Yeltsin implemented this agreement, which came as a huge shock to Najibullah.[27]

Not only that, but to improve the Russian economy, Yeltsin cut off the continuance of supplies of food, fuel, and all other forms of aid to Afghanistan. The cutting off of 'fuel and food' had an immediate crippling impact on the Najibullah regime. Suddenly, Najibullah was short of money to buy the loyalties of militia commanders like Dostum. As Najibullah realized the untenable condition, on 18 March 1992, he offered to transfer power to an interim Government that would be established under the United Nations plan.[28] On 10 April, the new United Nations Secretary General, Boutros Boutros-Ghali, said warring parties have agreed to form a 'pre-transition council' that will hand over power to an interim Government. But on 15 April, Muslim rebels claimed control of the country's main military base, 35 miles north of the capital, and started marching toward Kabul.[29]

Meanwhile, Najibullah sent a message to the Afghan Mission in New York through a letter from Foreign Minister Abdul Wakil to the Secretary General agreeing to the peace plan. On the evening of 15 April 1992, Indian Ambassador Vijay Nambiar was called by Tokhi to his office and informed of the decision Najibullah had taken to leave Kabul as soon as the UN could arrange for his move, which would probably be the same night. Shortly after this, around 10 pm, Najib spoke to the Indian Ambassador personally on the phone to express his gratitude for the arrangements that had already firmed up for the UN to take him to Delhi as a first stop.[30]

But suddenly, all hell broke loose when Vijay Nambiar was woken up at 3:30 am on 16 April 1992 by a phone call from the UN-OSGAP and told that Dr Najibullah wished to speak to him. Najibullah explained how his route was blocked by rebels, which forced him not to go to Delhi. Nambiar met him immediately at the UN office, where UN office bearer Mr Benon asked the Indian Ambassador whether India would consider offering asylum to Najibullah. The Indian Ambassador immediately sought a response from the MEA in Delhi. But he was informed, without much delay, by Foreign Secretary J.N. Dixit that 'it would not be advisable at the current juncture for the Government of India to consider grant of asylum for the former President'.[31] The Indian Foreign Service officers agreed with the fact that Najibullah's presence at any of the Indian properties within Afghanistan would make the functioning of the Indian Mission inside Afghanistan untenable. The Indian Ambassador feared a strike by elements from the Hekmatyar outfit. Therefore, the asylum request of Najibullah was turned down by the Ministry of External Affairs bureaucrats. The exact involvement of political leadership, especially that of Prime Minister Narsimha Rao, is not clear, but as the situation unfolded, the Indian Foreign Service officers, who risked their lives for long in Afghanistan, were guided by the safety of their staff and not by humane considerations. The strange thing was that, although Najibullah's asylum request was rejected on the grounds of possible threat to Indian strategic interests and safety of Mission personnel, his family was already given asylum in New Delhi a month before, that was in March 1992. It was not possible without the overruling of bureaucratic advice by political leadership to grant a visit/asylum to Najibullah's family in March 1992, which was formalized in April 1992.

President Najibullah handed over power to a group headed by Afghan Deputy Defence Minister, General Mohammed Nabi Azimi. It was also announced by Russian news that the Security Minister, General Ghulam Farook Yaqubi, had committed suicide.[32] But diplomats suspected that it may not have been a suicide as Yaqubi may have been killed for complicity in the flight of Najibullah, perhaps by Azimi, who discovered the attempted flight in time, ordered an airport lockdown, and changed the password of the final ring of airport security with the collusion of Dostum.[33]

On 17 April, Herat fell to rebels. Muslim rebels took up positions on the outskirts of the capital and demanded the surrender of the Government.[34] The Peshawar Agreement signed on 24 April 1992 set up an Islamic State of Afghanistan. As per the Peshawar Accord, it was decided that a 51-person body, headed by Sibghatullah Mojaddedi of Jabha-i-Nijat-Milli, would go inside Afghanistan so that they could take over power from the rulers of Kabul, completely and without any terms and conditions during the two months. After this period, Professor Burhanuddin Rabbani of Jamiat-i-Islami would remain as the President of the Transitional Islamic State of Afghanistan and the head of the Leadership Council for four months. The Prime Ministership was assigned to the Hizb-e-Islami, Afghanistan of

Gulbuddin Hekmatyar. The Deputy Prime Ministership and the Ministry of the Interior were offered to Ittehad-e-Islami, Afghanistan of Abdul Rasul Sayyaf. The Deputy Prime Ministership and the Ministry of Education were given to Hizb-e-Islami of Maulvi Khalis. The Deputy Prime Ministership and the Ministry of Foreign Affairs were offered to the Mahaz-i-Milli Islam headed by Pir Sayed Ahmad Gilani. The Ministry of Defence was offered to Jamiat-e-Islami of Professor Rabbani and Ahmad Shah Massoud. The Supreme Court was offered to the Harkat-e-Inqilab-e-Islami organization led by clergyman Mohammad Nabi Mohammadi.[35]

Hekmatyar rejected the offer to join the Government as Prime Minister and refused to sign the accord. Hamid Karzai became the Foreign Minister,[36] who later arranged numerous meetings of the Indian Ambassador with the Afghan Interim President. During his meeting with the Indian Ambassador, Sibghatullah Mojaddedi spoke warmly of the 'Sirhind connection' of the Mojaddedis and the spiritual debt he owed to India. When Pakistan wanted a hasty solution on the Durand Line and decided to push for a settlement with the Mojaddedi Government, Kabul once again looked for Delhi's support. To the surprise and dismay of Pakistan, Sibghatullah Mojaddedi paid a visit to Delhi soon afterwards and revived contacts with Indian leaders.[37]

In June 1992, Burhanuddin Rabbani took charge as President, with effective leadership being exercised by Ahmed Shah Massoud. Subsequently, Rabbani also took the same view and refused to compromise on the Durand Line. Pakistan tried its best to get the Durand Line recognized as the international border between the two countries. However, every time such a proposal was mooted, Afghan leadership from all ideological backgrounds refused to bite the bait. As stated earlier, the Durand Line, as understood by the Afghan leaders from all ideological leanings, was a vestige of colonial India. As we will see in subsequent developments, even when the Taliban, who were touted as the Pakistani proxy forces, ruled the country from 1996 to 2001, they refused to recognize the Durand Line as the international boundary.

Meanwhile, Hamid Karzai was replaced by Najibullah Laffrai as Foreign Minister. Indian Mission staff were stranded in Kabul as there was no pause in the bombardment to allow for evacuation. The foreign missions of various countries tried to work out an evacuation plan for foreign diplomats. The troubled time lengthened to almost four and a half months, and at the end of August 1992, an assurance came from the Afghan Foreign Ministry through the intercession of Ambassador Amir Osman of Pakistan. A period of assured pause in the bombardment of the airport area was agreed upon to arrange the evacuation of Kabul's remaining diplomatic personnel. This process was agreed upon for the morning of 28 August between 5 am and 9 am. Breaking the promised pause, the bombing of the airport area started during take-off. The three aircraft, arranged by Russia to evacuate all remaining Asian and European diplomatic personnel, came under attack. One aircraft was ablaze while the remaining two made their way to Dushanbe safely.[38]

It was believed by international observers that India lost contact with Afghanistan. Pakistan played her cards well and convinced the rebel leaders that India was supporting the Soviet-backed Communist government in Kabul. Pakistan successfully kept India out of all the international discussions on Afghanistan, stating that India had no locus in the whole process. India's attempt to re-establish ties with the Pashtun tribal leadership proved difficult, especially in the face of the presence of Najibullah's family in India and the Government's unconditional offer of continued support to them. Rebel leaders refused to engage with India immediately because Najib was still alive in the UN compound in Kabul while his family was in New Delhi.

In New Delhi, Ahmad Sarwar, Afghanistan's Ambassador to India, who was also the brother-in-law of Najibullah, was rescued from the Afghan Embassy by Indian police on 17 April 1992. He was threatened by a rival group inside the Embassy. Ambassador Sarwar left the Embassy with his wife, two daughters and the family of the ousted Afghan President. Mr Najibullah secretly sent his wife and three daughters to India in March 1992. His family was at the Ambassador's official residence until their escape before dawn on 17 April 1992. Indian Foreign Office spokesman Aftab Seth informed that India had responded to a request from Mr Sarwar for protection and assistance to leave the Embassy because a situation had developed where it was unsafe for him.[39] India claimed that everything it had done concerning Najibullah had been done in accordance with the UN Secretary General's plans for a peace process in Afghanistan.

In hindsight, it is easily discernible how India adopted strange yardsticks in responding to the unfolding situations. Even seasoned foreign service officers at the Indian Foreign Ministry have succumbed to the slippery slope and made untenable diplomatic decisions. They rejected Najibullah's asylum request in the dead of night of 16 April while they accepted the same request from Najibullah's family in broad daylight on 17 April.

The transitional phase in Afghanistan has been greatly complicated. A conflict situation has arisen involving various Afghan groups. Intense fighting erupted around Kabul, forcing the closure of several diplomatic missions, including India.[40] It was thought that India, for the time being, had lost its diplomatic link with Afghanistan. But soon, the President of Afghanistan, Professor Burhanuddin Rabbani, made a stopover in New Delhi on 30 August 1992, two days after the Indian Mission was shut down in Kabul.[41] He again made a transit visit on 5 September 1992. The Afghan Minister of State for Foreign Affairs, Mr Najibullah Laffraei, visited Delhi in November 1992. All these visits were unfolding while there was no functional Indian Mission in Afghanistan, but India still managed to maintain useful exchanges with the new leadership in Afghanistan.

In September 1992, at the request of Abdul Rashid Dostum and with the approval of the Jami'at Government, the Ministry of External Affairs sent a special mission headed by Ambassador Hamid Ansari not to Kabul but to Mazar-i-Sharif.[42] Ambassador Vijay Nambiar was also part of this mission, where India offered Rs 5 crores worth of assistance through the Office of UN Coordinators for Afghan Refugee Rehabilitation and an equal amount bilaterally during 1992. India supplied relief items worth Rs 1.5 crores to Afghanistan through UNCOA. As part of India's bilateral commitment, Indian relief supplies worth Rs 4.7 crores of essential items, as well as medicines and medical equipment, were also completed during 1992.[43] For the first time, India openly made contact with non-Pashtun leaders of Afghanistan like Uzbek Commander Abdul Rashid Dostum, Tajik Commander Ahmed Shah Massoud, and Burhanuddin Rabbani, although contact with the Northern Alliance was old but secret.

Indian Ambassador left Kabul on 28 August 1992 along with all remaining foreign diplomats in Afghanistan. It was reported by the Indian Foreign Ministry that the Embassy was shut down, but its operation was not completely ended. Vijay Nambiar returned to Mazar-e-Sharif again in September 1992 to distribute commodities at the request of General Dostum. He returned to India in October 1992 after a farewell meeting with President Rabbani and a farewell dinner hosted by Foreign Minister Salman Gailani.[44] Soon there was talk of restarting diplomatic contact with the new dispensation in Kabul.

Mujahideen Rule: Testing Time

Once the Rabbani Government was stabilized, India reopened its diplomatic mission in Kabul in January 1993, for which it had to pay a price. Shrapnel from a rocket fired by Hizb-e-Islami forces of Hikmatyar from Charasyab killed one of the India-based security guards. The annual report of MEA for the year 1993–1994 states that 'Owing to a serious deterioration in the security situation, the Indian Mission in Kabul had to be temporarily closed down in February 1993'. Even when the Indian Mission was shut down, India maintained useful official exchanges with the Afghan leadership. The Foreign Minister of Afghanistan, Mr Hidayat Amin Arsala, visited New Delhi from 16 to 21 July 1993. As a humanitarian gesture to the people of Afghanistan, India donated Rs 1.4 crores worth of medicines and tea to Afghanistan under the UN's assistance programme.[45] The Mission was reopened in September 1993.[46] It was amazing on the part of India to maintain the Mission under the tremendous strain of civil war and daily bombings.

The Indian Embassy was fully functional in the midst of daily unabated rocket firing. Indian Chargé d'Affaires Mr Azad Singh Toor narrowly escaped a barrage of rocket fire from Hizb-e-Islami forces on 31 December 1993, which was aimed at Shash Darak where the Indian Embassy residence was located. The security conditions deteriorated again and demanded that the Mission be temporarily closed down again in January 1994.[47] Kabul remained unsafe during 1994, and, therefore, India contemplated having a Consulate in Herat. The Governor of Herat, General Ismael Khan, offered all help to the Indian reconnaissance team that had arrived in the city. The team stayed with the Governor of Herat. However, logistical and other factors made it impossible to open any diplomatic presence in Herat. Thereafter, the reconnaissance teams were even been sent to Kabul twice by the Government of India to study the living conditions. The team leader met Ahmed Shah Massoud and other Afghan dignitaries in Kabul.[48] However, it was not possible to open the Mission until 1995.

Pakistan helplessly heralded a series of policy failures in Afghanistan. Gulbuddin Hekmatyar, Pakistan's trump card, failed to deliver the promised breaking of the Rabbani–Massoud alliance in Kabul. Therefore, Pakistan developed its force, and the Taliban was born around October 1994. The word Taliban in Pashtu means 'students', the plural of ṭālib. The Taliban are students of madrassas or religious seminaries. During the national struggle against the Soviet Army, the Taliban fought alongside the Mujahideen, mainly under the leadership of Mohammad Nabi of Harakat-i-Inqilab-i-Islami, one of the seven sanctioned Mujahideen leaders in Pakistan. The Taliban were influenced by the teachings of Islam in Pakistan, where they had migrated with millions of other Afghans after the Soviet invasion. There, they attended religious madrassas, while many of them also remained active fighting the Soviets on the battlefields.

They are the followers of the 'Deobandi' school of thought, preached by mullahs (clerics) in Pakistani madrassas. The Deobandi School emerged as a reform movement in British India intending to rejuvenate Islamic society. The Pakistani version of the Deobandi schools in Afghan refugee camps was, however, often run by inexperienced and semi-literate mullahs associated with Pakistan's Jamaat-e-Ulema-e Islam (JUI) political party. Saudi funds and scholarships, during the Afghan struggle against the Soviets, in combination with a lack of appreciation on the part of the Mullahs for the reformist Deobandi agenda, brought the schools and their curricula closer to ultraconservative Wahhabism, which claims to teach strict adherence to the practices of the Prophet Mohammad and the Four Rightful Caliphs.[49] The Taliban's close ties with the Deobandi schools and, in turn, their association with JUI and its links with the religious, military, and political establishments of Pakistan and Saudi Arabia have been prime sources of political, financial, and military aid for the group.

There are several versions of how a small group of Taliban, led by Mullah Muhammad Omar, took control of areas around Kandahar in 1994. According to the widely circulated account, Mullah Omar started his movement with fewer than 50 armed madrassa students in his hometown of Kandahar.[50] The most credible and often-repeated story of how Mullah Omar first mobilized his followers is that in the spring of 1994, neighbours in Singesar told him that the local governor had abducted two teenage girls, shaved their heads, and taken them to a camp where they were raped repeatedly. Thirty Taliban with only 16 rifles freed the girls and hanged the governor from the barrel of a tank.[51] Later that year, two militia commanders killed civilians while fighting for the right to sodomize a young boy.[52] These gory yet faithful incidents, the Taliban claim, marked the beginning of their campaign in Afghanistan. Though this action was violent and shocking, many local Afghans saw it as justified and in accordance with their interpretation of Islamic justice. The Taliban, under Mullah Omar, presented themselves as moral crusaders determined to end the widespread lawlessness, corruption, and moral decay that had plagued Afghanistan during the civil war period. Their swift, decisive, and uncompromising enforcement of *Sharia* law resonated with large segments of the population, especially in rural and conservative areas. As a result, despite the gruesome nature of such incidents, the Taliban's popularity began to grow unexpectedly. Many Afghans, exhausted by years of chaos and violence under competing warlords, saw the Taliban as a force that could restore order, justice, and religious morality. The movement's rise was not only based on military success, but also on its perceived legitimacy in the eyes of those who valued a return to traditional Islamic governance and social stability. The Taliban then moved in and disarmed other groups in the area. They began consolidating their position and procuring weapons by winning the allegiance of several local military commanders. The Taliban's first major military activity was in 1994 when they marched northward from Maiwand and captured Kandahar city and the surrounding provinces, losing only a few dozen men. On 12 October 1994, with the support of ISI, they captured an arms depot at Spin Boldak, on the Afghanistan–Pakistan border. The depot had been guarded by Hekmatyar's men. Major General Nasrullah Babar, Benazir Bhutto's aide, and Colonel Imam, Pakistani Consul General at Herat, helped the Taliban, and gradually the Taliban started gaining control over province after province.[53] Brigadier Sultan Amir, known by his *nom de guerre* Colonel Imam, was a United States-trained former Colonel in Pakistan's spy agency. He spent 20 years running insurgents in and out of Afghanistan. He was training the Taliban to conquer Afghanistan in 1994.[54]

As fate would have it for Colonel Imam, in March 2010, he was captured and kidnapped by the Pakistani Taliban in northern Waziristan. A founding patron of the Taliban in Afghanistan, he died in the hands of a younger generation of Taliban militants in the tribal badlands of Pakistan in January 2011. He became a victim of the vicious forces he helped create.[55] Nasrullah Baber also died due to illness during the same period in January 2011.

The advancing Taliban, trained by Colonel Imam and ISI, continued their forward march and captured Kandahar, Uruzgan, Zabul, Paktia, and Paktika before the end of November 1994. By February 1995, they had defeated Gulbuddin Hekmatyar, and Kabul was within range of their artillery fire. Ahmed Shah Massoud, with his superb military skill, forced the Taliban to retreat in early March 1995. Herat was under the control of Ahmed Shah Massoud.

There was a major escalation in the conflict in Afghanistan in January 1994, which continued through the year and further aggravated the political and security situation in Afghanistan. The Government had, however, been able to resume some technical cooperation (training facilities, scholarships, medical facilities, etc.) during 1994. Dr Abdul Rehman, Afghan Minister for Civil Aviation, visited New Delhi twice in March and July 1994 as a Special Envoy of the Afghan President. Mohammadullah Naqid, Afghan Minister of Martyrs and Disabled Affairs, visited India in March 1994. Sayed Noorullah Emad, the Afghan Agriculture Minister, paid a visit to India in October 1994.[56] These visits during 1994 resulted in the supply of tea, medicines, etc., worth Rs 1 crore as relief assistance to various provinces of Afghanistan such as Herat, Kabul, and Jalalabad.[57]

One of the primary reasons for highlighting visits by Afghan Government officials to India, which otherwise looks normal, is that Afghanistan was not a normal country, and its Government was not recognized by many countries throughout the annals of the post-Zahir Shah era. Following the end of Mohammad Zahir Shah's reign in 1973, Afghanistan experienced a period of significant political upheaval. A long list of heads of state adorned the seat of power at the Arg Palace. From 1973 to 2001, nine heads of state ruled the country with as many cabinets. Mohammad Daud Khan's rule was followed by Nur Mohammad Taraki, Hafizullah Amin, Babrak Karmal, Mohammad Najibullah, Abdul Rahim Hatif, Sibghatullah Mojaddedi, Burhanuddin Rabbani, and, finally, Mullah Mohammed Omar. Every time there was a change at the Arg Palace, there were speculations about the end of India's contact with Afghanistan. Therefore, explanations about these visits were significant. The list of dignitaries visiting New Delhi in an official capacity was not a mere visit or boring narration of the list of Afghan Ministers' visits to India, but it is an iteration of the importance of India in the eyes of the Afghans no matter who ruled Kabul.

As the security situation in Kabul improved, a major diplomatic effort was launched to persuade foreign governments to reopen their embassies. India reopened its Embassy on 2 May 1995. Iran, Pakistan, and Indonesia had already opened their missions, while Turkey restarted its Mission after India's arrival. Once India established formal diplomatic relations with the new Government, the Rabbani Government returned the courtesy in equal measure. There was a great deal of mutual respect and appreciation of each other's aspirations between India and Afghanistan. India's Chargé d'Affaires Mr Azad Singh Toor explained, 'there was hardly a month when Rabbani would not call [the] Indian [Chargé d'Affaires] for some meaningful conversation'.[58]

The situation has been further exacerbated by Pakistan's direct interference by employing its proxy force, the Taliban. The peace initiative launched by the United Nations under the Special Envoy of the UN Secretary General Ambassador Mehmoud Mestiri, suggesting transfer of power as an interim arrangement, was not found acceptable by all factions.[59] During the year 1995, Minister of Civil Aviation Abdul Rehman, Minister of Power and Irrigation Fariduddin Rafi, and Minister of State for Foreign Affairs Najibullah Lafrai visited India.[60] India in return, supplied tea, medicines, cooking oil, milk, and woollen garments worth about Rs 1.6 crores as bilateral humanitarian assistance.

On 5 September 1995, Rabbani and Massoud received news that their Governor, Ismael Khan, had lost Herat to the Taliban. Pakistan's role in mobilizing 25,000 men for the Herat attack was confirmed[61] and the next day, a large mob ransacked the Pakistani Embassy in Kabul and stabbed Ambassador Qaji Humayun and a few other diplomats. A staff member was killed. The Ambassador had to be airlifted to Jalalabad for treatment. The Embassy, which had earlier served as the Embassy of the British Empire, had been razed to the ground. Pakistan closed its Embassy after this incident. It was reopened only after the Taliban captured Kabul on 27 September 1996.[62] Given the rocket attacks and air raids carried out by the Taliban, Kabul airport was closed down in October 1995, and the Ariana flight of Afghanistan started operating from Bagram Airbase, 70 kilometres to the north of Kabul. The attack on Pakistan's Embassy in Kabul was a turning point. From this point onwards, Pakistan started backing the Taliban more proactively.[63] In the first meeting held after the attack on 7 May 1996 between Afghanistan and Pakistan officials, there were only a few hours of discussion focusing on Pakistan's demand for compensation for the attack.[64]

In February 1996, Ahmed Shah Massoud attended an Iftar party hosted by India's Chargé d'Affaires at his residence, where he spoke about India in glowing terms and praised India for all its assistance and for keeping its Embassy open in Kabul despite tough living conditions. It was extremely difficult for the few foreign embassies to sustain their presence. As a reward for their resilience and courage, President Rabbani awarded the 'Syed Jamaluddin Award' to three Chargé d'Affaires from India, Iran and Turkey and also to the Ambassador of Indonesia.

As the Taliban attack grew, with the mediation of Iran, President Burhanuddin Rabbani met Gulbuddin Hekmatyar, and the latter was ready to join the Kabul regime as Prime Minister in June 1996. However, the Taliban continued rocket fire, which delayed his swearing-in ceremony until the evening of 26 June 1996.[65] When Gulbuddin Hekmatyar was sworn in as Prime Minister of Afghanistan on 26 June 1996, the Government of India was so pleased with the new developments that Prime Minister H.D. Deve Gowda sent a congratulatory message to the new Prime Minister. Thereafter, when India's Chargé d'Affaires paid a call on Hekmatyar, the latter praised India's stance in resolving the Afghan conflict without taking anybody's side. The new Afghan Prime Minister also honoured the invitation of India's Chargé d'Affaires for the reception held on 15 August 1996.[66]

Despite the growing prominence of the Taliban, Kabul's relations with India grew phenomenally, and New Delhi was the only place from where the Afghan National Airlines Ariana operated its regular flights.[67] Even during such heightened tension, India set up a month-long camp to provide artificial limbs to Afghan amputees in Kabul and treated around 1100 Afghans in August–September 1996.[68]

In September 1996, the Taliban captured Jalalabad and Surobi before turning their guns towards Kabul. The whole plan was shaped by Saudi Arabian General Intelligence Chief Prince Turki al-Faisal. The Indian Chargé d'Affaires explained that on 24 September 1996, Civil Aviation Minister Dr Abdul Rahman, accompanied by another Minister, came to the Indian Embassy residence and said, 'India had shown its friendship towards Afghanistan by extending a lot of aid and assistance. The time has now come for Afghanistan to express its friendship towards India even at the cost of our lives'.[69] In *Bollywood-style* dialogue delivery, the Afghan Minister explained to Azad Singh Toor that 'they would stop the advancement of [the] Taliban towards Kabul until the Indian Embassy was closed'.[70]

Being assisted by Pakistan, Saudi Arabia, and the US, the Taliban were fully equipped with modern weapons.[71] He explained to the Indian representative that Ahmed Shah Massoud had decided to retreat towards the Panjshir Valley in the north. On 25 September 1996, the Indian officials packed their bags and rushed towards Bagram Airbase, from where a special Ariana plane was ready to take them to Delhi on 26 September 1996. American officials emphatically denied the assertion that the United States offered the movement covert support. American diplomats' frequent visits to

Kandahar, the headquarters of the Taliban's governing body, were mainly described as exploratory.[72]

Ahmed Shah Massoud also sent an emissary to Dr Najibullah to accompany him towards Panjshir, which the former Afghan President declined. Dr Najibullah said, 'I have been the President of Afghanistan. What would be my place in history if I also ran away like a coward? What will the people of Afghanistan say about me?'

The Taliban, backed by tanks and armoured vehicles, entered the city at 3 am on 26 September without any resistance from Government troops and captured all key installations, including the Presidential palace. Shortly before his death, Najibullah had made a frantic call by shortwave radio, sometime after 3 am, to another United Nations post in Kabul to say his guards had vanished and he needed some security.[73] Immediately after the entry of the Taliban into Kabul, they headed towards the UN premises, killed Dr Najibullah and his younger brother, and hung their bodies from the nearby lamppost. Najibullah's bodyguard was also hanged. The Taliban attackers reached the Indian Embassy and inquired about the whereabouts of the Indian Ambassador. The servant at the residence informed the invading Taliban that the Indian Ambassador had left for India.[74] The Taliban met minimal resistance from the Government forces loyal to the Prime Minister and the President, who destroyed their ammunition stock before fleeing.

The Taliban announced the capture of the city through public address systems in mosques. After fierce fighting overnight, the city was reported to be very calm on 27 September 1996, with people and traffic moving normally. Taliban chief Mullah Muhammed Omar, appointing a six-member interim Government, announced that his militia would enforce a complete and pure Islamic system in Afghanistan. In a special decree issued from his Kandahar headquarters, Omar said the former Government of President Rabbani had collapsed and the new six-member council would look after Government affairs during the interim period.[75] Mullah Muhammad Rabbani has been named as the acting chief of the council, which included several key Taliban leaders. Omar promised protection to all foreign missions in Kabul but dismissed all Afghan Ambassadors abroad and asked the host countries to ensure that the diplomats did not misuse Afghan property and funds. Omar appealed to the people who had fled the city to return and asked the traders to carry on their business as usual. Afghanistan Ambassador to India Massoud Khalili said on 27 September 1996 that the priority of the besieged Afghan Government was to recapture Kabul from the hands of the Taliban Islamic militia without inflicting civilian casualties. Defending the retreat by forces loyal to President Burhanuddin Rabbani and Prime Minister Gulbuddin Hekmatyar, Mr Khalili said it was a tactical decision to avoid a bloodbath in the Afghan capital. The Taliban militia hanged General Jafzar and Tokhi, the two aides of former President Najibullah, on 28 September 1996.[76]

Taliban Rule: The Missing Years in India–Afghanistan Relations

With the takeover of Kabul by the Taliban militia on 27 September 1996, a new dimension was added to the unstable condition of Afghanistan. On the military front, the Taliban made significant advances during January 1997 against the combined forces of the Northern Alliance, consisting of General Abdul Rashid Dostum, Commander Ahmad Shah Massoud, and Hizb-e-Wahdat leader Karim Khalili. By January 1997, the Taliban were in control of two-thirds of the country. However, since February 1997, there has been no significant forward movement by them. The forces of the Northern Alliance had been able to keep them in check in the two main battlefronts, Ghorband Valley and Badghis.[77]

Pakistan thought that it had successfully removed India from the soil of Afghanistan, which was true on paper. India continued to recognize the Government of Professor Rabbani, and although regular contact was not possible, Indian officials maintained occasional contact at various levels.[78] India participated in the Conference on Afghanistan on 29 and 30 October 1996 held in Teheran and attended the UN Secretary General's meeting in New York on 18 November 1996 to discuss issues related to Afghanistan. Indian representatives attended the meeting of the International Forum on Assistance to Afghanistan held on 21 and 22 January 1997 in Ashkhabad, Turkmenistan.[79]

Curiously, in its December 1996 policy statement on Afghanistan, the State Department called on other nations to 'engage' with the Taliban in hopes of moderating their policies. But the statement came as the Taliban were tightening still further their Islamic social code, particularly the taboos that had banned women from working, closed girls' schools, and required all women beyond puberty to cloak themselves from head to toe in burqas.[80] The result was that not a single one of the member countries of the United Nations had recognized the Taliban Government, and none had come forward with offers of reconstruction aid.[81] Later, only three countries – Saudi Arabia, the United Arab Emirates, and Pakistan –recognized the Taliban regime.

The Taliban, consequent to the major offensives it had launched in July 1998 in Northern Afghanistan, succeeded in capturing several cities in Northern and Central Afghanistan, driving out the forces of General Abdul Rashid Dostum and Hizb-e-Wahdat. However, Commander Ahmad Shah Massoud put up a strong resistance to the Taliban advances into his traditional areas of influence and recaptured, in October–November 1998, all of Takhar province and some areas in Kunduz.[82] India continued to send humanitarian assistance to Afghanistan both bilaterally and through the UN. After the devastating earthquake in Afghanistan on 30 May 1998, a plane load of relief material was sent on 11 June 1998. A consignment of 30 tonnes of vegetable oil was sent through the UN in July 1998. A consignment of medical equipment, medical supplies, and medicines worth Rs 40 lakhs was sent to the Indira Gandhi Institute for Child Health, Kabul, in October 1998.[83]

After the September 1996 retreat, the Northern Alliance receded to the northern Afghan provinces of Takhar, Kunduz, and Badakhshan. For five years, between 1996 and 2001, India ran Afghanistan contact from the Tajik capital of Dushanbe, which is closer to the Afghan provinces of Kunduz, Takhar, Badakhshan, and Mazar-e-Sharif. Ambassador Bharath Raj Muthu Kumar coordinated military and medical assistance that India was secretly giving to Massoud and his forces. The cooperation began immediately after the Taliban takeover of Kabul. After the Taliban takeover, on 3 October 1996, Amrullah Saleh, who looked after Kabul's interests in the Tajik capital, called Mr Muthu Kumar to inform him that 'Commander Massoud' would like to meet him.[84] The Indian Ambassador was readily available to facilitate all help to Ahmed Shah Massoud. In Dushanbe, Massoud maintained a house on Karamova Ulitse. He had his staff, and Mohammed Saleh Registani looked after the affairs of his house. It was here that the Indian Ambassador regularly began meeting Ahmed Shah Massoud, discussing the bewilderingly shifting fortunes of the battles in Afghanistan where money was enough to swing fighters. The Commander did not speak English, and Amrullah, who later became the Intelligence Chief of Afghanistan under Hamid Karzai, interpreted for him. The Indian Ambassador subsequently had his number two on the mission, Dr S.A. Qureshi, on hand for interpretation.

Ahmed Shah Massoud categorically told Ambassador Muthu Kumar, 'I need India's support'. The foreign service officer reported back to Delhi, explaining the fact that 'He is battling someone we should be battling. When Massoud fights the Taliban, he fights Pakistan'. India supported Ahmed Shah Massoud with utmost sincerity. The Commander's wish list kept growing. On one occasion, when New Delhi agreed to send only a fraction of the requirement, Mr Muthu Kumar sent a message explaining Massoud's predicament. In December 1998, Jaswant Singh, a former soldier who became External Affairs Minister, read the cables. He directly called Mr Muthu Kumar and gave him a message to deliver to the Commander: 'Please assure him that he will have his requirements'. Short of sending heavy equipment, India provided extensive assistance to the Northern Alliance – uniforms, ordnance, mortars, small armaments, refurbished Kalashnikovs seized in Kashmir, combat and winter clothes, packaged food, medicines, and funds through his brother in London, Wali Massoud. Assistance would be delivered circuitously with the help of other countries that assisted with this outreach. The logistics of procurement and delivery were handled by the Military Intelligence wing in New Delhi. The supplies arrived regularly at Dushanbe, and the Tajik customs ensured the smooth transfer to Farkhor, at the border between Tajikistan and northern Afghanistan, where Massoud maintained around ten helicopters for his war efforts. New Delhi also helped maintain the helicopters with spares and service. Between 1996 and 1999, India gifted two Mi-8 helicopters.[85]

The Taliban launched three major campaigns against the forces of the Government of Afghanistan, especially those of Commander Ahmad Shah Massoud in 1998 and early 1999. These campaigns sought to drive Massoud out of Afghanistan. However, Massoud was able to hold his ground in the Shomali Plains as well as north of the Hindukush.[86]

Jaswant Singh invited Ahmed Shah Massoud to New Delhi towards the end of May 2001. He spent four days in Delhi. This was a closely guarded visit, as Jaswant Singh would say 'any number of terrorist groups from Afghanistan and Pakistan were vying to take his life'. During various sessions of interactions, Ahmed Shah Massoud explained to the Indian Foreign Minister how he was managing the rigorous demands of that oscillating war, of uncertain supplies, and of keeping Panjshir Valley fed and looked after.[87]

Talking about the Tirich–Mir Pass, close to the border with Pakistan-occupied Kashmir, Massoud explained to Jaswant Singh whether a threat or an attack on the Panjshir Valley could occur through this pass, thus catching his forces from the rear. Massoud explained how this was not a militarily sustainable venture. Merely a small patrol, maybe five to seven strong, could take their lives in their hands and go over that pass into the Tajik-dominated Panjshir. 'Were it to stupidly do so, there was only one fate it would meet,' he had said. Upon the conclusion of the visit, India escorted Massoud back to Afghanistan by a circuitous route, not flying over Pakistan.[88]

India established a frontline hospital at Farkhor to treat the wounded soldiers of the Northern Alliance. Those requiring sustained treatment were sent to Delhi via Farkhor and Dushanbe, with the visas furnished in double-quick time. Also, at Farkhor, where the Embassy had scouted for a hospital, an isolation clinic had been refurbished with two operating theatres, 24 beds for the convalescing and an ICU of between six to eight beds, depending on the requirement. Five doctors and 24 paramedics ran the hospital, which also had an OPD for locals. The medical outreach project had been valued at that time at $7.5 million. The hospital had a helipad for the convenience of the wounded. Indian officials began flying up to Dushanbe to meet Massoud and also have themselves photographed with him. The policy grew more substantial when Tajikistan President Emamoli Rahmon indicated he would like a technical stopover in New Delhi on his way back from Vietnam, on 22 January 1999. Prime Minister A.B. Vajpayee invited him for lunch at his residence, and ways were discussed to deepen the ties. New Delhi was interested in an airbase in Aini to maintain a forward presence in the area. It had been used by the Russians who maintained Su-25 aircraft, subsonic and heavily armed. After they withdrew, it fell into disuse, and India lengthened the runway, upgraded the airbase, did a ferry run, flew a flag there too and stationed a Commandant with the rank of Group Captain with four officers under him. The Aini airbase has no IAF aircraft on the ground but is part of India's well-equipped training mission in Tajikistan.[89]

On 24 December 1999, Pakistani terrorists hijacked an Indian Airlines flight, IC-814, from Kathmandu to Kandahar via Amritsar, Lahore, and Dubai. An agreement was reached as a humiliated Indian Government sent Foreign Minister Jaswant Singh to personally deliver three dreaded terrorists, Maulana Massoud Azhar, Saeed Omar Sheikh, and Mushtaq Ahmed Zargar to the hijackers at Kandahar Airport in exchange for the safety of the airline's passengers. Three high-ranking officers of the ISI were present in Kandahar to strike a deal when on 31 December 1999 the Indian Government freed the three terrorists.[90] Notwithstanding India's lack of recognition of the Taliban, India established direct contact with the Taliban during the hijacking, and the role played by the Taliban during this crisis was noted.[91]

On 9 September 2001, Massoud fell victim to a suicide attack at Khoja Baha-ud-din in the Takhar Province. Two Moroccan Arabs, claiming to be journalists from Belgium, managed to get an interview with Massoud. Khalili, the Afghan Ambassador in Delhi, was visiting Massoud and sitting next to him when the assassination was carried out. Khalili had a miraculous escape, but Massoud suffered fatal injuries. Later, the French secret service disclosed on 16 October 2003 that the camera used by Massoud's killers had been stolen from Grenoble, France, in December 2000 and travelled through Pakistan to Panjshir. India's cooperation with the Northern Alliance, which spread over several years, went through many difficulties and challenging phases, but was consistent and covered many areas. Of great use to the Northern Alliance, particularly to Ahmad Shah Massoud and his forces, was the hospital India established, manned, and operated at Farkhor, on the Afghanistan–Tajikistan border.[92] It was to the Farkhor medical facility run by India that Massoud was brought when he was assassinated on 9 September 2001.

With the tragic death of Massoud, India lost a great window to the Afghan theatre. Ahmad Shah Massoud, often referred to as the 'Lion of Panjshir', was not only a legendary Afghan military commander but also a vital strategic ally of India. Known for his resistance against both the Soviet occupation and later the Taliban regime, Massoud shared India's vision of a stable, sovereign, and moderate Afghanistan. His deep mistrust of Pakistan's role in the region, especially its support for the Taliban, further aligned his interests with those of Indian policymakers. For Indian strategists, Massoud represented a crucial entry point into the complex Afghan theatre. His influence in northern Afghanistan, particularly through the Northern Alliance, provided India with a reliable and ideologically compatible partner on the ground. Through Massoud, India was able to maintain a strategic presence in the region, gather intelligence, and counterbalance the growing influence of Pakistan-backed Taliban forces. The tragic assassination of Ahmad Shah Massoud on 9 September 2001 – just two days before the 9/11 attacks – was not only a devastating blow to Afghanistan's anti-Taliban resistance but also a significant setback for India's regional policy. The killing of Massoud was accompanied by attacks on American soil by al-Qaeda terrorists. Famous as the 9/11 attacks, al-Qaeda's terror campaign in America changed the game in Afghanistan. Probably, Pakistan strategized Massoud's killing as a new vista to capture Panjshir Valley. But fate had something else in store.

Notes

1 Bill Keller, Last Soviet Soldiers Leave Afghanistan After 9 Years, 15,000 Dead and Great Cost, *New York Times*, 16 February 1989.
2 V.K. Nambiar, My Years in Kabul, 1990–1992, ICWA Sapru House Special Series on Afghanistan, Vol. 2, 2018, p. 3.
3 Henry Kamm, Pakistan Officials Tell of Ordering Afghan Rebel Push, *New York Times*, 23 April 1989, p. 1.
4 Henry Kamm, Pakistan Officials Tell of Ordering Afghan Rebel Push, *New York Times*, 23 April 1989, p. 1.
5 John F. Burns, Afghans: Now They Blame America, *New York Times*, 4 February 1990, p. 22.
6 John F. Burns, After Jalalabad's Defense, Kabul Grows Confident, *New York Times*, 30 April 1989, p. 16.
7 Time to Talk About Afghanistan, *New York Times*, 22 September 1989, p. 34.
8 John F. Burns, UK Cuts Off Arms to Afghan Faction, *New York Times*, 19 November 1989, p. 11.
9 J.N. Dixit, *India's Foreign Policy: 1947–2003* (New Delhi: Picador Publication, 2004), p. 143.
10 Azad Singh Toor, India-Afghanistan Relations: Observations from the 1995–96 Period of the Indian Embassy in Afghanistan, ICWA, New Delhi, Vol. 3, 2018, p. 7.
11 Robert Pear, US Weighs Shifts in Afghan Policy, *New York Times*, 14 January 1990, p. 1.
12 John F. Burns, Kabul Journal; In Power Still, Afghan Can Thank His 4-Star Aide, *New York Times*, 10 May 1990, p. 4.
13 Annual Report of Ministry of External Affairs 1990–91, New Delhi, India, p. iii.

14 Appendix XV– VVIPs Visits to India during 1990–91, Annual Report of Ministry of External Affairs 1990–91, New Delhi, India, p. A-27.
15 V.K. Nambiar, My Years in Kabul, 1990–1992, ICWA Sapru House Special Series on Afghanistan, Vol. 2, 2018, p. 8.
16 V.K. Nambiar, My Years in Kabul, 1990–1992, p. 10.
17 Appendix XV–VVIPs Visits to India, Annual Report of Ministry of External Affairs 1991–92, New Delhi, India, p. A-28.
18 V.K. Nambiar, My Years in Kabul, 1990–1992, ICWA Sapru House Special Series on Afghanistan, Vol. 2, 2018, p. 9.
19 Annual Report of Ministry of External Affairs 1991–92, New Delhi, India, p. A-28.
20 Annual Report of Ministry of External Affairs 1991–92, New Delhi, India, p. 8.
21 Annual Report of Ministry of External Affairs 1991–92, New Delhi, India, p. iii.
22 V.K. Nambiar, My Years in Kabul, 1990–1992, ICWA Sapru House Special Series on Afghanistan, Vol. 2, 2018, p. 16.
23 V.K. Nambiar, My Years in Kabul, 1990–1992, p. 17.
24 V.K. Nambiar, My Years in Kabul, 1990–1992, p. 17.
25 Amitabh Bachhan, Facebook, FB 313 – #Tuesday #Memoir: Khuda Gawah, 27 August 2013.
26 Amitabh Bachhan, Facebook, FB 313 – #Tuesday #Memoir: Khuda Gawah, 27 August 2013.
27 Coup to Rebel Victory, *New York Times*, 26 April 1992, p. 14.
28 Edward A. Gargan, Afghan President Agrees to Step Down, *New York Times*, 19 March 1992, p. 3.
29 Coup to Rebel Victory, *New York Times*, 26 April 1992, p. 14.
30 Special Report, Najibullah In-Law Flees, *New York Times*, 17 April 1992, p. 1.
31 V.K. Nambiar, My Years in Kabul, 1990–1992, ICWA Sapru House Special Series on Afghanistan, Vol. 2, 2018, p. 24.
32 Najib arrested; Generals take over Kabul, *The Hindustan Times*, 17 April 1992.
33 V.K. Nambiar, My Years in Kabul, 1990–1992, ICWA Sapru House Special Series on Afghanistan, Vol. 2, 2018, p. 27.
34 The Associated Press, Afghan Guerrillas Order Kabul Army to Surrender City, *New York Times*, 18 April 1992, p. 1.
35 Peshawar Accord, 25 April 1992, retrieved on 25 January 2011 from http://incore.hq.unu.edu/services/cds/agreements/pdf/afgan2.pdf.
36 Coup to Rebel Victory, *New York Times*, 26 April 1992, p. 14.
37 Azad Singh Toor, India-Afghanistan Relations: Observations from the 1995–96 Period of the Indian Embassy in Afghanistan, ICWA, New Delhi, Vol. 3, 2018, p. 5.
38 V.K. Nambiar, My Years in Kabul, 1990–1992, ICWA Sapru House Special Series on Afghanistan, Vol. 2, 2018, pp. 26–27.
39 Special Report, Najibullah In-Law Flees, *New York Times*, 17 April 1992, p. 1.
40 Annual Report of Ministry of External Affairs 1992–93, New Delhi, India, p. 23.
41 VVIPs visit during the year 1992, Annual Report of Ministry of External Affairs 1992–93, New Delhi, India, p. 162.
42 V.K. Nambiar, My Years in Kabul, 1990–1992, ICWA Sapru House Special Series on Afghanistan, Vol. 2, 2018, p. 37.
43 VVIPs visit during the year 1992, Annual Report of Ministry of External Affairs 1992–93, New Delhi, India, p. 162.
44 V.K. Nambiar, My Years in Kabul, 1990–1992, ICWA Sapru House Special Series on Afghanistan, Vol. 2, 2018, p. 37.

45 Annual Report of Ministry of External Affairs 1993–94, New Delhi, India, p. 8.
46 Appendix XIII–VVIPS visits to India during 1993, Annual Report of Ministry of External Affairs 1993–94, New Delhi, India, p. 172.
47 Azad Singh Toor, India-Afghanistan Relations: Observations from the 1995–96 Period of the Indian Embassy in Afghanistan, ICWA, New Delhi, Vol. 3, 2018, p. 2.
48 Azad Singh Toor, India-Afghanistan Relations: Observations from the 1995–96 Period of the Indian Embassy in Afghanistan, ICWA, New Delhi, Vol. 3, 2018, p. 2.
49 Ahmad Rashid, 'The Taliban: Exporting Extremism', *Foreign Affairs*, November 1999.
50 Kamal Matinuddin, *The Taliban Phenomenon, Afghanistan 1994–1997* (Oxford: Oxford University Press, 1999), pp. 25–26.
51 John F. Burns, How Afghans' Stern Rulers Took Hold, *New York Times*, 31 December 1996, p. 1.
52 Ahmad Rashid, *Taliban* (London: Penguin, 2000), p. 25.
53 Ahmad Rashid, *Taliban* (London: Penguin, 2000), p. 27.
54 Carlotta Gall, Former Pakistani Officer Embodies a Policy Puzzle, *New York Times*, 3 March 2010.
55 Jane Perlez, Onetime Taliban Handler Dies in Their Hands, *New York Times*, 24 January 2011.
56 Annual Report of Ministry of External Affairs 1994–95, New Delhi, India, p. 9.
57 Annual Report of Ministry of External Affairs 1994–95, New Delhi, India, p. 9.
58 Azad Singh Toor, India-Afghanistan Relations: Observations from the 1995–96 Period of the Indian Embassy in Afghanistan, ICWA, New Delhi, Vol. 3, 2018, p. 2.
59 Annual Report of Ministry of External Affairs 1995–96, New Delhi, India, p. 8.
60 Annual Report of Ministry of External Affairs 1995–96, New Delhi, India, p. 8.
61 Ahmad Rashid, *Taliban* (London: Penguin, 2000), p. 39.
62 Azad Singh Toor, India-Afghanistan Relations: Observations from the 1995–96 Period of the Indian Embassy in Afghanistan, ICWA, New Delhi, Vol. 3, 2018, pp. 16–17.
63 Azad Singh Toor, India-Afghanistan Relations: Observations from the 1995–96 Period, p. 17.
64 Country Report: Pakistan-Afghanistan, The Economist Intelligence Unit, 15 Regent Street, London SW1Y 4LR, United Kingdom, 1996, p. 16.
65 Azad Singh Toor, India-Afghanistan Relations: Observations from the 1995–96 Period of the Indian Embassy in Afghanistan, ICWA, New Delhi, Vol. 3, 2018, p. 17.
66 Azad Singh Toor, India-Afghanistan Relations: Observations from the 1995–96 Period, p. 6.
67 Azad Singh Toor, India-Afghanistan Relations: Observations from the 1995–96 Period, p. 7.
68 Annual Report of Ministry of External Affairs 1996–97, New Delhi, India, p. 8.
69 Azad Singh Toor, India-Afghanistan Relations: Observations from the 1995–96 Period of the Indian Embassy in Afghanistan, ICWA, New Delhi, Vol. 3, 2018, p. 18.
70 Azad Singh Toor, India-Afghanistan Relations: Observations from the 1995–96 Period, p. 18.
71 Azad Singh Toor, India-Afghanistan Relations: Observations from the 1995–96 Period, p. 6.
72 John F. Burns, How Afghans' Stern Rulers Took Hold, *New York Times*, 31 December 1996, p. 1.

73 Associated Press, Guerrillas Take Afghan Capital as Troops Flee, *New York Times*, 28 September 1996, p. 1.
74 Azad Singh Toor, India-Afghanistan Relations: Observations from the 1995–96 Period of the Indian Embassy in Afghanistan, ICWA, New Delhi, Vol. 3, 2018, p. 18.
75 Azad Singh Toor, Taliban captures Kabul, *The Hindustan Times*, 28 September 1996.
76 Azad Singh Toor, Taliban captures Kabul, *The Hindustan Times*, 28 September 1996.
77 Annual Report of Ministry of External Affairs 1996–97, New Delhi, India, p. 8.
78 Annual Report of Ministry of External Affairs 1996–97, New Delhi, India, p. 8.
79 Annual Report of Ministry of External Affairs 1996–97, p. 9.
80 Annual Report of Ministry of External Affairs 1998–99, New Delhi, India.
81 John F. Burns, How Afghans' Stern Rulers Took Hold, *New York Times*, 31 December 1996, p. 1.
82 Annual Report of Ministry of External Affairs 1998–99, New Delhi, India.
83 Annual Report of Ministry of External Affairs 1998–99, New Delhi, India.
84 Bharat Raj Muthu Kumar's interview with V. Sudarshan, How India Secretly Armed Afghanistan's Northern Alliance, *The Hindu*, 1 September 2019, p. 1.
85 Bharat Raj Muthu Kumar, interview with V. Sudarshan, How India Secretly Armed Afghanistan's Northern Alliance, p. 1.
86 Annual Report of Ministry of External Affairs 1999–00, New Delhi, India, p. 1.
87 Jaswant Singh, *A Call to Honour: In Service of Emergent India* (New Delhi: Rupa & Co, 2007), p. 238.
88 Jaswant Singh, *A Call to Honour: In Service of Emergent India* (New Delhi: Rupa & Co, 2007), p. 239.
89 Bharat Raj Muthu Kumar's interview with V. Sudarshan, How India Secretly Armed Afghanistan's Northern Alliance, *The Hindu*, 1 September 2019, p. 1.
90 Saroj Kumar Rath, *Fragile Frontiers: The Secret History of Mumbai Terror Attacks* (London: Routledge Publication, 2018), p. 53.
91 Annual Report of Ministry of External Affairs 1999–00, New Delhi, India, p. 1.
92 Jaswant Singh, *A Call to Honour: In Service of Emergent India* (New Delhi: Rupa & Co, 2007), p. 239.

6
NAVIGATING THE CHESSBOARD IN THE 21ST CENTURY

On 11 September 2001, two days after the death of Ahmed Shah Massoud, 19 al-Qaeda terrorists hijacked four American jetliners and flew two jetliners into both towers of the World Trade Center in Manhattan, New York, while they dashed another aeroplane into the Pentagon, outside Washington, in parallel attacks on quintessential symbols of American financial and military power. One wall of the Pentagon – the fortress-like headquarters of the Defense Department across the Potomac River that was built at the beginning of World War II – also tumbled to the ground.[1] One plane went down in Pennsylvania, with its intended target being Camp David, the Presidential retreat in Maryland.

On 7 October, nearly a month after the attacks, the US and its partners started a campaign against the intransigent Taliban, who refused to surrender Osama bin Laden, the mastermind of the 9/11 attacks. Pakistan tacitly supported the Taliban in their decision not to surrender before the United States. Code-named 'Operation Enduring Freedom', the US retaliation against al-Qaeda and their host Taliban Government of Afghanistan began with some 50 Tomahawk missiles dropped on Kabul, Kandahar, Jalalabad, and Kunduz from 40 aircraft of the US and coalition partners on the first night of the attack. The house of Taliban supremo Mullah Omar was hit, along with other military bases and oil installations in Kabul, Kandahar, and Herat.[2] The Taliban Government collapsed rather quickly as the entire spectrum of Taliban leadership fled urban centres in no time. The US relied on the battle-hardened prowess of Northern Alliance fighters, who helped the US fight with the Taliban on the ground.

DOI: 10.4324/9781003627678-6

On the evening of 11 September 2001, the Cabinet Committee on Security, the apex decision-making body of the Government of India, was convened under the leadership of Prime Minister Atal Bihari Vajpayee. The committee had 'expressed its great horror at this crime that has been perpetrated and has offered its deepest condolences and sympathy to the people, government and the President of the United States of America'.[3]

On 12 September, India's External Affairs Minister Jaswant Singh clarified to the press that 'India will provide whatever assistance required from India to the United States to fight the menace of terrorism. India's offer of assistance, as mentioned in the Prime Minister's letter to President Bush, was unambiguous and unconditional'.[4] On 16 September, Prime Minister Atal Bihari Vajpayee had a ten-minute telephone conversation with President George W. Bush, who called the Prime Minister from his Camp David office. The Prime Minister said that the Government and people of India share the pain and anger of the American people and that India would extend its fullest cooperation in bringing the terrorists to justice.[5]

Having commenced their military gains on 9 November 2001, when they captured Mazar-e-Sharif, the United Front forces quickly established control over most provinces of Afghanistan. Bamiyan, Faryab, Badghis, Samangan, Takhar, Ghor, Baghlan, and parts of Kunduz fell on 11 November 2001. Herat fell on 12 November, and Northern Alliance forces entered Kabul on 13 November 2001.

On 18 December 2001, with pomp and ceremony, despite the continuous drizzle, the American Embassy building in Kabul reopened, having been closed since 31 January 1989. With the reopening of the United States mission in Kabul, America resumed its diplomatic, economic, and political engagement with Afghanistan.[6] Barely four days later, on 22 December 2001, Hamid Karzai was sworn in as head of an interim power-sharing Government in Afghanistan[7] along with a 29-member cabinet, including two women, in ceremonies in Kabul before 2000 international dignitaries and Afghan leaders.[8] India's External Affairs Minister Jaswant Singh travelled to Kabul through Dushanbe in the helicopter of deceased Northern Alliance leader Ahmed Shah Massoud to reach the swearing-in ceremony. India renewed her contact with the Government of Afghanistan as most of the members of the new cabinet were erstwhile Northern Alliance cadres. The new Government had a six-month mandate, after which, on 20 June 2002, Afghan elders again re-elected him through the Loya Jirga for the next two years.[9]

Although India officially opened her office of the Consulate General of India, which was first opened in Herat with effect from 1 September 2002,[10] six doctors and seven paramedics were dispatched to the Indira Gandhi Hospital for Children in November 2001.[11] That was before the war against the Taliban was over and also before Hamid Karzai took over as head of the interim administration. A second group of doctors and technicians was sent to Kabul on 30 December 2001 to set up a camp for fixing artificial limbs (Jaipur foot) for Afghan amputees.[12]

An inquiry had been made by me at the Ministry of External Affairs, Government of India, through the invocation of the Right to Information Act to know the exact date of the restarting of the Indian Mission in Afghanistan. The Consulate of Herat, in its letter dated 31 March 2019, stated that the first consulate of India was opened in Herat on 1 September 2002. However, the Annual Report of the MEA for the year 2001–2002 states that

> on 21 November 2001, India's Special Envoy on Afghanistan, S.K. Lambah, led a diplomatic mission to Kabul, Afghanistan. From the same date, the Liaison Office of the MEA became operational in Kabul. It was subsequently upgraded to an Embassy on 22 December 2001, after the inauguration of the new Afghan Interim Administration on that day.[13]

The MEA website in its bilateral visit section[14] explained that the 'India Liaison Office' had been upgraded 'to Embassy in March 2002'. There is a lack of clarity regarding the exact timing of India's reopening of its embassy in Afghanistan following the fall of the Taliban. Various branches of the Indian government have offered differing accounts, leading to conflicting narratives. This inconsistency is particularly evident in the records from the Ministry of External Affairs (MEA), which themselves reflect contradictory positions on the matter.

Irrespective of the start date, besides the Indian Mission in Kabul, India had four consulates located in Mazar-e-Sharif, Herat, Kandahar, and Jalalabad. India participated in all the international conferences on Afghanistan, including the Bonn Agreement of 5 December 2001, the Washington Conference on 21 November 2001, the Islamabad Conference from 21–29 November 2001, the Brussels Conference on 20–21 December 2001, and the Tokyo Conference on 21–22 January 2002.

As the collective defence clause of NATO was invoked, all 19 member countries under the umbrella of the International Security Assistance Force (ISAF) and later the Resolute Support Mission participated in the US war on terror. However, NATO is a dynamic organization. Between 2001 and 2025, twelve new members joined the alliance, reflecting its continued appeal and relevance. By 2021, when the United States decided to withdraw from Afghanistan, ten of these new members had already joined NATO. As signatories to the collective defense clause under Article 5, they were automatically bound to participate in NATO's mission in Afghanistan.

Alongside the original nineteen member states, these ten countries became involved in the war on terror as part of the alliance's response. All of them rushed to the region to assert their influence. Suddenly, Afghanistan was abuzz with grants, investments, reconstructions, and a new chessboard for competing strategic struggles among nations. Pakistan lost its disproportionate influence, which it used to enjoy when its supposedly proxy force, the Taliban, ruled the country. However, owing to its geographical location and America's reliance on Pakistan as the sole supply route, it remained one of the important players in Afghanistan. China seized the opportunity and initiated another round of Great Game[15] by investment and increase of strategic presence. Iran and other Central Asian countries participated with the same vigour to assert their strategic objectives in Afghanistan.[16]

Afghanistan responded well to the call of the world and made the best of it. Despite massive complaints of corruption and misuse of grants, Afghan leaders ensnared the whole world into the trenches of Afghanistan. India was not immune to this snare. It was as if Afghanistan's history had come back to haunt the powerful. Lord Curzon, the colonial India's viceroy's words proved prophetic. In 1908, speaking at the annual dinner of the Royal Asiatic Society in London, Lord Curzon said: 'If the Society exists and is meeting in 50 or a 100 years hence, Afghanistan will be as vital a question as it is now'.[17]

Relying on her age-old relations, India renewed her contact with Afghanistan with confidence. India's Foreign Service Institute organized a special three-month training course for 20 Afghan diplomats from 18 February 2002. The programme aims at building professional skills required in diplomatic assignments and includes several training modules on language and computer proficiency, various aspects of diplomacy, foreign policy, international relations, topical global issues, and economic diplomacy.

Immediately after the restarting of diplomatic relations, Afghan Interior Minister Mr Yunus Qanooni visited India on 7 December 2001; Labour and Communication Minister Mr Mirwais Sadiq visited New Delhi on 10 December 2001; Foreign Minister Dr Abdullah Abdullah visited India from 13–19 December 2001; Light Industry Minister Mohd Arif Noorzai visited India in January 2002; Civil Aviation Minister visited India on 25 January 2002; Deputy Defence Minister General Abdul Rashid Dostum arrived in Delhi on 31 January 2002; and Vice President Muhammad Mohaqeq visited India on 30 January 2002.[18] The Chairman of the Afghan Interim Administration, H.E. Hamid Karzai, paid a state visit to India on 26–27 February 2002.[19]

There were regular bilateral exchanges, including the state visit of President Hamid Karzai in March 2003. He was conferred an honorary doctorate by Himachal Pradesh University, his alma mater. Suddenly, India became the erstwhile cousin country where everyone from Afghanistan wanted to go. Due to the flurry of all these visits, Delhi earned the sobriquet of 'Winter Capital of Afghanistan'.

India's Role in the Reconstruction of Afghanistan

As per information provided by the Ministry of External Affairs, from 2002 to March 2019, India committed $3 billion for the reconstruction, development, education, health, infrastructure, capacity building, and other related activities in Afghanistan.[20] Ever since the removal of the Taliban from Kabul in October 2001 and the installation of Hamid Karzai's interim administration, Afghanistan looked towards India with great expectations for all-round development. India reciprocated appropriately, and in 2002, a line of credit of US$100 million was offered to the Afghan Government for various reconstruction and rehabilitation projects. India also announced grants of US$10 million and US$1.5 million for immediate utilization by the Afghan Interim Administration.[21] A year later, in 2003, India's commitment added up to US$400 million. Over time, India's contribution increased. Total support from India rose to $550 million in the year 2005–2006. A year later, in 2006–2007, India increased its cumulative pledge of assistance by US$150 million, raising it to US$750 million.

Although the Taliban fled from Afghan cities and ceded ground to their rivals, they took shelter in the countryside and Pakistan and continued to attack the coalition forces present on the soil of Afghanistan. They attacked the Government forces led by Hamid Karzai in equal measure. Soon, it was realized by observers that the new condition was a mere repetition of the Soviet invasion of Afghanistan in 1979. The only difference was that in the present time, the Soviets were replaced by the Americans and their allies, while the Taliban had the same set of backers except for the Americans. Afghanistan again descended into a civil war.

Despite the deteriorating security conditions in the country and continued terrorist threats to the Embassy, Consulates, projects and personnel, India's commitment to Afghanistan's reconstruction and development has remained unwavering. Prime Minister Dr Manmohan Singh announced a further pledge of US$450 million during President Karzai's visit to India in September 2008, taking the total Indian pledge for Afghanistan to US$1.2 billion. The Union Cabinet of India approved the construction of Afghanistan's new Parliament building in November 2008.[22] By 2009–2010, India's bilateral assistance to Afghanistan had crossed US$1.3 billion.[23] Dr Manmohan Singh, during his visit to Afghanistan from 12 to 13 May 2011, announced a further increase in India's aid commitment by US$500 million, thus raising the cumulative Indian commitment to US$ 2 billion.

Hamid Karzai left office in September 2014. He proved to be a close friend of India. Afghanistan received $2 billion in military and monetary aid from India over his 13 years in office. Dr Ashraf Ghani assumed office as the President of Afghanistan in September 2014. During Dr Ghani's visit to India on 14–15 September 2016, India furthered its financial commitment by pledging an additional US$1 billion for capacity and capability building[24] taking the total grant to US$3 billion.

India remains the largest donor to Afghanistan in the region. From 2003 until 2021, India offered training to Afghan teachers, diplomats, journalists, satellite television channels, lawyers, judges, agricultural engineers, bankers, and municipal officers, to mention a few. A major issue for children is the country's impoverished schools, which have been damaged by civil war and the Taliban administration. In 2003, India contributed to the school feeding programme by distributing protein-fortified biscuits, which were distributed through the World Food Programme. In that year, 972,000 Afghan children received a package of 100 grams of biscuits from India every day. In 2007–2008, the number of beneficiaries grew to 1.2 million schoolchildren daily in 31 provinces, and since 2008–2009 nearly 2 million Indian biscuits have been supplied to about 2 million schoolchildren on school days, covering 32 out of 34 provinces in Afghanistan. India helped the Afghan Government in many areas of developmental activities in all 34 provinces of the country before the Taliban takeover in 2021.

Reconstruction Is Not Easy

India's reconstruction efforts continued despite the growing deterioration in the internal security situation in Afghanistan and amidst the increasing Taliban influence and attacks on Indian workers and projects. A UN study in September 2007 documented that there has been a seven-fold increase in the number of suicide attacks since 2001. After the removal of the Taliban from the seat of power, they fled to Pakistan, where its intelligence agency ISI sheltered them and 'sanctuaries and logistics were provided, training was provided, ideological bases were provided'.[25] Since Pakistan does not want an Indian footprint in Afghanistan, Taliban fighters became its Trojan Horse against Indian interests.

Indian officials had been bearing the brunt of Pakistan-sponsored terrorist attacks in Afghanistan. On 19 November 2005, an Indian official from India's Border Roads Organization, Mr Maniyappan Raman Kutty, who was working on the Zaranj–Delaram Road Project was abducted by suspected Taliban militants. The Government of India had made every effort to seek the safe release of the abductee, in cooperation with Afghan authorities, but on 23 November 2005 the decapitated body of Kutty was dumped by the Taliban at a roadside in Delaram in Nimroz province. In February

2006, the tragic killing of an Indian engineer, Bharat Kumar, occurred and a few months later, in April 2006 another official K. Suryanarayan was killed by militants. In 2006, three attacks involving the lobbing of grenades into the premises of the Indian Consulate at Kandahar and rocket attacks on the campsites of an Indian road construction company tested the morale of Indian reconstruction workers. Despite these setbacks, India reiterated its commitment to Afghanistan's reconstruction.

Indian workers, who had been working on the Zaranj–Delaram Road Project, suffered a terrorist attack on 3 January 2008. Two Indian and 11 Afghan security personnel were killed, and several others were injured. A few months later, a suicide bomber attacked the Indian Embassy in Kabul on the morning of 7 July 2008, in which five Embassy personnel were killed along with 60 Afghan nationals. The attack on the Indian Embassy was among the worst of the terrorist strikes in Afghanistan. Determined investigations by the Government of Afghanistan and also by the Government of India concluded that the attack was planned and executed by elements based in Pakistan.[26]

A year later, on 8 October 2009, there was a terrorist attack targeting the Indian Embassy in Kabul which killed at least 17 Afghans. There was a terrorist attack on the morning of 26 February 2010 in Kabul targeting residential facilities, used mainly by Indian nationals. Six Indians, including one officer of the Army Medical Corps and two officers from the Army Education Corps, engaged in medical and humanitarian work, one employee each of the Indian Consulates General in Herat and Kandahar, a member of an ICCR-sponsored visiting cultural troupe, and a senior official of Power Grid Corporation of India Limited fell victim the same day. The profile of Indian victims in Afghanistan amply explains the massive nature of Indian involvement in the reconstruction of the country.

On 23 May 2014, three days before the swearing-in ceremony of Mr Narendra Modi as Prime Minister of India, there was an attack on the Indian Consulate in Herat. When Hamid Karzai came to India for the swearing-in ceremony, he privately informed that the Pakistan-based terror group, Lashkar-e-Taiba, wanted a hostage situation at the Herat consulate of India.

The Taliban militants are unorthodox advocates of violence. They don't even seem to spare their benefactors. Although Saudi Arabia was among the three countries that recognized the Taliban regime during their 1996–2001 period and also provided financial support, they never hesitated to shelter Saudi dissident Osama bin Laden. Not only this, but when the Saudis wanted Osama extradited to Riyadh, they refused to hand him over to the Saudi regime. The killing of Colonel Imam of Pakistan's ISI by the protégé of the Taliban is already documented in the previous chapter. The United

Arab Emirates was the last country which recognized the Taliban regime. But the UAE's recognition never deterred the Taliban from sparing the UAE Ambassador in Kandahar. On 10 January 2017, in a deadly attack, the Taliban killed the United Arab Emirates Ambassador along with five of his diplomatic aides at the Governor's guesthouse in Kandahar. Investigations show that the Quetta Shura, the Taliban's leadership council operating out of Pakistan, planned the attack. Central to its execution was the Governor's cook Sayed Mahboob Agha, a 'sleeper' who had provided information to the Taliban in return for money for more than a decade. Mr Agha had been promised about US$ 30,000.[27] These attacks were against their own benefactors, who had been standing with the Taliban through thick and thin. Therefore, attacks against Indian interests were natural and aggravated by their sponsors in Pakistan.

The Search for Alternative Trade Routes

India has long been facing the challenge of importing tradable goods from Afghanistan. Despite the huge potential for mutual trade, considering the landlocked nature of Afghanistan, overland trade has always been a troubled subject. Overland trade can only be possible via Pakistan, making it a significant stumbling block to promoting mutual trade. The route from India used to be known as the Silk Road highway in ancient times, and more recently the same route, which remained in Pakistan, acted as supply arteries for NATO supplies reaching troops in Afghanistan. The route is the primary trade corridor for Afghan goods seeking markets in India and vice versa. The corridor extends from Kabul to the Torkham border crossing with Pakistan, then on to Peshawar and Wagah at the Indian border.[28] From Wagah, the goods are shifted to Indian trucks for the last stage of the journey to the wholesale markets in New Delhi.

Pakistan, which continues with its anti-India intransigence, allowed Afghan goods to reach India by overland routes with numerous conditions. As per the conditions, Afghan goods could reach India, but Indian goods were not allowed to go to Afghanistan using the same route. Pakistan signed an agreement with Afghanistan, namely the 'Afghanistan Transit Trade Agreement' (ATTA) in 1965, which was meant to facilitate overland transit between Afghanistan and Pakistan. The agreement guaranteed duty-free transit between the two countries. However, the agreement did not grant Pakistan reciprocal rights to export goods across Afghan territory to neighbouring countries. That is why, although the ATTA treaty allowed Afghan transit up to the Indian border, in reality, Pakistan allowed Afghan vehicles up to Peshawar and, thereafter, Pakistani trucks were used to transport goods towards the Indian border. Signed on 2 March 1965, the ATTA expired in September 2009. The ATTA was superseded in 2010 by the Afghanistan–Pakistan Transit Trade Agreement (APTTA).

The APTTA was signed on 28 October 2010, and since then the trade corridor has been governed by its provisions, which provide free movement and transit of goods between the two countries without any procedural bottlenecks. However, illegal tariffs are rampant along the trade corridor, with shippers contending with more than a dozen *ad-hoc* checkpoints along the corridor where government and non-government actors extract illegal tolls, creating delays for the goods and breaks in the cold chain. Afghan transporters are generally not allowed to go beyond Peshawar, forcing exporters to rely on Pakistani rather than Afghan shippers.

Besides, the APTTA is a confusing agreement. There are all types of media reports which explain the expiration of the APTTA agreement in 2015.[29] However, the agreement contains an automatic renewal provision and, as per its provision cited in Article 54 (3), 'The Agreement shall remain in force for five years from the date it comes into force'. The next subpoint 54 (4) specifies that 'This agreement shall be automatically renewed for a further period of five years thereafter, subject to such modification as may be agreed upon unless terminated by either Contracting Party in accordance with Article 56'. Article 56 (1) states that 'This agreement may be denounced by either Contracting Party on the basis of valid justifications thereto, after one year from the date of its entry into force, by means of written notification addressed to the other Contracting Party'.[30]

Although the treaty provided transit access up to the Indian border town of Wagah, Afghan trucks have been stopped at Peshawar. In 2015, when President Ghani was on a state visit to India, he stated that if Pakistan continued to stop Afghan trucks at Peshawar, 'We will not provide equal transit access to Central Asia (for Pakistani trucks)'.[31] Pakistan never amended its decision, and two years later, on 22 October 2017, the Afghan President issued a decree banning Pakistani trucks from crossing into the country.[32] The transport ministry said the trucks will only be allowed up to the border crossing, where Pakistani trucks will have to offload their goods and transfer them to Afghan trucks. Pakistani trucks have, until then crossed into Afghanistan at the Torkham and Spin Boldak borders and many transport their goods through the borders into other Central Asian countries.

In December 2017, it was reported that Kabul had unilaterally abandoned the APTTA and sought a new trade accord with India as a partner. Pakistani officials contended that the argument of abandoning the APTTA by Kabul carries no weight, as in 2015 this agreement was renewed until 2020.[33] On 1 April 2021, it was reported that Pakistan and Afghanistan signed a protocol for a three-month extension of the APTTA. The protocol was signed by the Adviser to Prime Minister on Commerce and Investment, Abdul

Razak Dawood from Pakistan, and Afghanistan's Minister of Industry and Commerce, Nisar Ahmad Ghoriyani, over video-link, simultaneously in Kabul and Islamabad.[34] In June 2021, the Pakistan–Afghanistan transit trade agreement extended for another six months.[35]

Against this backdrop, India continues to search for alternative routes to Afghanistan so that mutual trade can flourish despite the spoilsport played by Pakistan. In 2003, the trilateral India–Iran–Afghanistan meeting was held in Tehran from 4–5 January 2003. In the meeting, the three countries expressed their support for the development of alternative access routes to Afghanistan through the Chabahar Port of Iran via the Milak–Zaranj–Delaram road stretch in Afghanistan. This was the first time that Chabahar Port was discussed by the three countries.

An Inter-Governmental Memorandum of Understanding was signed between India and Iran on 5 May 2015. As per the contract, India committed to construct two terminals (five berths) at Chabahar Port according to the specifications agreed under the Inter-Governmental MoU. Nearly 13 years after the signing of the trilateral agreement, on 11 April 2016, India, Iran, and Afghanistan finalized the text of the Agreement on Establishment of International Transport and Transit Corridors among the three countries (Chabahar Agreement) in the 2nd Trilateral Meeting of Experts in New Delhi. The draft agreement provides the necessary legal framework for the movement of goods and passengers across the territories of the parties via Chabahar Port in Iran, thus affording India a reliable sea-land access route to Afghanistan and also to other Central Asian countries.[36]

On 23 May 2016, India, Iran, and Afghanistan signed the document for the final agreement.[37] A contract for the development of the Chabahar Port with an estimated cost of US$ 235 million was also signed between India Ports Global Private Limited (a consortium of Jawaharlal Nehru Port Trust and Kandla Port Trust) and Arya Banader of Iran. The contract envisages the development and operation for ten years of two terminals and five berths with cargo handling multi-purpose and general capacities.[38] This involves the investment of an amount of nearly US$ 85 million for the procurement of port equipment. Besides, India has agreed to provide a US$ 150 million credit facility to Iran through the Export–Import Bank of India (EXIM Bank) for the Chabahar Port development.[39]

Phase I of the Chabahar Port was formally inaugurated on 3 December 2017, but before its formal inauguration, the first shipment of wheat from India to Afghanistan was diverted and trans-shipped through the Chabahar Port.[40] Phase I of Chabahar Port has partially been operationalized by Iranians and was inaugurated on 3 December 2017. After 2017, only the second phase was under development, but India was not involved in the development of the second phase of Shahid Beheshti Port.[41]

The operationalization of the port was a major victory for India–Afghanistan relations. For the US, reaching Afghanistan through Iran was unthinkable as the two countries have been at loggerheads for decades. The topography of Central Asian states was too uneven and costly to consider a supply route. Therefore, Pakistan's Karachi Port remained the sole hope for America. However, owing to India's position to Iran and Afghanistan, India suggested the innovative Chabahar Port as an alternative to Pakistan's intransigence and monopoly over the supply line. India always works to provide genuine solutions to complex problems. The U.S. war on terror in Afghanistan was significantly constrained by Pakistan's strategic control over the primary supply route through the Karachi port, which served as the main logistical hub for coalition forces. Recognizing this dependency and its geopolitical implications, India sought to reduce Pakistan's leverage by leveraging its longstanding ties with Iran and Afghanistan to establish an alternative supply corridor. The Chabahar port in Iran emerged as a strategic solution, offering a viable route that bypassed Pakistan entirely. This initiative not only aimed to undermine Pakistan's monopoly over access to Afghanistan but also positioned India as a proactive and constructive player in the region. Despite the involvement of major global powers in Afghanistan, it was India's practical and forward-looking approach that introduced a credible alternative, thereby securing its special and influential role in Afghan affairs. Besides the Indian exports of food products, the port has also handled several shipments and trans-shipments from Russia, Brazil, Thailand, Germany, Ukraine, and the UAE.[42]

The Chabahar Port was not the end of innovative thinking to devise a solution to the problem of connectivity with Afghanistan. India continues to search for alternative and reliable access routes to the landlocked country, bypassing Pakistan. During Afghan President Ghani's visit to India in September 2016, Prime Minister Modi discussed the idea of an air freight corridor, and amazingly, before the inauguration of the Chabahar Port, the first flight from Delhi to Kabul, establishing an air freight corridor, left from Delhi on 18 June 2017.[43] The first flight from Kabul to Delhi was received on 19 June 2017. The air connectivity allows greater access to markets in India and enables Afghan farmers quick and direct access to the Indian markets for their perishable produce.[44] The air freight corridor had been expanded to Kandahar and Herat in Afghanistan and Kolkata and Mumbai in India. This link worked until the Taliban takeover of the country in August 2021.

Owing to the maritime route connecting India with Afghanistan through Iran, coupled with the establishment of the direct air freight corridor, bilateral trade shoots up exponentially. The total India–Afghanistan trade turnover in 2007–2008 was Rs 978.3 crores, compared to Rs 550 crores during the same period in 2006–2007.[45] Bilateral trade crossed

$1 billion as a result of initiatives including the air freight corridor.[46] By 2020, the total bilateral trade between India and Afghanistan stood at $1.5 billion.

After the operation of the Chahbahar Port and air freight corridor, India–Afghanistan trade was never held hostage to Pakistan's monopoly. Although it may sound strange, the two countries continue to search for other areas of cooperation with Pakistan. The Turkmenistan–Afghanistan–Pakistan–India project (TAPI) is so bewildering that Pakistan readily consented to cooperate with India and Afghanistan. The TAPI gas pipeline project involves the construction of an approximately 1700 km pipeline from Turkmenistan's South Yolotan-Osman field through Herat and Kandahar in Afghanistan to Multan in Pakistan and finally extending up to the India–Pakistan border near Fazilka.[47] The Turkmenistan–Afghanistan–Pakistan (TAP) project was first announced in May 2002. India joined the consortium in 2008. In 2014, the TAPI Pipeline Consortium Ltd (TPCL) was incorporated. The Shareholders Agreement of TPCL was signed on 13 December 2015, under which Turkmenistan holds an 85 per cent share and India, Pakistan, and Afghanistan hold 5 per cent shares each. The Asian Development Bank is the Transaction Advisor for the project.[48]

According to an ADB-commissioned report, the estimated cost of the project is US$15 billion. As per the Inter-Governmental Agreement, signed on 11 December 2010 among the four participating countries, the parties have guaranteed the security and safety of that part of the TAPI pipeline crossing their respective territories.[49] However, despite the promise of completion of the project by 2020, considering the geopolitical situation in the region, the project is delayed. The 214-kilometre Turkmen segment of the TAPI was completed in March 2020 after several delays. Despite promising feasibility studies in 2018, the next step of construction in Afghanistan has been delayed.[50] Security of the pipeline, especially in Afghanistan and Pakistan, is a big issue as the onus of providing a secure supply of petroleum products is on the concerned state where the pipeline is running. On 6 February 2021, a delegation from the Taliban visited the Turkmen capital, Ashgabat. In a meeting held with Turkmenistan's foreign affairs minister, Raşit Meredow, the Taliban declared their support for the pipeline project.[51] However, no progress was possible until September 2024, when construction commenced on the Serhetabat–Herat segment. In December 2024, the Foreign Ministers of Afghanistan and Turkmenistan conducted a site visit near the border, wherein they resolved to expedite the project through intensified technical dialogue and strategic collaboration. As of 2025, the construction of the TAPI pipeline in Afghanistan exhibits sluggish progress. Notwithstanding these endeavours, persistent challenges, including security vulnerabilities and financial constraints, continue to impede progress. Construction in

Pakistan can only be started when the pipeline reaches Pakistan. All these steps may take considerable time before the pipeline reaches India.

India Even Elbowed Out the US While Signing a Strategic Partnership Agreement

During the state visit of Indian Prime Minister Dr Manmohan Singh to Afghanistan in May 2011, the two countries agreed to establish a strategic partnership covering all areas of mutual interest.[52] A few months later, on 4 October 2011, Dr Manmohan Singh and Mr Hamid Karzai proclaimed a formalized Strategic Partnership Agreement in New Delhi.[53]

The strategic partnership is one of the most secretly implemented agreements whereby both governments have been silent on the exact nature of cooperation. The agreement was provocative for the Pakistanis because it paved the way for India to train and equip Afghan security forces.[54] Answering a question at the Lok Sabha, Minister of State for External Affairs Mr V.K. Singh said, 'India has imparted training to personnel of the Afghan National Security Forces (ANSF) as per the requests received from the Afghan authorities and based on our capacity'.[55] From the geopolitical perspective, the issue of training military personnel and signing a strategic treaty with India had huge repercussions for Pakistan. The Pakistan Army understands that by offering army training to Afghanistan, India not only creates sizeable favourable generals but also keeps a finger on the pulse of Afghan defence forces. Apart from that, such dealings would enable India to gain prestige in the eyes of Afghans. Pakistan feared that the strategic agreement was an instrument to isolate Pakistan.

Pakistan was agitated after the signing of the strategic partnership agreement. On 28 March 2013, President Karzai's spokesman, Mr Aimal Faizi, was quoted by AFP saying that Pakistan 'demanded we cut all ties to India, send army officers to Pakistan for training, and sign a strategic partnership'. Although Pakistan's Foreign Office spokesman rejected Faizi's comments the next day, pointing out that it was Mr Karzai who had proposed a bilateral strategic partnership agreement – which did not include India,[56] but the underlying feelings in Pakistan were conveyed covertly to Afghanistan.

India was the only country with which Afghanistan has signed such an agreement. The Afghans did not do this with even their prime benefactor and donor, the United States. However, later, on 1 May 2012, President Barack Obama and President Karzai signed a similar treaty, the 'Enduring Strategic Partnership Agreement between the Islamic Republic of Afghanistan and the United States of America'.[57] Pakistan tried to sign a similar pact in 2013, but the Afghan regime refused and while then National Defence Service Chief Mr Rahmatullah Nabil resigned from his position in protest. Mr Ajmal Faizi stated that the Afghan public would 'stone us' to death if 'we signed the

SPA with Pakistan' as they know the suicide bombers that kill civilians and armed forces in Afghanistan come from Pakistan.[58]

Although India edged out all other powers to befriend Afghanistan, the India–Afghanistan Strategic Partnership was not a fully automated happy agreement. In August 2015, the Afghan side complained that 'We can't understand what the agreement means if we can't even schedule a meeting for three years'.[59] After President Ashraf Ghani took charge in 2014, he made a decisive shift towards mending fences with the Pakistan Army, including visits to the Pakistan General Headquarters inviting the Army and intelligence chiefs to Kabul, and signing a MoU between intelligence agencies NDS and ISI, even as his Government joined talks with the Taliban hosted by Pakistan. Ghani refused to honour his predecessor's agreement with India, and there was no way to mend fences on India–Afghanistan relations until an opportune moment came or Pakistan made some mistakes. India reacted sharply and refused to play ball with Afghanistan amidst its shift towards Pakistan at the cost of India.

That opportunity came to India when the ISI and NDS signed a memorandum of understanding on 18 May 2015 to share intelligence and bolster cooperation in their fight against militancy. On 10 December 2015, NDS Chief Rahmatullah Nabil, a vocal critic of the ISI, resigned owing to his disapproval of the agreement. Ghani's endeavour to repair relations with Pakistan faltered when the NDS chief rejected his demand to sign the document and resigned instead. Former ISI Chief Asad Durrani opined that 'It is difficult to consider him Pakistan's friend'.[60] In Pakistan, Ghani said, 'I made a political sacrifice coming to you. Pakistan is unpopular in Afghanistan'.[61] Ashraf Ghani thought that after one visit to Pakistan, he could turn the region on its head. Soon, Ghani realized that friendship with Pakistan was neither easy nor trustworthy. After his failure with Pakistan, he looked towards India. As relations gradually improved with India, President Ghani visited India on 27–29 April 2015. Signalling a change of heart, during his visit, the Afghan President reiterated that '*Kabuliwala* has done more to give us a brand which we could not buy with a billion dollars of investment'.[62] Nobel Laureate Rabindranath Tagore wrote a short story in 1892 about a homesick Afghan Pathan in India and his love for a little Bengali girl in Kolkata who reminded him of his daughter back in Kabul. In this story, Tagore called the Pathan '*Kabuliwala*'.

Reciprocating Ghani's visit, Prime Minister Modi visited Kabul on 25 December 2015, where he dedicated the Parliament building constructed with Indian cooperation to the Afghan nation. The Afghan Parliament building was constructed in Kabul with the assistance of the Government of India at an approximate cost of Rs 969 crores.[63] During President Ghani's visit to India on 14 September 2016, it was agreed that the Strategic Partnership

Council, headed by the External Affairs Minister of India and the Foreign Minister of Afghanistan, would meet shortly.[64] However, information about the first Strategic Partnership Council meeting is not currently available publicly. The second Strategic Partnership Council meeting was held in New Delhi on 11 September 2017. To further improve India–Afghanistan relations, India signed an extradition treaty with Afghanistan on 14 September 2016.

Until 2011, India mainly provided discreet training to Afghan security forces in an unstructured manner, with officers attending largely theoretical courses. Once, in 2007, two platoon-sized units of 30 men each were trained. Under the India–Afghanistan pact, weapons such as rifles, rocket launchers, and artillery would help fill equipment gaps, and pilots would be trained on simulators in India.[65] Starting in 2004 and continuing until 2015, the Indian Army trained over 5000 Afghan Army personnel, including officers. Though the agreement to impart military training was made between the two neighbours in the year 2004, the number started picking up only after 2014. Annually, the Indian army trained approximately 1000 Afghan military personnel.[66]

India had been training thousands of Afghan soldiers and provided eight Mi-35 helicopters to the Afghan Air Force, four during 2015/2016 and four more in 2018. This aid marks a significant departure from India's previous policy of providing only non-lethal military assistance.[67] India had been contributing to the all-round development of Afghanistan and, in the process, earning massive goodwill. All this training stopped after the Taliban takeover of Afghanistan. Nevertheless, in 2021, India provided vaccines and COVID19.-related medicines and medical equipment by air to Afghanistan.[68]

Although, until 2021, India–Afghanistan relations were at their natural height, the US decision to enter into peace negotiation with the Taliban without the participation of the Afghan Government and withdrawal of troops from Afghanistan before 11 September 2021 spelt doom for India–Afghanistan relations. The ISI had been indoctrinating and brainwashing the Taliban cadres on how India was indirectly participating in NATO operations by providing military hardware. Indian interests in Afghanistan had been continuously under attack by the Taliban insurgents as they placed India among the league of occupying forces. Unlike the post-Soviet era and post-Najibullah era, when India had the time and opportunity to befriend insurgents, this time, India was caught unprepared because the insurgents were anti-India from the outset, and Pakistan had the advantage of running the Taliban's daily activities from its soil. Therefore, the US departure was a rude shock for India.

The US–Taliban peace talks agreed on the withdrawal of US troops. The talks proceeded while the elected Government was not involved in the negotiation process . India reiterated its position, stating that

> there is widespread international consensus for a peace deal in Afghanistan. If the democratically elected Afghan Government is kept out of the loop, such a deal would not only render the deal illegitimate but also discredit the election and democracy at one go.[69]

However, without adhering to any of the precautions, the United States signed a deal with the Taliban on 29 February 2020 that set the stage to end America's longest war. The chief American envoy, Zalmay Khalilzad, signed on behalf of the United States. Mullah Abdul Ghani Baradar, the Taliban deputy and a figure from the original Taliban Government, signed for the Taliban in Doha, Qatar. The agreement, which followed more than a year of stop-and-start negotiations and conspicuously excluded the American-backed Afghanistan Government, was not a final peace deal. It was filled with ambiguity.

The war cost US$2 trillion and took the lives of more than 3500 Americans and coalition troops. Other than that, the war killed tens of thousands of Afghans.[70] From the outset, the Taliban refused to recognize the Afghan Government, and they insisted that they would sign the agreement with the US only. The Taliban successfully defended the narrative that the Afghan Government was a puppet in the hands of Americans and that such a Government could not sustain even a few hours in the absence of US support. Therefore, the Taliban made it clear that the Afghan Government could not be a party in the negotiation. The US, while signing the deal with the representative of the Taliban who called themselves the Islamic Emirates of Afghanistan, mentioned more than a dozen disclaimers that the US does not recognize the Islamic Emirates of Afghanistan. The Taliban never consented to stop violence – not even during the negotiation and not after the signing of the agreement. The agreement lays out a timetable for the final withdrawal of the United States troops from Afghanistan. From the start of the talks, late in 2018, Afghan officials were troubled that the Taliban had blocked them from participating.

Taliban guerrillas successfully humbled the might of the US Government and the collective strength of NATO forces in a two-decade-long war. A day before the signing ceremony at the Doha Sheraton Hotel, the Taliban's multimedia chief described it as a historic landmark for proclaiming 'the defeat of the arrogance of the White House in the face of the white turban'. The Taliban resurrection was a striking study of modern guerrilla warfare where the insurgents successfully defeated their adversaries with sheer determination and dedication. Strategic analysts and observers may agree with the fact that the US policy of continuing to be a bedfellow with Pakistan, the mentor and host of Taliban insurgents, proved devastating. The US intelligence provided threadbare details of Pakistan's double game as early as 2001. However, the US strategists have fallen into the Pakistani trap and ended up withdrawing from a costly war.

Against this backdrop, it was challenging and unviable for India to expect friendly behaviour from the Taliban. The US Special Representative, Mr Khalilzad, opined that India needs to speak to the Taliban directly to discuss security concerns. When Russia convened an intra-Afghan meeting on 9 November 2018, wherein regional countries were invited and Taliban representatives were present, India sent two retired foreign service officials, Mr Amar Sinha and Mr T.C.A. Raghavan, as non-official participants. The Ministry of External Affairs in India clarified that no direct conversation between the two sides was part of the agenda, and the Indian representatives did not speak at the deliberations attended by a delegation from the political office of the Taliban in Doha.

India consistently advocated for the US presence in Afghanistan, not knowing how long. For India, there was another factor that was working in her favour. Because of the US presence, Afghan and Pakistani militants were glued to the Afghan theatre. Once the US and NATO troops vacated the country, Pakistani militants turned their eyes to Kashmir and other regions in South Asia. India's social capital build-up in Afghanistan was also lost, and all aid and reconstruction were reduced to dust.

India missed the opportunity in Moscow to initiate contact with the Taliban. But soon, without losing time and to avoid collateral damage, it rechristened its policy and opened dialogue with the Taliban. India, for the first time, opened channels of communication with Afghan Taliban factions and leaders, including Mullah Baradar. The move marked a significant shift from New Delhi's position of not engaging with the Afghan Taliban in any way and comes at a time when key world powers were veering around to the position that the Taliban would play some part in any future dispensation in Kabul.[71]

The Taliban's resurgence in Afghanistan in August 2021 marked a pivotal turning point in South Asian geopolitics, reshaping the strategic landscape. India, which had long been a key player in Afghanistan's development and diplomacy, faced an abrupt diplomatic void as its official representation ceased with the Taliban's takeover. Despite enduring popularity among the Afghan populace due to humanitarian aid and developmental projects, India's influence waned without formal diplomatic channels. In stark contrast, Pakistan swiftly capitalized on the power vacuum, leveraging its ties with the Taliban to strengthen its foothold in Afghanistan. This shift allowed Pakistan to assert greater influence over Afghan internal affairs. As India's strategic presence diminished, Pakistan's ascendancy underscored a significant realignment of regional power dynamics, leaving India grappling with the loss of its long cherished civilizational contact.

Notes

1 James Barron, World Trade Center Is Toppled, *New York Times*, 11 September 2001.
2 Raj Chengappa, Destination Kabul, *India Today*, New Delhi, 22 October 2001.
3 Jaswant Singh, *A Call to Honour: In Service of Emergent India* (New Delhi: Rupa & Co, 2007), pp. 258.
4 MEA, Government of India, EAM's Meeting with Media, 12 September 2001.
5 MEA, Government of India, Prime Minister Speaks to President George W. Bush, 16 September 2001.
6 Amy Waldman, A Nation Challenged: Kabul; Unsealing Time Capsule at the American Embassy, *New York Times*, 18 December 2001.
7 Reuters, Excerpts From Speech by Afghan Leader Hamid Karzai, *New York Times*, 23 December 2001.
8 Robert D. McFadden, An Overview: December 22, 2001: New Leaders in Kabul, Pledges of Support and the Cleanup Operation, *New York Times*, 23 December 2001.
9 Carlotta Gall and James Dao, A Buoyant Karzai Is Sworn In as Afghanistan's Leader, *New York Times*, 20 June 2002.
10 Ashvini Kumar, Vice Consul, Consulate General of India, Herat, No. HER/551/07/2011, 31 March 2019.
11 MEA, Afghans First: India at Work in Afghanistan, 2004, p. 11.
12 Annual Report of Ministry of External Affairs for 2001–02, New Delhi, India, pp. 1–2.
13 Annual Report, Ministry of External Affairs, Government of India, 2001–2002, p. 1.
14 MEA, Government of India, https://eoi.gov.in/eoisearch/MyPrint.php?0357?000/0001, accessed on 19 January 2020.
15 Saroj Kumar Rath, The Great Game Has a New Leader, *Fountain Ink*, 2 June 2015, p. 12.
16 Saroj Kumar Rath, A New Round of Great Game, *Fountain Ink*, 5 May 2015, p. 23.
17 George Nathaniel Curzon, *Speeches by Lord Curzon of Kedleston, Viceroy and Governor-General of India* (Calcutta: Office of the Superintendent of Government Printing, 1908).
18 Annual Report, Ministry of External Affairs, Government of India, 2001–2002, p. 2.
19 Annual Report, Ministry of External Affairs, Government of India, 2002–2003, p. iv.
20 Janesh Kain, Afghan-Iran Section, PAI Division, Ministry of External Affairs, Government of India, No. J.II/551/04/2019, 19 March 2019.
21 Annual Report of Ministry of External Affairs, 2002–2003, New Delhi, India, p. iv.
22 Annual Report of Ministry of External Affairs for 2008–09, New Delhi, India, p. iii.
23 Annual Report of Ministry of External Affairs for 2009–10, New Delhi, India, p. iii.

24 Annual Report of Ministry of External Affairs for 2016–17, New Delhi, India, p. i.
25 Elizabeth Roche, Ashraf Ghani in India: Afghan President Asks Pakistan to End Support for Terror Groups, *Mint*, 25 October 2017.
26 Annual Report of Ministry of External Affairs for 2008–09, New Delhi, India, p. iii.
27 Mujib Mishal, In Anatomy of an Afghan Bombing, Clues of a Tangled War, *New York Times*, 31 March 2017.
28 USAID, Commercial Horticulture and Agricultural Marketing Program (Champ), Afghanistan-India Overland Trade Corridor Trade Development Report, May 2017, p. 4.
29 Suhasini Haider, India turns down Pakistan's Offer for Talks on Transit Trade to Afghanistan, *The Hindu*, 28 October 2017.
30 Agreement Between the Governments of the Islamic Republic of Afghanistan and the Islamic Republic of Pakistan, Afghanistan Pakistan Transit Trade Agreement, 2010 (APTTA), pp. 22–23.
31 Haidar, Suhasini. Pakistan Must Open Wagah for Trade, *The Hindu*, 30 April 2015.
32 Mir Haidar Shah Omid, Ghani Bans Pakistani Trucks from Entering Afghanistan, *Tolo News*, 22 October 2017.
33 Khalid Mustafa, Kabul Abandons APTTA, Seeks New Transit Accord, *The News*, 23 December 2017.
34 Sajjad Hussain, Pak-Afghan Transit Trade Accord Extended for Three Months, *Outlook*, 1 April 2021.
35 ANI, Pak-Afghan Transit Trade Agreement Extended for Another Six Months, *ANI News*, 10 June 2021.
36 Sushma Swaraj, Chabahar Port, Lok Sabha Starred Question No: 152, Lok Sabha Debate, Government of India, 4 May 2016.
37 Agreement on the Establishment of an International Transport and Transit Corridor among the Governments of the Republic of India, the Islamic Republic of Afghanistan and the Islamic Republic of Iran (Chahbahar Agreement), Ministry of External Affairs, Government of India, 2016.
38 Ministry of External Affairs, List of Agreements/MOUs signed during the visit of Prime Minister to Iran, 23 May 2016.
39 Sushma Swaraj, Lok Sabha Debate, Starred Question No. 192, 15 March 2017.
40 Ministry of External Affairs, India-Afghanistan: A Historic and Time-Tested Friendship, 3 January 2019.
41 Minister of Shipping, Lok Sabha Debate, 8 February 2018.
42 S. Jaishankar, Address by the External Affairs Minister on 'Chabahar Day' at the Maritime India Summit 2021, 4 March 2021.
43 Ministry of External Affairs, India-Afghanistan: A Historic and Time-Tested Friendship, 3 January 2019.
44 Media Centre, India and Afghanistan Establish Direct Air Freight Corridor, Ministry of External Affairs, Government of India, 19 June 2017.
45 Annual Report of Ministry of External Affairs for 2018–19, New Delhi, India, pp. ii–iii.
46 Annual Report of Ministry of External Affairs for 2018–19, New Delhi, India, pp. 7–8.
47 Preneet Kaur, Unstarred Question No. 1707, Lok Sabha, Parliament of India, 10 August 2011.
48 V.K. Singh, Unstarred Question No. 1823, Lok Sabha, Parliament of India, 13 February 2019.

49 Dharmendra Pradhan, Unstarred Question No. 4024, Lok Sabha, Parliament of India, 27 March 2017.
50 Special Correspondent, Delayed Implementation of TAPI Construction Owes to Stalled Afghan Peace Process, *New Delhi Times*, 5 April 2021.
51 Zenon Bekdouche, TAPI Pipeline After Taliban Visit? *Novastan*, 24 February 2021.
52 Ministry of External Affairs, Joint Declaration between India and Afghanistan on the occasion of the visit of Prime Minister of India, 12 May 2011.
53 Ministry of External Affairs, Text of Agreement on Strategic Partnership between the Republic of India and the Islamic Republic of Afghanistan, 4 October 2011.
54 Jack Healy and Alissa J. Rubin, Afghanistan Favors India and Denigrates Pakistan, *New York Times*, 4 October 2011.
55 V.K. Singh, Unstarred Question No. 282, Lok Sabha Debate, Parliament of India, 25 February 2015.
56 Tolo News, Afghan Government Repeats Claim of Pakistan's 'Unacceptable' Demands, 30 March 2013.
57 Office of the Press Secretary, Fact Sheet: The US–Afghanistan Strategic Partnership Agreement, White House, 1 May 2012.
58 Anita Joshua, Pakistan Denies Asking Afghanistan to Snap Ties with India, *The Hindu*, 29 March 2013.
59 Suhasini Haidar, India Rebuffs Afghanistan on Strategic Meeting, *The Hindu*, 29 August 2015.
60 A.S. Daulat, Asad Durrani, and Aditya Sinha, *Spy Chronicles: RAW, ISI and the Illusion of Peace* (Noida: HarperCollins Publisher, 2018), p. 240.
61 A.S. Daulat, Asad Durrani, and Aditya Sinha, *Spy Chronicles: RAW, ISI and the Illusion of Peace* (Noida: HarperCollins Publisher, 2018), p. 240.
62 Press Trust of India, Tagore's Kabuliwala Has Given Us a Brand: Afghan President Ashraf Ghani, *The Indian Express*, 28 April 2015.
63 V.K. Singh, Unstarred Question No. 1823, Lok Sabha, Parliament of India, 13 February 2019.
64 India-Afghanistan Joint Statement during the visit of the President of Afghanistan to India, PMO, 14 September 2016.
65 Sanjeev Miglani, Analysis: With an Eye on 2014, India Steps Up Afghan Role, *Reuters*, 9 November 2011.
66 Pradip R. Sagar, Afghanistan Wants More Military Cooperation with India. *The Week*, 11 December 2017.
67 Department of Defence, Enhancing Security and Stability in Afghanistan, Report to Congress in Accordance with Section 1225 of the Carl Levin and Howard P. 'Buck' McKeon National Defense Authorization Act for Fiscal Year 2015 (P.L. 113-291), as amended, June 2019, p. 20.
68 Annual Report of Ministry of External Affairs for 2020–21, New Delhi, India, p. 9.
69 Vinay Kumar, Speech at the Afghan Institute of Strategic Studies, 27 November 2019.
70 Mujib Mishal, Taliban and US Strike Deal to Withdraw American Troops from Afghanistan, *New York Times*, 29 February 2020.
71 Rezal H. Laskar, In a Huge Shift, India Opens Channels with Afghan Taliban Factions and Leaders, *Hindustan Times*, 9 June 2021.

7
FROM GRANDEUR AND GLORY TO AN OSCILLATING BOND

The India–Afghanistan bond is a stunning story of great ancient common inheritance. It is also a remarkable tale of a shared interaction that oscillates and swings in the modern era. Mutual economic, social, and cultural factors have shaped its evolution from ancient grandeur to modern oscillations. Historically, economic exchanges and socio-religious similarities fostered strong ties. Other factors, including linguistic connections and migratory patterns, facilitated deep-rooted community interactions across centuries. Culturally, the Gandhara civilization and the spread of Buddhism enriched bilateral relations, while Islamic conquests and the influence of Persian and Turkic cultures further intertwined their histories. In the modern era, economic interests, such as infrastructure projects and regional connectivity, continue to drive relations alongside social dynamics influenced by regional strategic interests. The Taliban takeover in 2021 highlighted the fluctuating nature of these bonds, yet the enduring cultural and historical legacy remains pivotal. Common interests and multifaceted forces like economic benefits, social interactions, and cultural bonhomie will continue to shape India–-Afghanistan relations.

The Grecians' pulsating admiration for Indian civilization during the ancient era had extensively been documented by Greek scholars. Greek literature enthusiastically captured every aspect of Indian history. As a byproduct, Greek literature offers a tremendous amount of information relating to the region that later became Afghanistan. They conform to the claim that present-day Afghanistan was an inalienable part of India during the ancient era. As explained in the first chapter, myriad Greek sources offer precise details about the topography, demography, ethnic composition, religious

DOI: 10.4324/9781003627678-7

beliefs, and political order prevailing in the region. Like their Grecian neighbours in the west, the Persians were equally curious about their neighbour in the east.[1]

Even if we ignore the Grecian and Persian endorsement, the monumental *Rig Veda*[2] denotes a geographical, physical, and historical description of Afghanistan, a region that was well within the ambit of ancient India.[3] Potentates, court chroniclers, and scholars from the Indian heartland treated Afghanistan as an integral part of the Indian realm.

During the Buddhist era, Buddhism became one of the great binding forces for the people of the region. Curiously, the religion is no longer popular either in India or in Afghanistan in the contemporary era, but in ancient times, Buddhism used to be the common religious denominator of the region where a large mass of the population followed Buddhist principles with great fun and fare. Although Buddhism originated from the *Rig Veda*, it claimed a separate identity; therefore, people of the region joined a new pantheon together, showing the similarity in their thought systems. The incorporation of Buddha as an avatar of the Sanatan/Hindu pantheon proffers credence and gravitas to the common Buddhist connections. It is no coincidence to find the tallest Buddha statues (55 m and 38 m high) in the world at the cliffs of Bamiyan Valley in Afghanistan. Ancient residents of Afghanistan carved numerous caves, forming a large ensemble of Buddhist monasteries, chapels, and sanctuaries along the foothills of the Bamiyan cliffs, dating from the 3rd to 5th centuries CE. There are other groups of caves that exist in the tributaries of Bamiyan, including the Kakrak Valley caves, where more than 100 caves dating from the 6th to 13th centuries[4] are still standing to tell the ancient tale. Despite attempts at destruction, Buddha's colossal statues still adorn the cliffs of the Bamiyan Valley. It speaks volumes how Gautama Buddha's appeal reverberated across Afghan soil.

In 629 CE, when the pious Hiuen Tsang travelled through Afghanistan to enter India, there was no sign of Islam or separate Afghan identity. The Afghans were proud of their Buddhist lineage and remained part of the Indian realm with the ease of a pebble crossing still water. The heavy concentration of Buddhist viharas and pagodas in Afghanistan was not without deep linkages and mutual coherence with Indian philosophy. The notion that 'only some parts of present-day India share resemblance with the sociocultural or geographical conditions of modern-day Afghanistan' and 'most of the subcontinent remains largely different from the ancient Afghan way of life or the Afghan topography' is untrue. Afghans were obsessed with Magadh, which was not a peripheral state. Similarly, the compilation of a portion of the *Rig Veda* in Afghanistan and the extensive inclusion of Afghan geography in the Mahabharata reiterate India's deep affiliation with the Afghan landscape.

Veda, Buddhism, and the Mahabharata are subjects with pan-Indian appeal and assert influence on the Indian thought system. In other words, all over India, people have been well acquainted with Afghan topography. The ancient maxim quoted by Abul Fazl in his *Ain-i-Akbari* at the end of the 16th century amplifies the bond with vivid images. He wrote, 'The wise of ancient times considered Kabul and Kandahar as the twin gates of Hindustan, the one leading to Turkestan and the other to Persia'.[5]

The lament that the 'Indian subcontinent remains largely different from the Afghan way of life or the Afghan topography' is antithetical to historical reality and does not stand scholarly scrutiny. Abul Fazl reiterated that the Subah of Kabul 'comprises Kashmir, Pakli, Bimbar, Swat, Bajaur, Kandahar and Zabulistan'.[6] Not only did Akbar's court poet incorporate Kashmir within the Kabul Subah, but he 'looked upon Kashmir as a holy land full of sacred places, hermits' retreats and quiet natural scenes, appropriate to be the retired abode of the recluse'.[7] In other words, Kashmir was administratively part of the Kabul Subah. Historically, it was a revered heartland of sages who engaged in deep penance for years and produced remarkable works across a wide range of disciplines – including dance, drama, philosophy, music, art, science, mathematics, and astronomy, to name a few. Renowned as a center of wisdom and learning, Kashmir served as a spiritual sanctuary for hermits and seekers from across the Indian subcontinent. Kabul and Kashmir reflect the profound intellectual and administrative ties that historically connected Afghanistan and India. The fact that Kabul's day-to-day affairs were run from Delhi has been aptly explained in detail by Akbar's Persian courtier.

Afghanistan was never separated or cut off from Pataliputra, Purushapura, Indraprastha, or Delhi. Afghans had not been practising Islam until the 11th century CE, although the presence of Islam was noted in the 7th century CE. They were avid practitioners of Hindu–Buddhist religious ideas for many centuries. The separation of Afghans as a unique ethnic group far detached from India until the arrival of Islam cannot withstand academic scrutiny. It was debated at length in the first chapter how the people and potentates from Balkh to Kandahar used to descend to the Peshawar plateau during harsh winters. There were no religious, cultural, or ethnic lines separating people in these territories.

The separate ethnic identity of the Afghans is a modern argument advanced by contemporary historians. With the rise of Islam and the creation of a separate country, especially after 1747 CE, Afghanistan diverged from India. The Durand Line of 1893 further reduced the region to a landlocked impoverished state. The end of civilizational contact with India spelled doom for the growth of Afghan society and considerably restrained economic development. The rugged and unproductive terrain of Afghanistan could not sustain its vast population. For millennia, the region was fully integrated with India, and the productive plains of India used to feed the population and offered scope and opportunity to cope with routine climatic upheaval. The divergence of Afghanistan from India and its subsequent Islamic leaning proved an extreme disadvantage in the ensuing era. The region remained an impoverished, violent outpost, a stark contrast to the rich and peaceful plains of India.

Although the two countries sustained unceasing contact, their individual growth and development from the medieval era to today are a striking study in contrast. India continued her civilizational journey unabated. Defying even ancient Greece, Egypt, and Mesopotamia, India retained her original character. But Afghanistan succumbed to the onslaught of a new religion and resultantly comprehensively changed her character when compared with her ancient past.

Afghanistan embraced a new religion and accepted a new way of life; India remained the same – ancient and robust. A strange but vivid fact about India is that its history is different from the civilizational history of Greece, Mesopotamia, and Egypt. Before the development of archaeology as a subject, the inhabitants of Egypt and Iraq had no information about their ancestors. They were living a separate life, cut off from their history. Similarly, the people of Greece knew nothing about Greek history except vague ideas concerning the glory of Periclean Athens, even though the 5th century BC was a period of political hegemony, economic growth, and cultural flourishing in Athens. This age was also known as classical Greece, the golden age of Athens, or the age of the Great Emperor Pericles. But the Greeks were unaware of such a great story of their own. Although archaeology as a subject started in the 17th century, it became popular only in the 19th century.

In Greece, its residents were worshippers of the Sun, Moon, Venus, Mars, and scores of other celestial deities. It was archaeologists who told Greece what its history was. But by then, it was too late. The Greeks had completely broken their connection with their past. After the arrival of Jesus Christ, Christianity overwhelmed Europe. The Greeks and Europeans adopted Christianity. Followers of the Christian faith called the adherents of all other religions uncivilized and living in darkness; therefore, proselytization and crusades were initiated side by side.

In the Arab world, people in Iraq used to worship idols before the arrival of Prophet Muhammad. Not only Iraq but the entire Arabia remained worshippers of 360 idols installed in various parts of their country.[8] The people of Mecca were one step ahead because there was a very famous black stone[9] – the Kaaba, which they used to worship with great devotion. They also worshipped animals. When Prophet Muhammad started preaching his new religion – Islam, and especially when he preached against the idols in Mecca, there was a loud outcry against him. Ultimately, he was driven out of Mecca, barely escaping with his life. We know every emperor of the great Egyptian civilization was a worshipper of nature and celestial gods. After the arrival of Prophet Muhammad, followers of Islam spread the ideological concept of Jihad or holy war in the name of Islam. Those who refused to accept Islam were either killed, converted into slaves, or called 'Kafirs'. A tax called 'Jizya' was imposed on the 'Kafirs' for not accepting Islam. A vast swath of Asia adopted Islam. For many years, Afghanistan resisted the allure of the glory and glare of the new religion, but not after the 11th century. Like the Greeks and Europeans, the Arabs and Afghans broke with their past and adopted a new religion; they embraced Islam.

The original religions of these civilizations became extinct in a mere few centuries. All these civilizations, knowingly or unknowingly, separated from their past and adopted a new religious life completely contradictory to the belief system of their ancestors. In the subsequent era, people became separated from their history. They replaced the religion of their ancestors with new religions.

The entire swathe of Asia, Africa, and Europe witnessed fast changes. It was natural for Afghanistan to flow with the current and, in the course of time, adopt a new religion. Change was not limited to Afghanistan, and it was not as if India did not witness transformation. Massive changes occurred in the way of life and religious practices in India. The prolonged dominance of Islamic rulers at the seat of power in India necessitated an unprecedented adjustment in the socio-religious life in India. A vast number of Indians embraced Islam. Not only did Afghanistan become an Islamic nation, but India's eastern and western fronts also subscribed to Islamic ideas. Pakistan and Bangladesh cut off from India and embraced Islam, while India also retained a huge Islamic population, which was enough to become the third largest Islamic population in the world after Indonesia and Pakistan.

Nevertheless, amid this religious tumult and socio-cultural change, India continued with its ancient character. Indians never broke ties with its ancestors. Indian religions – primarily Hinduism and Buddhism – stood against the prolonged and sustained onslaught of outside religions. Hinduism, although interacting closely with other religions, pursued its age-old traditions with confidence. To practise the religion with impunity and to sustain the ideological onslaught of other religions, Hindu sages who imagined such a situation mentioned in the Holy *Bhagavad Gita* that

> It is far better to practice one's own religion, even imperfectly, than to follow another's religion flawlessly. It is preferable to face destruction while practicing one's own faith than to engage in the practices of another's faith, for following someone else's path is perilous.[10]

If we make an analysis of the religious practices available in ancient Greece, Iraq, Egypt, and India, the similarity of deities and methods of worship can easily be deciphered. However, if we look at all these civilizations from the prism of ancient life and ancient religious practices, India is the only civilization that has not only succeeded in maintaining its ancient character but also brilliantly continued with the ancient practices even in the present time. Even today, the legends known to the common Indian recall the names of their ancestors who lived about a thousand years before Jesus Christ, and even today, traditional Brahmins perform their daily worship with the same hymns composed by their ancestors thousands of years before the birth of Jesus Christ. Both India and Afghanistan changed a lot over thousands of years, but only Afghanistan lost its original character.

It was not easy for India to stand against the appeal of those new religions. India faced countless invasions, but she maintained her ancient character. Afghanistan lost everything and became a different country entirely cut off from its ancient past. Both India and Afghanistan were under the control of Persians, Turks, and Mongols/Mughals for many centuries. But while Hinduism and Buddhism sustained in India, both these religions gradually faded from Afghanistan as Afghans adopted a new religion.

For Afghanistan, the transition from Hinduism to Buddhism was smooth, but the transition from the Hindu–Buddhist precept to Islam was tenuous. It became an extension of what Muhammad bin Tughlaq would have said: '*My kingdom is diseased, and no treatment cures it. If I suppress a revolt in one place, they break out in another*'. Ever since Afghanistan dissociated from India, its situation has been identical to what Tughlaq endured six centuries ago. Once a cradle of Hindu–Buddhist civilization where religion, culture, and commerce grew in parallel, Afghanistan, in contemporary times, is the exact opposite of its ancient past.

Modern scholars confine their research and analysis mostly to Afghanistan's complex admixture of tribes and races, where tribal ethics, ethnic distinctions, religious divides, and linguistic differences are debated at great length. Although there is no official census of tribes or ethnic groups in Afghanistan, most writers explain ethnic division with great fervour. It is generally believed that the Tajiks comprise 30 per cent, Hazaras consist of 15 per cent, and Uzbeks account for 8 per cent, who are collectively pitted against Pashtuns, who form the majority among the tribes with a whopping 40 per cent of the population. Not only this, within the Pashtuns, there is rivalry between the Durrani and Ghilzai Pashtuns. Then there is the Shia–Sunni conflict, and tribal divisions add their bit to this confusing picture. Other important areas of research on Afghanistan include the Great Game struggle, the Soviet Union's occupation of Afghanistan, and the United States' war on terror. Study and research on Afghanistan by modern scholars remain confined to these subjects only, and Afghanistan is hostage to these topics.

That is why modern literature on Afghanistan misses India's contact. Owing to the intrinsic focus on recent subjects, many historical accounts tend to overlook or oversimplify the intricate cultural, political, and economic exchanges between India and Afghanistan. This longstanding interaction is often overshadowed by more dominant geopolitical concerns, such as colonialism or modern political ideologies. The illustrious subject of India–Afghanistan relations reflects centuries of mutual influence and shared heritage. It provides rich historical explanations that extend beyond simplistic portrayals of conflict and rivalry. This study is a compelling departure from conventional narratives surrounding South Asian history.

Notes

1 Athenaeus. *The Deipnosophists: Banquet of the Leashed Athenaeus*, Vol. I, Trans. C.D. Yonge (London: Henry G. Bohn, 1853–1854), p. 82.
2 *Rig Veda*, Mandal – 10, Sukta – 75, Sloka – 5.
3 Upendra Nath Ghoshal, *Ancient Indian Culture in Afghanistan* (Calcutta: Greater India Society, 1928), pp. 1–6.
4 World Heritage Conservation, Cultural Landscape and Archaeological Remains of the Bamiyan Valley, UNESCO, https://whc.unesco.org/en/list/208/
5 Abul Fazl, *Ain-i-Akbari*, Vol. II. Translated by H.S. Jarett (Calcutta: Royal Asiatic Society of Bengal, 1949), pp. 408–409.
6 Abul Fazl, *Ain-i-Akbari*, p. 349.
7 Abul Fazl, *Ain-i-Akbari*, p. 350.
8 J.L. Nehru, *Glimpses of World History* (New Delhi: Penguin, 2004), p. 165.
9 J.L. Nehru, *Glimpses of World History*, p. 165.
10 श्रेयान्स्वधर्मो विगुनः परधर्मात्स्वनुष्ठितात् । स्वाधर्मे निद्धानम् श्रेय: परधर्मो भयावहः ॥; *Bhagavad Gita*, Chapter 3, Karma Yoga, Verse Number 35.

BIBLIOGRAPHY

Primary Sources

A.K. Bakshi, Vice Consul, Vice Consulate of India, Kahdahar, Annual Consulate Report from the Vice Consulate of India, Kandahar, No. F. 1-S/60, April 26, 1960, NAI.

A.K. Damodaran, Additional Secretary, 'Hinduism, Truth & Corruption', D.O. No. 479/AS/82, April 3, 1982. Cabinet Secretariat, Bikaner House Annex, Shahjahan Road, New Delhi, File No. FIII/103(16)/82, Note on 'Hinduism, Truth and Corruption Prepared by Cabinet Secretariat', MEA, GOI, 1982.

Agreement Between Afghanistan and India Regarding Radio-Telegraphic Communication between Their Respective Countries, Certificate of Registration No. 2005, Signed at Kabul, December 14, 1949, Ministry of External Affairs, Government of India, File No. 1-I/1/Afghanistan/49, 1949, NAI.

Agreement Between the Governments of India and Pakistan Regarding Security and Rights of Minorities, Signed by Jawaharlal Nehru and Liaqat Ali Khan, Ministry of External Affairs, Government of India, New Delhi, File No. PA50B1228, April 8, 1950, NAI.

Annual Consular Report, 1971, Embassy of India Kabul, No. KAB/PV/414/1/72, February 29, 1972, NAI.

Annual Report for 1959 from Kabul, Research and Intelligence Branch, MEA, GoI, File No. 3(14) R&I/60-I, 1960, NAI.

Annual Report for 1971 from Kabul, MEA, GOI, File No. HI/1011 (14)/72-I, 1972, NAI.

Annual Report from Afghanistan (Kabul), Research and Intelligence Branch, MEA, GoI, File No. 3(13)-R&I/51, 1951, NAI.

Annual Report on Afghanistan (Kabul) for 1954, Research and Intelligence Branch, MEA, GoI, File No. 3(14)-R&I/55, I, II, & II, 1955, NAI.

Annual Reports Etc – 1977 From Kandahar, MEA, GoI, File No. HI/1011/13/78-III, 1977, NAI.

Annual Report from Jalalabad, File No. 3(14)-R&I/60-II, 1960, MEA, GoI, NAI.

Annual Reports from Kabul for the year 1976, MEA, GoI, File No. HI/1011 (13)/77-I, Part-I, 1977, NAI.

Annual Report of Ministry of External Affairs 1978-79 to 2020-2021, MEA, New Delhi, India.
Ashvini Kumar, Vice Consul, Consulate General of India, Herat, No. HER/551/07/2011, March 31, 2019.
Brij Kumar, Charge d'Affaires, Monthly Political Report for January 1967, Secret, Embassy of India, Kabul, MEA, GoI, No. KAB/101/67, February 8, 1967, NAI.
Brij Kumar, Monthly Political Report for February 1967, Secret, Embassy of India, Kabul, MEA, GoI, No. Kab/101/67, March 7, 1967, NAI.
Brij Kumar, Monthly Political Report for May 1967, No. KAB/101/67, MEA, GoI, June 10, 1967, NAI.
Brij Kumar, Monthly Political Report for December 1967, Secret, Embassy of India, Kabul, MEA, GoI, No. KAB/101/67, February 4, 1968, NAI.
Central Intelligence Agency, Durand Line, Office of Research and Reports, Confidential, July 1961.
Chancery, Embassy of India, Kabul, Annual Consular Report of Indian Missions/Post Abroad - 1976, No. KAB/PV/414(3)/77, March 16, 1977, NAI.
Col. Deewan Singh, Special Intelligence Report Number 2/6/63, Strained Pak-Afghan Relations and their likely Effects, No. 192(a)/MAK/62, February 28, 1962, NAI.
Copy of Letter from Shri Mehr Singh, Ministry of External Affairs, New Delhi to Shri G.L. Puri, No. F.1/54/1327/17, September 17, 1955, NAI.
Cultural Relations Officer, Embassy of India, Kabul, Annual Commercial Report of the Embassy of India, No. 5/23, November 2, 1951, NAI.
D. Murugusan, Charge d'Affairs, Annual General Report, No. F. 2/25/60, June 28, 1960, NAI.
Department of Defence, Enhancing Security and Stability in Afghanistan, Report to Congress In Accordance With Section 1225 of the Carl Levin and Howard P. "Buck" McKeon National Defense Authorization Act for Fiscal Year 2015 (P.L. 113-291), as amended, June 2019.
Director of Central Intelligence, *The Soviet Invasion of Afghanistan: Implications for Warning, Interagency Intelligence Memorandum* (Washington DC: Department of Defence, NARA, October 1980).
Durand Line Agreement, Agreement between Amir Abdur Rehman Khan, G.C.S.I., and Sir Henry Mortmer Durand, K.C.I.E., C.S.I, November 12, 1893, Kabul.
Dwarka Dheesh, Second Secretary, Annual Consular Report of Indian Missions/Posts Abroad for the Year – 1977, No. KAB/PV/414(3)/78, February 2, 1978, NAI.
Extension of Trade Arrangement Exchange of Letters, Kabul, 12 September 1962, Government of India, Ministry of Commerce And Industry, Kabul, September 12, 1962.
G.L. Puri, Cultural Relations Officer, Embassy of India, Kabul, The Economic Report for Afghanistan for the Period From 1 April 1952 upto 31 March 1954, No. G. 27/Muscat/55, MEA, GoI, June 19, 1955 (by the time G.L. Puri prepared the report he was transferred to Muscat), NAI.
H.A.K. Barathi, Monthly Note on Pakhtoonistan Activities, Secret, No. MII/503(4)/67, June 16, 1967, NAI.
H.A.K. Barathi, Note on Pakhtoonistan Activities for the Month of November, 1967, Secret, No. MII/503(4)/67, MEA, GoI, January 15, 1967, NAI.
H.A.K. Barathi, Note on Pakhtoonistan Activities for the Month of December 1967, Secret, Historical, Research and Intelligence Section, MEA, GoI, No.2702/68, May 10, 1967, NAI.
H.N. Haksar, Ambassador of India, Embassy of India, Kabul, Annual Political Report for the year 1959, No. 1/SES/59, December 22, 1959, NAI.

Hodding Carter 3d, Spokesperson, State Department, Government of United States, NARA, December 22, 1979, National Archives Identifier: 54495.
I.S. Hassanwalia, Note on Pakhtoonistan Activities 1967, Intelligence Bureau, Ministry of Home Affairs, DIB U.O.No.1/PTS(FP)/67(1), March 6, 1967, NAI.
India-USSR: Strains in Relations, Director of Intelligence Report, Department of Defence, NARA, Washington DC, November 1986.
J.N. Dhamija, Ambassador of India, Embassy of India, Kabul, Report for the Month of April 1962, No. 1/PS/62, May 6, 1962, NAI.
J.N. Dhamija, Ambassador of India, Kabul, Monthly Political Report for September 1962, Secret, No. 1/PS/62, October 8, 1962, NAI.
J.N. Dhamija, Ambassador of India, Kabul, Note of the Ambassador to MEA, Secret, No. C-22/PC, December 12, 1962, NAI.
J.N. Dhamija, Ambassador of India, Kabul, Political Report for the Month of October 1962, Secret, No. 1/PS/62, November 8, 1962, NAI.
J.N. Dhamija, Ambassador of India, Kabul, Note on Chinese Aggression and Afghan Policy, Secret, No. C-22/PC, November 15, 1962, NAI.
J.N. Dhamija, Ambassador of India, Kabul, Political Report for the Month of August 1962, Secret, No. 1/PS/62, September 18, 1962, NAI.
J.N. Dhamija, Ambassador of India, Kabul, Secret Note on Chester Bowles Visit to Afghanistan, sent to Mr. B.F.H.B. Tyabji, Special Secretary, MEA, New Delhi, No. 1/PS/62/J, March 3, 1962, NAI.
J.N. Dhamija, Ambassador of India, Kabul, Secret Note on Durand Line, to Mr. B.F.H.B. Tyabji, Special Secretary, MEA, New Delhi, No. 1/PS/62/3, February 4, 1962, NAI.
Janesh Kain, Afghan-Iran Section, PAI Division, Ministry of External Affairs, Government of India, No. J.II/551/04/2019, March 19, 2019.
Jawaharlal Nehru. *Constituent Assembly of India (Legislative) Debates*, Vol. 1, Part-1 (New Delhi: Government of India Press, 1949).
Jimmy Carter, Soviet Invasion of Afghanistan and US President Jimmy Carter's Imposed Peacetime Reprisals, White House, Government of United States, NARA, December 28, 1979, National Archives Identifier: 652980.
K.C Bhardwaj, Monthly Report for July 1979, No. JAL/101/1/78, Consulate of India, Jalalabad, August 11, 1979, NAI.
K.D. Bhasin, Charge d'Affaires, Annual General Report of the Indian Embassy Kabul, D. O. No. 5/23, January 24, 1951, NAI.
K.L. Mehta, Ambassador, Embassy of India, Kabul, 'Political Report for the Month of March 1974 (Part I)', No. KAB/101/1/74, April 1974, NAI.
L. Mansingh, First Secretary, Embassy of India, Kabul, Political Report for the Month of April 1974-Part-I, No. KAB/101/1/74, MEA, GoI, May 8, 1974, NAI.
Letter of Evidence & Commission of Appointment in Favour of Wing Commander Rup Chand as Indian Ambassador to Afghanistan, Ministry of External Affairs, Government of India, File No: 1(6)-PT, 1948, NAI.
M. Sahai, Press Attaché, Main Trend of Afghan Press During January to June 1951, Secret, Publicity Wing, Embassy of India, Kabul, Annual Report from Afghanistan (Kabul), Research and Intelligence Branch, October 1, 1951, Ref. No. 3(13)-R&I/51, 1951, MEA, GoI, NAI.
M.K. Malik, Consul General, Monthly Report for April 1978, Consulate of India, Jalalabad, No. JAL/101/1/78, May 2, 1978, NAI.
M.K. Malik, Consul General, Monthly Report for July 4, 1978, Consulate of India, Jalalabad, No. JAL/101/1/78, July 4, 1978, NAI.
M.K. Malik, Consul General, Monthly Report for August, 1978, Consulate of India, Jalalabad, No. JAL/101/1/78, September 5, 1978, NAI.

M.K. Malik, Consul General, Monthly Report for September, 1978, Consulate of India, Jalalabad, No. JAL/101/1/78, October 3, 1978, NAI.

M.K. Malik, Consul of India, Annual Consular Report for the Year 1977, Jalalabad, No. JAL/414/2/78, March 7, 1978, NAI.

M.K. Malik, Consulate of India, Jalalabad, Monthly Report for April 1978, No. JAL/101/1/78, May 2, 1978, NAI.

M.K. Malik, Monthly Report for February 1979, No. JAL/101/1/78, Consulate of India, Jalalabad, March 5, 1979, NAI.

M.K. Malik, Monthly Report for March 1979, No. JAL/101/1/78, Consulate of India, Jalalabad, April 8, 1979, NAI.

M.K. Malik, Monthly Report for April 1979, No. JAL/101/1/78, Consulate of India, Jalalabad, May 1, 1979, NAI.

M.L. Choudhary, Consul, Consulate of India, Jalalabad, Monthly Political Report for the Month of May 1967, No. JAL/101(1)/66, June 1, 1967, NAI.

M.L. Choudhary, Consul, Consulate of India, Jalalabad, Monthly Political Report for the Month of July 1967, No. JAL/101(1)/66, August 3, 1967, NAI.

MEA, Afghans First: India at Work in Afghanistan, Government of India, 2004.

MEA, Government of India, EAM's Meeting With Media, September 12, 2001.

MEA, Government of India, Prime Minister Speaks to President George W. Bush, September 16, 2001.

Military and Air Attaché, Embassy of India, Kabul, Monthly Intelligence Report Number 10/61 For the Month of December 1961, N.150/MAK/62, January 11, 1962, NAI.

Ministry of External Affairs, "Agreement on Strategic Partnership between the Islamic Republic of Afghanistan and the Republic of India", Government of India, 4 October 2011.

Ministry of External Affairs, India-Afghanistan: A Historic and Time-tested Friendship, 2017.

Ministry of External Affairs, "Supplement to the Report of the Ministry Of External Affairs 1979–80", Annual Report 1979-1980 Supplement.

Monthly Political Report for June 1967, Embassy of India, Kabul, Secret, MEA, GoI, No. KAB/101/67, July 13, 1967, NAI.

Monthly Political Report, Historical, Research and Intelligence Section, MEA, GoI, File No. HI/1012(I)/67, 1967, NAI.

NARA, Moving Images Relating to Intelligence and International Relations, 1947–1984, National Archives Identifier: 652980. Central Intelligence Agency, April 12, 1981.

NARA, Moving Images Relating to US Domestic and International Activities, 1982–1999, US Information Agency, August 24, 1982, National Archives Identifier: 54188.

National Archives and Record Administration, Afghanistan Report: Moving Images Relating to International Development Programs and Activities, 1979–1991, 1980, National Archives Identifier: 2733355.

P.K. Thakkar, Consulate of India, Kandahar, Monthly Record of Events of the Month of March 1978, No. KAN/101/1/77, April 4, 1978, NAI.

P.K. Thakkar, Consulate of India, Kandahar, Monthly Record of Events of the Month of May, 1978 – Coup d'etat in Afghanistan, No. KAN/101/1/77, May 7, 1978, NAI.

P.K. Thakkar, Consulate of India, Kandahar, Monthly Record of Events of the Month of June 1978, No. KAN/101/1/77, June 6, 1978, NAI.

P.K. Thakkar, Consulate of India, Kandahar, Monthly Record of Events of the Month of July 1978, No. KAN/101/1/77, July 2, 1978, NAI.

P.K. Thakkar, Consulate of India, Kandahar, Monthly Record of Events of the Month of August 1978, No. KAN/101/1/77, August 3, 1978, NAI.
Political Report for the Month of March 1974 (Part I), No. KAB/101/1/74, April 10, 1974, NAI.
Political Reports (Other than Annual) from Kabul, Historical, Research and Intelligence Section, MEA, GoI, File No. 6(1)-HI/62, 1962, NAI.
Political Reports Etc. (Other than Annual Reports) From Kabul/Pakhtoonistan, MEA, GoI, File No. HI/1012(1)/74, 1974, NAI.
Political Reports for the year 1978 from Jalalabad, MEA, GoI, File No. HI/1012/2/78, 1978, NAI.
Research Department, Foreign Office, UK (1947) A Survey of Anglo-Afghan Relations, Part – I, 1747-1919, Part-II, 1919–1947, London: Foreign Office, IOR/L/P&S/12/1321.
Rup Chand, Ambassador of India, Embassy of India, Kabul, Secret, No. A-21/51, February 1, 1951, NAI.
Rup Chand, Ambassador of India, Embassy of India, Kabul, Secret, Note No. A-21/51, File No. 3(13)-R&I/51, 1951, NAI, February 1, 1951, NAI.
S. Haider, First Secretary, Embassy of India, Kabul, "Annual Political Report for the Year 1971", No. KAB/101/1/71, May 15, 1972, NAI.
S.K. Singh, Ambassador of India, Kabul, Annual Political Report, Kab/101/1/77, March 26, 1978, NAI.
Treaty of Friendship Between the Govt. of India and the Royal Govt. of Afghanistan, Ministry of External Affairs, Government of India, New Delhi, File No. 1-I/2/Afghanistan/50,1950, January 4, 1950, National Archives of India.
Vinay Kumar, Speech at the Afghan Institute of Strategic Studies, November 27, 2019.

Secondary Sources

A. Foucher, *Notes on the Ancient Geography of Gandhara*. Trans. H. Hargreaves. Calcutta: Superintendent Government Printing, 1915.
A. Sarkar et al., "Oxygen Isotope in Archaeological Bioapatites from India: Implications to Climate Change and Decline of Bronze Age Harappan Civilization." *Science Report*, Vol. 6 (2016), Article No. 26555.
A.B.M. Habibullah, *The Foundation of Muslim Rule in India* (Calcutta: Calcutta University, 1945).
A.S. Daulat, Asad Durrani, and Aditya Sinha, *Spy Chronicles: RAW, ISI and the Illusion of Peace* (Noida: HarperCollins Publisher, 2018).
Abul Fazl Allami, *Ain-i-Akbari*, Trans. Col. H. S. Jarrett (Calcutta: Asiatic Society of Bengal, 1938).
Adam K. East, "Afghani Groups: The Peshawar Seven", *Executive Intelligence Review*, October 13, 1995.
Adi Shankara, *Complete Works of Sri Sankaracharya* (Srirangam: Vani Vilas Press, 1910).
Ahmad Rashid, *Taliban* (London: Penguin Publication, 2000).
Ahmad Rashid, "The Taliban: Exporting Extremism", *Foreign Affairs*, November 1999.
Al-Biruni, *Al-Beruin's India*, Vol. 2, Trans. Edward C. Sachau (London: Kigan Paul, Trench, Trubner & Co. Ltd., 1910).
Aleksandr Antonovich Lyakhovskiy, "Inside the Soviet Invasion of Afghanistan and the Seizure of Kabul, December 1979", Working Paper 51, Woodrow Wilson International Centre, January 2007.

Alexander Cunningham, *The Ancient Geography of India*, Vol. I (London: Trubner and Co., 1871).
Amitabh Bachhan, "Facebook, FB 313 - #Tuesday #Memoir: Khuda Gawah", August 27, 2013.
Aristotle, *Poetics*, Trans. Ingram Bywater (Oxford: Claredon Press, 1920), p. 7; Aristotle. *The Metaphysics of Aristotle*, Trans. Thomas Taylor (London: David, Wilks, and Taylon, 1801).
Arrian, *The Anabasis of Alexander*, Trans. E.J. Chinnock (London: Butler and Tanner, 1884).
Arrian, *The Anabasis of Alexander or, the History of the Wars and Conquests of Alexander the Great*, Vol. V. Trans. E.J. Chinnock (London: Hodder and Stoughton, 1884).
Arrian, *Indica of Arrian*, Trans. Watson McCrindle (Bombay: Educations Society's Press, 1896).
Asta Olesen, *Islam and Politics in Afghanistan*, Vol. 3 (Oxford: Psychology Press, 1995).
Athenaeus, *The Deipnosophists: Banquet of the Leashed Athneaeus*, Vol. I, Trans. C.D. Yonge (London: Henry G. Bohn, 1853–54).
Athenaeus, *The Deipnosophists: Banquet of the Leashed Athneaeus*, Vol. I, Trans. C.D. Yonge (London: Henry G. Bohn, 1930).
Azad Singh Toor, *India-Afghanistan Relations: Observations from the 1995–96 Period of the Indian Embassy in Afghanistan*, Vol. 3 (New Delhi: ICWA, 2018).
B.B. Lal, *Indian Archaeology 1969–70 – A Review* (New Delhi: Indian Archaeological Survey of India, 1970).
B.K. Thapar, *Indian Archaeology 1976–77 – A Review* (New Delhi: Indian Archaeological Survey of India, 1977).
B.K. Thapar, "New Traits of the Indus Civilization at Kalibangan: An Appraisal", in N. Hammond (ed.), *South Asian Archaeology* (London: Duckworth, 1973).
Barbara Graziosi, *Inventing Homer: The Early Reception of Epic* (Cambridge: Cambridge University Press, 2002).
Claudius Ptolemy, *The Geography*, Vol. VI, Trans. E.L. Stevenson (New York: New York Public Library, 1932).
Claudius Ptolemy, *The Geography*, Vol. VII, Trans. E.L. Stevenson (New York: New York Public Library, 1932).
Country Report: Pakistan-Afghanistan, *The Economist Intelligence Unit 15 Regent Street* (London: SW1Y 4LR United Kingdom, 1996), p. 16.
Ctésias, *Histoires de l' Orient*, Trans. Janick Auberget (Paris: Les Belles Letters, 1991).
D.D. Kosambi, "Notes on the Kandahar Edict of Asoka", *Journal of the Economic and Social History of the Orient*, Vol. 2, No. 2 (May 1959) p. 113–127.
Dilip Mukerjee, "Afghanistan under Daud: Relations with Neighbouring States", *Asian Survey*, Vol. 15, No. 4 (April 1975), p. 306.
Diodorus Siculus, *Library of History*, Trans. C.H. Oldfather (Cambridge: Harvard University Press, 1933).
E. Hultzsch, *Inscription of Asoka*, Pliny. *Natural History*, Vol. VI, Trans. H Rackham (London: William Heinemann, 1942), Vol. I (Oxford: Clarendon Press, 1925).
E. Maxon, *Agathonia: A Romance* (New York: Public Library, 1844).
E.J.H. Mackay, *Further Excavations at Mohenjo-daro*, Vol. 2 (New Delhi: Government of India).
Edward Thornton, *A Gazetteer of Countries Adjacent to India on the North-West*, Vol. I (London: W.M.H. Allen and Co., 1844).

Erik Zurcher, *The Buddhist Conquest of China: The Spread and Adaptation of Buddhism in Early Medieval China*, Vol. I (Leiden: Brill Publication, 1972).
F.J. Goldsmid, *Eastern Persia: An Account of the Journeys of the Persian Boundary Commission 1870–72*, Vol. 2 (London: MacMillan and Co., 1876).
Fa-hien, *FoéKouéKi, ou, Relations des royaumesbouddhiques: voyage dans la Tartarie, dansl'Afghanistan et dansl'Inde, exécuté, à la fin du IVe siècle, par ChyFaHian*, Trans. Jean Pierre Abel Rémusat (Paris: l'Imprimerie Royale, 1836).
Fa-hien, *A Record of Buddhistic Kingdoms, being an account by the Chinese Monk Fa-hien of His Travels in India and Ceylon (A.D. 399–414), in Search of the Buddhist Books of Discipline*, Trans. James Legge (Oxford: Oxford University Press, 1886).
Farah Abidin, *Suba of Kabul Under the Mughals: 1585–1739* (New Delhi: Patridge India Publication, 2014).
G.P. Tate, *The Kingdom of Afghanistan: A Historical Sketch* (Bombay: Bennett Coleman and Co., 1911).
George Grierson, *Linguistic Survey of India*, Vol. X (Calcutta: Government Press, 1922).
H.C. Rawlinson, "Notes on a March from Zoháb, at the Foot of Zagros, along the Mountains to Khúzistán (Susiana), and from Thence through the Province of Luristan to Kirmánsháh, in the Year 1836", *Royal Geographic Society Journal*, Vol. IX, No. 26 (1839).
H.G. Rawlinson, "Early Contacts Between India and Europe", in A.L. Basham (ed.), *A Cultural History of India* (Oxford: Oxford University Press, 1997).
H.H. Wilson, *Ariana Antiqua: A Descriptive Account of the Antiquities and Coins of Afghanistan* (London: East India Company, 1841).
H.P. Francfort, "Excavations at Shortugai in Northeast Afghanistan", *American Journal of Archaeology*, Vol. 87, No. 4 (1983), pp. 518–519.
H.P. Francfort, *Second Campagne de fouilles sur le sit.e proto-historique de Shortugai (Afghanistan du N.E.): 10 avril - 2 juin 1978, mss., Kabul, 1978* (Paris: Klincksieck Publisher, 1978).
Han-sung Yang et al., *The Hye Cho's Diary: Memoir of the Pilgrimage to the Five Regions of India*, Trans. Han-sung Yang et al. (Berkeley: California University Press, 1984).
Hecataeus, "Fragment 294a", in F. Jacoby (ed.), *Fragmente der Griechischen Historiker*, Vol. 1 (Berlin: Weidmann, 1923).
Hecataeus, *Hecataei Milesii Fragmenta: Scylacis Caryandensis Periplus*. Edit. Rud Henr Klausen (Berolini: Impensis G. Reimeri, 1831).
Hein G. Kiessling, *Faith, Unity, Discipline: The ISI of Pakistan* (New Delhi: Harper Collins, 2016).
Herbert Cushing Tolman, *A Guide to the Old Persian Inscription* (New York: American Book Company, 1893), p. 146.
Herodotus, *The Histories of Herodotus*, Vol. I, Trans. George Rawlinson (London: John Murrey, 1860).
Herodotus, *The Histories of Herodotus*, Vol. II, Trans. George Rawlinson (London: John Murrey, 1860).
Herodotus, *The Histories of Herodotus*, Vol. III, Trans. George Rawlinson (London: John Murrey, 1860).
Herodotus, *The Histories of Herodotus*, Vol. IV, trans. George Rawlinson (London: John Murrey, 1860).
Hiuen Tsang, *Si-Yu-Ki: Buddhist Records of the Western World*, Vol. I, Trans. Samuel Beal (London: Kegan Paul, Trench, Trubner & Co. 1884).

Homer, *The Odyssey*, Trans. W. Lucas Collins (London: William Blackwood and Sons, 1879), p. 13; Homer, *The Odyssey*, Trans. E.V. Rieu (London: Clays Ltd, 1946).
I-Tsing, *A Record of the Buddhist Religion As Practiced in India and the Malay Archipelago, 671–695 AD*, Trans. J. Takakusu (Oxford: The Clarendon Press, 1896).
J.N. Dixit, *An Afghan Diary: Zahir Shah to Taliban* (New Delhi: Konark Publishers, 2000).
J.N. Dixit, *India's Foreign Policy: 1947–2003* (New Delhi: Picador Publication, 2004).
J.P. Joshi, *Excavation at Surkotada and Exploration in Kutch. Memoirs of the Archaeological Survey of India No. 87* (New Delhi: Archaeological Survey of India, 1990).
Jaswant Singh, *A Call to Honour: In Service of Emergent India* (New Delhi: Rupa & Co, 2007).
Jaswant Singh, *Jinnah: India-Partition Independence* (New Delhi: Rupa Publication, 2009).
Jawaharlal Nehru, *The Discovery of India* (New Delhi: Penguin Publication, 2004).
Jawaharlal Nehru, *The Glimpses of World History* (New Delhi: Penguin, 2004).
Jean Pierre Ferrier, *History of the Afghans*, Trans. Original Unpublished Manuscript by Captain William Jesse (London: John Murrey, 1858).
Jean W. Sedlar, *India and the Greek World: A Study in the Transmission of Culture* (Princeton, NJ: Rowman and Littlefield Publication, 1980).
Kalidasa, *Raghuvamsa* (Bombay: Gopal Narayan & Co. 1952), Hymns 89–91, p. 102.
Kamal Matinuddin, *The Taliban Phenomenon, Afghanistan 1994–1997* (Oxford: Oxford University Press, 1999).
Koichiro Matsuura, *Chanting of Vedas in India an Outstanding Example of Heritage and form of Cultural Expressions* (Paris: UNESCO, November 7, 2003).
Krishna Chandra Sagar, *Foreign Influence on Ancient India* (New Delhi: Northern Book Centre, 1992).
M. Sharif and B.K. Thapar, "Food-producing Communities in Pakistan and Northern India", in Vadim Mikhaĭlovich Masson (ed.), *History of Civilizations of Central Asia* (New Delhi: Motilal Banarsidass Publication, 1999).
M. Witzel, "Vedas and Upaniṣads", in Gavin Flood (ed.), *The Blackwell Companion to Hinduism* (Blackwell Publishing Ltd., 2003).
M.A. Stein, *Kalhana's Rajatarangini*, Vol. 2 (Srinagar: Gulshan Publisher, 2007).
Madhu Sarup Vats, *Excavations at Harappa: Being An Account of Archaeological Excavations Carried Out at Harappa Between the Years 1920–1 And 1933–4* (New Delhi: Manager of Publications, 1940).
Mahavamsa, Trans. Wilhelm Geiger (London: Oxford University Press, 1912).
Major General Samay Ram, *The New Afghanistan Pawn of America* (New Delhi: Manas Publication, 2004).
Megasthenis, *Indica*, Trans. E.A. Schwanbeck (Bonn: Sumptibus, 1846).
Mirza Kalichbeg, *The Chachnamah* (Karachi: Commissioners Press, 1900).
Mohamed Kasim Ferishta, *History of the Rise of the Mohamedan Power in India Till the Year AD 1612*, Translated from the original Persian by John Briggs, Vol. I & II (London: Oriental Translation Fund, 1829).
Mohammad Ayub Khan, *Friends Not Masters: A Political Autobiography* (London: Oxford University Press, 1967).
Mohammad Yousaf and Mark Adkin, *Afghanistan the Bear Trap* (New Delhi: Bookwise Pvt. Ltd, 2007).

Mohan Lal, *To Balk, Bokhara and Herat* (New Delhi: National Archives of India and Three Rivers Press, 2011).
Mohan Lal, *Travels in the Punjab and Afghanistan and Turistan to Balkh, Bikhara and Herat and a Visit to Great Britain, Germany* (London: Murry and Co. 1946).
Muhammad Babur, *Babarnama*, Vol. I, Translated from original Turki Text by Annette Susannah Beveridge (London: Luzac & Co, 1922).
Nanjio's Catalogue of the Chinese Buddhist Books, No. 1492; Nanjio Bunyiu, *A Catalogue of the Chinese Translation of the Buddhist Tripitaka the sacred canon of the Buddhists in China and Japan compiled by order of the Secretary of State for India* (Oxford: At the Clarendon Press, 1883).
Nārāyaṇa, *The Hitopadeśa*, Trans. A.N.D. Haksar (New Delhi: Penguin Publication, 1998).
Olaf Caroe, *The Pathans: 550 BC – AD 1957* (London: Macmillan and Co., Ltd., 1958).
P. Bernard et al., *Fouilles d'Ai Khanoum I (Campagnes 1965–68): Memoires de la Delegation archeologique francaise en Afghanistqn, XXI* (Paris: Klincksieck Publisher, 1973).
Panini, *The Ashtadhyayi of Panini*, Vol. IV, Chapter – 2, Hymn – 99, Trans. Srisa Chandra Vasu (Benares: Sindhu Charan Bose Publication, 1896).
Panini, *The Ashtadhyayi of Panini*, Vol. VI, Chapter – 1, Hymn – 153, Trans. Srisa Chandra Vasu (Benares: Sindhu Charan Bose Publication, 1896).
Parashuram Lakshman Vaidya, *The Harivamsa* (Poona: Bhandarkar Research Institute Publication, 1971).
Patrick Clawson, *Eternal Iran* (London: Palgrave Macmillan Publication, 2004).
Paul Pelliot, *Un Bibliotheque Medieval Retrouvee au Kan-sou* (Annee: Bulletin de l'Ecole Francaise d'Extreme-Orient, 1908).
Percy Sykes, *A History of Afghanistan* (London: MacMillan and Co., 1940).
Phylarchus, *Historiarum Reliquiae*. Edit. A. Brueckner (Vratislaviae: Apud Georgium Phillippum Aderholz, MDCCXXXIX), p. 31; Athenaeus, *The Deipnosophists: Banquet of the Leashed Athneaeus*, Vol. I, Trans. C.D. Yonge (London: Henry G. Bohn, 1930).
Pliny, *Natural History,* Vol. VI, Trans. H Rackham (London: William Heinemann, 1942).
R.C. Majumdar, *An Advanced History of India. Part – 2* (New Delhi: Macmillan, 1967).
Raza Ali, "The Shadow War" (Unpublished Manuscript).
Richard Salomon, *Five Kharosthi Inscriptions*, Bulletin of the Asia Institute, Vol. 10 (Bloomfield Hills, MI: Asia Institute, 1996).
Romesh C. Dutt, *The Ramayana and Mahabharata* (Whitefield: Kessinger Publication, 2012).
S. Radhakrishnan, Speech at the Indo-Afghan Society, Kabul, May 13, 1963, 'President Radhakrishnan's Speeches and Writings; May 1962–May 1964', Publication Division, Government of India, February 1965.
S.R. Rao, *Lothal: A Harappan Port Town, 1955–62*, Vol. II (New Delhi: Archaeological Survey of India, 1985).
Samuel Beal, *Travel of Fah-hien and Sung Yun: Buddhist Pilgrims from China to India* (London: Trubner and Co, 1869).
Saroj Kumar Rath, *Fragile Frontiers: The Secret History of Mumbai Terror Attacks* (London: Routledge Publication, 2018).
Satya Shrava, *A Comparative History of Vedic Literature* (New Delhi: Pranava Prakashan, 1977).
Selected Speeches of Indira Gandhi: January 1966–August 1969, *Ministry of Information and Broadcasting* (Publications Division, India, 1971).

Shaman Hwui Li, *The Life of Hiuen-Tsiang*, Trans. Samuel Beal (London: Kegan Paul, Trench, Trubner & Co, 1911).
Sir Mortimer Wheeler, *Charsada: A Metropolis of the North-West Frontier* (London: Oxford University Press, 1962).
Sten Konow, *The copper plate Grant of Valabhi king Siladitya in Epigraphia Indica XI* (New Delhi: Manager of Publications, 1911).
Strabo, *The Geography of Strabo*, Vol. VII, Trans. Horace Leonard Jones (London: William Heinemann, 1917).
T.H. Holdich, *The Indian Borderland, 1880–1900* (London: Cambridge University Press, 2012).
The Zenda Avesta: The Sacred Books of the East. Edit. Max Muller (New York: The Christian Literature Company, 1898).
V.D. Mahajan, *History of Medieval India* (New Delhi: S. Chand Publication, 1988).
V.K. Nambiar, *My Years in Kabul, 1990–1992*, ICWA Sapru House Special Series on Afghanistan, Vol. 2 (New Delhi: Indian Council of World Affairs, 2018).
V.S. Agrawala, *India As Known to Panini: A Study of the Cultural Material in the Ashtadhyayi*, Vol. VI (Allahabad: Law Journal Press, 1953).
Valmiki, *Ramayana, Uttarakhand*, Trans. M.N. Dutt (Calcutta: Girish Chandra Chakravarty, 1891).
Vincent A. Smith, *Rulers of India: Asoka, The Buddhist Emperor of India* (Oxford: Clarendon Press, 1901).
Vishnu Sarma, *Panchatantra*, Trans. Chandra Rajan (New Delhi: Penguin Publication, 1993).
Vishweshwar Anand Vedic Research Institute, *Atharva Veda* (Hoshiarpur: VVRI Publication, 1961).
Vishweshwar Anand Vedic Research Institute, *Rig Veda* (Hoshiarpur: VVRI Publication, 1963).
Vyasadev, *The Mahabharata*, Sabha Parvan, Chapter – 51, No. 3, Trans. G.C. Vaidya (Bombay: Ramchandra Govind & Son).
W.K. Fraser Tytler, *Afghanistan: A Study of Political Developments in Central and Southern Asia* (London: Oxford University Press, 1967).
W.M. Crindle, *Ancient India: As Described in Classical Literature – A Collection of Greek and Latin Tests Relating to India* (London: The Hakluyt Society, 1897).
Walter K. Anderson, 'India in Asia: Walking on a Tightrope', *Asian Survey*, December 1979.
William Darlymple, *Return of a King: The Battle for Afghanistan 1829–1842* (London: Blumsbury Publication, 2013).
William Moorcroft and George Trebeck, *Travels in the Himalayan Provinces of Hindustan and the Punjab in Ladakh and Kashmir: In Peshawar, Kabul, Kunduz, and Bokhara 1819–1825* (New Delhi: Asian Education Service, 2004).
William Smith, *Dictionary of Greek and Roman Geography* (Boston: Little, Brown, and Co., 1980).

Newspapers

Afghan Islamic Press
Asia Times Online
DNA
Jang
Kabul Times
Khaama Press
La Mode

Long War Journal
Mid-Day
Pro Publica
Radio Kabul
The Asian Age
The Boston Globe
The Daily Mail
The Dawn
The Economic Times
The Express Tribune
The Guardian
The Hindu
The Hindustan Times
The Huffington Post
The Indian Express
The Los Angeles Times
The New York Times
The Observer
The Pioneer
The Telegraph
The Times
The Times of India
The Wall Street Journal
The Washington Post
The Washington Times
Wikileaks

INDEX

9/11 attacks xxi, xxiii, xxvii, 151, 155–156

Abbas the Great, Shah 6
Abdullah, Dr Abdullah 158
Abdullah bin-Amar 32
Abdul-Rahimzay, Abdul Malik 71–72
Abouseid, Sultan 6
Abu Bakr 31
Achaemenid Empire 37
Achakzais 95
Adi Shankara 14
Adkin, Mark xxii
   Afghanistan: The Bear Trap, The Defeat of a Superpower xxii
Afghan–Baluch Boundary Commission 46
Afghan Hindus xiv
Afghanistan 32
   American intervention in 159
   anti-regime activities of rebels 104
   boundaries 46–48, 64
   bribery and corruption in 57
   British interaction with xx–xxi
   British–Russian shadow fight in xxiii
   Chinese investments in 158
   civil war in 103–123
   collapse of 43–44
   1978 coup in 89–96, 98, 104
   as 'Democratic Republic of Afghanistan' 93
   ideas of Islam 48–49
   Indian consulates in 157
   Indian families in xiv–xv, 56, 77, 82, 89
   intelligence system 72
   Joint US–USSR announcement of aid stoppage to 136
   July 1973 coup d'etat in 80
   as key to India 42–43
   language issues 45
   Mujahideen rule in 140–141
   new religion 178
   orthodox population 93
   Pakhtoon problem 74
   Pakistan-sponsored terrorist attacks 160
   Russian interests in 64–65
   Soviet intervention in 45, 105–108, 111–112
   Soviet military and economic assistance 131
   Soviet withdrawal from 115, 120, 129–131
   Taliban rule and attacks xiv, xxii, 141–151, 160–162, 169–172
   tensions between Afghan Sikhs and Hindus 117
   transitional phase in 139
   UN's assistance programme 140–141
   US Afghan policy 119
   US sanctions 103–104
Afghanistan–Pakistan Transit Trade Agreement (APTTA) 163

Index

'Afghanistan Transit Trade Agreement' (ATTA) 162
Afghan Mujahideen 101, 109, 123
Afghan National Liberation Front 100
Afghan–Pakistan relations 75, 168, 171–172
  Afghan refugee camps in Pakistan 98
  border issues xii, 60, 64, 74–75, 95, 101
Afghans 6, 177
Afghan Sikhs xiv, 117
Agha, Afandi 100
Agha, Sayed Mahboob 162
Ahmadzai, Mohammad Najibullah xxi, xxvii, 118, 120–121, 129, 132–134
  defence of Jalalabad 130
  fall of 136–140, 146
  India policy toward Afghanistan during 131–135
  official visit to India, 1988 121
  proclamation of a ceasefire 120
  Soviet assistance and 131
Ahmed, Fakruddin Ali 81
Aiz, Governor Mohammad Ayub 93
Akbar, Emperor 42
Akbar, Mohd. 100
Akhundzadeh, Abdur Rab 94–95
Al Beruni 32, 35
Alexander's campaign 11
Alexander the Great 13, 37
Ali, Brigadier Syed Raza 100–101
Amin, Hafizullah 96, 105–107, 143
Amir, Brigadier Sultan 142
Amu Darya basin 1
Anglo-Afghan War xiv
  First xx, 37
  Second 1878 xx, 44–45
  Third, 1919 45
Ansari, Mohammad Hamid 72
Antiochus (Antiochus II Theos) 13
April Revolution of 1978 89–96, 98
Arachosia 3
Arrian 10–11
Arsala, Hizb-e-Islami 140
Artaxerxes II Mnemon, King 9
Aryadesa 5
Aryan race xviii, 41
Asa Mai temple 132
Ashoka, Emperor 12
Atharva Veda 2
Athenaeus 9

Aurangzeb, Emperor 42
Azhar, Maulana Massoud 150, 155
Azimi, General Mohammed Nabi 137
Aziz, Dr Abdul Ghaffar 73

Babar, Major General Nasirullah 130, 142–143
Babur, Ziauddin 38
Bachchan, Amitabh 134–135
Bactria 3
Badakhshan 39
Balban, Ghyasuddin 36
Baluchistan 46
Bamiyan valley xi, xxvi, 7, 17–19, 21, 40, 73, 156, 176
Baradar, Mullah Abdul Ghani 170–171
Basharmal, Dr Khudaidad 90
Batanjal xvii
Battle of Buxar 44
Battle of Plassey 44
Beg of Kunduz, Mir Muhammad Murad 44
Behramuddin, Major 90
Bharana 15
Bharata, King 7
Bhimapala 33
Bhutto, Benazir 81–82, 129–130, 142
Biden, Joe xxix
Biloo 135
Bindusara 11
Bokhara 10
Bolan Pass xi, 1
border issues xii–xiii, 60, 64, 68, 74–75, 95, 101
Boundary Commission 46
Boutros-Ghali, Boutros 136
Bowles, Chester 62–63
Brahmarashtra 5
Brahmarashtra/Jambudvipa 5
Brahmin kingdom of Kabul 33
Breschna, Abdullah 73
Brezhnev, Leonid I. 107, 109
British India–Afghanistan Agreement xiii
Buddhism xxv, 3, 15–17, 20, 33, 38, 48, 176–177, 179
  in Balkh 17
buffer state theory xx
Bulganin, Nikolai Alexandrovich 64
Burnes, Sir Alexander 44
Bush, George W. 156
Butler, Elizabeth xx

Callatians 9
Caroe, Sir Olaf 61, 81
  The Pathans xxvii
Carter, Hodding 91
Carter, Jimmy 103, 107
Caspatyros 6
Central Revolutionary Council (CRC) 91
Central Treaty Organization (CENTO) 65
Chabahar Agreement 164
Chabahar Port development xxvii, 164–165
Chakravarty, Nikhil 117–118
Chand, Rup xxvi, 54
Chandragupta, King 10
Charsada 7
Chauhan, Prithviraj 34
Chinese–Indian border dispute 68
Chopra, B.R. 73
Choudhury, Moinul Haq 79
Chou En-lai 66, 69
Christianity xviii, 178
Chu Sanzcing Ji Ji 15
Cold War politics 103–108
Coll, Steve xxii
  Ghost War xxii
Communist Party in Afghanistan 93
Conolly, Captain Arthur xxiii
Ctesias 14
Ctesias of Cnidos 9–10
  about Indians 10
Cuellar, Javier Perez de 114
  Five-Point Peace Proposals 133
culture of ancient India 8
culture of India 4
Curzon, Lord 157
Cyrus the Great 36–37

Dahir, Raja 32–33
Dalrymple, William 37
  Return of a King: The Battle for Afghanistan 1839–1842 xxi
Danavas 15
Daoud, Limer Ali Sardar Mohmad 58, 62, 65, 71, 91, 95, 106
  on Kashmir issue 62
Dari Persian language 45
Darius, King 3, 6
Darius I, King 8
Dawood, Abdul Razak 163–164
Deimachus 11, 13–14
  Deipnosophists 11–12

'Democratic Republic of Afghanistan' 93
Dengzongpa, Danny 135
Deo, Arvind 109
'Deobandi' school of thought 141–142
Dhamija, J.N. 60–63, 65–67, 70, 72–73
Diodorus Siculus 10
Dionysios 11, 13
Dixit, J.N. 114–115, 118, 137
Dodge, Tony xxii
Dost, Shah Mohammed 113
Dostum, General Abdul Rashid 131, 135, 137, 140, 147, 158
Dubs, Adolph 103
Durand, Sir Mortimer H. 46, 68
Durand agreement/Durand Line 1, 46–48, 60–61
Durand Line xii–xiii, xx, xxv–xxviii, 1, 46–47, 60–62, 76, 138, 177
Durjodhan, King 7
Durrani, Ahmad Shah 43
Durrani, Asad xv, 168
Durranis (Sadozai) 43–44, 180

Elgin, Lord 46
Eliot, Theodore 91
Ellenborough, Lord 37
Elliot, Sir H. xvii, 32
Emad, Sayed Noorullah 143
Eratosthenes 11
Etemadi, Mohammad Nur Ahmad 76
Etemadi, Nur Ahmed 69
Ethiopians 8

Fa-hien 16
Faizi, Aimal 167
Farhadi, Rawan 97
Fazl, Abul xix, 42, 177
Ferishta, Abul Qasim 36
Firdausi 33–34
Five Countries of India (Wu-t'ien) 5
Foguo ji (Fo-Kue-Ki) 16
Four Rightful Caliphs 141
French, David: *The British Way in Counterinsurgency* xx
  The British Way of War Reconsidered xx

Gall, Carlotta: *The Wrong Enemy* xxii
Gandarians 3–4, 8–9
Gandhara xii, 3, 8, 16, 19, 43, 175
Gandhari lambs 1–2

Gandhi, Indira 59, 79, 81–82, 110–111, 113, 115, 118
Gandhi, Rajiv 121–122, 132, 134
Geneva Accords 122
Ghani, Dr Ashraf 160, 168
Ghaznavids 38
Ghazni, Mahmud 59
Ghori, Muhammad 34
Ghoriyani, Nisar Ahmad 164
Ghurids 38
Gilani, Pir Sayed Ahmad 138
Goldsmid, Sir Frederick John 46
Gommans, Jos J.L. xix
 The Rise of The Indo-Afghan Empire, c. 1710–1780 xix
Gorbachev, Mikhail 118–119, 121, 136
Gowda, H.D. Deve 145
Great Game struggle xx, xxiii–xxiv, xxv, 44, 180
Grecian and Chinese scholars xii, 4
Greco-Bactrian Kingdom 37
Greek literature xii, 175
Gromov, Lieutenant General Boris 122
Gromyko, Andrei 112
Gul, Islam 90
Gul, Lieutenant General Hamid 130

Haq, General Zia-ul 99, 101, 114
Harakat-i-Inquilab-i-Islami (Islamic Revolutionary Forces) 103
Harivamsa Purana 2
Harmandir Sahib Temple 117
Hart, B.H. Liddell xx
 The British Way in Warfare xx
Hastinapur 7
Hatif, Abdul Rahim 143
Hazaras 40, 180
Heathcote, T.A. xix
 The Afghan Wars, 1839–1919 xix–xx
Hecataeus 8
Hecataeus of Miletus 3
Hekmatyar, Gulbuddin 99, 119, 130–131, 137–138, 143, 145
Herat xv, xxix, 3, 6, 38–40, 43, 89, 92, 137, 141–144, 155–157, 161, 165–166
Herodotus xi, 1, 6, 8
 about Indians 9
 Histories 8
 Indika 9
Hezb-i-Islami (Party of Islam) 102

Hidayat, Gazi 97
Hijrat 31
Hikmatyar, Gulbuddin 100
'*Hindu*' (term) 5
Hindu Afghans 116
Hindu Gods and Goddesses 14
Hinduism 38, 48, 179
Hindu Shahi dynasty 32–33
Hiuen Tsang xi, 3–5, 17–19, 176
 Si-Yu-Ki or *The Record of the Western Kingdom* 17
Hizb-e-Wahdat 147
Hizb-i-Islami (Party of Islam) 102, 130–131, 137–138, 140–141
Holdich, Colonel T.H. 46
Homer 8
Hopkirk, B.D. xxiii
 The Making of Modern Afghanistan xxiii
Hopkirk, Peter: *Foreign Devils on the Silk Road: The Search for the Lost Cities and Treasures of Chinese Central Asia* xxii
 The Great Game: The Struggle for Empire in Central Asia xxi
Humayun, Qaji 144
Hussain, Dr Zakir 75, 81
Hwui-seng 17
Hwuy-wei 16
Hwuy-ying 16
Hye Ch'o 20–21

Ibn Battuta 35
Ikhwan-ul-Musalmeen (IUM) party 97, 99–100
India: Afghan policy 108–123
 Aryan invasion xviii
 Chinese thoughts about xii, 15–22
 descriptions of 8–15
 establishment of Muslim empire 34, 38
 Khalji dynasty 35–36
 Lodi dynasty 35
 Mughal dynasties 38
 Pokhran nuclear test 81
 stance on Russian and Cuban 96
 Sultanate dynasties 36
 Tughlaq dynasty 35
 Turks campaign against 34
India–Afghanistan relations 1
 Afghanistan's dealings with superpowers, role of 63
 Afghans dynasties 35–36

Index

Agreement on Establishment of International Transport and Transit Corridors (Chabahar Agreement) 164
attacks against Indian Consulate 115–116
beads trade 4
bonds of friendship 58
boundary agreements 46–48
catalyst of change in 44–49
common ancient destiny 7
communication links 45
cultural commonalities 4, 181
economic assistance 4, 57, 133, 181
film shooting xv, 134–136
food aid 160
importance of Kandahar and Jalalabad 59
imports and exports 55–56
Indian scholars on xvi
India's influence at Royal Palace 69–70
'Jawaz Nama' (Trade permit) 56
language issues 45
literature on xvi–xvii
in military 81, 169
opening of land routes 73–74
in radio-telegraphic communication 54
reconstruction and rehabilitation projects in Afghanistan 159–162
religious affinity 1–2
same landmass, similar population, and homogeneity of religion 7–15
Strategic Partnership Agreement xxix, 167–172
during Taraki era 96–103
in trade 55–58, 165–166
trade routes 162–167
Treaty of Friendship 53–54, 63
visa agreement 82
India–China war 65–66
India–Chinese dispute 58
India–Iran–Afghanistan trilateral meeting 164
Chabahar Port development 164–165
Indian Airlines flight, hijack of 150
India–Pakistan dispute: Afghan factor 111–112
Kashmir issue 55, 60, 62
shooting down of a Pakistani plane 74

Indira Gandhi Institute for Child Health, Kabul 133, 148, 156–157
Indo-Afghan Joint Commission 131
Indo-Afghan Society 72
Indo-Afghan Wars xiv
International Security Assistance Force (ISAF) 157
Inter Services Intelligence (ISI) 100–102, 168–169
'invincible Afghan' myth 36–37
Islamic Emirates of Afghanistan 170
ITEC Programme 73
Itehad Islami (Islamic Unity) 102
I-tsing, Monk 5–6, 20

Jabha-i-Nijat-Milli (Afghan National Liberation Front) 102, 137
Jain, Dr L.C. 57
Jaipur foot 133
Jaitley, P.C. 73
Jalalabad xiv–xv, xx, 59, 75, 77, 82, 90, 92, 115, 122, 130, 143–145, 155, 157
Jalalabad attacks xv
Jalalar, M.K. 97
Jalali, Ali Ahmed xxiii
  A Military History of Afghanistan xxiii
Jamaat, Tablighi 95
Jamiat-e-Islami 100, 102, 138
Jamil-ur-Rehman 79
Jandar, Maulvi 98
Jashan celebration 54–55
Jirga, Loya 156
Johnson, Rob xx
  The Afghan Way of War Culture and Pragmatism: A Critical History xx

'Kafir' (non-believers) 97
Kafirs 179
Kakar, M. Hassan xxiii
  Afghanistan: The Soviet Invasion xxiii
Kalinga War 12
Kambojas 2
Kandahar Consulate 89
Kandahar xiv–xv, xvii–xviii, xxix, 3, 12–13, 33, 38–40, 42–43, 59, 72, 77, 82, 89, 92–95, 115–116, 129–130, 142–143, 146, 150, 155, 157, 161–162, 165–166, 177
1978 coup 89–96, 98
Kanishka of Gandhara 19

Kanwar, Lala Raj 54
Kapiladharinas 18
Kapisi 3
Karmal, Babrak 92, 104, 106–107, 113, 118, 120, 143
Karzai, Hamid 42–43, 138, 148, 156–158, 160–161, 167
Kashmir dispute 55, 60
  plebiscite question 62
Kashmiri, Mohan Lal 44
Kaul, T.N. 110
Kautilya's Arthashastra 2
Kennedy, John F. 62
Keshmand, Sultan Ali 117
Keskar, Dr B.V. 55
KGB 118
Khalili, Karim 147
Khalili, Massoud 146
Khalilzad, Zalmay 170–171
Khalis, Maulvi 98
Khalq Democratic Party of Afghanistan 91, 93, 99, 106
Khan, Abdul Gaffar Khan 74
Khan, Abdullah 6–7
Khan, Amanullah 59
Khan, Ayub 62, 76
  Friends Not Masters 75–76
Khan, Daoud 57
Khan, General Ismael 141
Khan, Genghis 6, 38–39
Khan, Ismael 144
Khan, Khizr 36
Khan, Lieutenant General Yunus 92
Khan, Marshal Shah Wali 66
Khan, Mohammad Daoud 80–81, 143
Khan, Najibullah 54
Khan, Sardar Najibullah 53–54
Khan, Shah Mahmood 57
Khan, Sultan Muhammad 81
Khan of Herat, Abdullah 6
Khotanese language 16
Khrushchev, Nikita 64
Khyber Pass xi, xiii, 42, 46
Kipling, Rudyard xxiv
  Kim xxiv
Krishnan, N. 110
Kshatriya, King 18
Kumar, Bharath Raj Muthu 148, 161
Kumbh Melas 15
Kunzru, Pandit Hriday Nath 55
Kutty, Maniyappan Raman 160
Kwuy-king 16

Laden, Osama bin 155, 161
Laffrai, Najibullah 138–139, 144
Lalliya, King 32–33
Lambah, S.K. xxvii, 157
Lang, Taimur 35
lapis lazuli 4
Lashkar-e-Taiba 161
Levy, Adrian xxiii
  The Exile xxiii
Little Rajagriha 17

MacMunn, Sir George xviii
  Afghanistan From Darius to Amanullah xviii
  The Martial Races of India xviii–xix
MacNeill, Sir John xxiii–xxiv
Madhyadesa 5
Mahabharata 7, 176
Mahabharata xxvi
Mahaz-i-Milli Islam (National Islamic Front of Afghanistan) 102
Mahmud of Ghazni 32–34
Mainwandwal, Prime Minister 74
Major 2nd Rock Edict 13
Mamluk or Slave dynasty 35
Manchanda, Dr S.S. 73
Mandal Commission 132
Marriet, Ogayar Fillip Jean 116
Massoud, Ahmed Shah xxvii, 115, 131, 138, 141, 143–151, 156
Massoud, Wali 149
Matanga, Kasyapa 15–16
Maurya, Chandragupta 10–11, 13
Mauryan dynasty of Pataliputra 11
Mazar-e-Sharif xxix, 134, 156
McMahon, A.H. 46
McMahon Line 46, 60
Megasthenes 10, 13–14
  Indika 10
Mehrgarh 1
Memoir of a Pilgrimage to the Five Regions of India 20
Menon, K.P.S. 121
Meredow, Rasit 166
Mestiri, Mehmoud 144
Milak–Zaranj–Delaram road 164
Ming-ti 15
Ming-ti, Emperor 15–16
Minority Agreement (Nehru–Liaqat Agreement) 55
Minor 4th Rock Edict 12
Mishra, Brajesh 109–111
Mishra, Shyam Nandan 109

Misri, Vikram xxix
Modi, Narendra 161, 165
Mohammad, Prophet 31
Mohtat, Abdul Hamid 133
Mojaddedi, Sibghatullah 100, 122, 131, 137, 143
Moksha Mahaparishad 18
Moorcroft, William 44
Mughal-era Zafar Mahal 36
Muhammad, Abu Abdullah xvii
Muhammad, Prophet 31, 36, 141, 178–179
Mujahideens 101–103
Mujavats 2
Mukund, J. 73
Muttaqi, Maulvi Amir Khan xxix

Nabi, Lieutenant Colonel Ghulam 92
Nabil, Rahmatullah 167
Nagnajit, King 7
Naim, Aziz 100
Naim, Sardar 58, 60, 66–70, 100
Nambiar, Vijay K. 132, 136–137, 140
Nanak, Guru 90
Naqid, Mohammadullah 143
Narain, Govind 81
Nasser, Gamal Abdel 68
National Directorate of Security (NDS) 168
National Front for the Liberation of Afghanistan (NFLA) 98–99
Nearchus 13
Nehru, Jawaharlal xxv, 5, 44, 53–54, 58–59, 63
Nicholls, Sir Jasper 37
Nikator, Seleukus 11
Nirgranthas or Digambara Jainas 18
'Noble Land' *(Aryadesha)* 5
Noorzai, Mohd Arif 158
North Atlantic Treaty Organization (NATO) xxix, 65, 157–158, 162
North Eastern Frontier Agency (NEFA) 66
Northern Alliance xxvii, 120, 147–151, 155–156
Nuclear Non-Proliferation Treaty (NPT) 109

Oakley, Robert B. 130
Obama, Barack 167
Office of Secretary General in Afghanistan and Pakistan (OSGAP) 133

Omar, Caliph 31–32
Omar, Mullah Muhammad 142, 146
Onesicritus 13
Operation Enduring Freedom 155
Operation Storm 333 106
Osman, Amir 138
Osman, Caliph 32

Pakhtoonistan movement xxvi–xxvii, 74
Pakistan: admission to UN 77
  air strikes against India 79
  backed Taliban forces 150–151
  bilateral agreements with Afghanistan 121
  Jamaat-e-Ulema-e Islam (JUI) political party 141
  Karachi Port 165
  mission in Kabul 116–117
  Pashtunistan issue 77
  'Proximity Talks' with 120
  Soviet intentions in 110; *see also* Afghan–Pakistan relations
Pakistan–Afghanistan transit trade agreement 163–164
Pakistan–Bangladesh–India Tripartite Agreement 79
Pandavas xi, 7
Pandit, Kalhana 32
Panini, Sage 2–3
  Ashtadhyayi 2
  history of region 2
Parapamisus (Hindukush Mountain range) 11
Parchamists 104
Parthasarathi, G. 110
Pashtu language 41, 45, 47, 67, 81
Pashtunistan movement 76–77, 80–81
Pashtuns 35–36, 40–41, 47–48, 55, 63, 76–77, 99, 118, 180
Pashtunwali customs 47
Pasupatas 18
Pectra 21
People's Democratic Party of Afghanistan (PDPA) 92, 104, 123
Peshawar 43
Peshawar Accord 137
Philadelphus 13
pilgrimage to India 15
Pliny 10
Prakanva (Fergana) 2
Prakasa, Sri 55
Prasad, Rajendra 58

Prevention of Trafficking in Narcotic Drugs and Psychotropic Substances 132
Ptolemy 13
Ptolemy, Claudius 3
Purushapura or Peshawar 19
Pushakalavati 7
Pushkala 7
Puzanov, Aleksandr M. 105

Qadir, Abdul 92
Qanooni, Yunus 158
'Quetta Scandal' of 1983 101
Qureshi, Dr S.A. 148

Rabbani, Dr Burhanuddin xxvii, 98–99, 119, 131, 137, 139, 143, 145
Rabbani, Mullah Muhammad 143, 146
Radhakrishnan, Dr Sarvapalli 58, 72–73
Rafi, Fariduddin 144
Rafiqi, Governor 90
Raghavan, T.C.A. 171
Rahim, Major Abdul 90
Rahman, Amir Abdul 68, 145
Rahmon, Emamoli 150
Ram, Atma 44
Ram, Major General Samay 113, 116, 118, 130
Ramayana 7
Ramdasi, V.G. 73
Ranibai, Queen 32
Rao, P.V. Narasimha 111–114, 122, 134
Rashid, Ahmed: *Descent into Chaos* xxii
  Pakistan on the Brink xxii
  Taliban: Militant Islam, Oil and Fundamentalism in Central Asia xxi
Rashid, Salman 36
Ratebzad, Anahita 107, 118
Rawlinson, Lieutenant Henry xxiii
Reagan, Ronald 119
Redman, Nicholas xxii
Registani, Mohammed Saleh 148
Rehman, Amir Abdur 46
Rehman, Dr Abdul 143
Rehman, Lieutenant General Akhtar Abdul 101
Resolute Support Mission 157
Right to Information Act, India 157
Rig Veda xi, xxvi, 1–2, 6, 176
Rock Edicts 12–13

Rohillas 42
Rouf, Brigadier General Tohmas 93
Royal Asiatic Society in London 157

Sadaqat 100
Sadiq, Mirwais 158
Saikal, Amin xxii
  Modern Afghanistan: A History of Struggle and Survival xxii
Saleh, Amrullah 115
Samanid dynasty xiii
Sanatana 5
Sanger, David: *The Inheritance* xxii
Sangharamas 17, 19
Sapta Sindhu '*Hapta Hindu*' 5
Sarwar, Ahmad 139
Sathe, R.D. 109, 111, 113
Saul, 'Malek Thalut 6–7
Sayaf, Rasul 119
Sayyaf, Abdul Rasul 138
Sayyid, Mufti Muhammad 132
Sayyid, Rubaiya 132
Schofield, Victoria xxiii
  Afghan Frontier xxiii
Scylax 8
  intelligence report 8–9
Seistan (Iran)–Baluchistan boundary 46
Sengyou 15
Seth, Aftab 139
Seth, Radha Krishan 56
Sevan, Benon 133
Shah, Ahmad xiii, 39, 54
Shah, King Ali Zahir 58, 67
Shah, King Mohammad Zahir 57, 80, 143
Shah, Nadir xiii, 35, 43
  title of '*Dur-i-Durran*' 43
Shah, Qadir 92
Shahreyar, Sepahbad 34
Shahzad, Syed Saleem xxii–xxiii
  Inside Al Qaeda and the Taliban xxii–xxiii
Sheikh, Saeed Omar 150
Shekhar, Chandra 133
Sherzad, Mr 72
Shia–Sunni conflict 180
Shinwari, Maulvi Fazal Hadi 98, 100
Shortugai 1
Shruti literature 14
Silk Road highway 162
Sindhu Gandhara 3
Singh, Avtar xv
Singh, Charan 109–110

Singh, Deewan 65
Singh, Dr Manmohan 159, 167
Singh, Jaswant 148–149, 156
Singh, Khushwant 35
Singh, Natwar 116
Singh, S.K. 93, 113, 118, 122
Singh, Vishwanath Pratap 123, 132–133
Singh, V.K. 167
Sinha, Amar 171
Sirajuddin, Captain 92
Skandha-dhatu-ayatanas 19
South East Asia Treaty Organization (SEATO) 65
Strabo 3, 10–11, 14
Strategic Partnership Agreement xxix, 167–172
Subuktigin 33, 36
Sulemankhel, Mohd. Gul 100
Sung-yun 17
Sunni Hanafi sect xiv
Sun-yun 17
Suryanarayan, K. 161

Tabeev, F.A. 115
Tagore, Rabindranath xvii, 168
　Kabuliwala xvii, 168
Tajiks 40–41, 102, 105, 180
Taliban rule and attacks in Afghanistan xiv, xxii, 141–151, 160–162, 169–172
Tanai, Lieutenant General Shahnawaz 131
T'ang dynasty 17
Tantrik practices 18
Tao-ching 16
TAPI Pipeline Consortium Ltd (TPCL) 166
Taraki, Noor Mohammad 91–92, 95, 104–106, 143
Tarikh-i-Salatin-I Afghana 35
Tate, G.P. 40
Tawans, Musa 100
Taxila Takšašila (Takshasila) 7
Thakkar, P.K. 93
Thapar, General P.N. 73, 75
Three Jewels 20–22
Thurium 8
Tirich–Mir Pass 149
Toor, Azad Singh 141, 144–145
treaties: 'Indo-Afghan Trade Treaty,' 1950 55–56
　Treaty of Friendship 53–54, 63

Treaty of Gandamak 1879 xx, 45–46
Tughlaq, Ghyasuddin 36
Turkie, Prince 101
Turkmenistan–Afghanistan–Pakistan (TAP) project 166
Turkmenistan–Afghanistan–Pakistan–India project (TAPI) 166
Turks 5, 20–21, 32–33, 36, 38–39, 41, 48

Udbhandapura (Und) 33
UN General Assembly (UNGA) Sessions 114
United States–Pakistan relations 62–63
US–Taliban peace talks 169–170
Uzbeks 39–41, 105, 180

Vajpayee, Atal Bihari 96–97, 150, 156
Vajrabodhi 20
Vitkevitch, Captain xxiv
Vorontsov, Yuli 109, 122

Wahhabism 141
Wakhan Corridor 68
Wakil, Abdul 120, 136
Waldheim, Dr Kurt 114
Wang Ocheonchukguk Jeon 20
Wasifi, Azizullah 92
Watanjar, Mohammed Aslam 131
Watanyar, Colonel Aslam 92
Weigley, Russell xx
　The American Way in War xx
Woodward, Bob xxiii
　Obama's War xxiii
World Food Programme 160

Xerxes, King 3, 9

Yadgar, Ahmad 35
Yaqubi, General Ghulam Farook 137
Yeltsin, Boris 136
Ye-tha (Ephthalites or White Hun) 17
Yogic postures in India 15
Yousaf, Brigadier Muhammad 101, 103
Yue-Chi (Kushan) 3, 19

Zabulistan 21
Zaher, Mohammed 67
Zaranj–Delaram Road Project 160–161
Zargar, Mushtaq Ahmed 150
Zend-Avesta 2
Zhang Qian 16
Zoroastrians 2

For Product Safety Concerns and Information please contact our EU representative GPSR@taylorandfrancis.com
Taylor & Francis Verlag GmbH, Kaufingerstraße 24, 80331 München, Germany

www.ingramcontent.com/pod-product-compliance
Lightning Source LLC
Chambersburg PA
CBHW050533300426
44113CB00012B/2068